Vatican Diplomacy and The Armenian Question: The Holy See's Response to The Republic of Armenia 1918-1922

Mario Carolla

Translated from the Italian by Cynthia Quilici

Gomidas Institute
London

FUNDAÇÃO
CALOUSTE
GULBENKIAN

This publication has been made possible with the generous support of the Calouste Gulbenkian Foundation.

Published by Taderon Press by special arrangement with the Gomidas Institute.

© 2010 Mario Carolla. All Rights Reserved.

ISBN 978-1-903656-98-3

For more information please contact
Gomidas Institute
42 Blythe Rd.
London, W14 0HA
ENGLAND
Web: *www.gomidas.org*
Email: *info@gomidas.org*

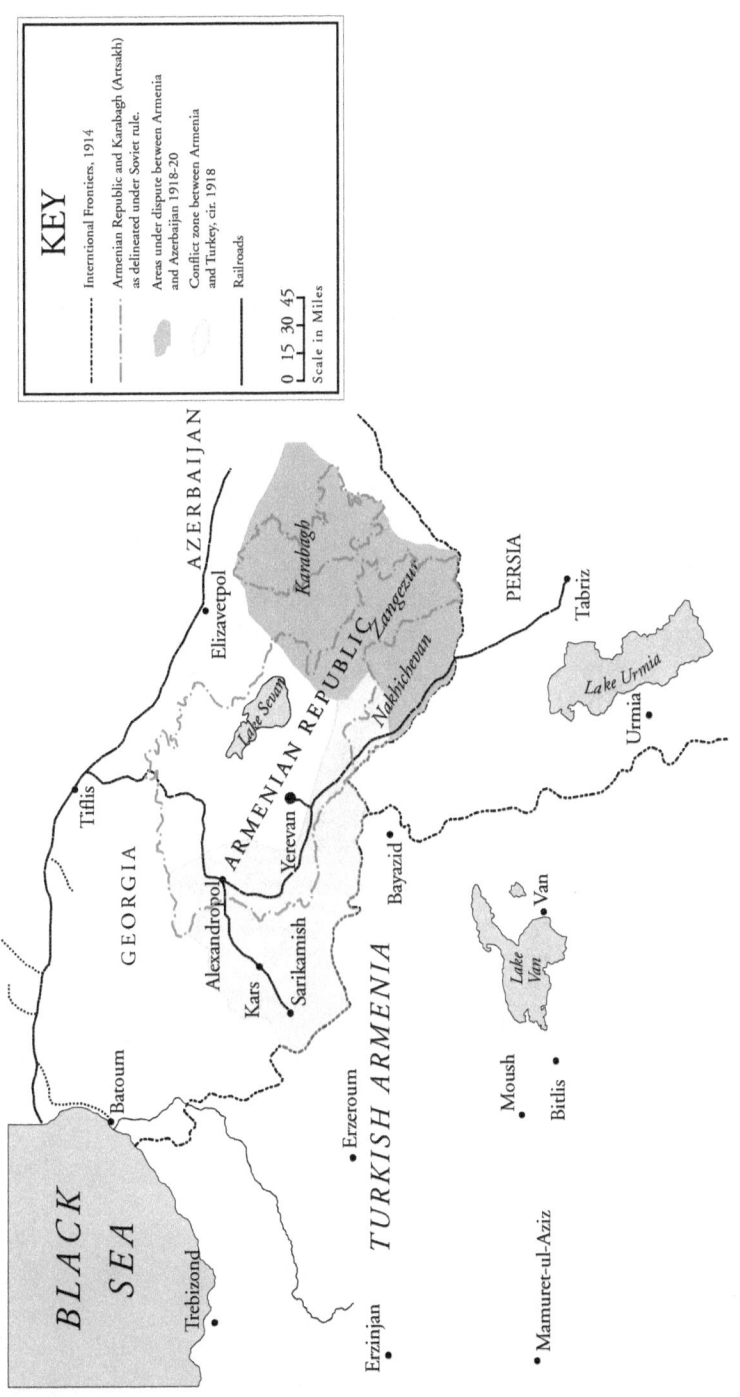

Acknowledgements

There are many people to whom I owe sincere thanks: first of all, Professor Boghos Levon Zekiyan, who for twenty years has been following and encouraging my Armenian studies. It was upon his advice that this thesis was first published in Italy.

Professor Aldo Ferrari maintained contacts within the Armenian community in Italy, who favored him with a generous financial contribution towards the book's Italian publication.

Professor Antonia Arslan was the guardian angel who made possible its publication in the USA, and Professor Siobhan Nash-Marshall tended the relationship with the American publisher.

Special thanks also to His Exc., the Most Rev. Claudio Gugerotti, Apostolic Nuncio in the Caucasus and ex-Official for the Armenian Church of the S. Congregation for the Oriental Churches, for having, with exceeding courtesy, assisted in my consultation of the Congregation's archives.

Not least, I would like to express my gratitude to Mons. Marcello Camisassa, past director of the archives of the Vatican Secretariat of State, and to F. Joseph Metzler, O.M.I., past director of the Vatican Secret Archives, who helped me with great willingness and care in tracking down material in the archives for which they were responsible.

Finally, Cynthia Delfino Quilici was the very scrupulous and mindful translator of the English edition.

TABLE OF CONTENTS

INTRODUCTION	1
I. THE HOLY SEE FACING THE ARMENIAN QUESTION	5
II. THE RUSSIAN REVOLUTION AND ARMENIAN INDEPENDENCE	7
III. INITIAL ARMENIAN-VATICAN CONTACTS	9
IV. THE REUNIFICATION OF ARMENIA	19
V. FATHER DELPUCH'S MISSION	24
VI. THE PARIS PEACE CONFERENCE	30
VII. THE LONDON AND SAN REMO CONFERENCES	35
VIII. TOWARDS THE TREATY OF SÈVRES	39
IX. THE KEMALIST OFFENSIVE AND THE FALL OF THE DASHNAKS	44
X. MONSIGNOR MORIONDO'S MISSION	49
XI. NEW VATICAN DIPLOMATIC INITIATIVES ON BEHALF OF ARMENIANS	58
XII. THE REPORTS OF THE APOSTOLIC DELEGATE IN BEIRUT	61
XIII. FATHER KALATOSOFF'S MISSION	68
CONCLUSIONS	73
VATICAN DOCUMENTS	75
LIST OF DOCUMENTS FROM THE VATICAN ARCHIVES	343
BIOGRAPHICAL GLOSSARY	363
BIBLIOGRAPHY	365

INTRODUCTION

The object of this work is the study of the Vatican's conduct surrounding the brief emergence of the Armenian Republic between 1918 and 1920, and the events immediately thereafter, up until early 1922.

With the goal of reconstructing pontifical actions of the period, the examination of diplomatic documents was paramount. Of particular importance were the archives of the [Vatican's] Secretariat of State (*Archivio della S.C. degli Affari Ecclesiastici Straordinari*; AAEESS), of the Congregation for the Oriental Churches (*Congregazione per le Chiese Orientali*; CO) and the Vatican Secret Archives (*Archivio Segreto Vaticano*; ASV).

One hundred and twenty-five documents were collected and transcribed in their entirety, with the exception of a few which were extremely lengthy and partially transcribed, i.e. those parts which were within the scope of the present study. Only eight of the documents we collected have been previously cited, and only one transcribed, by Andrea Riccardi,[1] who had found copies in the Vatican Archive of Extraordinary Ecclesiastical Affairs (*Archivio della S.C. degli Affari Ecclesiastici Straordinari*; AAEESS), while another was cited and partially transcribed by Morozzo della Rocca,[2] but only with regard to Georgia.

Other documents found by Riccardi, again in the Archive of Extraordinary Ecclesiastical Affairs, are now complementary to those published here, as we shall cite further on.

The documents collected for the current work, while being all of those available in the Vatican Archives up to now, do not constitute a complete body of documentation, seeing as they engage different aspects of the Armenian question (religious, political, diplomatic and humanitarian) in an incomplete and unsystematic way. But then, they regard an area (the Transcaucasus) whose connections with the rest of the world were—

---

1 Andrea Riccardi, "Benedetto XV e la crisi della convivenza multireligiosa nell'Impero ottomano." *Benedetto XV e la pace–1918*, G. Rumi, ed., Brescia: Morcelliana, 1990, pp. 83–128, v. *infra*, in the documents of the present work, doc. n° 53; doc. n° 98; doc. n° 99; doc. n° 50; doc. nn° 90–93 (cited in the order followed by Riccardi).

2 Roberto Morozzo della Rocca, *Le Nazioni non muoiono*, Bologna: Il Mulino, 1992, p. 323, v. *infra* doc. n° 27.

especially during that period—extremely problematic, due to the wars in the region and the collapse of the two bordering Russian and Turkish empires. Moreover, the acceleration of events, over a relatively brief period (1918-22) was such that news reaching the Vatican was often out-of-date. This explains the difficulty in making and carrying out rapid decisions, as Riccardi and Morozzo della Rocca have stressed.[3]

In any case, the documentation in this work should be useful in filling certain gaps, seeing as almost all of those studying the Armenian question have worked on archives and testimonies of Armenian, Turkish, United States and other European origin. Most of that material is of Armenian origin.

Richard Hovannisian's work on the period of the Armenian Republic's independence is outstanding among these.[4] His bibliography is certainly the largest and most complete, but it totally excludes the Vatican Archives and those of the Italian state.

Sidari has been the only author so far to have used previously published Italian documents, along with material from Turkish archives; however, he was not able to utilize sources from the Vatican Archives.[5] Only Naslian, as an Armenian Catholic bishop, was able to publish in his memoirs documents of the Holy See that were in his possession, limited to the massacres and pontifical humanitarian efforts in the years 1914–28.[6]

The Vatican Archives were made accessible to all scholars, without distinction for nationality or faith, by Leo XIII in 1880. Currently, documents up until 1939 are available.

The opening of the Vatican Archives has permitted the publication of studies on the Armenian question, such as those previously mentioned, by Riccardi and by Morozzo della Rocca (the latter only indirectly related to Armenia).

---

3 Riccardi, *op. cit.*, p. 95; Morozzo della Rocca, *op. cit.*, p. 57.
4 Richard G. Hovannisian, *The Republic of Armenia*, vol. I, Berkeley: University of California, 1971.
5 Francesco Sidari, *La questione armena nella politica delle Grandi Potenze: dal Congresso di Berlino al Trattato di Losanna 1878–1923*, Padova: CEDAM, 1962.
6 Jean Naslian, *Les mémoires de Mgr. Jean Naslian sur les événements politico-religieux en Proche-Orient de 1914 à 1928*, Beyrouth: ed. Naslian, 1951, 2 volumes.

As for Pipes[7] and Carr,[8] these writers dealt with Armenia primarily in relation to the birth of the Soviet Union and the problem of nationalities[9] within that entity.

Armenian historians, albeit using diverse tones, have concentrated their attention on the violence suffered by the Armenians at the hands of the Turks during and soon after the First World War, with the object of conserving its memory and denouncing it before the public opinion of the world. In substance, their thesis maintained that the Turkish empire was guilty of genocide, aided by a lack of engagement on the part of the Western Powers. This thesis is largely supported by the memoirs of foreign witnesses such as the U.S. ambassador to Constantinople, Henry Morgenthau.[10] Other non-Armenian historians concur with this thesis as well.

As for the attitude of these historians, whether Armenian or not, towards the independent Republic, one finds a consensus that the Republic was a major event in the history of the Armenian people. Indeed, notwithstanding its brief duration—due not in small part to the lack of Western support— the Republic permitted the aggregation of the Armenians into a part, however small, of ancient Armenia, with their own political and administrative organization. Therefore, this study particularly bears in mind the republic's dramatic politico-military vicissitudes, without which the motives for the Vatican's attention towards the Armenians would not be understood. While it's certain that the genocide carried out by the Young Turks would be sufficient in explaining the Holy See's sympathy for Armenians, the possibility of the rebirth of a free Armenia, the hostility of many neighboring countries towards that outcome, and the substantial

---

7 Richard Pipes, *The Formation of the Soviet Union. Communism and Nationalism 1917–1923*, Cambridge Mass.: Harvard University Press, 1964.
8 Carr, Edward H., *La rivoluzione bolscevica 1917–1923*, Torino: Einaudi, 1964.
9 Translator's Note: *Nationalities*. The author and the document writers use this term to refer to that which might be more often called "ethnicities" in modern English parlance. Nationality, ethnicity and religious identification is discussed at length in document number 83.
10 Henry Morgenthau, *Ambassador Morgenthau's Story: the Documented Account of Armenian Genocide*, New York: New Age Publishers, 1975; *United States Diplomacy on the Bosphorus: the Diaries of Ambassador Morgenthau 1913-1916*, ed. and intro. Ara Sarafian, London: Gomidas Institute, 2005.

indifference of the Great Powers combined in heightening the Vatican's concerns for the people of Ararat.[11]

---

[11] For a general history of the Armenians and their culture *cfr.* V. Brjusov, *Annali del popolo aarmeno*, it. trans., introd. and notes by A. Ferrari, Milano: Greco & Greco ed., 1993; G. Dedeyan, (ed.), *Storia degli armeni*, it. ed. B. L. Zekiyan and A. Arslan, Milano: Guerini, 2002; A. Ferrari, *L'Ararat e la gru. Studi sulla storia e la cultura degli armeni*, Milano: ed. Mimesis, 2003; *Documenti Diplomatici italiani*, I–V, Firenze: Commissione per la pubblicazione dei Documenti Italiani sull' Armenia, 1998–2005. For a study of the Armenian question *ccfr.* Boghos Levon Zekiyan, "Questione armena? per puntualizzare la situazione attuale: schizzo di una sintesi storica" in idem, *L'Armenia e gli armeni. Polis lacerata e patria spirituale:la sfida di una sopravvivenza*, Milano: Guerini, 2000, pp. 41–69.

I. THE HOLY SEE FACING THE ARMENIAN QUESTION

On April 24th, 1915, the government of the Young Turks began the frightful Armenian genocide, which cost over one million lives in just a few short years.[12]

The Holy See exerted itself in every way possible to avoid or at least to limit the deportation and massacre of the Armenian people, as Riccardi shows on the basis of ample documentation.[13] Many steps were taken through the Apostolic Delegate in Constantinople, Mons. Dolci,[14] as well as, on September 10th, 1915, a personal letter from Pope Benedict XV to Sultan Mohammed V. It was an unprecedented gesture that resounded in the European press at the initiative of the Vatican, which wanted to give the measure a public character.

In the letter, the pope showed that he was already aware of the massacres of Armenian civilians and—expressing the belief that this was occurring against the sultan's wishes—urged him to intervene to stop the killings. Benedict XV didn't exclude the possibility that among the Armenians there might be rebels, who should, in any case, be tried and sentenced according

---

12 The bibliography of the genocide is vast; among the best [TN. Italian language] works on the subject: V. Dadrian, *Storia del genocidio armeno. Conflitti nazionali dai Balcani al Caucaso*, it. ed. by A. Arslan and B. L. Zekiyan, Milano: Guerini, 2003; *Armin T. Wegner e gli Armeni in Anatolia, 1915. Immagini e testimonanze*, Milano: Guerini, 1996; C. Mutafian, *Metz yeghern. Breve storia del genocidio degli armeni*, Milano: Guerini, 1995; Marco Impagliazzo, *Una finestra sul massacro. Documenti inediti sulla strage degli armeni 1915–1916*, Milano: Guerini, 2000; Y. Ternon, *Gli Armeni 1915–1916: il genocidio dimenticato*, it. tr. Milano: Rizzoli, 2003. For the Armenian diaspora *cfr.* D. M. Lang, *Armeni: Un popolo in esilio*, Bologna: Calderini, 1989.
13 Riccardi, *op. cit.*, pp. 98–105.
14 G. M. Croce, "I rappresentanti pontifici a Costantinopoli (1814–1922). Tra missione e diplomazia." *Roma/Armenia. Catalogo della Mostra Vaticana*, C. Mutafian, ed., Roma: De Luca, 1999, pp. 349–351.

to the law. He stressed that it was necessary to avoid involving defenseless civilians in any repression and, further, an appeal was made for imperial clemency toward the guilty.[15] This last request would seem to show a remarkable level of sympathy on the part of the pontiff for the Armenian people, even as they countered oppression.

The pope's letter had a twofold effect: firstly, it served to partially mitigate the Turkish persecution, especially of Catholics; secondly, it profoundly irritated the Ottoman government. Mohammed V, personally receiving Mons. Dolci, declared himself to be facing such a widespread Armenian conspiracy that the Turkish authorities were obliged to undertake mass deportations without distinguishing between peaceful and rebellious Armenians.

The sultan repeated the same position in his letter of reply to the pope.[16] The Holy See also attempted the diplomatic route, primarily with the Austrian and Bavarian governments,[17] achieving a certain amount of success, as shown by the warm thanks that the patriarch of the Armenian Apostolic Church in Constantinople, Zaven, sent to the pope in 1919 upon his return from deportation.[18]

Perhaps the most important step that Benedict XV took in support of the Armenians, though, was the *Note to the Leaders of the Belligerent Peoples* of August 1st, 1917.[19] In this document, at point 5, an appeal was made for the "structuring of Armenia", on par with that requested for the Balkan states and for Poland. It's significant that the pope had considered Armenian aspirations just as legitimate as those of the European countries. In both cases, the questions were to be handled, to the extent possible, by respecting the will of the interested peoples. Thus Benedict XV anticipated the spirit of Wilson's "Fourteen Points" of January 8th, 1918.[20] In the latter, however, the independence of Poland was called for unequivocally, while a more generic expression was used concerning the nationalities subject to the Ottoman Empire.

---

15 Riccardi, *op. cit.*, pp. 104–105.
16 *Op. cit.*, pp. 106–108.
17 *Ibid.*, pp. 105–106 and 110–111.
18 Doc. n° 40 of [?] March 1919, Constantinople - Dolci to Gasparri - AAEESS, *Asia* 57, 1, n° [?] and doc. n° 41 of 6 March 1919, Constantinople - Dolci to Gasparri - AAEESS, *Asia* 57, 1, n° [?].
19 "Una Nota del Sommo Pontefice ai capi dei popoli belligeranti." *L'Osservatore Romano*, 17 August 1917.
20 Naslian, *op. cit.*, p. 539.

II. THE RUSSIAN REVOLUTION AND ARMENIAN INDEPENDENCE

The events of war and of the October Revolution brought the Russian region of the Transcaucasus to proclaim its independence and, soon afterward, to split itself along the lines of the three major nationalities which it had comprised: Armenian, Azeri and Georgian. In May of 1918 the three states were officially established.

Ex-Russian Armenia,[21] now governed by the socialist party *Dashnaktsutiun*, or Armenian Revolutionary Federation (ARF), signed a demanding but ephemeral peace treaty with Turkey on June 4th. This accord would fall in November with the defeat of the Central Powers, but at the time it seemed necessary in order to put an end to the new massacres of Armenians following the Ottoman advance.

Regarding the relations between Turkey and the new Caucasian states, on June 26th, 1918, in the Turkish newspaper *Hilal*, an interview appeared with the secretary of the Azeri delegation, who had traveled to Constantinople to conclude a treaty of friendship with Turkey.

In this interview—a copy of which the apostolic delegate Dolci had sent to Secretary of State Cardinal Gasparri—the head of the Azeri delegation, Mehmed Emin Bey, declared that a treaty of friendship had been signed between the Azeris and the Turks and that relations among the three Caucasian republics were good.

For the moment, the cordiality of Turkish-Azeri relations was significant and perfectly comprehensible, since the Turks represented the Azeris' only hope of retaking Baku, which had been occupied in a coup by Armenian communists and Dashnaks. However, the Azeri delegate had made partially inexact declarations when he had spoken of the inexistence of an Armenian government. Actually, after the declaration of independence, the Armenian National Council ran a *de facto* government with full executive powers for a month, sending its own delegates to Constantinople, for example, as apostolic vice-administrators of the Armenian Catholics, noted in passing in a letter to their superior dated June 21st, 1918:[22]

---

21 On the Russian Armenians *cfr.* A. Ferrari, *Alla frontiera dell'impero. Gli armeni in Russia 1801–1917*, Milano: ed. Mimesis, 2000.
22 Doc. n° 14 of 21 June 1918, Tiflis - F. Kalatosoff and F. Kapojan to Mons. Der Abramian - AAEESS, Asia 57, 2, n° 81691.

[...] I have now heard that Mr. Ferdinando Tactagian is leaving for Constantinople as a member of the Armenian Delegation, to carry out peace talks; [...]

Finally, a government was formed on June 30th, 1918, i.e., four days after the Azeri declaration. Evidently contrasts among the Armenian factions were serious, but not enough so to impede the building of a normally structured executive.

In reality, Mehmed Emin Bey's statements would seem to have been an excuse for the Azeris to make ever more exorbitant demands on Armenian territory that had just been, as we have already said, reduced to 11,000 square kilometers.

The Turkish strategy was, essentially, aimed not only at reducing Armenia but surrounding her with hostile Muslim neighbors, in view of a final attack that would wipe out the country.[23] Even Christian Georgia practiced a policy of occupation with respect to Armenia, in the districts of Borcialo and Lori.[24]

Confronted with such generalized hostility, the Armenians acted to obtain the most authoritative international recognition possible.

---

23 Sidari, *op. cit.*, p. 124.
24 Sidari (in *ibid.*, p. 125) quoted by M. Varandian, *Le conflit arméno-géorgien et la guerre du Caucase*, Paris, 1919: "Ormai i rapporti tra i due paesi si erano inaspriti, e divennero tesi quando la Georgia (luglio 1918) spinse fuori dal suo confine quindicimila Armeni, in maggior parte donne e bambini, che per sfuggire agli Azerbaigiani si erano rifugiati in un villaggio di frontiera georgiano. Le truppe di quello Stato, che aveva la pretesa di assumersi la protezione del Caucaso, spinsero, con la punta delle baionette, quel gregge umano sino al limite del confine, ove ad attendere erano gli Azerbaigiani che massacrarono la maggior parte di quei disgraziati. Gli Armeni, che non erano in quel momento in grado di affrontare la Georgia, serbarono un astio profondo che sboccò, dopo pochi mesi, in una lotta aperta tra i due popoli che per secoli avevano vissuto in pace reciproca" ["By now relations between the two countries had soured and become tense when Georgia (in July of 1918) expelled from its borders fifteen thousand Armenians, mostly women and children, who in order to escape from the Azerbaijanis had taken refuge in a Georgian border village. The troops of that State, which had the pretention of assuming for itself the protection of the Caucasus, pushed that herd of humans at bayonet point up to the limit of the border where, to await them, were Azerbaijanis who massacred most of those unfortunates. The Armenians, who in that moment were not able to confront Georgia, harbored a deep rancour that found outlet, a few months later, in an open struggle between the two peoples who for centuries had lived in mutual peace."] pp. 72–73.

III. INITIAL ARMENIAN-VATICAN CONTACTS

Gradually, as the Turks advanced, the massacres of Armenians and of other Christians began again.

Relaying the news and asking for protection, calls were made to the Holy See from the Armenian Catholic bishop Der Abramian,[25] and from the eminent lay member of the Armenian Apostolic Church, Boghos Nubar Pasha, of whom we shall relate more further on.[26] To the latter, Cardinal Gasparri responded by telegram that the Holy See had already acted in the desired sense.[27] In fact, Gasparri had directed an encoded message to the Apostolic Nuncio in Monaco, in order that he take steps with the Chancellor of the German Empire in favor of the Armenians. The Chancellor's response was transmitted to Gasparri by the chargé d'affaires Schiappi.[28] In it, the German Chancellor—after having reported on a step taken by the Imperial government towards the Ottoman government, whereupon the most ample assurances had been given of positive Turkish disposition towards peaceful Armenians—called upon the Vatican Secretary of State to employ all his influence to impede the protests sponsored by the Armenian Revolutionary Committees in Switzerland. The Chancellor also mentioned Nubar, who would have been asked (by the Armenian

---

25 Doc. n° 1 of 5 March 1918, Rome - Der Abramian to the pope - AAEESS, *Asia* 57, 2, n° 59711; doc. n° 2 of 6 [or 7] March 1918, Rome - Der Abramian and others to the pope - AAEESS, *Asia* 57, 2, n° 59712.
26 Doc. n° 3 of 8 March 1918, Paris - telegr. from Nubar to the Vatican - AAEESS, *Asia* 57, 2, n° 57889.
27 Doc. n° 4 of 9 March 1918, Rome - telegr. from Gasparri to Nubar - AAEESS, *Asia* 57, 2, n° 57889. In fact, Gasparri had addressed an encryption to the Apostolic Nuncio in Monaco asking him to intervene with the Chancellor of the German Empire in favor of the Armenians, as can be inferred from doc. n° 9, p. 72, which makes reference to it.
28 Doc. n° 9 of 20 March 1918, Monaco - Schiappi to Gasparri - AAEESS, *Asia* 57, 2, n° 63502.

Committees, probably) to intervene with the British government in order to obtain military aid for the rebels.

On March 11th, Boghos Nubar addressed a letter of thanks to Gasparri for the pope's intervention on behalf of his compatriots and profited from that occasion to warn that the Turks, in turn, had been accusing the Armenians of having committed atrocities against Muslims.[29] According to Nubar, it was really just a Turkish pretext for giving themselves over to new anti-Armenian violence. On March 13th he sent another telegram to Gasparri in which he expressed the warmest thanks of the Armenian National Delegation.[30]

The succession of tragic news prompted Benedict XV to address the sultan directly once again, on March 12th, 1918.[31]

The sultan's reply, dated May 15th, 1918, arrived at the Vatican in the second half of June.[32] Therein, Mohammed V declared once more that, on the part of the Ottomans, there were no persecutory intentions whatsoever toward the Armenians. It was just that the Armenians were guilty of massacring the Muslim population of the Turkish territories just abandoned by the Russians. The sultan assured that peaceful Armenians had nothing to fear, and that he hoped for the re-establishment of good relations between the Armenians and the Muslims. As one can see, Mohammed V did not deviate from the official Turkish position placing the preponderance of responsibility on Armenians in their conflicts with Muslims.

In the meantime, the Holy See had taken some further steps in regard to the Turkish government through Mons. Dolci.[33] He had spoken to the German ambassador, Count Bernstorff, and to the acting Turkish foreign minister, Halil Bey, and had received soothing news about the fate of

---

29 Doc. n° 5 of 11 March 1918, Paris - Nubar to Gasparri - AAEESS, *Asia* 57, 2, n° 60608.

30 Doc. n° 6 of 13 March 1918, Paris - Nubar to Gasparri - AAEESS, *Asia* 57, 2, n° 59729. Evidently Nubar had already founded the Armenian National Delegation of which we will speak in regard to the Peace Conference.

31 Riccardi, *op. cit.*, p. 115. He found the handwritten letter in the Archive of Extraordinary Ecclesiastical Affairs, *Austria* 57.

32 Doc. n° 11 of 15 May 1918, Constantinople - The sultan to the pope - ASV, *Guerra* [War], *1914–18*, 244, 112, n° 67801, (in the transl. in French); Mons. Dolci's letter of accompaniment: doc. n° 12 of 14 June 1918, Constantinople - Dolci to Gasparri - *ibid.*; Gasparri's reply to Dolci: doc. n° 13 of 20 June 1918, Rome - handwritten draft from Gasparri to Dolci - *ibid.*

33 Doc. n° 7 of 19 March 1918, Constantinople - Dolci to Gasparri - ASV, *Guerra* [War], 1914–18, 244, 112, n° 66827.

Turkish Armenians, while through other channels the Apostolic Delegate received word of new deportations. Dolci had managed to get the Turkish press not to give too much publicity to presumed Armenian violence in the territories reoccupied by the Turks. On March 29th, the Apostolic Delegate gave notice of having needed to appeal once again to the German ambassador and to the Turkish foreign minister to prevent the deportation of Armenians from Ankara. Interestingly, the Vali of the city was opposed to the deportation. Mons. Dolci's action led to the Ottoman government's military commander's recall to Constantinople. Gasparri replied, thanking the Apostolic Delegate for the work carried out.[34]

A letter from the priests F. Kalatosoff and F. Kapojan, left in Tiflis as his vicars by the Apostolic Administrator Mons. Der Abramian, written June 21st but arrived in Rome in September, testifies as to the difficulties of postal communications, gives news of massacres, even of Catholic priests, and tells of the misery and confusion that reigned in the Caucasus.[35]

The Chaldean bishop Manna wrote to Gasparri on June 22nd, 1918 to ask, seeing the impossibility of continuing to send aid to the Christians of the Caucasus and of Persia via Russia, whether the cardinal were able to indicate a safer alternate route. He also gave news of rumors about the killing of the Nestorian patriarch.[36]

Gasparri responded that money could be sent through Dolci, whom he would quickly ask for more precise news regarding the fate of the Christians.[37]

In fact, he sent an encrypted telegram to Mons. Maglione, representative of the Holy See in Bern, such that he in turn would telegraph Dolci asking for confirmation of the slaying of the Nestorian patriarch.[38] This testifies as to the circuitous complications to which the Holy See was forced to resort in order to communicate with Dolci.[39]

---

34 Doc. n° 8 of 24 June 1918, Rome - handwritten draft from Gasparri to Dolci - ASV, *Guerra* [War], 1914–18, 244, 112, n° 66827.
35 Doc. n° 14 of 21 June 1918, Tiflis - Kalatosoff and Kapojan to Der Abramian - AAEESS, *Asia* 57, 2, n° 81691.
36 Doc. n° 15 of 22 June 1918, Rome - Manna to Gasparri - ASV, *Guerra* [War], 1914–18, 244 K 12 c, 306, n° 66909.
37 Doc. n° 16 of 25 June 1918, Rome - handwritten draft from Gasparri to Manna - *ibid.*
38 Doc. n° 17 of 26 June 1918, Rome - handwritten draft from Gasparri to Maglione - *ibid.*
39 Riccardi indicates another: Rome - Nunciature of Vienna - Constantinople. RICCARDI, *op. cit.*, p. 95.

Gasparri also sent a telegram to Mons. Pacelli, then Apostolic Nuncio to Monaco, asking him to sound out the German government on the possibility of sending help to the Christians of the Caucasus and Persia.[40] Pacelli replied that the government had declared itself willing to do so, but that he doubted the practical possibility of sending aid, especially to Persia.[41]

Meanwhile, the Armenian Republic initiated its first diplomatic contacts with the Holy See.

In July of 1918 the Apostolic Delegate to Constantinople, Monsignor Dolci, cordially received an Armenian delegation. The ambassadors had arrived to sign a peace agreement with the Turks and, mindful of the action taken by the Holy See on behalf of those deported during the massacres of World War I, did not want to fail to thank its representative.

But the discussion soon drifted towards strictly political themes, the Armenians giving thanks to pontifical efforts "in favor of the... Nation", a discreet but significant allusion to the Note sent by Benedict XV to the belligerent nations in 1917.

Even the Armenian delegates' admission of the Great Powers' hostility towards the new Republic appears to have been an invitation to the Holy See, not particularly veiled, to take up Armenia's defense even more.[42]

Worthy of note are the Armenian delegates' affirmations of German support for Georgia, not least in opposition to Azeri pan-Turkism which would have favored Turkish expansion in the oil-producing region of the Caucasus, causing the exclusion of Germany from the area.

Unfortunately, the document is missing its concluding pages, which prevents us from deepening, as it would merit, the study of the extent of Germany's and Austria's awareness of the massacre of Armenians on the part of the Young Turks.

Regarding the Vatican's posture towards the Armenian Republic, this can be better inferred from Dolci's successive dispatch of August 9th. In it, it is true, an explicit reference to the national question is lacking, but the underlined cordiality of the meeting on the part of Mons. Dolci and his haste in returning the visit show that the Holy See was not timid in

---

40 Doc. nº 19 of 9 July 1918, Rome - telegr. from Gasparri to Pacelli - ASV, 244 K12c, 306, nº 68898.
41 Doc. nº 20 of August 1918, Monaco - copy of the encrypted telegram from Pacelli to Gasparri - *ibid.*
42 Doc. nº 21 of 18 July 1918, Constantinople - Dolci to Gasparri - AAEESS, *Asia* 57, 2, nº [...]61.

beginning to take a position on the matter. The religious question itself is proof; it is a fact that the Armenian delegates demonstrated themselves to be "convinced schismatics", but their president's desire to see official relations soon established with the Holy See was noted with satisfaction and almost with relief by the pontifical representative.[43]

On October 24th, on the occasion of the Armenian delegation's return home, Mons. Dolci reported to Card. Gasparri, pontifical Secretary of State, and to Card. van Rossum, Prefect of *Propaganda Fide*, having encouraged the Armenians and the Georgians to consider the pope's charitable commitment and, given his immense spiritual authority, the possibility that political consolidation of Armenia might come about together with spiritual union with Rome.

Even Dolci's observation about Catholicism's natural respect towards constituted power sounded favorable for the new States.

Dolci reminded Gasparri and van Rossum of the Armenian insistence upon cementing diplomatic relations with the Vatican.[44]

Concerning the more strictly political aspect of developments, the pope's decision to establish the see of the Armenian Catholic Patriarch in Yerevan, in the newborn Republic, directly or through a representative, was also highly appreciated.

That decision might appear insignificant but, in a moment in which the Armenians were beginning a brief period of liberty, any recognition of them at all as a People and as a State was vital.

In fact, it was so much so that on November 4th Mons. Dolci was forced to relate to Cardinal Gasparri that, in the general satisfaction over the local transfer of the Catholic Patriarch, on October 30th an Armenian newspaper found reason to maintain that the pope had already provided for recognizing the republic diplomatically. The Catholic Patriarch should have sent an Apostolic Delegate of his own to the Yerevan government. Aside from the absolute ignorance of canon law (only the pope could send a similar representative), the attempt to exploit, in an exclusively political fashion, a measure that originally had, as always, a mainly pastoral character,

---

43 Doc. n° 22 of 9 August 1918, Constantinople - Dolci to Gasparri - AAEESS, *Asia* 57, 2, n° 81286.
44 Doc. n° 27 of 24 October 1918, Constantinople - Dolci to Gasparri - AAEESS, *Russia* 540 bis, n° 85097; doc. n° 28 of 24 October 1918, Constantinople - Dolci to van Rossum - CO, 106, 4, 2, 3, n° 1191.

is evident. Certainly the article in the newspaper *Jamanak* demonstrated the deep need Armenia had of receiving international support.[45]

After all, Mons. Dolci, receiving the Armenian delegates in a farewell visit on October 23rd, had already read them the pontifical Note of 1917, and the pope's 1915 letter to the sultan in which he called for an end to the massacres. In fact, Dolci told Cardinal Gasparri that publicizing the documents should not be greatly delayed, because knowledge of them would contribute enormously to raising the prestige of the Holy See. The reference was, in particular, to the pope's mention of Armenian independence.[46]

On December 20th, 1918, Damadian, who represented Nubar Pasha's National Delegation in Italy, made an appeal based on the passage in Benedict XV's *Note* regarding Armenian independence, in a letter to Cardinal Gasparri in which he also thanked the Holy See for the goodwill shown during the massacres, and again pleaded for support for the republic and its re-organization within its historical boundaries in order that Armenia reassume her role as a vanguard of Christianity and civilization in the East.[47]

In the audience Gasparri conceded to Damadian on December 20th, the latter probably conveyed, for information's sake, a copy of a memorandum addressed to the U.S. ambassador to the Italian state. Therein, after having recalled the Armenian military contribution to the Entente's victory, the National Delegation asked for Allied recognition of the Armenian Republic and the reunification of Russian Armenia with Turkish Armenia, under the guarantee of the League of Nations or one of the Entente Powers. The western powers had reason to favor an independent Armenia, considering that the country found itself on a plateau where two spheres of influence met: that of Great Britain to one side and that of Germany and of Turkey to the other. Armenia could thus become a buffer state between those Great Powers, so as to diminish possible frictions between them and, above all, to

---

45 Doc. n° 30 of 4 November 1918, Constantinople - Dolci to Gasparri - AAEESS, *Asia* 57, 2, n° [?].
46 Doc. n° 32 of 25 October 1918, Constantinople - Dolci to Gasparri - AAEESS, *Asia* 57, 1, n° 85098.
47 Doc. n° 35 of 20 December 1918, Rome - Damadian to Gasparri - AAEESS, *Asia* 57, 2, n° 84492.

block the realization of the pan-Turanist[48] dream by representing a barrier between Muslims and Christians:[49]

> [...]
> 3º - Une Arménie indépendante servirait les intérets de la paix établissant un Etat-Tampon entre l'influence germanique au Nord-Ovest et l'influence britannique au Sud-Est. Elle éléverait une véritable barrière entre l'Asie Mineure et le Turkestan, et empecherait ainsi la réalisation du rêve pantouranien qui est une réelle et grande menace pour la paix du monde et la Civilisation.
> [...]

On January 3rd, 1919, Damadian turned once again to Gasparri, advising him that the secret accords of 1916 regarding a partition of the Ottoman Empire among France, Britain and tsarist Russia—despite having lapsed after the Russian revolution—seemed confirmed by an Anglo-French declaration of November 8th, 1918.[50] This, therefore, jeopardized the reunification of Armenia, depriving her of the Turkish part and of a possible outlet on the Mediterranean.

> [...]
> Votre Eminence ne saurait ne pas se rendre compte combien ces accords, s'ils étaient appliqués comme bases du réglement du sort de la nation arménienne seraient préjudiciables aux intérêts de l'Arménie, qui réclame, à juste titre, *l'unification de tout son territoire historique, du Caucase à la Méditerranée,* baigné du sang de ses martyrs et de ses héros, *pour en constituer un Etat arménien libre et indépendant sous la garantie internationale des Puissances Alliés et des Etats-Unis d'Amérique ou de la Société des Nations, dès qu'elle serait réalisée*
> [...]

Damadian, then, asked the Holy See that—on the occasion of a visit, considered by him to be imminent, by President Wilson to the Vatican—

---

48 Translator's Note: *Pan-Turanism*. Distinct from its subset, pan-Turkism, a movement that sought to unite Turks with other ethnic groups (Tartars, Magyars, Finns among others) arguing linguistic connections in establishing racial classifications.
49 Doc. nº 31 of 11 October 1918, Rome - Memorandum of the Armenian National Delegation to the U.S. ambassador to Rome - AAEESS, *Asia* 57, 2 nº 84492.
50 It was not possible to ascertain the content of said declaration.

the pope promote the Armenian requests regarding all of historical Armenia belonging to the government of Yerevan.[51] It does not appear that a visit by Wilson to the Vatican was expected. However, the reference to the American president was motivated by Wilson's declarations in favor of the autonomy of the non-Turkish zones of the Ottoman Empire.

In January of 1919 the Peace Conference between the Allies and Turkey opened in Paris. Armenia gained representation, but the Delegation of the Republic of Yerevan found themselves side by side with the so-called Armenian National Delegation headed by Bogos Nubar Pasha, an Egyptian Armenian who had organized the Eastern Legion for the French during the war.

Nubar, a member of the Armenian upper-class, strongly connected to the Apostolic patriarchate, represented a conservative nationalism hostile to the ARF, it being a socialist party. Nubar was the spokesman for the Turkish-Armenians and he strenuously defended their importance before his co-nationals from the eastern zone.

With difficulty, and with the mediation of the Armenian Apostolic Church, success was achieved in making the two groups collaborate, "confederating" them into the Delegation of Integral Armenia in which Nubar and the ARF of Yerevan maintained their respective autonomy.[52]

Another difficulty arose for the Armenians from their complex relationship with the Russian monarchist general Denikin.

The Armenian government had declared its own neutrality in the Russian civil war but had added that Armenia would have been a country friendly to any Russia respecting the independence of the Republic.[53] On this basis, the government sent semi-official Armenian representatives both to the Bolsheviks and to the White forces, not least in order to try and obtain food and other aid. Denikin sent many times the amount requested, but little or nothing arrived at its destination because Georgia and Azerbaijan, hostile to Armenia over border issues, intercepted the aid.[54] When Denikin realized that supplies sent to Armenia went to benefit only Georgia and Azerbaijan, with whom Armenia was in conflict, he suspended all shipments.[55] In fact, of all the Caucasian states, only Armenia received

---

51 Doc. n° 36 of 3 January 1919, Rome - Damadian to Gasparri - AAEESS, *Asia* 57, 2, n° [?].
52 Hovannisian, *op. cit.*, p. 262.
53 Hovannisian, *op. cit.*, p. 360.
54 *Ibid.*, p. 361.
55 *Ibid.*, p. 364.

declarations of friendship on Denikin's part because, in his project of restoring a single and indivisible Russia, he could not tolerate the separation of Georgia and of Azerbaijan, while he was disposed to accept Armenia's autonomy, especially if, in peace treaty negotiations, she were able to obtain reunification with the Turkish territories all the way to Cilicia, and thus with the outlet to the Mediterranean. Also, in Paris—albeit only in private conversations with the president of the Armenian delegation Avedis Aharonian—Russian anti-Bolshevik exponents declared themselves in agreement over the independence of Armenia alone.[56]

However, the suspicion that a White victory could signify the reinstatement of Russian dominion over Armenia remained a shadow over relations between Denikin and top Armenian politicians.[57]

Pipes gives news of a formal accord in March of 1920, by which Armenia agreed to host retreating White forces and obtained from Denikin in exchange arms, munitions and financial aid.

While Armenian politicians debated these difficulties, the patriarch of the Armenian Catholics, Terzian, on January 15th, 1919, took the initiative of addressing a personal letter to the French premier Clémenceau, to Lloyd George, to Albert of Belgium and to Wilson.

It was evidently an unofficial intervention by the Armenian Catholic Church. Cardinal Marini, Prefect of the Sacred Congregation for the Oriental Church, was informed of it by Dolci after the fact,[58] but it does not appear that the Holy See even minimally disavowed the patriarch's initiative.

The missive was particularly directed to Clémenceau, as leader of the power apparently closest to Armenian interests. Terzian, after having recalled the sufferings of the Armenian people and their benevolence towards the Entente, expressed in no uncertain terms the hope that the recipients work towards assuring Armenia's independence within her historic borders: eastern and western Armenia and Cilicia.[59]

---

56 *Ibid.*, pp. 365–366 and 375–376.
57 *Ibid.*, p. 363.
58 Doc. n° 37 of 28 January 1919, Constantinople - Dolci to Marini - CO, *Armeni e Caucaso* [Armenians and the Caucasus], 105, 3, 5, n° 1525.
59 Doc. n° 38 of 15 January 1919, Constantinople - copy of the letter from Terzian to Clémenceau, Lloyd George, Albert of Belgium and Wilson - CO, *Armeni e Caucaso* [Armenians and the Caucasus], 105, 3, 5, n° 1525. Published by Naslian, *op. cit.*, vol. II, pp. 943–944.

The request was a risky one, since it had to do with claiming an enormous territory that was also inhabited by large Muslim minorities.

Terzian, as bishop, did not neglect to confront specifically religious problems that, for the Church, were equally as important as political ones, if not more so. The division of the Armenians into Apostolics, Catholics and Protestants required that the Constitution not reserve a privileged status to any one confession; otherwise the Catholics, who were a minority, would have suffered from discrimination. The Catholic Church thus had to be able to freely develop its own religious and charitable institutions for the good of Armenia herself.[60]

Finally, given that during the massacres the Turks had confiscated or otherwise alienated a variety of assets belonging to Armenians, it was indispensable that the new republic should receive congruous economic reparations. Such requests, as one may see, were quite concrete and show the support of the Catholic Church, especially of the Armenian Catholic Church, for the national claims.[61]

It does not appear that a response was given to the messages.

---

60 Doc. n° 38 cit.
61 *Ibid.*

IV. THE REUNIFICATION OF ARMENIA

The first act of the Delegation of Integral Armenia was the presentation, in February 1919, of a memorandum which requested the reunification of the two historical zones of Armenia with the addition of Cilicia and an outlet to the Mediterranean, vast areas of southeastern Anatolia inhabited by Muslim Turks and Kurds, and lastly the city of Kars and some territories contested by Georgians and Azeris. The new Armenian state should be placed under Allied tutelage or that of the League of Nations, which she asked to join. It was requested also that Armenia be placed under the fiduciary mandate of a western power for the first twenty years. Other minor dispositions regarded the reparations that Turkey should pay Armenians as compensation for the massacres, and the punishment of those responsible.[62]

The exorbitance of the Armenian requests could not avoid an uncertain response at best from the Great Powers, who in May began discussion over the fiduciary mandate. The candidacy of the USA was proposed for this responsibility, but the British observations—according to which it would neither be opportune to divide the ex-Turkish Empire into multiple mandates, nor should France be the one to exercise administration over the enormous territory that would result should partition not take place—provoked the decisive opposition of the French premier Clémenceau. President Wilson remained disturbed by the rivalries among the European allies and decided to accept with reservations the British proposal of a mandate the U.S. should accept regarding Armenia alone, for humanitarian reasons.[63]

Between the spring and summer of 1919 the advisability of a mandate and who should be entrusted with it was discussed, but nothing more. As far as sending contingents to safeguard the new governments in the Caucasus, Great Britain had been the first to move, but the pressure of public opinion against the war pushed the government to announce an

---

62 Sidari, *op. cit.*, pp. 132–133.
63 *Ibid.*, pp. 139–146.

upcoming withdrawal that, however, came to be continually put off. In place of the British it seemed for a while that the Italians might arrive; Orlando announced the creation of a contingent of 85,000 men, but the fall of his government, replaced by one under Nitti's leadership, put everything back under discussion. Nitti was hostile to the use of Italian troops abroad and, moreover, the fact that the allies should go into the Caucasus to counter Bolshevik penetration led him to fear the opposition of many Italian workers and the mutiny of the troops themselves.[64]

Armenia also encountered difficulty with the Entente over the problem of Upper Karabagh, in particular with the British, due to their pro-Azeri policy. Even today Karabagh is 70 percent Armenian, but juridically subject to the Republic of Azerbaijan.

In the Vatican, the question of Karabagh was signalled to Card. Marini by Dolci who sent an article about the massacres of Armenians perpetrated by the Azeri general Sultanov, nominated governor of Karabagh by the British.[65]

Perhaps it was precisely this Allied attitude that led the Armenians to overvalue every gesture of the Catholic Church as full diplomatic recognition. In fact, as in the case of the transfer of the patriarchate in Armenia, even the meaning of the patriarch's letter to the leaders of the European powers was distorted, transforming it into an exclusively political action.

In fact, on February 24th, 1919, Mons. Dolci indicated to Cardinal Marini of the Sacred Congregation for the Oriental Church that the newspaper *The Renaissance* had written of an alleged missive from the Pope himself to Wilson. As we can see, the Armenians' temptation to inflate and distort to their own advantage the moves made by the Catholic Church was too strong for them to resist. Even the unofficial letter of the Armenian Catholic patriarch had become a pontifical message![66]

---

64 Sidari, *op. cit.*, pp. 147–150.
65 Doc. n° 46, of 27 June 1919, Constantinople - Dolci to Marini - CO, *Armeni e Caucaso* [Armenians and the Caucasus], 105, 3, 5, n° 2375. British responsibilities and the indignation that these aroused in U.S. officers and diplomats present in the Caucasus as observers are treated at length in Hovannisian, (*op. cit.*, pp. 166–197) who also analyzes the possible reasons for Britain's clearly philo-Muslim policy.
66 Doc. n° 39 of 24 February 1919, Constantinople - Dolci to Marini - CO, 106, 4, 3, n° 1667.

Then, on March 18th, 1919, Mons. Dolci related, this time to Cardinal Gasparri, that the Armenian newspaper *Erivan* had highlighted the pope's dispatch of two delegates to Washington in order to promote the cause of a "united and independent greater" Armenia and to gain the benevolent attention of President Wilson.[67]

Actually, regarding these two articles, particularly the second, there is no hint of denial on Mons. Dolci's part concerning the news reported. The fact is that the pope's letter to Wilson has not been found, and there is absolutely no information regarding the dispatch of two delegates to Washington, either.

Certainly it's not a given that the pope should always have informed all of his delegates of diplomatic steps taken but, after the failure of Benedict XV's peace initiatives during the Great War, it is possible that he did not consider it useful to address new messages to the U.S. government.

The government of Yerevan, meanwhile, in honor of the first anniversary of independent Armenia, had decreed the reunification of the former Turkish provinces of Armenia with the former Russian ones, and had gone ahead with their partial occupation of territories, notwithstanding disputes with Nubar and his supporters regarding the identification of the Armenian people with the Caucasian Republic.

From the 21st to the 23rd of June the first free elections of independent Armenia were held, in which the ARF had 90 percent of the votes. The new government was headed by Alexander Khatissian, who assumed the offices of President of the Republic and Foreign Minister.

Over the summer of 1919, Armenia grew from 11,000 to 46,000 square kilometers annexing, among other places, Kars, and from May to July Nakhichevan.[68]

This consolidation of the Armenian Republic—linked, however, to the sad economic and religious conditions of the Armenian Catholics—led the Holy See to decide to send a Visitor Apostolic to the Caucasus.[69] Actually, this title aroused the opposition of the Apostolic Administrator still in office, Der Abramian. He had been summoned to Rome two years earlier to

---

67 Doc. n° 42 of 18 March 1919, Constantinople - Dolci to Gasparri - ASV *Guerra* [War], 1914–18, 244, 69, n° 90014.
68 Anahide Ter Minassian, *La République d'Arménie*, Bruxelles, Ed Complexe, 1989, pp. 119–129.
69 Doc. n° 45 of 2 March 1919, Tiflis - Kalatosoff to Dolci - transmitted 16 May 1919, Constantinople - Dolci to Gasparri - AAEESS, *Russia* 505, n° 1120.

report on his management of the Armenian Catholic Church of the Caucasus, given the accusations of authoritarianism against him. The nomination, then, of a Visitor Apostolic sounded to Der Abramian like a condemnation of his pastoral activity. He therefore asked, and obtained, in a letter to Mons. Papadopulos, Assessor of the Sacred Congregation for the Oriental Church,[70] which was also sent for the information of Card. Gasparri,[71] that the Visitor Apostolic be sent principally to the Georgian Catholic Church.[72]

On June 30th Card. Marini, Prefect of the Sacred Congregation for the Oriental Church, asked Card. Gasparri that the Holy See furnish its passport to the Visitor Apostolic F. Antonio Delpuch of the White Fathers (Missionaries of Africa), and obtain him a British pass, seeing as Great Britain controlled the Caucasus.[73]

Once again the destiny of the Republic seemed to take a positive turn, but a new and more terrible danger was already becoming apparent. While at the Paris Conference the Allies were engaged in passing off to one another the responsibility for a military intervention in the Caucasus in support of Armenia and of the other Republics, Turkey witnessed a resurgence of the conflict between the population and the armed forces on one side, and the Entente—in particular Greece, a member since 1917—on the other.

As is well known, the protagonist of the Turkish national revolt was Mustafa Kemal.

In July 1919, at Erzerum, in territory that would then be regained in several reconquests by Armenians, Kemal gave the rallying cry: not even one inch of Anatolia would be ceded to the Greeks and Armenians.

Under his impetus a fierce armed resistance quickly developed against the Greek invasion, a battle that would consequently be directed towards the Republic of Armenia.

In October 1919, while Kemal's revolt was in full course, Mons. Dolci wrote to Gasparri that the new situation had awoken strong apprehensions among Turkish Christians. He argued, however, that the alarm was "quite exaggerated" because, in his opinion, a renewal of Turkish violence against Christians would have been extremely counterproductive in terms of

---

70 Doc. n° 49 of 28 June 1919, Rome - Der Abramian to Papadopulos - AAEESS, *Russia* 540 bis, n° 92975.
71 V. doc. n° 48 of 1 July 1919, Rome - Der Abramian to Gasparri - *Ibid*.
72 Morozzo della Rocca, *op. cit.*, p. 81.
73 Doc. n° 47 of 30 June 1919, Rome - Marini a Gasparri - AAEESS, *Russia* 540 bis, n° 97077.

European public opinion and would therefore have provoked the ultimate collapse of the Ottoman Empire.[74]

Dolci also reported having had the opportunity to converse with the British High Commissioner in Constantinople, Admiral Robert. He had confirmed Dolci's impressions about the absence of danger to Christians.

Robert also made understood his conviction that Ukrainian, Georgian, and Armenian independence was detrimental, because it deprived the White tsarist armies of useful bases and rendered the Caucasus potentially subservient to German influence besides.

Dolci retorted that the reconstitution of Greater Russia would be the gravest error that Europe could commit. Whatever the political justifications expressed to Robert but not reported in the dispatch, the ecclesiastic's position had a precise motivation: orthodox, tsarist, Russia had never been benevolent towards her own Catholic subjects of any nationality, therefore her return would have signified a new period of difficulty and perhaps of persecution. Perhaps the fact did not escape Dolci that a fear of German influence on the day after her defeat appeared absurd, while the uncertainty of the civil war in Russia could certainly not exclude a Bolshevik victory (as then did come to pass). In this case the interests of the Holy See would have been equally compromised, and gravely so.

The independence of the small republics, then, was a preferable solution for the Holy See. It should then be considered that, as far as Armenia is concerned, she had always been—unique in the Caucasus—rigorously faithful to the Entente, while Georgia had always been inclined towards German protection and Azerbaijan, which Robert strangely did not even contemplate in his negativity, was openly Turkophile.[75]

---

74 Doc. n° 50 of 2 October 1919, Constantinople - Dolci to Gasparri - AAEESS, *Asia* 117, n° 10228.
75 *Ibid.*

V. FATHER DELPUCH'S MISSION

Delpuch's voyage, while originating with religious matters, could not avoid having a precise politico-diplomatic significance—again, according to the religious outlook of the Vatican.

Delpuch, in effect, was received with great cordiality by the three governments: the Azeri, the Armenian, and the Georgian.

Upon his arrival in Yerevan, Delpuch addressed a letter to the Armenian president Khatissian, also responsible for the country's foreign policy. In the missive, the Visitor Apostolic cited, in no uncertain terms, not only the pope's evident sympathy for the Armenians, which had expressed itself in continual humanitarian interventions to avoid or partially mitigate Turkish ferocity, but above all the pope's desire that Armenia would live finally in peace, that is, free and independent.

This phrase should suffice in making clear what the Holy See thought of the Republic of Armenia, because F. Delpuch would never have written it without being authorized by Rome to do so.

Obviously the good will should be reciprocal, Delpuch basically added, because the Armenian Catholics were a substantial minority in the nation and it was necessary that the Vatican could assure itself of the full possibility of assisting them religiously.

The State, therefore, should guarantee complete religious freedom, not only to worship, but also to establish solid structures such as private religious schools and hospitals endowed with real estate and assets. It has to do, notes Delpuch, with entities like schools, which would represent important centers of Armenian culture, since the basic subjects would be Armenian language, literature and history. The Church was, at any rate, ready to discuss the details of the accord.

Delpuch concluded with great tact, hoping to report good news to the pope who had spoken up first in defense of the Armenians. Thus he implied that, if Armenians really took freedom to heart, they should be ready to respect the religious freedom of minorities.[76]

---

[76] Doc. n° 51 of 21 October 1919, Yerevan - Delpuch to the Armenian Foreign Minister - AAEESS, *Asia* 126, n° 3643.

In early November, Khatissian replied very warmly, giving the most ample assurances possible to the Catholic Church, thanking the pope for his humanitarian efforts in the past and, in closing, trusting in the Vatican for additional support in the future.[77]

In the report of November 21st, Delpuch highlights the exquisite hospitality with which he was received by the Armenians, as well as by the Georgians and Azeris. Khatissian had told him of his knowledge of the personal letter that Benedict XV had sent to Sultan Mohammed V during the war in order to halt the massacres. The gesture had not failed to engender the highest appreciation among the Armenians, therefore the Church could be sure of acting freely in the exercise of its ministry.

Continuing his report, F. Delpuch noted that all the people with the most responsibility, of whatever social class, looked to Rome as a base of support and as an irreplaceable model. This was expressly demonstrated by the kindness shown the representative, even unofficial, of the pope. The Armenians were aware of F. Delpuch's rank as a simple priest, but his role of Visitor Apostolic sufficed to confer upon him great honors wherever he might visit. It is true that at the outset he was taken for an actual Nuncio even by Georgia and by Azerbaijan, but that did not prevent—once the misunderstanding was cleared up—the pope's envoy in any way from enjoying the greatest sympathies and arousing the highest of hopes in the Caucasian states.[78]

The report of Delpuch's which we examined was directed to Mons. Isaia Papadopulos, Assessor of the Sacred Congregation for the Oriental Church. This body was about to assume pastoral care of the Caucasus in a more direct way than in the past.

Before returning to Italy, Delpuch did not want to fail to pay a last visit to the Armenian President. During this visit, on November 27th, 1919, the priest, in addition to routine formal personal thanksgivings, emphasized that the pope, full of affection towards Armenia, would by all means support her noble and legitimate aspirations for independence. A people faithful to their Christian tradition, which had paid for such affiliation with unheard-of suffering, would not be forgotten by the Holy See.[79]

---

77 Doc. n° 52 of 3 November 1919, Yerevan - Alkhatissian and der Akopian to Delpuch - AAEESS, *Asia* 126, n° 3643.
78 Doc. n° 53 of 21 November 1919, Tiflis - Delpuch to Papadopulos - AAEESS, *Asia* 126, n° 3643.
79 Doc. n° 54 of 27 November 1919, Tiflis - Delpuch to Khatissian - CO, 106, 2, 3, n° 3228.

At the end of his mission in the Caucasus Delpuch wrote out a new and more exhaustive report for the Congregation for the Oriental Church.[80] In it—after having perceptively analyzed the political problems of the Caucasus and those more strictly religious, especially regarding relations internal to the Catholic community divided between Georgian Catholics and Armenian Catholics—he proposed practical measures to reinforce the Church's actions in the region.

Delpuch's primary consideration was that the Armenian government of the socialist *Dashnaktsutiun* party was indeed secular, but that it did not suppress religious freedom at least towards the Armenian Apostolic Church. Besides, the activity of the State had purely political goals and not ones based on class. And it was in fact this patriotic qualification that had earned them the full support of the Apostolic Church: many ecclesiastics were full members.[81]

Harmony, however, was far-off for Armenian political leaders and that weakened the newborn Republic, Delpuch noted worriedly; the sole factor for unification was hatred towards the neighboring Muslim Turks and Azeris, their age-old persecutors.[82]

Nevertheless, considering that the Caucasus was confined between Russia and Turkey, a federation among the three republics similar to the dissolved Transcaucasia seemed opportune to him.[83]

That notwithstanding, the rapport between Georgians and Armenians was also certainly not the best: many Georgians judged Armenians far too clever and unscrupulous in business dealings, while many Armenians considered Georgians lazy and hedonistic.

In the cities where the two groups both lived, all the wealth ended up in the hands of the Armenians. The Georgians, therefore, considered them their own ruin, and held against them the preference accorded by the Tsars over the course of centuries.[84]

It is true that the Georgians often acted as mediators, authentic agents of peace, in the conflict between Armenia and Azerbaijan, with whom they were on excellent terms; but the division between the two Christian peoples remained profound.

---

80 Doc. n° 55 n.d. [perhaps January 1920] - Report from Delpuch to the S. Congr. Oriental Church - CO, 106, 2, 3, n° 3516.
81 Doc. n° 55 cit.
82 *Ibid.*
83 *Ibid.*
84 *Ibid.*

Delpuch did not commit himself to judging the Armenian attitude towards the Georgians favorably, but he recognized that with the Muslims, as with the Azeris, the Armenians had not been able to establish a peaceful coexistence. For Delpuch, anyway, the hatred between Armenian and Azeri was that between oppressed and oppressor, and the Armenian struggle was dictated by motivations of self-defense, pure and simple. The detail is not irrelevant, because in the case of conflicts the Holy See has demonstrated a great deal of caution before sympathizing with one of the contenders; the fact that, at least in part, Delpuch pronounced himself in favor of the Armenians means that it was not morally possible to ignore or relativize with equidistance the Armenian people's sufferings.[85]

And precisely in order to put an end to her suffering, Armenia believed international recognition of the republic necessary and, at least in part, conclusive. Georgia and Azerbaijan hoped likewise, though having less need of it, perhaps, for the survival of their respective populations. To Delpuch, Georgia seemed the more suited to obtain a *de facto* recognition from the Holy See with the dispatch of a Prelate.

The Peace Conference, even at the end of 1919, delayed in recognizing the three republics *de jure*. Only Georgia and Azerbaijan had obtained a *de facto* recognition, an ambiguous formula that had not been applied to Armenia, however. Delpuch declared he did not want to investigate the cause (or rather judge the motive) for this attitude of the great powers'. He only noted that it was cause for great bitterness on the part of the interested parties, who now had even more reason to hope for pontifical recognition. The welcome shown the Visitor demonstrated as much.[86]

Certainly, notwithstanding Vatican sympathy, there were plenty of practical difficulties in establishing official relations. In the first place, as we have said, the turbulence itself of the situation in the Caucasus led the Holy See to maintain caution in its concrete steps. Besides, the low number of Armenian Catholics compared with Georgian ones suggested, at least provisionally, the sending of an apostolic representative just to Tiflis, the Georgian capital. He then could have had a secondary residence in Yerevan, staying there from time to time. A fixed see also in Azerbaijan, instead, did not seem necessary to Delpuch because in the Muslim states the pope's prestige was such that the governments showed themselves to be rather liberal towards Catholics.

---

85 *Ibid.*
86 *Ibid.*

According to Delpuch, it should probably not have to do with a Delegate or of a Nuncio, but another Visitor.

The Armenians and the Georgians had accepted.

In the last part of his report, Delpuch then described the dispatch of an unofficial envoy as the best temporary means of accommodating the requests of all the Caucasian republics, at the same time giving the region an ecclesiastical organization conforming to the needs of the Church.[87]

Delpuch underlined that the interest of the Holy See in attracting the local populations was to help fulfill them in that which they rightly sought, avoiding, however, hasty gestures that might then have aroused jealousies, resentments, reawakening age-old hatreds even among the Christians.[88]

The title of the pontifical representative should be that of Visitor Apostolic, the same carried by Delpuch. Precisely the sense of indeterminacy of this office permitted carrying out the preliminary work that would permit the establishment of normal relations in a more tranquil future. Besides, the Visitor would not be supervising only the Transcaucasus, but also the Russian north Caucasus, and his office would be limited in duration, according to Delpuch.

The residence, lastly, as proposed to Khatissian, would have been in Tiflis and subordinately in Yerevan.[89]

The report, supplied with observations on the religious state of the region that are beyond the object of this study, received a wholly positive welcome in Rome.

Cardinal van Rossum, Prefect of *Propaganda Fide*, in turn made his own commentary report for the Vatican vertices, in which he accepted all of Delpuch's proposals.

After having observed that, usually, the Holy See in similar cases went on to nominate a Delegate, he added that such a delegate should have jurisdiction and responsibilities delimited in a very precise way. In the Caucasus, instead, the loosening of canonical discipline, the relationship between the Armenian and Georgian clergy and the creation of complex structures like schools, hospitals etc., should be subject to extraordinary discretionary measures that did not enter into the responsibility of a normal diplomatic representative.[90]

---

87 *Ibid.*
88 *Ibid.*
89 *Ibid.*
90 doc. n° 56 n.d. - relation of van Rossum on Delpuch's report - CO, 106, 2, 3, n° 3825, pp. 6–8.

Moreover, noted van Rossum, a Delegate supervises one or more States, and the borders in the Caucasus had not yet been defined by the Great Powers, nor had the Holy See decided how many Delegates to send to the region.[91]

At any rate, should the pontifical envoy have demonstrated himself to be inferior to his duties or have offended the sensibilities of the populations, it would have been easier to recall a Visitor as opposed to a Delegate.[92]

The dispatch of a Delegate still remained, however, even for van Rossum, the goal at which to arrive.

For the meantime, it was opportune that the Visitor have jurisdiction over all the territories Delpuch indicated, including the Crimea. Southern Russia and the northern Caucasus would be provided for later on with the dispatching of another Visitor, like the one for the Ukraine.[93]

On January 13, 1920, Mons. Dolci communicated to Card. Gasparri that Delpuch, on November 12th, had announced to him his imminent return. In this letter, Delpuch related that—given the immense prestige of the Holy See and the parallel proselytizing carried out in Armenia by various American Protestant sects—it would be absolutely disastrous if the visit did not lead to concrete measures on the Vatican's part in favor of the Armenians, both from the religious-missionary point of view and the political one.[94]

The Vatican Secretary of State, for his part, had already hastened on January 15th of 1920 to send warm thanks to the Armenian President Khatissian for all the kindnesses lavished upon the Holy See's envoy. In this missive, Gasparri took the opportunity to restate once again the hope that Armenia safeguard the rights of the local Catholic Church, and to confirm the pope's wishes for every moral and material progress of the nation.[95]

F. Delpuch's mission had an exploratory sense; it was a move on the part of the Holy See to carry out an initial reconnaissance of the conditions in the Caucasus and of the concrete possibilities for reorganization of religious life and for establishing contacts with the three Transcaucasian republics.

The results of the mission, fairly positive, show the openness of the local governments to the Catholic Church's freedom of action.

---

91 *Ibid.*
92 *Ibid.*
93 *Ibid.*
94 Doc. n° 57 of 13 January 1920, Constantinople - Dolci to Marini - CO, 106, 2, 3, n° 3172.
95 Doc. n° 58 of 15 January 1920, Rome – handwritten draft of Gasparri to Khatissian - AAEESS, *Asia* 126, n° 3643.

VI. THE PARIS PEACE CONFERENCE

Finally, in January 1920, the moment arrived for the Holy See to promote the Armenian cause in a more specifically diplomatic arena.

The Armenian Apostolic patriarch Zaven, planning to go to the Paris Peace Conference, also invited the Lieutenant (*Locum Tenens*) of the Armenian Catholic patriarchate, Mons. Sayeghian, to accompany him in order to carry out a more coordinated and more powerful initiative.[96]

Cardinal Gasparri, urged to issue the necessary *nulla osta*, accepted the idea but— foreseeing that the Catholic patriarch Terzian would probably go to Paris as well—did not want to leave the ecclesiastical administration of the patriarchate completely uncovered and without a guide; thus he sent Mons. Naslian, the bishop of Trabzon, to France in Sayeghian's place.[97]

---

96 Doc. n° 59 of 20 January 1920, Constantinople - telegram encrypted from Cesarano to Gasparri - AAEESS, Asia 57, 2, n° 1066 : "Patriarca Armeno Gregoriano ha deciso di recarsi a Parigi per favorire causa armena ed ha pure invitato Luogotenente Sayeghian ad andarvi oppure inviare vescovo patriarcato armeno cattolico rappresentante. Al Luogotenente sembra che proposta gioverebbe interessi cattolici e prestigio patriarcato. Se Santa Sede trova proposta accettabile, si implora autorizzazione per partire con risposta telegrafica." ["Armenian Gregorian Patriarch has decided to go to Paris to promote Armenian cause and has even invited Lieutenant Sayeghian to go otherwise send bishop representative Armenian Catholic patriarchate. To the Lieutenant seems proposal would be good for Catholic interests and prestige of patriarchate. If Holy See finds proposal acceptable, authorization begged to leave with telegraphic reply."]

97 Doc. n° 60 of 28 January 1920, Rome - Gasparri to Cesarano - AAEESS, *Asia* 57, 2, n° 1066 : "In risposta suo cifrato N. 83 le significo che Santo Padre permette a Monsignor Giovanni Naslian di fare parte missione armena Parigi, quale rappresentante patriarcato armeno cattolico. Se detto Prelato è già in viaggio per Roma si recherà poi a Parigi di qui" ["In reply your encryption N. 83 I inform you that Holy Father permits Monsignor Giovanni Naslian to take part Armenian mission Paris, as representative Armenian Catholic patriarchate. If said Prelate is already en route to Rome he will then go to Paris from here"].

The choice of Mons. Naslian as representative of the Armenian Catholics showed itself to be an extremely fortunate one, as he was a tireless activist for the Armenian cause.

On March 12th he took the initiative of addressing French Catholic public opinion with an appeal to all bishops. In this—after having recalled and strongly emphasized the Turkish persecutions carried out, for the most part, precisely out of hatred for Christianity, and after having exalted the traditional friendship and recent alliance between France and the Armenians—Naslian summarized the desires of the new republic with clarity and firmness.[98]

These were: 1) the constitution of a free and independent Armenian state; 2) the extension of her territory and the concession of both an outlet to the sea and of borders along the zone of French occupation in the Middle East; 3) the return to Christianity of the Armenians forcibly converted to Islam; 4) the release of Armenian women and children held prisoner; 5) repatriation assistance for the survivors of massacres, dispersed throughout the Middle East; 6) disarmament of the Turks and guarantees for the lives of the Armenians; 7) the restitution of assets or compensation on the part of the Turks to individuals and to the Armenian religious communities.

Naslian's requests were along the lines of those presented by the Armenian delegates at the Paris Peace Conference.[99] In fact, at least as far as borders were concerned, their official memorandum laid out—in a much more detailed fashion however—the same requests about the borders of the new republic. In addition to everything Naslian asked for the Entente powers, beyond defining the borders of Armenia, to take on the burden of securing the new state with a mandate. This should be entrusted to a power acceptable to the Armenians and was not to last more than twenty years. The acting power would have had the task of evacuating the Turks from the occupied territories, punishing those responsible for the massacres of Armenians, distancing from Armenian borders the nomadic tribes which threatened them, and lastly of expelling from Armenia the Muslim colonies settled there in the period of Abdul Hamid and the Young Turks.

One last request by the delegates, not repeated in Naslian's appeal, was the right of Armenians living abroad to opt for Armenian citizenship within five years.

---

98 Doc. n° 63 of 12 March 1920, Paris - Naslian to French public opinion - AAEESS, *Asia* 57, 2, n [?].
99 Sidari, *op. cit.*, pp. 132–133.

Naslian, in support of his requests, addressed a memorandum to the French Premier. To Clémenceau, beyond that asked of the French bishops (excepting the return to the Church of those converted by force), he also directed specifically Catholic wishes; basically, he wished for continuous special French protection of the Armenian Catholic Church.[100]

Thinking that Armenia and in particular the Armenian Catholic Church would not be able to sustain themselves without French support, Naslian promised the Parisian government to coordinate the interests of the Armenian Catholic patriarchate with French interests.

In particular, Naslian asked France to open schools and universities in Armenia, to bestow scholarships in France to young Armenians, and to help the Armenian Catholic Patriarchate in the immense work of reconstruction of the twelve dioceses devastated by the Turks.

There does not appear to have been any response to the appeal.[101] Considering Clémenceau's secular convictions, after all, it's not really any wonder; and perhaps because Naslian's requests were excessive, as well. Let us recall that he was in Paris together with representatives of the Armenian Apostolic Church and of the Delegation of Integral Armenia.

On April 5th, 1920, writing to Cardinal Gasparri about the work at the Conference, Naslian confirmed Nubar's subjection before the Apostolic Patriarch Zaven, while the government delegation—perhaps precisely because it was more secular—appeared to him more prudent and equidistant; its position was actually closer to the interests of the Catholic Church.[102]

> [...]
> Overall, as Your Eminence will see, the arrangements that were made are very liberal and tolerant, and will be extremely good for the institutions that the Catholic Church would like to create and found in Armenia.
>
> [...]
> The Delegation of the Armenian Republic, it pleases me to say, was most explicit in favor of Catholicism in Armenia and in its ever more ample and liberal assurances.

---

100 Doc. 64 of 13 March 1920, Paris - Naslian to Clémenceau - AAEESS, *Asia* 57, 2, n° [?].
101 There is no trace of it in Naslian's memoirs.
102 Doc. n° 67 of 4 May 1920, Paris – handwritten letter from Naslian to Gasparri - AAEESS, *Asia* 57, 2, n° 5288.

The composition of the republican delegation, in Naslian's opinion, was much more authoritative—thanks to the professional qualities of its members, comprising former tsarist generals, economic experts and others—and displayed a much more serious and responsible attitude than that of Nubar.[103]

The assurances of the envoys from Yerevan appeared, at least formally, quite well-disposed towards the Catholics, perhaps more in order not to lose Vatican sympathies than for any special preference.

It should be said in fact, observed Naslian, that the republic had the natural tendency to favor every institution that might assist in national rebirth. And the Apostolic Church, with a widespread network in the country and having greater influence over the masses, was more able to contribute to a political effort. In any case, its members, like the bishop of Yerevan, demonstrated quite a notable activism with respect to the Catholic Patriarchate. Hence Mons. Naslian warned the Vatican against maintaining the *statu quo* in Armenian Catholic affairs. The clear impression must be given that they shall be second to none in the work of reconstruction, not least from a financial point of view.

The Apostolic bishop of Yerevan had made contacts with many Armenian communities in Europe and was preparing to go to America, basing his talks on three apodictic assertions: first, the freedom of worship guaranteed by the state is fully in line with Apostolic tradition (Naslian inserted here a "*sic*" of incredulity); second, the Apostolic Church is the oldest in the country and the most deeply-rooted in its people; third, it has shared with the people their vicissitudes and age-old suffering, therefore it has a right to special legal and financial support on the part of the state.

Naslian retorted to the contrary that it was the moment to profit from the confusion among the apostolic clergy after the persecutions, from the Republic's need for Vatican support, and from the general religious reshuffling that reigned in the country. However, to be incisive it was necessary to be active at all costs.[104]

But the principal purpose, perhaps, of this letter was to send Cardinal Gasparri the text of a document edited at the Conference of London, and there consigned to the Armenian delegates in order to have their observations on it. Said text was to have been made part of the peace treaty and regarded the totality of the obligations of the Armenian government, pertaining to ethnic or religious minorities and to the preferential economic

---

103 *Ibid.*
104 Doc. n° 67 cit.

and customs treatment to be accorded member countries of the League of Nations.

Naslian related to Gasparri that the discussion over the document had taken place in the presence of religious representatives as well. The document had been approved, with the addition of a clause to art. 5 regarding the right of control on the part of the Armenian government over the contemplative institutions.[105]

---

[105] *Attachment* to doc. n° 67 cit.

VII. THE LONDON AND SAN REMO CONFERENCES

The collapse of the Russian monarchists in January 1920 had as an effect the recognition, still only *de facto*, of the three Caucasian republics on the part of the Allies.

This recognition was possible because—having lost their greatest ally against communism in southern Russia—nothing remained to the Entente but to rely on the three republics of the Caucasus, governed by socialist parties but clearly anti-Bolshevik.

The Holy See very probably did not fail to send its congratulations, as we may infer from the request of Mons. Papadopulos, Assessor of the Sacred Congregation for the Oriental Church, directed to Mons. Cerretti, secretary of the Congregation for Extraordinary Ecclesiastical Affairs.[106] In April of 1920, Gasparri wrote to Aharonian, the President of the Delegation of the Armenian Republic to the Peace Conference, assuring him of papal interest in all matters having to do with Armenia.[107]

> Je n'ai pas manqué de transmettre au Saint Père l'expression des nobles sentiments que Votre Excellence a bien voulu formuler dans sa lettre du 3 Avril courant.[108]
>
> Sa Sainteté, vivement touché, m'a chargé de Vous confirmer encore une fois la sollicitude toute paternelle avec laquelle Elle suit les questions se rattachant au sort de la généreuse nation arménienne [...]

---

106 Doc. n° 62 of 6 March 1920, Rome - Papadopulos to Cerretti - AAEESS, *Asia* 126, n° 3643.
107 Doc. n° 66 of [?] April 1920, Rome - Gasparri to Aharonian - AAEESS, *Asia* 57, 2, n° 4764.
108 Gasparri had received two copies of the historical atlas of Armenia that had served as a basis for Armenian national claims, together with a letter of thanks from Aharonian for the pope.

Armenia's situation, however, did not improve as a result, and Allied differences in its regard remained significant. Talks moved to London in February 1920 and continued in San Remo in April.

A French willingness to send troops to the Caucasus via Anatolia and not the Black Sea met with tough British opposition. In fact, London saw in it merely an attempt to usurp the American fiduciary mandate, altering the equilibrium of the region to their disadvantage and threatening British interests in Syria, whose destiny had not yet been defined.

Amidst the mutual hostility of the Allied powers, the only unanimous decision was to place the republic under the protection of the League of Nations anyway, while the United States Congress had not yet come to a decision regarding the mandate in Armenia. On the other hand, American appeals not to abandon the weak nation to her age-old enemies provoked a contemptuous European response: since the Armenian question was tied to that of the imminent signing of the peace treaty with Turkey, the French declared that it should not be dependent on "the eccentricities of the American president."[109]

During April 20th's meeting at the San Remo Conference, the League of Nations presented a memorandum in which they excluded the assumption of a fiduciary mandate on their part, because that would have been contrary to article 22 of the founding Pact. That notwithstanding, the League would assume the responsibility of formally investing a Power with this duty, on the condition that satisfactory guarantees were received on several points:

I. Armenian financial resources, in the absence of which the Allied powers should advance the funds necessary to the survival of the state.

II. Armenian military resources: the lack of League's own army and the permanence of some Armenian territories in Turkish hands rendered Allied intervention indispensable to the region up until the time that she should be able to defend herself.

III. Access to the sea, essential to the country's economy and to connections between Armenia and the mandatory state.[110]

The Allied response to the League was the entrusting of military and financial problems to their respective experts, in addition to recourse to the generosity of rich Armenians for an initial round of fundraising.

The military question, however, remained thorny: according to the experts, four divisions would be needed for Armenia alone, plus another twenty-three in order to impose Turkish compliance with the future peace

---

109 Sidari, *op. cit.*, p. 172.
110 Sidari, *op. cit.*, pp.173–74.

treaty. The British and the French appeared contrary to sending their troops to the Caucasus. Armenia should be solely armed and equipped, with the eventual aid of European officials in training her army, but should be able to defend herself on her own, otherwise it would be better that she not exist. Let the Americans take care of sending divisions in aid to Yerevan, seeing as it means so much to them.

That notwithstanding, they came to a compromise: the USA would handle the financial stewardship, while the recruitment of new troops would be carried out by the Anglo-French.[111]

During the course of April—while in successive sessions the order of business was dealing the problem of Erzerum, a city in Turkish Armenia still in the hands of the Kemalists—Azerbaijan suffered a political upheaval, signaling a general change afoot in the order of things in the Caucasus: the Azeri communists took power with a revolt and obtained the intervention of the Red Army.

In the Karabagh, on the night between the 22nd and the 23rd of March, an Armenian insurrection took place against reunification with Azerbaijan. On April 4th the Azeri army carried out a ferocious repression, and on April 13th Armenia sent a contingent of her own in aid of the insurrectionists.[112]

On the same date, the pontiff received an appeal on the part of the delegate from Karabagh and Zangezur, Tigran Nazarian, such that he intervene with the Peace Conference against the reunification of those two provinces with Azerbaijan.[113]

On May 5th the Khatissian government came to be substituted with that of Hamazasp Ohandjanian, constituted entirely of the directorate of the ARF. This exceptional measure, contrary to a resolution approved at the ninth Party congress, was explained by the need to distance the republic from a mortal danger after the sovietization of Azerbaijan and the risk of a Russian invasion of Armenia. On May 10th a communist revolutionary committee proclaimed the Soviet Republic of Armenia and declared that the Dashnak government had been dismissed. Ohandjanian mobilized the faithful troops and Dashnak militants on the night between May 14th and 15th, and the revolt was soon put down.[114]

---

111 Sidari, *op. cit.*, pp. 174–180.
112 Ter Minassian, *op. cit.*, p. 202.
113 Doc. n° 69 of 13 April 1920, Rome - Tigran Nazarian to the pope - AAEESS, *Asia* 57, 1, n° 5293.
114 Ter Minassian, *op.cit.* pp. 210–211.

On April 30th, however, the authorities had already decided to send Levon Shant, a diplomat *sui generis* with a brilliant career as a playwright behind him, to Moscow. Shant was charged with negotiating with the Russians starting from the following conditions: 1) Russian recognition of Armenia including the Karabagh, the Nakhichevan and another territory contested with the Muslims, Zangezur; 2) acceptance of the reunification of Turkish Armenia with ex-Russian Armenia; 3) Russian non-interference in internal Armenian politics; 4) authorization for those Armenians who had taken refuge in the northern Caucasus to return to the country with their goods.

The Russians, led by Georgi Chicherin, promised to respect the Armenian government, to mediate with Mustafa Kemal regarding western Armenia, and to ask the Turks to cede the provinces of Van and Bitlis. Chicherin also accepted the repatriation of the refugees and the annexation of Zangezur and Nakhichevan to Armenia, but asked for a referendum for Karabagh and, in rebuking Armenia's ties to the Entente, admonished her not to obstruct the Kemalists in their struggle against "the Anglo-French imperialists".

On June 10th, Shant reported to his government that an initial accord had been reached and asked authorization to conclude it.

Yerevan hesitated, in order to maintain western sympathies, until, in July, the Russians interrupted negotiations, perhaps out of regard for the Azeri communists, and asked to resume the talks in Yerevan where they were represented by Boris Legran.[115]

---

115 *Ibid.*, pp. 205–207.

VIII. TOWARDS THE TREATY OF SÈVRES

The San Remo Conference ended on 26 April with a proposal for a Turkish peace treaty that, as far as regarded Armenia, entrusted the definition of the respective borders to the arbitration of President Wilson. Provisionally, the borders would remain the same, up until such time as those between Armenia and the other two Caucasian republics should be drawn up by the Allied Council following U.S. arbitration, unless an accord was arrived at directly by the three interested parties.[116]

In any case, the draft of the treaty was not very satisfactory to the Armenians, who realized that the Allied powers had every intention of abandoning them precisely at the moment the Kemalists, with the support of the Russians and sovietized Azerbaijan, threatened the Armenian Republic.

Mons. Naslian interpreted this Armenian disappointment in a letter to the Sacred Congregation for the Oriental Church. In it, he related as follows:[117]

> The affairs in Armenia are not comforting: in the Caucasus the definitive extermination of all the surviving Armenians threatens; means of defense are lacking and the Tartars in league with the Turks are decided to crush them, and perhaps they are already at work, so that before the diplomatic solution to the question arrives perhaps we shall bemoan the Turkish idea of a solution. Captain Poidebard, Jesuit, who is on his way back from Yerevan, told me a true final catastrophe is imminent, especially after the Bolshevik invasion, and thus he advised me to warn the Holy See so that it might in some way avert this disaster by intervening energetically wherever possible. I am waiting for a report from the Captain on the

---

116 Sidari, *op. cit.*, p. 195.
117 Doc. n° 70 of 27 May 1920, Paris - Naslian to Mons. [Papadopulos?] - CO, 106, 2, 3, n° 4363.

subject, and then I will lay out the case to the Holy Father. [...]

Almost contemporaneously, the Apostolic Delegate Dolci in Constantinople took in the bad mood of the Ottoman government. The latter had been called to sign a very onerous peace treaty, while it had already lost, to Kemal's benefit, all influence over the Turkish [Muslim] people. It is evident, then, that it was extremely recalcitrant to the idea of accepting the peace imposed on it at San Remo. In this regard Mons. Dolci, on June 1st, referred to Card. Gasparri that he had been summoned by the Grand Vizier to a meeting.[118] In it, Damad Ferid Pasha had asked Dolci:

> a) my opinion on the Peace Treaty of San Remo and, should this be favorable to the sovereignty and independence of the Ottoman State, to authorize the Grand Vizier to render this opinion of mine public.
>
> b) the intervention of the Holy Father with the Great Powers signatory to the Treaty so as to modify its conditions.

Dolci got out of this tight spot by saying that he was very sorry, but he had "categorical orders" from his superiors to refrain from expressing political judgments of any kind during the war; moreover, the Pontiff also "scrupulously" followed the principle of neutrality and, in addition, the insult had been made against him by his exclusion from the Peace Conference. The Grand Vizier then threw out some observations on the fact that:

> there where Greece enters the Turk and the Catholic should exit: that the Crescent and the Cross had always gotten along (*sic*):[119] that the Catholics in particular were always loved and assisted by the Sultan and that they always(!)[120] enjoyed the most ample freedom in the practice of their religious worship.

Gasparri, on June 18th, responded, approving of Dolci's comportment.[121] The response of the Secretary of State, though terse, lets it be openly understood that the Holy See approved of Dolci's reserve in not pronouncing himself in favor of a state often persecutory towards Catholics and Christians in general.

---

118 Doc. n° 71 of 1 June 1920, Constantinople - Dolci to Gasparri - AAEESS, *Austria* 576, n° 7232.
119 An eloquent comment added by Dolci.
120 V. note n° 119.
121 Doc. n° 72 of 18 June 1920, Rome – handwritten draft from Gasparri to Dolci - AAEESS, *Austria* 576, n° 7232.

Far different was the attitude of the Holy See towards the new Armenian requests for help.

To solicit Vatican aid, on June 8th, 1920, Boghos Nubar Pasha addressed himself directly to the pontiff. Nubar, after having thanked the pope for past help, pointed out that the European powers were, in reality, betraying the solemn promises they had made and thus the expectations of the Armenian people, while only the Holy See, with its spiritual authority, could, and showed that it would, sustain the cause of Armenian freedom. A people martyred, emphasized Nubar, because of their Christian faith and threatened to the extent that they were a bulwark against the surrounding Muslim world. Precisely the fact that at the San Remo Conference the Entente powers had not resolved the Armenian question, making a decision about her borders, made the Armenians fear that these could be drawn in such a way as to surround the country with hostile neighbors, which would have jeopardized Armenia's existence, especially if she were abandoned to herself on the strictly military level. In that case independence would have no practical meaning and the principles of "what's done is done" and the survival of the fittest would be enshrined.[122]

Unlike the Allies, Benedict XV did not delay in taking up the problem and charged Cardinal Gasparri with urgently advising the full satisfaction of the Armenians' wishes to the British representative to the Vatican, Count de Salis.

The note (of July 8th, 1920) was couched in extremely official and energetic terms towards the addressees. After having referred Nubar's requests, the Secretary of State advised that His Holiness had "ordered" him to petition the British government such that—true to its Armenophile traditions—it assure the Caucasian state common borders with her European allies and, in any case, such as to not cause her to risk annihilation on the part of neighboring Islamic peoples.

It is evidently a strong pronouncement on the part of the Holy See that it was not afraid of directly taking sides in favor of the Armenians, defending not only their persons and their independence as a republic, but consenting to enter into particulars such as the protection of the integrity of extensive borders. The allusion to the loyalty owed by Britain to its own commitments was a severe admonition not to abandon themselves to

---

122 Doc. n° 73 of 8 June 1920, Paris - Boghos Nubar to the pope - AAEESS, *Asia* 57, 1, n° 8131.

exclusively utilitarian considerations.[123] Maintaining Armenia in the situation in which she already found herself, a country surrounded by hostile neighbors and therefore without the possibility of receiving aid, meant the impossibility of any protective action on her behalf.

Soon afterwards, on July 9th, Gasparri wrote a very cordial letter to Nubar, informing him that his request had been immediately satisfied on the part of the Vatican, and that it was hoped that it would be fruitful. Meanwhile, Nubar was warmly thanked for the recognition expressed to the pontiff regarding past assistance and the leader of the Armenian National Delegation was assured that the Holy See would not cease to interest itself in the Armenian question and to sustain Armenia's rights.[124]

Not even the pope, however, obtained concrete answers from the Allies, and Armenian prospects worsened rapidly under the double assault of the Kemalist Turks and the Red Army, and of the substantial Allied withdrawal.[125]

In fact, on June 1st the United States Senate had refused to accept the mandate for Armenia because it was devoid of economic interest, while the Greek offensive against Kemal in Asia Minor, begun on June 22nd, did not spare Yerevan a definitive conflict with the Turks.

And yet at the Spa Conference the Allies had rejected Turkish protests over the peace treaty, which were based on the observation that, in order to respect the principle of nationality, it was necessary to limit Armenia to the Transcaucasian part. The addition of Turkish Armenia would bring a large component of Muslim Turks and Kurds to the new state, with the evident danger of continued civilian conflicts.

Allied firmness, however, compelled the Turks to sign the treaty at Sèvres on August 10th, 1920.[126]

Armenia was one of the countries signatory to the treaty, unlike Russia which—probably precisely in order to break out of her international isolation—beginning in July launched a diplomatic offensive to reach an agreement as much with the Armenians as with the Kemalists.

As far as the first were concerned, after the breaking-off of negotiations in July they had adopted a "wait and see" position, still more confident of

---

123 Doc. n° 74 of 8 July 1920, Rome - handwritten draft from Gasparri to Count de Salis - AAEESS, *Asia* 57, 1, n° 8131.
124 Doc. n° 75 of 9 July 1920, Rome - handwritten draft from Gasparri to Nubar - AAEESS, *Asia* 57, 1, n° 8132.
125 Ter Minassian, *op. cit.*, p. 212.
126 Sidari, *op. cit.*, p. 196.

help from the West than from the Bolsheviks. The assurances of their representative Shant that the Allies would see to the complete enforcement of the peace treaty led them to persevere in this position, but the arrival of the new Russian envoy Boris Legran—to put an end to the border skirmishes between the Bolsheviks and the Dashnak in territories contested by the Azeris—brought about an arrangement reached on August 10th. The accord provided for the temporary occupation of Karabagh, Nakhichevan and Zangezur by the Red Army. The definitive attribution of those zones, however, would be ratified by a successive Russian-Armenian treaty in an official form.

In this manner, the Russian troops and Kemalist troops from southeastern Anatolia joined up for the first time.[127]

As for the Kemalists, negotiations opened in Moscow on July 19th.

Kemal gave precise instructions to his representatives to refuse any territorial concession in Anatolia with respect to the Armenians, and to ask for Russian financial support along with a guarantee that no international treaty for Turkey would be recognized by the Russians without the ratification of the Assembly of Ankara.

The Russians accepted after some hesitation over Armenian borders. The Russian-Turkish treaty was sealed on August 24th, 1920.

On the other hand, naturally, Kemal refused the Treaty of Sèvres and the Parliament of Constantinople did not ratify it either.

Anyway, the treaty had arrived too late. The Armenians themselves ended up not having much faith in it.

In fact, between July and September, the Armenian Minister of War and of the Interior Ter Minassian decided to implement an extremely drastic plan: "Armenize Armenia", expelling the Muslim minority which after 1918 had gone on to grow with the expansion of the republic. From July through September of 1920 units of Armenian guerrillas were charged with "encouraging the departure" of Muslims by all means, to the point of physical elimination. This would have brought an absolute homogeneity to Russian Armenia.[128]

In reality these measures were counterproductive because they gave Kemal the pretext to intervene, nullifying the provisions of the Treaty of Sèvres.

---

127 Ter Minassian, *op. cit.*, pp. 205–215.
128 Ter Minassian, *op. cit.*, pp. 215–218.

IX. THE KEMALIST OFFENSIVE AND THE FALL OF THE DASHNAKS

On September 23rd, the Turkish nationalist leader ordered one of his lieutenants, General Kazim Karabekir, to invade northeastern Anatolia, that is to say western Armenia, with the support of the few Muslims the government of Yerevan had not yet had time to expel.

The Armenian army, demoralized and influenced by Bolshevik propaganda, disbanded practically everywhere; by now the population, exhausted by privation, believed that only the country's admittance of the Red Army and its rapid sovietization would bring peace and security.

In effect, Russia—not well-disposed to an excessive Turkish expansion towards the Caucasus—had sent Legran to Yerevan once again, to actuate a policy of penetration into Armenia through a provisory collaboration with the ARF government. The Armenians, left without other backing, received Legran on October 12th. He asked for the renunciation of the Treaty of Sèvres, rupture with the Entente, free transit in Armenia for Russian, Turkish and Azeri soldiers, the protection of Armenia by the Red Army and Russian mediation in the conflict with Kemal.

Ohandjanian's government, however, still refused to cut off ties with the Allies and to denounce the Treaty of Sèvres. On October 28th he agreed only to sign an accord that reaffirmed Russian recognition of Armenia, and Moscow's right to mediate between Yerevan and its Muslim, Turkish and Azeri neighbors.[129]

Anyway, in October of 1920 the situation had deteriorated so much as to lead the Catholic Armenian patriarch Terzian to fear the worst. On October 20th he resolved to solicit yet another intervention by the Holy See, writing to the Secretary of State in order to pass on another appeal from Boghos Nubar to the pope. Given the recurring expressions, it may originally have been part of a chronicle addressed to the French government and then by way of information to Benedict XV. The subject was Cilicia which, at the time the Yerevan Republic was about to fall, appeared an

---

[129] Ter Minassian, *op. cit.*, p. 224.

ultimate refuge under French protection. But the Treaty of Sèvres conceded almost all of Cilicia to the Turks and this would have represented a danger to the Armenian people's survival.

In the memo, Nubar—after having once again mentioned French promises to Armenians and the latter's heroism demonstrated in fighting during the First World War alongside the Entente—observed that, faced with Turkish advances even into Cilicia, the Armenians could barely defend themselves, and their collapse appeared imminent if the Allies did not take action. After the Armenians had so far compromised themselves in favor of western powers, it was unthinkable that the Kemalists would abstain from carrying out new massacres. Nubar, in a balanced manner, did not demand revising the provisions of the Treaty of Sèvres. He limited himself to asking that Turkey raise Cilicia to the status of an autonomous province with ample local self-government. The guarantee of all of this, however, must derive from western commitment to safeguarding the area militarily, but to do this effectively the French stationed in Cilicia must absolutely not withdraw, at least for the time being. Nor would the relocation of the Armenians as refugees be a fair solution, as it would once again become an endorsement after the fact.[130]

> La Délégation Nationale Arménienne qui, par son acte en date du 14 Août 1920 adressé au Conseil Suprême, a protesté contre cette injustice, est la première à reconnaitre qu'une fois le Traité signé, l' on ne saurait plus échapper à ses conséquences. Aussi, tout en regrettant que le Conseil Suprême n'ait pas tenu compte des légitimes aspirations de nos compatriotes au sujet de la Cilicie, la Délégation propose-t-elle de garantir la vie et la sécurité des 270.000 Chrétiens de ce pays en leur octroyant une autonomie administrative sous le contrôle ou la protection de la France, tout en conservant, d'après les termes du Traité, la souveraineté turque sur cette région. La Cilicie deviendrait ainsi une province privilégiés de la Turquie et son autonomie administrative lui serait octroyée par iradé de S.M. le Sultan, sans que cela pût en aucune façon donner lieu à des difficultés internationales.

Conveying the Armenian memorandum, Mons. Terzian warned that the Turks were again going ahead with out-and-out mass deportations as in 1915. He then bitterly observed that no Allied country had deigned to listen

---

130 Doc. n° 76 of 10 October 1920, Paris – Historical note by Nubar - AAEESS, *Asia* 57, 1, n° 13508.

to Nubar's repeated appeals, varied protests and requests. In light of such an experience, unfortunately routine, he deemed it possible to rely, as always, only on the Holy See, to the limits within which it was possible for it to act.[131]

The response was not long in coming: on November 6th Cardinal Gasparri answered Nubar directly, informing him that even prior to his communication the pope had been worried about the new dangers that everywhere threatened the Armenians. Gasparri did not name the governments to which Benedict XV had probably turned, but concluded that the pontiff would have reinforced his diplomatic pressures on behalf of the country rightly considered anew a victim of aggression.

The Church usually waits quite a while before attributing innocence and blame in the case of political and military conflicts, especially in a situation as complex as that of Armenia, in which diverse factors interacted: the opposing interests among the Entente Powers, the national claims based on the peoples' right to self-determination, and the problems derived from the need to provide for the establishment of a new stable and definitive order after the collapse of Empires. Therefore Gasparri's judgment is quite significant.[132]

On November 28th Gasparri sent a reply to Terzian as well, reassuring him of the pope's constant interest on behalf of Armenia.[133]

But in the meantime, events plunged forward at an ever-increasing pace.

On November 7th, the Turks entered Alexandropol. On November 18th, Armenia signed an armistice.

On November 20th, Legran returned to Yerevan and initiated a new series of contacts in order to gain the admittance of the Red Army into Armenia, but once again the Armenians refused.

On November 22nd, Wilson's arbitral ruling—by now useless—that attributed the greater part of the contested territories in northeastern Anatolia to Armenia, became public.

Meanwhile, an Armenian delegation left Yerevan on November 23rd to reach Alexandropol and conclude peace with the Kemalists. The Armenian

---

131 Doc. n° 77 of 20 October 1920, Paris – handwritten letter from Terzian to Gasparri - AAEESS, *Asia* 57, 1, n° 19169.
132 Doc. n° 78 of 6 November 1920, Rome - handwritten draft from Gasparri to Nubar - AAEESS, *Asia* 57, 1, n° 13138.
133 Doc. n° 80 of 28 November 1920, Rome - Gasparri to Terzian - AAEESS, *Asia* 57, 1, n° 13163.

representative Khatissian had instructions to offer Erzerum and Trabzon in exchange for Kars, Van with its lake, and Moush.

The Turkish general Karabekir asked, on November 25th, that Armenia renounce the Treaty of Sèvres. The Armenians, after consulting Yerevan, agreed to overturn their foreign policy guidelines and granted the Turkish request.

The Armenian behavior was based on these considerations: if the Entente had had the means of helping the Armenians and had meant to do so, the renunciation of the treaty, under threat, would not have invalidated it, while in the case of Allied withdrawal the Armenian posture would have at least served to establish good relations with their powerful Turkish neighbor.[134]

On November 28th the Armenians officially presented their border proposals to Karabekir. He scornfully rejected them the following day and presented an ultimatum: Armenia must be reduced to an area of 27,000 square kilometers, about the same dimensions as today's ex-soviet Armenia.

The Armenian delegation, facing the danger of an attack on Yerevan, consulted with their government and, on the evening of December 2nd, signed the treaty that, among other things, reduced the Armenian army to 1,500 men and placed the Nakhichevan under Turkish protectorate. Muslim exiles were to be allowed to return west within a year.[135]

But in the meantime, things had changed in Yerevan as well. On November 23rd the single-party Dashnak government had been forced to step down and had been replaced by a coalition of revolutionary socialists and left-wing Dashnak headed by Vratsian. His first act was to resume talks with Legran. While these were still going on, on November 29th a group of Armenian Bolsheviks seized Ijevan, proclaiming the birth of the Armenian Soviet Socialist Republic and invoking the protection of the Red Army, which arrived immediately.

Vratsian's government accepted this *fait accompli* and ceded their place to a coalition of five Bolsheviks and two Dashnak leftists satisfactory to Moscow. The exponents of the old regime were assured against any persecution.

The new coalition remained in power until the committee of Bolsheviks from Ijevan entered Yerevan. For his part, on December 1st, the Azeri communist leader Narimanov arrived at promising the right of Zangezur

---

134 Ter Minassian, *op. cit.*, p. 231.
135 *Ibid.*, p. 232.

and Nakhichevan to return to Armenia and even self-determination for the Karabagh![136]

Meanwhile, however, on December 6th the Red Army entered Yerevan. The treaty with Legran was immediately annulled, and the Bolshevik party established its own dictatorship, quickly sovietizing Armenia.

The Dashnaks were harshly persecuted and the attempts by some Armenian communists to obtain a revision of the treaty of Alexandropol with Moscow's mediation were abruptly frustrated by Lenin on December 12th.[137]

On December 16th the League of Nations refused Armenia admission into their circle.[138] The official motivations for the refusal were the impossibility of considering Armenia as a stable country, as required by article 10 of the Pact of the League of Nations. According to Mandelstam, a telegram from the three governments—French, British and Italian—to their representatives to the League of Nations certainly influenced the Assembly's decision.[139] In it, the impossibility of approving Armenia's request for admission was affirmed because the Treaty of Sèvres had not been ratified and the borders between Armenia and Turkey, as they had just been drawn by President Wilson, were difficult to guarantee and to enforce on the part of the League of Nations. This telegram was given ample publicity which naturally influenced the Assembly. Mandelstam observed, then, that developments in Armenia during these discussions (above all, the Armenian-Turkish peace treaty of Alexandropol and the entrance of the Red Army into Yerevan) did not influence only the three powers that had sent the telegram, but also directly influenced the Assembly itself. Mandelstam expressed, besides, the conviction that the Assembly of the Nations was more afraid of and conditioned by Turkish danger than by Soviet danger. For this reason, the rejection of the Armenian demand for admission must be considered a confession of impotence not in the face of Lenin, but in the face of Kemal.[140]

---

136 Ter Minassian, *op. cit.*, p. 238.
137 *Ibid.*, pp. 234–240.
138 Sidari, *op. cit.*, p. 228.
139 Mandelstam, A., *La Societé des Nations et les Puissances devant le problème Arménien*, Paris : Pedone ed., 1926, pp. 98–100.
140 *Ibid.*, p. 107.

X. MONSIGNOR MORIONDO'S MISSION

In the meantime, the Holy See had decided to adopt Father Delpuch's suggestions[141] regarding the sending of a new Visitor Apostolic. The nomination fell upon Mons. Moriondo, a Dominican, and bishop of Cuneo.

However, many months passed from the time of Delpuch's mission before Moriondo actually went to the Caucasus.

The first reason was probably due to the difficulty in obtaining timely and continual updates about the real regional situation. It was also necessary to find, among the bishops, the person suited to the delicate role—not an easy matter—and this person then had to be disposed to accept the position with all the risks, even physical ones, that it carried. Moriondo, as we shall better see later on, accepted the nomination only out of a spirit of obedience.

The exact date of his arrival in the Caucasus is unknown, but it must have been earlier than November 12th, 1920, when he sent an initial report to Rome regarding the general situation as well as his personal one. We do not know if this report arrived at the Vatican, but it had certainly been forwarded, because he spoke of it in a letter dated December 18th, with which we shall occupy ourselves further on.

Notwithstanding the fact that Moriondo's first report probably did not reach the Vatican, the Holy See had already been made aware of the Armenian situation, thanks in part to a letter of November 21st, 1920, from Mons. Naslian to Mons. Cerretti.[142] In it, the bishop of Trabzon, in broken Italian, after having mentioned the violence carried out by the Kemalists in Cilicia after the French withdrawal, begs pontifical intervention.[143] In an attached note, he expressed his requests in a list of points. In addition to

---

141 V. doc. n° 55.
142 Mons. Bonaventura Cerretti, at the time Substitute of the Sacred Congregation for Extraordinary Ecclesiastical Affairs.
143 Doc. n° 79 of 21 November 1920, Rome - Naslian to Cerretti - AAEESS, *Asia* 57, 1, n° 13508.

diplomatic pressures on western countries for aid, probably military, in Yerevan, he suggested an appeal by the pope to Kemal in order to mitigate anti-Armenian persecutions, and also an intervention with the Italian People's Party such that they involve their government—well-regarded, he asserted, by Turkish nationalists—in an action of solidarity with Armenia.[144]

In fact, Italy arrived at concluding an economic accord with the Kemalists a few months afterward, on March 12th, 1921.[145]

Naslian also asked for the support of Cardinal Mercier, Primate of Belgium, for contacts with the Belgian government and people and with the League of Nations itself. In short, it was necessary to mobilize the whole of Catholic public opinion on behalf of the Armenian issue, using hostility towards Bolshevism and towards Islam as leverage.[146]

But the more significant steps regarded the analysis of the situation in Christian- and Armenian-majority Cilicia. She should remain so, through the safeguarding of the 270,000 refugees returned there after the massacres; otherwise French interests themselves would be compromised to the advantage of the Muslim Arab and Turkish populations in western Asia. Even Naslian, like Nubar, no longer asked for the annexation of Cilicia to Yerevan, but for her administrative autonomy under Turkish sovereignty, however with French military control.

The important thing was not to consign the region to the Kemalists who, having neither signed nor accepted the Treaty of Sèvres, clearly were not disposed to enforcing it. Also, the government of Constantinople should obtain the restitution of the area only after having offered the necessary guarantees. Collaboration between the forces of the French occupation and local Armenian ones should be established on a footing of substantial parity.[147]

Naslian observed that the Entente, had it wanted to, could have succeeded in imposing upon Turkey respect for Armenian rights everywhere. In areas like Cilicia it would have sufficed to avail themselves of the strong indigenous contingents. Deploying battleships to the ports of western Armenia, that is, to that part claimed and partially occupied by the Turks, also seemed like a good measure to the bishop of Trabzon, as it had been with respect to Constantinople. The legitimate Turkish government

---

144 *Attachment* to doc. n° 79 cit.
145 Sidari, *op. cit.*, p. 243.
146 *Attachment* to doc. n° 79 cit.
147 *Attachment* to doc. n° 79 cit.

should have received serious threats from the Allied side. Eventual declarations of principle from the League of Nations were absolutely useless.[148]

The French had retorted that drafting the Christians to face the Turks would have meant paving the way for probable Armenian vendettas, presaging new Kemalist reprisals. For Naslian this fear was groundless, first of all because the Muslims were already at a maximum level of agitation against the enemy, and in second place because western strong-arming would fall back on Kemal himself. After all, the French would always have the possibility of putting a stop to Armenian violence when it reached a serious point. But, concluded Naslian, the only way to make the Turks—"a bloodthirsty race"—listen was the use of force, without which the deportations and the massacres would begin again. For that reason, he arrived at wishing for a very harsh intervention indeed.[149]

For the bishop, world peace itself required that the alliance between Turkish Kemalists and Russian Bolsheviks be broken, by attacking the member most actively hostile to the Christians.[150]

It is worth noting that, in the letter to Cerretti, Naslian affirms having sent his requests in accord with Patriarch Terzian.[151] This shows that the vertices of the Armenian Catholic Church were profoundly hostile both to the Bolsheviks and to the Kemalists. Against the latter, it must be emphasized that Naslian and Terzian expressed a very negative opinion, especially when compared with Dolci's optimism of October 1919.[152] On the other hand, a year had gone by and the Kemalists had carried out numerous massacres of Armenians and other Christians, including Catholics, as the two prelates attested.

Meanwhile, Moriondo hastened, on December 18th, to send another letter, probably to Cardinal Marini, Prefect of the Congregation for the Oriental Church.[153]

Moriondo observed that the situation was seriously compromised: the combined offensive of the Kemalists and of the Red Army had caused the

---

148 *Ibid.*
149 *Attachment* to doc. n° 79 cit.
150 *Ibid.*
151 Doc. n° 79 cit.
152 Doc. n° 50 cit.
153 Doc. n° 81 of 18 December 1920, Tiflis - Moriondo to Card. [Marini?] - CO, 106, 2, 3, n° 4999.

collapse of the Dashnak government in Yerevan. Only Georgia had resisted, but to observers her fall also appeared imminent.[154]

Certainly all of the Caucasus would return to Russia under a different government from the tsarist one, but still anti-Christian and especially anti-Catholic, according to Moriondo. Therefore he saw the pointlessness of continuing his stay in Georgia given the impossible task and the danger that faced the mission.[155]

Besides, it was not only the military news that distressed him: the local economy was in ruin as well, with galloping inflation and a freezing winter that claimed many victims from among the more humble ranks of the population. The religious situation was equally distressing, not least for the establishment of an antagonistic climate between the Georgian Menshevik government and the local orthodox church. Moriondo took up the latter's defense openly in the fight for the conservation of ecclesiastical assets and in the consequent legal suits that followed.[156]

The Visitor, deeply pessimistic over the future of the Church in the Caucasus, dissuaded the Holy See even from sending new missionaries, who would absolutely not be able to act, nor even lodge, in Tiflis. Word of new Kemalist violence in western Armenia had prompted him to intercede on behalf of the vanquished, receiving the most ample assurances regarding respect for the local populations. But from Moriondo's words emerges a substantial skepticism towards the Turkish government of Ankara and its promises and, ultimately, the facts bore him out. The Piedmontese bishop concluded by subscribing to the judgments of politicians and foreign diplomats, begging the Congregation for the Oriental Church to recall him home as soon as possible, and resigning himself to being unable to carry out any action in the Caucasus for a very long time to come.[157]

A month after Moriondo's letter, notwithstanding the fact that the Dashnak republic had fallen, the Treaty of Sèvres with Turkey was still considered useful by many Armenians towards salvaging what could be salvaged.

In fact, continuing to hope for western help, Mons. Naslian sent the Vatican a series of observations on the possibility of still saving the nation or at least of safeguarding Catholic interests in the zones that would have gone to Turkey anyway on the basis of the Treaty of Sèvres.

---

154 Doc. n° 81 cit.
155 *Ibid.*
156 *Ibid.*
157 Doc. n° 81 cit.

Starting from the observation of the country's division into a zone practically annexed by the Kemalists and a state occupied by the Red Army, Naslian concluded that Armenia's change of sides from the Entente to Russia had been forced, and thus Yerevan should not be considered adversely. Rather, it was precisely because of her sympathy toward the Entente that Armenia had been invaded by the Russians, therefore westerners should help her and not abandon her to her fate.[158]

The nation must be safeguarded in its physical survival as a people and in its independence as a state including both Russian and Turkish Armenia, and equipped with access to the sea. Therefore it was a vast territory that needed to be accommodated, even at the cost of sacrificing the birth of an independent Kurdistan.[159]

The renunciation of Cilicia on the basis of the Treaty of Sèvres was supposed to take place under the condition that secure guarantees be furnished regarding the Christians, but the problem for Naslian was that the Turks' division into two governments, neither one accountable for reciprocal decisions, posed a serious question as to the possibility of obtaining respect for the peace provisions. It would have been pointless for the Allies to threaten the occupation of Constantinople, because the Turks feared the presence of a free and potentially hostile Armenia more than [they were concerned for] the destiny of a city easily recuperable thanks to western suspicions and mutual jealousies. And in this Naslian probably saw correctly. If anything, he continued, it would be better to tie the restitution of the territories due the Turks to their honoring of all legal obligations towards Armenia. Even measures of a military nature were useless without the political will to render them effective.

If the Turkish demobilization order, for example, had not been carried out after the armistice of Moudros, all the more reason it would have become a dead letter now that Kemal had headed up a victorious revolt. Kemal himself had demonstrated his intentions, discharging soldiers along with all of their equipment, and saying that he considered as soldiers all Turks fit for military service. Thanks to volunteers, the Kemalist forces would grow even more. Besides, Kemal had remobilized the prisoners of war

---

158 Doc. n° 84 of 25 January 1921, Rome - Naslian, notes commenting on the Treaty of Sèvres - AAEESS, *Asia* 57, 1, n° 16169. For a commentary on the Treaty of Sèvres v. Mandelstam, *op. cit.*, pp. 70–88.
159 Doc. n° 84 cit.

returned to him by the Entente and thus had a strong army at his disposition.[160]

Naslian, anyway, showed himself to be very pessimistic about the future of his own country, since the League of Nations seemed incapable of taking effective decisions and the Great Powers were more inclined to safeguard their own often conflicting interests than to enforce the Treaty.[161]

Cardinal Gasparri, to whom Naslian turned, promised to involve himself in the desired sense but, significantly, warned that given the circumstances they should not deceive themselves about the Great Powers' response (that is, regarding their willpower and their chances of obtaining satisfaction from Kemal and from the new Bolshevik Armenia).[162]

> [...] foreseeing, however, the difficulties of the moment, I feel it my duty to add that it does not seem possible to harbor abundant illusions that the requests of the Holy See will be absolutely satisfied on the part of the various Governments involved.

The fact that even Cardinal Gasparri, so sensitive to the Armenian issue, would display such skepticism shows, rather eloquently, how much Armenian affairs had worsened. By now the Armenian collapse may have rendered almost useless any strictly political action, based, then, on a treaty like that of Sèvres which showed itself overridden by military developments.

Precisely because of these changes, Mons. Moriondo took the initiative of addressing himself directly to the pope on February 10th, 1921. Benedict XV had sent him the express order to remain in the region as long as possible and the Visitor naturally had obeyed, but repeated his mistrust regarding the success of a mission whose outcome depended in large part on the unfolding of events of war. Moriondo also added that he had never deluded himself, and that he had judged the optimism of his predecessor Delpuch ill-considered.

It should be said, however, that Delpuch's visit took place at a particular moment when, from a military point of view, Armenia did not appear compromised, much less defeated, while on a diplomatic level the Allies, though refusing to recognize her in a clear and definitive way, had not yet shown her substantial hostility, as later occurred.

---

160 *Ibid.*
161 Doc. n° 84 cit.
162 Doc. n° 85 of 18 February 1921, Rome - draft of Gasparri's reply to Naslian - AAEESS, *Asia* 57, 1, n° 16169.

The truth is that in Moriondo's time circumstances had changed and pessimism was certainly not unfounded.[163]

Two days after having written to the pope, the Visitor Apostolic turned to Cardinal Marini, from whom he had received a letter a few days earlier together with numerous offerings from the Congregation and from the pope.

Marini had sent the letter on December 17th, which testifies as to the difficulty in making connections, of which we have already spoken.

Responding to Marini, Moriondo confirmed his negative impressions, convalidated by the opinions of politicians and western diplomats and by the European press itself. It's true that, at the time, fear of a Russian invasion had been diminished due to the Entente's recognition of Georgian autonomy. The Menshevik government, however, promised nothing good regarding religion. The law on the separation between State and Church had not yet been approved, but the Georgian leaders were in fact applying it, requisitioning ecclesiastical assets and ignoring protests. According to Moriondo, there was no hoping for a fall of the government, because it had on its side the whole of the Georgian people, deeply socialist. Besides, the economic crisis and the cynicism of the Allies who denied all financial assistance inevitably pushed the Georgians towards Russia.[164]

But the situation in Georgia, in reality, deteriorated rapidly. In February 1921 an Armenian revolt—artfully instigated by the Bolsheviks in the district of Lori, formerly occupied by Georgia—offered the opportunity for the Red Army to invade this republic as well, which was conquered and sovietized in just a few days, notwithstanding a tenacious resistance.[165]

Mons. Moriondo decided to abandon Tiflis for Constantinople with the foreign diplomats and gave notice of it to Cardinal Marini in a rather terse telegram of March 2nd:[166]

> Cause events constrained to leave Tiflis with foreign legations am in Const.ple awaiting orders : Moriondo

Moriondo's flight, even though for comprehensible reasons, aroused irritation and perplexity in the Vatican, the fact notwithstanding that on

---

163 Doc. n° 87 of 10 February 1921, Tiflis - handwritten letter from Moriondo to the pope - CO, 106, 3, 5, 2, n° 5313.
164 Doc. n° 88 of 12 February 1921, Tiflis - Moriondo to Marini - CO, 106, 3, 2, n° 5293.
165 Ter Minassian, *op. cit.*, pp. 240–242.
166 Doc. n° 94 of 2 March 1921, Constantinople - telegr. from Moriondo to Marini - CO, 106, 5, 3, 2, n° 5287.

March 3rd the Visitor had sent an apposite letter to Marini recounting the facts and justifying his choice. Moriondo explained that, just after his letter of February 12th in which he agreed to remain, the Bolsheviks had attacked Georgia and this, to the bishop, seemed to totally extinguish the hope of being able to dedicate himself in peace to the religious mission. To the Georgian government there remained naught but to invite foreign diplomats to provide for their own security.

Analyzing the political situation, Moriondo observed that Vatican action under the Bolshevik occupation appeared practically unfeasible. Perhaps the Kemalist and Bolshevik allies would clash, once they had a common border, but that would not minimally affect the aims of evangelization of the Caucasus; rather, it would have made [the situation] even more turbulent and unbearable. By now, concluded the Visitor Apostolic, there was nothing he could do but wait there for the pontifical decision, ready to leave for Rome to narrate in detail the events in the region to the members of the Sacred Congregation for the Oriental Church.[167]

As we have said, the Holy See disapproved, courteously in form, but emphatically in substance, of Moriondo's departure from Tiflis. The Assessor of the Congregation for the Oriental Church, Mons. Papadopulos, asked that the acting Secretary of State Mons. Tedeschini telegraph Moriondo to remain in Constantinople and await new orders.[168]

The urgent communication reveals the fear that Moriondo, continuing to act on his own initiative, would abandon that city as well to reach Rome before new orders were issued.

Papadopulos, in a letter quickly sent, did not hide his disappointment over the Visitor's flight and, advising him of the now proximate arrival of F. Kalatosoff, ordered him to remain in Turkey rather than reach Italy. The Holy See, added Papadopulos, had foreseen the fall of Georgia, and for just this reason would have preferred that the Visitor not abandon the faithful entrusted to him. Maybe he could have moved to western Armenia under Turkish dominion; in that way, he would have kept in better contact with all the Christians of the Caucasus, ready to intercede on their behalf with any occupying power in the region. Such behavior would have avoided the scandal among the inhabitants over the disappearance of a pontifical envoy. However, concluded the Assessor, seeing as Moriondo was already in

---

167 Doc. n° 95 of 3 March 1921, Constantinople - Moriondo to Marini - CO, 106, 3, 5, 2, n° 5347.
168 Doc. n° 96 of 4 March 1921, Rome - Mons. Assessor to Tedeschini - CO, 106, 3, 5, 2, n° 5287.

Constantinople, he should limit himself to waiting for a propitious moment to return at least to Batum, even if not in the company of foreign diplomats. He should certainly not expose himself to pointless risks, but it was asked that he immediately continue to concern himself with the inhabitants of the Caucasus, giving them all possible attention and defend them, if necessary, from all persecution without any ethnic or religious distinction.[169]

The fact is, the mission of Mons. Moriondo was over, even though the bishop remained isolated in Constantinople for many months, as we shall see later.

In any case, Moriondo's expedition represented for the Holy See an initial abortive attempt to establish stable relations with the governments and peoples of Transcaucasia. In fact, given the brevity of his stay in the Caucasus and the acceleration of events, Moriondo ended up not even visiting Armenia, at least from what comes through in his reports.

---

169 Doc. n° 97 of 5 March 1921, Rome - Mons. Assessor to Moriondo - CO, 106, 3, 5, 2, n° 5287.

XI. NEW VATICAN DIPLOMATIC INITIATIVES ON BEHALF OF ARMENIANS

On November 23rd, 1920, the League of Nations, *in extremis*, charged Spain, Brazil and the United States, being Christian powers, with occupying themselves with the case of Armenia. The three countries appear to have responded willingly to the invitation, and the Armenian Catholic Patriarch Terzian did not let the occasion escape him to insist along those lines, addressing the interested ambassadors assembled in London. There, they were also to discuss the Armenian case, and Terzian—in order to pin these countries down even more—solicited and obtained from the Holy See pressure on their respective Vatican representatives. Writing to the Secretary for Extraordinary Ecclesiastical Affairs, Mons. Cerretti, Terzian advised an urgent intervention, maintaining that the three countries would be very influential and thus useful to the Armenian cause during the conference of the Powers. Perhaps the patriarch himself did not harbor many illusions about the possibility of being useful to his people in this way, since he observed that the appeal would, at any rate, have given the Catholic Church the consolation of having done everything possible for Armenia.[170]

In any case, Cardinal Gasparri addressed, in an extremely worried tone, an explicit invitation to the ambassadors of Spain[171] and Brazil[172] (the United States did not have official relations with the Holy See) such that their governments might undertake concrete initiatives regarding the Armenian question.

---

170 Doc. nº 90 of 28 February 1921, Rome - Terzian to Cerretti - AAEESS, *Asia* 57, 1, nº 17537.

171 Doc. nº 91 of 1 March 1921, Rome – handwritten draft from Gasparri to the Marquis of Villasireda, Spanish amb. to the Holy See - AAEESS, *Asia* 57, 1, nº 17537.

172 Doc. nº 92 of 1 March 1921, Rome - handwritten draft from Gasparri to Magalhas de Azevedo, Brazilian amb. to the Holy See - *ibid.* Text virtually identical to doc. nº 91.

Both the individuals questioned responded in a reassuring tone that they would see to the matter, but the type of action taken is unclear. In substance, they limited themselves to humanitarian measures, at least as far as Brazil was concerned.

The Brazilian ambassador responded a first time to Gasparri on March 3rd, saying that he had passed on to his government the pope's requests.[173] On March 31st he related that the president of Brazil had taken to heart the appeal conveyed to him by the Holy Father and had given instructions to the Brazilian ambassador in Paris to earnestly sustain the Armenian cause with the League of Nations.[174]

In turn, the Spanish ambassador declared on April 16th that his government would willingly participate in any diplomatic action in favor of Armenia.[175]

The Holy See, however, must not have had much confidence in the western powers if on March 9th, 1921, Card. Gasparri, in the name of the pope, addressed himself directly to Kemal to ask him to respect the lives and assets of the Christians of Turkey.[176]

The appeal is particularly significant in that it is directed to a rebel general not yet vested with any legitimate power in his country. Perhaps it is for this reason that it was not the pope who addressed himself personally to Kemal, as he had done with the sultan in the two letters sent to him during the war.

Kemal, on his part, must have been quite pleased with the honor shown him and he did not miss the occasion of assuring the greatest benevolence towards the Armenians and other Christians in a very long telegram sent directly to the pope.[177] To his response, Kemal also attached extracts of the inaugural speech upon the opening of the Turkish Grand National Assembly of Ankara on April 24th, 1920, and of that held on March 1st, 1921. In both, he declared that he considered the protection of Christians, as long as they were peaceful, a cardinal element of his politics. However, as

---

173 Doc. n° 93 of 3 March 1921, Rome - the Brazilian ambassador to Gasparri - AAEESS, *Asia* 57, 1, n° 17537.
174 Doc. n° 100 of 31 March 1921, Rome - the Brazilian amb. to Gasparri - AAEESS, *Asia* 57, 1, n° 17537.
175 Doc. n° 104 of 16 April 1921, Rome - the Spanish amb. to Gasparri - AAEESS, *Asia* 57, 1, n° 17537.
176 Doc. n° 98 of 9 March 1921, Roma - handwritten draft of the telegram from Gasparri to Kemal - AAEESS, *Asia* 117, n° 17569.
177 Doc. n° 99 of 12 March 1921, Angora - French transl. of Kemal's reply telegram to the pope - n° 17569.

the sultan had done, Kemal, too, rejected responsibility for the violence against Christians.

The pontiff's step is significant since it shows that Benedict XV either did not consider the Turks a bloodthirsty people and so fanatical as to be unable to have a dialogue with (unlike Naslian), or anyway—whether with the sultan or whether with Kemal—he wanted to try all avenues in order to mitigate the fate of the Christians in the East.

XII. THE REPORTS OF THE APOSTOLIC DELEGATE IN BEIRUT

The Delegation of the Republic led by Aharonian and the unofficial National Delegation of Nubar Pasha continued to exist for some time in exile.

Between February and March 1921, in London, both participated in the Conference in which the Entente laid the basis for a revision of the Treaty of Sèvres in favor of Turkey. The Allies offered the Armenians an ill-defined "national Armenian homeland in eastern Anatolia", following a formula proposed for the Jews in Palestine.

The Republican Delegation maintained a clear opposition to any solution other than an independent and united Armenia. They also recalled the anti-Bolshevik revolts in affirming that a legitimate government existed in Yerevan: that of Vratsian in the mountains of Zangezur.

The Kemalist opposition, at each concession, however, brought about the failure of every accord.[178]

By now the Armenians' possibilities for survival were ever more bound, on one side, to the communist Republic of Yerevan, and on the other, to the creation of a national Armenian homeland, or rather, an autonomous state in Turkey.

One request to the latter end was advanced to the United States government on April 8th, 1921, by the President of the Armenia-America Society, with a precise proposal of resolution addressed to the Congress. The proposal, however, entailed supplying a loan of 25 million dollars.[179] And for that it went unheeded.

As for the Vatican, for several months it was interested in the reports of the Apostolic Delegate in Beirut, Mons. Giannini, about his activities on behalf of the Armenians and other Christians, especially in Cilicia.

---

178 Ter Minassian, *op. cit.*, pp. 250–251.
179 A copy of these requests was found in the archives of the Vatican Segretariat of State and is cited in documents nn° 101, 102, 103.

On May 7th, Giannini had already addressed Cardinal Gasparri to remind him of the fate of Cilicia, informing the Holy See of the action carried out in its regard.

At the Conference of London, in March, France had committed to withdraw from Cilicia. As is evident, that would have represented a mortal blow for the local Christians who were openly aligned with the Entente. Even the ample promises of Bekir Sami Bey, Kemal's envoy to the Vatican, did not reassure Giannini about the Armenians' defense. It is true that Bekir himself had not appeared very hostile towards the Armenians when he had been governor of Beirut, for example, but his political militancy, Giannini retained, would still prevent him from truly opposing persecutory orders of his government. For that matter, he had never shown himself very obliging towards the missionaries.

But Giannini, in an error common to Vatican diplomats, considered Kemal and all the Turkish nationalists a mixed bag of Islamic fanatics and Bolshevik sympathisers. This misunderstanding was possible, in the beginning, because Kemal maintained an alliance with communist Russia for tactical reasons while he had not yet taken power in hand and drastically secularized Turkey. In reality, once in possession of the country, he would found a decidedly nationalist and secular regime, implementing a complex politics of maneuvering between Russia and the western powers. So, exclusively on the level of realpolitik, French disengagement from the East did not have the negative effects for Paris that Giannini predicted, as we shall see.

In 1921, anyway, it was still easy to fool oneself about the true intentions of Kemal who, later, did not prove to be any better towards Christians than his predecessors.

Giannini found reason to sustain his thesis about Kemal's pan-Islamic ideas in the fact that Bekir was Circassian—therefore not of Turkish nationality—and yet he served Kemal in a common struggle against Greece and the Christian minorities in Turkey.

Precisely this Turkish strategy should have, in Giannini's opinion, called for a policy of firmness on the part of France and the other Allies. Also, during the war, the Entente had weighed too much in favor of the Armenians to be able to then abandon them to Turkish vendettas. An act of that kind would be shameful, and dearly paid for later, because if Kemal were truly a pan-Islamist he would be inclined to re-annex the Arab Middle East, including the French mandates of Syria and Lebanon.

France could have limited itself to a few forceful acts to intimidate the Turks, and peace in Cilicia would have been assured; in fact, perhaps she could in future be able to proceed with the evacuation of the French from the province, against reliable promises of a broad autonomy for Armenians under Turkish sovereignty. For France there were political motives, but also economic ones, that counseled a provisory maintenance of French control in Cilicia, because this region alone was rich enough to compensate France for the expenses of the Eastern campaign.[180]

On May 14th Giannini wrote once again to Gasparri to strongly recommend that he receive a certain Arshag Tchobanian, a poet and member of Nubar's National Delegation who, after a mission in the Levant, had headed for Europe to raise awareness in Christian countries on behalf of Armenians and Cilicia. Despite not being Catholic, Tchobanian gained Giannini's trust through his respect towards the Church. In any case, added the Delegate, it would be to the credit of the Holy See to continue to interest itself in the Armenian cause, at this point ignored by the Powers, and perhaps this might favor religious reunification. Anyway, there was a duty to help the Armenians and their representatives even apart from confessional interests because it concerned a people threatened with death.[181]

In reality, Tchobanian wasn't able to pass through Rome, but he sent a letter to Gasparri about Cilicia from Paris, via Diran Noradunghian, advisor to the Armenian National Delegation which came to Rome to thank the pope.[182]

To render his efforts more effective Giannini informed Gasparri of having submitted a memorandum on the Armenian problem to the French admiral de Bon, commander of the fleet in the eastern Mediterranean. De Bon, judged by Giannini to be a fervent Catholic, seemed the most appropriate person to transmit the wishes of the pontifical representative to his government. The delay, then, in the French evacuation cast a ray of hope on the future of Cilicia.[183]

Giannini, in the note to de Bon, figures at hand, demonstrated that in substance the region was inhabited almost in equal measure by Christians

---

180 Doc. n° 106 of 7 May 1921, Beirut - Giannini to Gasparri - AAEESS, *Asia* 57, 1, n° 21439.
181 Doc. n° 107 of 14 May 1921, Beirut - Giannini to Gasparri - AAEESS, *Asia* 57, 1, n° 21439.
182 V. doc. n° 117 of 27 November 1921, Paris - handwritten letter from Tchobanian to Gasparri - AAEESS, *Asia* 117, n° 26036 A.E. and doc. 118 of 28 November 1921, Paris - G. Noradunghian to Gasparri - *Ibid.*
183 Doc. n° 107 cit.

and Muslims. The latter, however, were by no means all Turks, but rather mostly Alawi and Nizari. Only a fifth of all the inhabitants were of Turkish ethnicity. As for the Christians, they were almost all Armenian, the most numerous and oldest group residing there.[184]

Often the Armenians spoke in Turkish, admitted Giannini, but only because it was the official language, so that should not automatically include them in the proper Turkish population. If a political hegemony were to be recognized from among the ethnic groups, if anything it would have to be Armenian.[185] But Giannini was not asking much; he limited himself to begging once again for a political and administrative autonomy under French military protection, with the prohibition of the Turks from establishing their own garrisons. The inhabitants could, or rather should, provide for their own defense with territorial militias. Giannini ended in repeating that the political interest of France was at stake.[186]

Several days afterward, on May 19th, Giannini completed a trip to Cilicia which he related to Gasparri in a report from June 18th.

In it, he said that the French High Commissioner had responded to the petition, addressed to him on May 14th by the Apostolic Delegate, that he intervene on behalf of the Christian population of Zeytun which risked being massacred. The response, however, was completely negative and the French High Commissioner sought to gloss over the refusal with an invitation to the Holy See to take the initiative in coordinating eventual western diplomatic measures with the Turks in favor of the Christians. In fact, France refused to continue to act on behalf of the religious minorities.[187]

Giannini, however he judged the French attitude, agreed that the Vatican should not cease its Armenophile efforts, also in order avoid arousing scandal within Catholic public opinion. For Giannini, the problem was that diplomatic pressure had no value without military support. On the contrary, perhaps it would be counterproductive for Eastern Christians, since it would irritate the Turks without intimidating them. The recognition of Kemal's government on the part of the Entente seemed to him sheer foolishness: welcomed into the assembly of the Powers, Turkey would figure that she was able to impose her own policy towards the Christians,

---

184 Attachment to doc. n° 107 cit.
185 *Ibid.*
186 *Ibid.*
187 Doc. n° 108 of 18 June 1921, Beirut - Giannini to Gasparri - AAEESS, Asia 57, 1, n° 22655.

mistaking benevolence for weakness. The Turks, according to Giannini, were only capable of bowing before strength; otherwise, their actions would continue up until the complete extermination of the Christians. Between a victorious armed intervention and the utter undoing of Christian minorities and their western "friends", there was no middle ground.[188]

To conserve men and means France had chosen a conciliatory policy regarding Kemal, and that served to encourage the constant toll of the ongoing guerilla warfare carried out by various bands of Syrian Muslims, multiplying the casualties and the expenses for Paris.[189]

Giannini observed that it was necessary to put pressure on the French political world, on the Church, and on public opinion to induce the government to a decisive policy. And in contribution to this he had prepared an appeal to Cardinal Dubois, archbishop of Paris, which he attached to the letter to Gasparri.[190]

In his memorandum, Giannini recapitulated all the reasons for a clear French military involvement in the region, aiming at a secure autonomy for Turkish Cilicia under international control.

His affirmation that even moderate Muslims in Cilicia dreaded the return of complete Turkish domination was interesting.[191]

To this missive, Gasparri finally replied on July 5th with a terse note that acknowledged receipt of all the material sent by Giannini.[192]

This had nothing to do at all, however, with Vatican disinterest towards the Armenian cause—unjustified after so many official stands had been taken—but probably, rather, it was prudent encouragement to Giannini to proceed with the work carried out but to beware, however, of going beyond the limits of operation which, for an ecclesiastic, should be strictly religious. What's more, Giannini was also Vicar for Latin Rite Catholics in the East. Therefore perhaps Gasparri wanted the Delegate to consider his need, and above all the need of his faithful, to live alongside the Turks for some time to come.

Giannini also hazarded to send an umpteenth memorandum to Franklin Bouillon, a still-influential French ex-minister and parliamentary deputy, just back from Ankara. To Giannini, Bouillon's radical-socialist militancy

---

188 *Ibid.*
189 *Ibid.*
190 Doc. n° 108 cit.
191 *Attachment* to doc. n° 108 cit.
192 Doc. n° 109 of 5 July 1921, Rome - draft of Gasparri's reply to Giannini - AAEESS, *Asia* 57, 1, n° 22655.

didn't represent an insurmountable obstacle to a French clarification on the Armenian issue. Consequently, after having sought to speak with Bouillon, he addressed a memorandum to him, a copy of which he attached to his report to Cardinal Gasparri about it. In this report, Giannini admitted that the Frenchman was known for his Turkophile positions. These had earned him an unofficial assignment from the government of Paris, desirous of exploring the situation in Anatolia. But the Turkish military and civil progress so highly praised by Bouillon after his trip did not convince the Apostolic Delegate in the least: the Turks could have even resorted to outright deception for propagandistic purposes, certain that the French visitor was already well-disposed towards them and openly inclined to a friendly Franco-Turkish accord. But even admitting the successes of the Kemalist administration, these only meant that the Turks were stronger than two years earlier, and an eventual conciliation was possible only on condition of reciprocal commitment, beginning with the problem of the Christian minorities.[193]

> [...]
> If France is not disposed, and I do not believe that she can be, to lose everything, not only in Cilicia but also in Syria, it will be necessary that, sooner or later, she decide to impose her will on the Turkish nationalists by force. Not a completely easy thing today, I agree, but not, certainly, beyond her means, despite everything. After all, much less difficult today than tomorrow: without taking into account that the right blow struck at the right time would curtail the politics of half-measures practiced up till now and which threatens to perpetuate itself with successive, uninterrupted expenditures of money and blood, much greater than that which it would take to give the coup de grâce and, what's more, harmful beyond words to France's reputation whether in the face of friends or of enemies.
> [...]

The practical difficulties lay, for Giannini, in the Turks' evident bad faith, which could be effectively faced only by an ultimate military effort against Anatolia, in such as way as to crush Kemal's every offensive capacity and aspiration. Only then could an accord be signed that maintained an autonomous Cilicia under Turkish sovereignty, but without Turkish

---

193 Doc. n° 110 of 17 July 1921, Beirut - Giannini to Gasparri - AAEESS, *Asia* 57, 1, n° 24161.

garrisons, rather, French ones. Still starting from the supposition that Kemal was pan-Islamist and that after Cilicia he intended to annex Syria as well— in order to be connected to the holy places of Islam, Mecca and Medina— Giannini observed that a definitive military push would be necessary anyway sooner or later, but that the longer it was put off, the more difficult and bloody it would be. A rapid execution on her part, instead, would permit France to live in peace in the Middle East for a long time, maintaining besides the promises of protection made to the Christians who, he recalled, represented the majority in Cilicia.[194]

Giannini's appeal to Bouillon does not appear to have achieved any real effect; on October 20, 1921, France sealed an accord with Kemal using none other than Franklin Bouillon as plenipotentiary.[195]

Moreover, the Apostolic Delegate acted in his own name, but Cardinal Gasparri was certainly constantly informed about it and never disavowed him.

In effect, Giannini seemed to reveal a substantial incomprehension of the weariness over the war common to the governments as well as the people of Europe. He advocated France's military involvement in Cilicia, not only in order to defend the rights of the Armenians of the region, but to fight pan-Islamism. In his harshness, he demonstrated himself to be very different from Dolci in how the latter had implicitly judged Kemal in October 1919.[196] On the other hand, almost two years had passed and Kemal had shown that he was by no means better than his predecessors towards Armenians.[197]

It does not appear that there were further strictly political stances assumed by the Holy See; for a certain time there was no lack of pastoral and humanitarian efforts that took the place of political activity. In fact, that was the Vatican's typical style of engagement, especially after other avenues had been precluded.

---

194 *Attachment* to doc. n° 110.
195 Sidari, *op. cit.*, p. 247.
196 Doc. n° 50 cit.
197 Mandelstam, *op. cit.*, p. 99.

XIII. FATHER KALATOSOFF'S MISSION

The Armenian Mekhitarist father Dionysius Kalatosoff,[198] replacement for the Apostolic Administrator of the Armenian Catholics Mons. Der Abramian, reported on events in the Transcaucasus for the Holy See.

Kalatosoff returned to Rome provisionally at the end of April 1921 and used the occasion to report on the situation to Cardinal Marini. The difficulties of the war and a battle between Kemalists and Russians at Batum had not permitted him to reach his destination, Tiflis. Anyway, thanks to an envoy from the new communist Georgian government, it had been possible for agents of the Italian shipping companies to reach Batum after the Turks had been driven out. Kalatosoff had entrusted letters and offerings for the Armenians to the agent from Lloyd Triestino, Marco Ballovich. He had promised to report on the outcome of his trip and on the possibility of Kalatosoff's proceeding at least as far as Batum.[199]

Meanwhile, Kalatosoff had not wasted his time and, as he recounted to Marini, had quickly entered into contact with many Russian and Georgian refugees and even with Georgian communist agents in Constantinople.

The effect of these encounters was the belief that a new apostolic action would not be impossible in the region, but would require special documentation from the Holy See, not so much for the envoy's personal protection as to underline the official character of the mission.

It was necessary to demonstrate to the new communist governments that the priest sent to the Caucasus had the pope's explicit mandate to organize assistance for the Catholics, Armenian and non-Armenian, even in the Crimea and in the North Caucasus. Kalatosoff noted, *en passant*, that the Vatican seemed well-regarded even by the Bolsheviks and that, anyway, it would be a grave mistake to leave the Catholics of the region without

---

198 Regarding F. Kalatosoff, I have in preparation a brief study which I hope will see the light as soon as possible.
199 Doc. nº 105 of 3 May 1921, Rome - Kalatosoff to Marini - CO, 106, 3, 5, 2, nº 5638.

spiritual guidance, and ecclesiastical assets without adequate safeguarding.²⁰⁰

As we mentioned, between summer and fall of 1921 F. Kalatosoff finally succeeded in returning to the Caucasus.

We do not know whether he left before or after Mons. Moriondo's recall home. Moriondo had written to Cardinal Marini from Constantinople on July 30th, complaining of having been left practically abandoned to himself. Therefore, he insisted once and for all upon his return to Italy.²⁰¹

Considering his pressing requests, the Assessor of the Sacred Congregation for the Oriental Church, Mons. Papadopulos, urged Mons. Pizzardo, Substitute of the Secretariat of State, to propose Moriondo's nomination to the Consistorial Congregation for an Italian diocese. It was not just a matter of satisfying the Piedmontese bishop, but primarily in order not to leave 50,000 Catholics too long without guidance and protection, as well as to belie certain inferences about Moriondo's presumed nomination as Apostolic Delegate of Constantinople.²⁰²

The hard trials to which the memorandum referred were the massacres and the deportations of Christians that accompanied Kemal's victories as much in the east as in the west.²⁰³ From August 23rd to September 13th, 1921, the Turkish leader delivered an attack along the Sakarya river that forced the Greeks to retreat.

The French and the Italians, who on the basis of the Treaty of Sèvres had obtained spheres of economic influence in Anatolia, hastened to abandon her. Armenian Cilicia—which had received so many promises of assistance from the French—was at the mercy of the victors, and 60,000 refugees had left the region by January 1922.²⁰⁴

These Armenians headed to Syria and Lebanon, then many of them transplanted themselves to the Americas. The first government to manifest its willingness to accept them was Brazil. Naslian wrote to Gasparri requesting that he apply his good offices to the conditions of relocation.²⁰⁵

---

200 *Ibid.*
201 Doc. n° 111 of 30 July 1921, Constantinople - Moriondo to Marini - CO, 106, 3, 5, 2, n° 6331.
202 Doc. n° 116 of 10 November 1921, Rome - Memorandum for Mons. Pizzardo (Substitute Secr. of State) - CO, 106, 3, 5, 2, n° 5278.
203 V. note n° 197 and, for the Greeks, Mandelstam, *op. cit.*, pp. 232–241.
204 Ter Minassian, *op. cit.*, pp. 254–256.
205 Doc. n° 113 of 30 August 1921, Constantinople (Pera) - Naslian to Gasparri - AAEESS, *Asia* 117, n° 25108.

Naslian sent Gasparri further news of massacres of Christians, in particular Catholics, by the Kemalists, already noted to an extent as demonstrated by an encrypted telegram from Gasparri to Dolci of August 11th, 1921.[206]

On October 13th, 1921, a treaty of friendship analogous to that with Russia was signed by Kemal with the three Republics of the Caucasus which, on March 12th, 1922, would unite in the Transcaucasian Soviet Federative Socialist Republic, to then enter, in December of 1922, into the Union of Soviet Socialist Republics.[207]

As for the Bolsheviks, they now sought to establish contacts with the Catholic Church, perhaps in particular following the death of Benedict XV on January 22nd, 1922, and the election of the new pope, Pius XI.

In this regard Papadopulos, on March 3rd, 1922, received an appeal from don Francesco Agagianian, Vice-Rector of the Armenian College of Rome as well as future patriarch and cardinal, that insistently entreated the nomination of a pontifical representative to be sent to the Caucasus. Agagianian, perhaps out of imprecision or out of ignorance of diplomatic nuances, called him an Apostolic Delegate; at any rate, he advised that this would be the only possible provision and therefore only right and fair for the local Christians, and also for possible future evangelization in Russia itself. The Armenian priest added the conviction that a pontifical representative, being a symbol of the Holy See's humanitarian action, would be benevolently accepted by whatever local government, even a Bolshevik one. In support, he cited some of the phrases that the Armenian Education Commissioner Evangouloff had pronounced in front of Armenian clergymen in order to reassure them of the communist government's maximum support for eventual Vatican missions.[208]

Evangouloff had been minister for Caucasian affairs and a member of the Imperial Council under the Tsar and, during the Armenian Republic, one of the most important personages in the Armenian world of the Caucasus.[209] Earlier in that role, in an appeal to Delpuch, he had hoped for a strong

---

206 Doc. n° 112 of 11 August 1921, Rome – Handwritten draft of the encrypted telegr. from Gasparri to Dolci- AAEESS, *Asia* 117, n° 23784 and doc. n° 114, of 1 September 1921, Constantinople (Pera) - Naslian to Gasparri - AAEESS, *Asia* 117, n° 25109-. On the massacres of Catholic Armenians at the hands of the Kemalists v. NASLIAN, *op. cit,* vol. II, *passim.*
207 Ter Minassian, *op. cit.*, pp. 253–254.
208 Doc. n° 119 of 3 March 1922, Rome - Agagianian to Papadopulos - CO, 106, 3, 5, 2, n° 7439.
209 Doc. n° 82 of 23 January 1921, Rome - Delpuch to Marini - CO, *Armeni e Caucaso* [Armenians and the Caucasus] 1921–22, 106, 3, 5, 2, n° 5145.

presence of the Catholic Church in his country. He did not weigh in favor of the reunification between the two churches, but he had declared that only the Catholic Church was capable of assuring Armenian spiritual and cultural rebirth. The Apostolic Church, on the other hand, constrained for centuries to occupying themselves with merely political matters such as representing the Armenians to the sultan, seemed to suffer from spiritual impoverishment.[210]

It is unknown how much Agagianian's words might have convinced the Holy See of the effective possibility for collaboration between the Catholic Church and the communist regimes; in any case, having sent Kalatosoff to Tiflis proved to be a necessary move for exploring any possibility of action in the region.

The Mekhitarist clergyman, after having carried out his investigation, abruptly returned to Constantinople on March 15th, 1922, as a telegram to Rome from the Apostolic Delegation reveals.[211]

Papadopulos warned Cesarano not to allow Kalatosoff to proceed to Rome, but to have him send directly the report that was understood he could not have sent from Tiflis for security reasons. The Apostolic Delegation of Constantinople, in the person of its deputy Cesarano, would occupy itself with particular provisions in support of the Christians according to Kalatosoff's suggestions. The Vatican would take care of answering the most urgent requests right away, leaving the other decisions to be made to a new Visitor Apostolic for the Caucasus who, it was hoped, would leave around June.[212]

As we shall see, the dispatch of the pope's official and unofficial representatives to the region did not end with Kalatosoff.

The new pope Pius XI, in fact, while continuing fully with the policy of defending Christians throughout the East on an eminently humanitarian plane, did not quickly abandon the hypothesis of establishing an official permanent representative of his in the Caucasus.

As for Father Kalatosoff, the report requested by the Holy See was sent from Constantinople on a date that was impossible to establish with precision. Probably still in the spring of 1922, Kalatosoff, after having worriedly reported rumors of Bolshevik infiltrations even within the Catholic communities of the region and indeed within the Vatican, warned that the communist party had seen to disseminating the Transcaucasus with

---

210 Doc. n° 83 of 23 October 1920, Tiflis - Evanguloff to Delpuch - CO, 106, 3, 5, 2, n° 5145.
211 Doc. n° 121 of 15 March 1922, Constantinople - telegram from Cesarano to the S. Congr. Or. Ch. - CO, 106, 3, 5, 2, n° 7506/7439.
212 Doc. n° 122 of 18 March 1922, Rome - Mons. Assessor [Papadopulos] to Cesarano - CO, 106, 3, 5, 2, n° 7506/7439.

numerous spies, for the most part cultured and attractive young women, to better keep an eye on every social class within the population. They were certainly the priest's personal fears, confirmed, however, by observations of reality and by confidential conversations that Kalatosoff himself had had with communist leaders, one on his way back from Moscow, and one in Constantinople functioning as an ambassador through an assignment as head of the "Central Institute of Reunited Commerce" of the Caucasus.[213]

Kalatosoff was informed of the Vatican's decision to send another Visitor to the Caucasus, and this gladdened him. But the failure of Moriondo's mission drove him to recommend the nomination of quite a different person.

The new Visitor should leave willingly, know divers languages and, above all, show himself to be patient and respectful towards the local mentality; moreover, he should be disposed to remain for at least five years.

These requests, and the reasons Kalatosoff raised for them, testify as to the great fear in Catholic ecclesiastical circles that a cowardly and at the same time diffident attitude like that of Moriondo would provoke a scandal among the faithful, benefiting eventual propagandistic moves by local governments. Indeed, Moriondo's flight had been received with scorn by the communists, who told Kalatosoff that they knew well enough not to make generalizations about people and that they respected any pontifical representative in view of the notable humanitarian activity of the Holy See.

In particular, Visitors of Italian nationality seemed to appeal to the communist governments of the Caucasus out of a presumed friendship towards the government of Rome, which is why Kalatosoff was reproached with Moriondo's departure as a vile and unjustified gesture.

Kalatosoff did not go so far as to give credit to the promises of his Georgian and Armenian interlocutors, but confirmed the desire that the pope choose his 'ambassador' well. Besides having precise juridical guarantees (or rather diplomatic documents that would officially attest to his functions), the candidate should combine an upright religious life with a broadness of spirit and affability in his ways, as did the first Visitor, F. Delpuch, as a matter of fact.[214]

The Holy See, anyhow, in 1921 had already planned to send another Visitor in the person of Adrian Smets. He, however, was able to visit the Caucasus only in 1923, profiting from a purely humanitarian mission on behalf of victims of the famine in the Volga region.[215]

---

213 Doc. n° 123 [n.d.] Constantinople - secret handwritten report from F. Kalatosoff to the S. Congr. - 106, 3, 5, 2, n° 7632, pp. 9–12 and 15–16.
214 Doc. n° 123 cit.
215 Morozzo della Rocca, *op. cit.*, p. 323, note 18.

CONCLUSIONS

The analysis of our body of documents seems to demonstrate the Vatican's sympathies for the Armenian people and for an independent Armenia with sufficient clarity, even though the two parties never arrived at the establishment of diplomatic relations. This was due to the fact that the Holy See showed extreme caution in making official moves in the absence of a clear and stable international framework. And certainly the period between 1918 and 1922, especially in the Caucasus, was exceedingly confused and turbulent.

Something new that emerges from the documents collected in the Vatican Archives is the degree of trust and esteem that the Holy See enjoyed among Armenian politicians. Their appeals, in fact, are quite numerous, and hold a particular importance because they are the work of members of the Apostolic Church such as Nubar, or of laypersons as were the Dashnak militants. In both cases, these were people well outside of the Catholic Church and therefore their words take on a particular relevance.

It is also worth noting that the support provided to Armenia was completely disinterested; the understandable desire for the reunification of the Apostolic Church with the Catholic Church was never a *conditio sine qua non* for charitable aid and diplomatic support.

Solidarity originated from considerations of a humanitarian nature, towards a people beset by too many false friends and true enemies, and who—in concrete terms—faced extinction.

VATICAN DOCUMENTS

About the Documents

The following documents are the author's original Italian transcriptions, along with transcriptions in French and Spanish. The Italian texts have been translated into English. These are marked as "[Translation]" after each document, but in a few places, where the translation is for a minor sentence, the translations simply appear in square brackets after the Italian. Sizeable French citations have not been translated into English.

1

5 March 1918, Rome – Der Abramian to the pope – AAEESS,
Asia 57, 2, n° 59711

Administrator Apostolicus
Armeno - Catholicorum
in Imperio Russiaco

Beatissimo Padre,

Con sommo dolore, con l'animo straziato ho letto ieri sul giornale un dispaccio col seguente titolo "MASSACRO DI RUSSI A TREBISONDA. Parigi 1 Marzo. L'agenzia dei Balcani ha da Pietrogrado che al momento della rioccupazione di Trebisonda migliaia di sbandati russi sono stati fucilati e annegati. Sono stati gettati a mare molti sacchi pieni di ragazzi armeni; uomini e donne sono stati crocifissi e tutte le giovani donne e le fanciulle sono state abbandonate alla soldatesca" (La Tribuna del 2 Marzo 1918).

A questa funestissima notizia mi pare di sentire, col cuore lacerato, l'eco delle grida di disperazione e desolazione di una gran parte del mio povero gregge che si trova nel Caucaso. Specialmente quelli che si trovano a Batum, Artvin, Kars ecc. circa 20.000 armeni cattolici con 25-30 preti stanno in pericolo imminente: se il Governo Turco è entrato ovvero sta per entrare, allora avranno la stessa terribile sorte di quei di Trebisonda.

Io non ho altra speranza, dopo DIO, che la protezione morale di Vostra Santità, che trovi un mezzo, senza indugio, di sollevare i suoi lontani disgraziati figli che tutti con me unanimemente gridano a VOSTRA SANTITÀ "DOMINE, SALVA NOS, PERIMUS"

Intanto chinato al bacio dei SS. Piedi chiedo umilmente la Benedizione Apostolica e ho l'onore di dichiararmi di vostra Santità

Umilissimo e Devotissimo figlio e servo.

[Translation]

Armenian-Catholic
Apostolic Administrator
in Imperial Russia

Most Blessed Father,

With the greatest of pain, with a breaking heart, yesterday I read a dispatch in the newspaper with the following title: "RUSSIAN MASSACRE IN TRABZON. Paris, March 1. The Balkan news agency has word from Petrograd that during the re-occupation of Trabzon thousands of Russian refugees were shot and drowned. Many sacks full of Armenian children were thrown into the sea; men and women were crucified, and all the young women and girls were abandoned to the soldiery." (*La Tribuna* of March 2nd, 1918).

With this tragic news I seem to hear, tearing at my heart, the echoes of the cries of desperation and desolation of a great part of my poor flock in the

Caucasus. Especially those living in Batum, Artvin, Kars etc.: around 20,000 Armenian Catholics and 25–30 priests are in imminent danger; if the Turkish government has gone in, or is about to go in, then they will have the same terrible fate as those of Trabizon.

I have no other hope, beyond GOD, that the moral protection of Your Holiness find means, without delay, to comfort your distant wretched children who are crying with me unanimously to YOUR HOLINESS "DOMINE, SALVA NOS, PERIMUS"[216]

For now, bowed to the kiss of the Holy Feet, I humbly ask the Apostolic Blessing and have the honor of professing myself Your Holiness's

Most Humble and Devoted son and servant

2

6 or 7 March 1918, Rome – Der Abramian and others to the pope – AAEESS, *Asia* 57, 2, n° 59712

Beatissimo Padre,

La Russia, cedendo ora le provincie d'Armenia conquistate negli ultimi anni, in potere e balia del Governo Turco, dà le mani libere alla barbarie mussulmana per la continuazione delle stragi e deportazioni del 1915 delle popolazioni Armene già in parte ripopolate in quelle regioni, per portare a compimento l'iniquo suo progetto dell'intiera distruzione della nostra Nazione. Con sommo dolore e trepidazione si apprendono già le notizie di quel che fanno i Turchi nel loro ingresso a Trebisonda.

Per opera benefica di V. Santità, nel 1915, la sorte degli infelici Armeni, era stata mitigata, almeno in parte. Molto maggiore sarebbe stato certamente l'effetto della valida protezione della S. Sede, se V. Santità fosse stato informato prima che succedessero quegli eccessi di barbarie.

Altro magnanimo atto di V. Santità, col quale ha voluto mostrarci tutta la paterna sollecitudine verso la nostra travagliata e decimata Nazione, vedemmo nella Nota Pontificia ai Capi dei popoli belligeranti, nella quale ha voluto l'assetto dell'Armenia: per questo augusto atto di V. Santità, la Nazione Armena sarà eternamente riconoscente.

Nel presente terribile momento, gli Armeni corrono pericolo di essere distrutti non solo nelle provincie di Ardahan, Kars e Batum nelle quali si trovano in gran numero e che per le condizioni della pace colla Germania dovranno essere cedute alla Turchia.

Affinché si possa risparmiare un sì orribile sterminio, non vediamo altro rifugio e rimedio che nella validissima protezione ed efficace interessamento di V. Santità: e ciò umilmente imploriamo per tutta la Nazione Armena ed in special modo per i Cattolici, i quali benché pochi in proporzione dei non

---

216 Translator's Note: "Lord, save us, we are perishing"; Matthew 8:25.

uniti, perdettero però cinque Vescovi diocesani, molti del Clero sia regolare sia secolare, e molte migliaia di Fedeli sono morti sia per morte violenta sia per i disagi e tormenti sopportati nelle deportazioni.

 Intanto, sicuri che V. Santità, accogliendo benevolmente la nostra umile preghiera, vorrà venire in aiuto, in questo momento urgente della nostra infelice Nazione, ci prostriamo al bacio dei SS. Piedi con figliale devozione e con incrollabile attaccamento alla Vostra Persona, Vicario di G. Cristo in terra

firmato
+ Pietro Kojunian Arciv. di Calcedonia
Procuratore Patriarcale
S. Der Abramian
Amm. Apostolico degli Armeni
di Russia
P. Giovanni Torossian Proc. Gen.le
dei Mechitaristi di Venezia

[Translation]
Most Blessed Father,

Russia, now ceding the Armenian provinces conquered in recent years to the power and mercy of the Turkish government, gives free hand to Muslim barbarities, the continuation of the 1915 massacres and deportations of the Armenian populations already partially re-established in those regions, in order to bring to completion their iniquitous plans for the complete destruction of our Nation. With great pain and trepidation we are already hearing the news of what the Turks are doing during their entry into Trabizon.

Through the beneficent work of Your Holiness in 1915, the fate of the unfortunate Armenians had been at least partially mitigated. The effects of the Holy See's valuable protection would have been far greater if Your Holiness had been informed before those barbaric excesses had occurred.

Another magnanimous act on the part of Your Holiness, with which you have wished to show us complete paternal solicitude towards our afflicted and decimated Nation, we saw in the Pontifical Note to the Heads of the Belligerent Peoples, in which you called for the restructuring of Armenia; for this august act on the part of Your Holiness, the Armenian Nation will be eternally grateful.

In the present terrible moment, the Armenians run the risk of being eliminated, not least in the provinces of Ardahan, Kars and Batum, where they reside in great numbers and which according to the conditions of the peace treaty with Germany should be ceded to Turkey.

In order that they be spared such a horrible extermination, we see no other refuge nor remediation than in the precious protection and vigorous intervention of Your Holiness; therefore we humbly plead for the entire

Armenian Nation and especially for the Catholics who, even though few in proportion to those not united [to the faith], have lost, however, five diocesan bishops; many of the Clergy, both regular and secular, and many thousands of Faithful are dead, whether by violence or by the torments and hardships endured during the deportations.

Meanwhile, safe in knowing that Your Holiness, benevolently receiving our humble prayer, will come to our aid in this pressing moment for our unhappy Nation, we prostrate ourselves to kiss the feet of Your Holiness with filial devotion and a steadfast bond to Your Person, Vicar of J. Christ on Earth

signed

+ Pietro Kojunian, Archbishop of Chalcedon

Patriarchal Advocate

S. Der Abramian

Apostolic Adm. of the Russian Armenians

P. Giovanni Torossian

Adv. Gen'l. of the Venetian Mekhitarists

3

8 March 1918, Paris – telegr. from Nubar to the Vatican – AAEESS, *Asia* 57, 2, n° 57889

Encourage[217] par les sentiments de compassion que le tres St Pere temoigne aux Armeniens la Delegation National Armenienne fait une fois encore tres respectuesement appel a sa protection et a son auguste intervention afin que la reoccupation turque des provinces abandonnees par russes ne renouvelle crimes et attrocites qui ont ensanglante Armenie et ne lui porte dernier coup fatal stop Communiques officiels ottomans avouent exces sanguinaires deja commis et il est urgent qua Sa Saintete etende sa main protectrice sur malheureses populations sans defense et empeche leur extermination.

Boghos Nubar Delegation Nationale Armenienne 12 Avenue Trocadero

4

9 March 1918, Rome – Gasparri's reply telegr. to Nubar – AAEESS, *Asia* 57, 2, n° 57889

Je m'empresse de Vous assurer que avant d'avoir reçu votre télégramme le Saint Siège avait déjà fait des pressantes démarches dans le but désiré. Cardinal Gasparri

---

217 [*sic*] The entire document is without accents.

5

11 March 1918, Paris – Nubar to Gasparri – AAEESS, *Asia* 57, 2, n° 60608

Eminentissime Seigneur,

J'ai l'honneur de confirmer le télégramme de remerciements que je viens d'adresser à Votre Eminence et de La prier de vouloir bien offrir au Très Saint Père le très respectueux hommage de la plus profonde gratitude de la Délégation Nationale et de tous les Arméniens pour sa très Auguste intervention en faveur de nos compatriotes des provinces que les armées turques réoccupent. Dans les tragiques circostances actuelles, seules les démarches de Sa Sainteté peuvent exercer une action sur les Gouvernants turcs et sauver de l'extermination cette malheureuse nation chrétienne.

Je me fais un devoir, à ce propos, de rectifier une erreur qui s'est glissée dans mon premier télégramme. La trasmission dénaturée des dépêches qui m'étaient parvenues m'avait fait dire que les crimes déjà commis étaient reconnus par les communiqués ottomans mêmes, quand au contraire ce sont les Turcs qui accusent les Arméniens de s'être livrés à des excès sur les Musulmans. Mais les faits n'en sont nullement modifiés et cette fausse accusation des Turcs n'est, au contraire, qu'un sinistre présage car, fidèles à leur tactique, c'est pour donner d'avance un semblant de justification à leurs crimes et pour avoir un prétexte aux atrocités qu'ils préparent et qui sont déjà commencées, qu'ils attribuent des actes criminels aux Arméniens, les traitant de bandes rebelles, quand ces derniers ne font que tenter de défendre leurs foyers et d'échapper à l'extermination.

Dans l'espoir que, grâce à la pression du Saint Siège, ce nouveau coup pourra être évité, je prie Votre Eminence de vouloir bien agréer la nouvelle assurance de ma plus haute considération.

6

13 March 1918, Paris – telegr. from Nubar to Gasparri – AAEESS, *Asia* 57, 2, n° 59729

Delegation Nationale Armenienne exprime plus chaleureux remerciements a Votre Eminence pour son telegramme et la prie de vouloir bien offrier au Tres Saint Pere tres respectueux hommage de profonde gratitude pour Son Auguste intervention dernier espoir de salut. Nubar

7

19 March 1918, Constantinople (received 22 June 1918) – Dolci to Gasparri – ASV, *Guerra* [War], 1914–18, 244, 112, n° 66827

Eminentissimo Principe,

Il 12 corrente avevo l'onore di ricevere il seguente Cifrato distinto dal N° 14: "V.S. Illma faccia, Nome Santo Padre, le più vive istanze presso cotesto Ministro Esteri e presso… (indecifrabile), affinché i poveri armeni siano rispettati dai turchi rioccupanti territorio attribuito loro nel trattato pace con Russia…(altri numeri indecifrabili)".

Prima d'intervenire presso questo Governo, credetti opportuno intervistare il giorno stesso del recapito del Cifrato, questo Signore Ambasciatore Conte Bernstorff; e, dopo avergli partecipato l'incarico che l'Eminenza Vostra degnavasi affidarmi, gli dimandavo il suo efficace concorso.

L'Ambasciatore mi dichiarò di esser ben lieto che il Santo Padre mi avesse assegnato si nobile e caritatevole missione, la quale giungeva opportunamente per facilitargli l'azione già iniziata per la causa degli armeni.

Interrogato da me sulle atrocità che i turchi attribuiscono agli armeni della Russia e che gli armeni di Costantinopoli, alla loro volta, rigettano sui turchi, mi rispose dicendo: che nella guerra, di atrocità se ne commettono anche fra i popoli i meglio inciviliti. Immagini quindi, Monsignore, quello che può accadere laggiù ove si combatte per odio di razza.

Mi disse infine che Enver Pacha lo aveva assicurato di aver inviato ordini ai comandanti delle truppe, vietanti qualsiasi atto di rappresaglia contro gli armeni.

Nei giorni susseguenti, i giornali locali tratteggiavano vivamente le atrocità commesse dagli armeni in modo da impressionare il pubblico, e fra questi, "L'HILAL" di cui rimetto qui due articoli, l'uno del 13, e l'altro del 14 corrente.

Il quindici, alcune persone armene degne di fiducia, si presentavano a questa Delegazione per prevenirmi nel più stretto segreto che questo Governo aveva decretato la deportazione degli armeni, non esclusi neppure quelli di Costantinopoli, e mi supplicavano a nome dei loro connazionali, d'interporre a nome del Santo Padre, i miei uffici presso il Governo, onde far sospendere tali misure che si sarebbero risolte in un vero disastro per tutta la nazione.

Corsi tosto, nuovamente, dall'Ambasciatore di Germania per metterlo confidenzialmente al corrente di questa comunicazione fattami. Egli, pure lasciandomi intravedere la possibilità di questa misura, riteneva però la decisione prematura, stante che il Cabinetto non si sarebbe assunto una responsabilità si grave senza attendere l'arrivo del Gran Vizir. Mi disse che avrebbe subito telegrafato a von Kuhlmann, il quale trovandosi a Bucarest insieme col Gran Vizir avrebbe potuto interporre i suoi valevoli uffici presso quest'ultimo.

Ieri, diciotto, conforme le istruzioni telegrafiche dell'Eminenza Vostra intervenni presso questo Signor Ministro degli Esteri interinale, Alil Bey, trovandosi il titolare di questo dicastero pure a Bucarest. Il Ministro, accogliendo con la massima deferenza l'intervento del Santo Padre a tutela degli armeni, m'incaricò di rassicurare Sua Santità che nei territori rioccupati non s'incontravano più armeni i quali colle loro famiglie avevano abbandonato quei luoghi portandosi al dilà della frontiera russa.

Non vi rimangono, mi soggiunse, che delle bande armene, le quali lottano per la ritenzione di quelle regioni appartenenti all'integrità territoriale dell'Impero Ottomano.

Facendo poi subito cadere il discorso sulle atrocità commesse contro la razza turca, mi ripeté ciò che egli mi aveva già detto nell'intervista del 25 febbraio, che mi pregiai portare a conoscenza dell'Eminenza Vostra con Rapporto N° 740; cioè che le bande armene avevano commesso i più orribili delitti contro la razza turca; che esse avevano saccheggiato, devastato e bruciato le abitazioni in tutte le terre dalle quali furono costrette, nei combattimenti, a ritirarsi; e che nel loro odio belluino non avevano risparmiato neppure le fanciulle, i vecchi, le donne incinte. Mi dichiarò inoltre che queste atrocità erano state commesse in Erzinghian ed Erzerum; e che la devastazione da tali bande perpetrata si estendeva da Van a Trebizonda; conchiuse dicendo che di tutte queste nefandità avrebbe redatto un esposto per comunicarlo alle Potenze.

Rappresentando poi al Ministro che la Stampa Europea esprimeva seri timori che il Governo Ottomano procedesse a misure di rappresaglie contro gli armeni esistenti nell'Impero, specialmente a nuove deportazioni, intercedevo sempre nel Nome Augusto del Santo Padre per far sospendere tali misure nel caso che il Governo intendesse di ricorrervi.

Richiamavo la sua attenzione sui due articoli già accennati del giornale "HILAL", facendogli osservare che la Stampa turca si era dipartita da quella saggissima decisione da lui presa e comunicatami nell'intervista del 25 Febbraio, di non abbandonare alla pubblicità le particolareggiate notizie di crudeltà armene. Esse avrebbero potuto, soggiungevo, eccitare il popolo turco a rappresaglie contro gli armeni dell'Impero, che sono irresponsabili di quanto hanno commesso i loro connazionali della Russia. Mi fermai a fargli notare che, degli eccessi ai quali il popolo si lascia trascorrere, la responsabilità cade sempre sul Governo, quantunque esso sia quanto mai alieno da ispirare e permettere tali atti e che nell'opinione pubblica è vivo ancora il ricordo della prima repressione armena.

Il Ministro, relativamente a nuove misure di rappresaglia contro gli armeni dell'Impero, negò categoricamente ch'esse fossero nella mente del Governo e mi diede l'incarico di rassicurare il S. Padre che tutte le voci di deportazione erano destituite di fondamento e che il Governo era anzi disposto a concedere a tutti gli armeni, sudditi ottomani, completa amnistia.

Quanto alla pubblicazione degli articoli mi disse che essa fu subito repressa, come sarebbe subito represso qualunque atto ostile della popolazione turca contro quella armena. Infatti all'infuori di quelli menzionati, non sono più comparsi nei giornali, per quanto mi consta, articoli contro gli armeni; la stampa anzi prende ora la loro difesa lodando il contegno pacifico degli Armeni dell'Impero. Di ciò ho ricevuto assicurazioni anche dall'Ambasciatore di Germania.

Di tale intervista col predetto Signore Ministro degli Esteri mi sono affrettato a trasmettere all'Eminenza Vostra il riassunto col seguente cifrato: Nº 24.

"Conforme istruzioni cifrato nº 14 essendo oggi 18 intervenuto nome Augusto Santo Padre questo Ministro Esteri interinale m'incarica portare a conoscenza Sua Santità che tutti gli armeni dei territori che rioccupano le truppe turche hanno colle loro famiglie traversato frontiera russa. Solamente, le truppe turche incontrano negli accennati territori delle bande armene armate che lottano per la ritenzione di quei luoghi e dove esse hanno commesso le più atroci crudeltà contro la razza turca. Avendo la stampa turca pubblicato tali atrocità sono pure intervenuto Nome Augusto S. Padre presso questo Ministro per scongiurare agli armeni nell'Impero Ottomano ogni pericolo; specialmente quello della deportazione di cui essi temevano e per cui avevano ricorso a questa Delegazione. Ministro Esteri m'incarica di rassicurare anche su questo punto Santo Padre che tale pubblicazione è stata dal Governo repressa, che nessun atto ostile sarà commesso contro gli armeni dell'Impero e che la minaccia di deportazione è destituita di ogni fondamento. Mi aggiunse ancora che Governo è disposto concedere amnistia armeni Impero. Segue rapporto. Ossequi."

Lieto intanto che la magnanima bontà del Santo Padre si sia novellamente estesa a protezione di questa nazione armena, m'inchino al bacio della Sacra Popora e con sensi di alta stima e somma venerazione ho l'onore di raffermarmi...

[Translation]
Most Eminent Prince,

The 12th of this month I had the honor to have received the following encoded message distinguished by the Nº 14: "Y. Most Ill. make, name Holy Father, the most active petitions with Foreign Minister there and with... (indecipherable), in order that the poor Armenians be respected by the Turks reoccupying territory attributed them in the peace treaty with Russia... (other indecipherable numbers)".

Before intervening with this government, I believed it opportune to interview, the very same day as the receipt of the encrypted message, the Lord Ambassador Count Bernstorff here and, after having shared with him the charge with which Your Eminence deigned to entrust me, I asked his effective contribution.

The Ambassador said that he was quite pleased that the Holy Father had assigned me such a noble and charitable mission, which arrived conveniently to facilitate action he had already initiated on behalf of the Armenians.

Questioned by me about the atrocities that the Turks attribute to the Russian Armenians and that the Armenians of Constantinople, in turn, throw back onto the Turks, he responded by saying: in war, atrocities are committed even among the most civilized of peoples. Imagine then, Monsignor, what could happen over there, where they are fighting each other out of racial hatred. Finally, he told me that Enver Pasha[218] had assured him of having sent orders, to the commanders of the troops, forbidding any act of reprisal against the Armenians.

In subsequent days, the local newspapers painted vivid pictures of atrocities committed by the Armenians in such a way as to frighten the public, among these "L' HILAL", from which I enclose two articles, one from the 13th, and the other from the 14th of this month.

On the 15th, several trustworthy Armenians presented themselves to this Delegation to forewarn me in strictest secrecy that the government here had decreed the deportation of the Armenians, including even those of Constantinople, and they begged me in the name of their compatriots to interpose, in the name of the Holy Father, my offices with the government so as to suspend these measures, which would be a true disaster for the whole nation.

I quickly rushed, again, to see the German ambassador to keep him confidentially abreast of this communication made to me. Even allowing that I might imagine the possibility of this measure, he retained, however, that the decision was premature, it being that the Cabinet would not have assumed such a serious responsibility without waiting for the Grand Vizier's arrival. He told me that he would immediately telegraph von Kuhlmann[219] who, being in Bucharest with the Grand Vizier,[220] would be able to interpose his good offices with the latter.

Yesterday, the eighteenth, following Your Eminence's telegraphed instructions, I intervened with the interim Lord Minister of Foreign Affairs here, Alil Bey, finding the holder of this office also to be in Bucharest. The minister, receiving with the greatest of deference the Holy Father's intervention to safeguard the Armenians, charged me with reassuring His Holiness that in the reoccupied territories there were no more Armenians to be found, as they and their families had abandoned those places and moved to the other side of the Russian border.

There remain, he added, only some Armenian bands struggling to retain those regions belonging to the territorial integrity of the Ottoman Empire.

---

218 Minister of War.
219 German foreign minister.
220 Talaat Pasha. Both were in Bucharest for the Peace Conference with Romania (March 7th, 1918, never ratified).

Quickly changing the subject to the atrocities committed against the Turkish race, he repeated that which he had already told me in the interview of February 25th, which I prided myself in bringing to the knowledge of Your Eminence with Report Nº 740: that is, that Armenian bands had committed the most horrible crimes against the Turkish race; that they had sacked, destroyed, and burned dwellings in all the lands from which they were constrained to retreat during the fighting, and that in their beastly hatred they had not spared even the young girls, the elderly, the pregnant women. He declared, besides, that these atrocities were committed in Erzinghian and Erzerum, and that the devastation perpetrated by these bands extended from Van to Trabizon; he concluded saying that he would put together an account of all these wicked acts and communicate it to the Powers.

Representing, then, to the Minister that the European Press expressed serious fears that the Ottoman Government would proceed with reprisal measures against the existing Armenians in the Empire, especially new deportations, I interceded again in the August Name of the Holy Father to suspend such measures in the case that the government intended to recur to them.

I recalled his attention to the two articles already mentioned, from the newspaper "HILAL", making him observe that the Turkish Press had departed from that very wise decision he had made and communicated to me in the interview of February 25th, not to release to the public detailed news of Armenian cruelty. Such news could have served, I added, to incite the Turkish people to reprisals against the Armenians of the Empire, who are not responsible for the acts committed by their Russian co-nationals. I ended by pointing out that, for the excesses that the people allow to occur, the responsibility always lies with the Government, however extraneous it may be to inspiring and permitting such acts, and that in the public's opinion the memory of the first Armenian repression is still alive.

The Minister, relative to new measures of reprisals against the Armenians of the Empire, denied categorically that these were in the mind of the Government, and charged me with reassuring the Holy Father that all the rumors of deportations were baseless and that, rather, the Government was disposed to concede complete amnesty to all Armenians who are Ottoman subjects.

As far as the publication of the articles is concerned, he told me that this was quickly suppressed, as would be suppressed any hostile act of the Turkish population against the Armenian. In fact, as far as I know, no other articles against the Armenians have appeared in the newspapers beyond those mentioned; the press, indeed, now takes up their defense, praising the peaceful demeanor of the Armenians of the Empire. I have also received assurances of this from the German Ambassador.

Of this interview with the aforesaid Lord Minister of Foreign Affairs I hastened to transmit to Your Eminence a summary with the following encoded message: N⁰ 24.

"As per instructions encryption n⁰ 14 today being 18th intervened in August Name Holy Father interim Foreign Minister here charges me bring to attention His Holiness that all the Armenians from the territories that the Turkish troops are reoccupying have crossed Russian border with their families. In the mentioned territories Turkish troops encounter only armed Armenian bands fighting to retain those places and where they have committed the most atrocious cruelties against the Turkish race. The Turkish press having published such atrocities I also intervened August Name Holy Father with this Minister to avoid any danger to the Armenians in the Ottoman Empire; especially that of deportation which they feared and for which they had turned to this Delegation. Foreign Minister charges me to reassure also on this point Holy Father that such publication was suppressed by the Government, that no hostile act shall be committed against the Armenians of the Empire and that the threat of deportation is completely baseless. Adds further that Government is disposed concede amnesty Armenians of Empire. Report follows. Deepest respects."

Meanwhile, pleased that the magnanimous goodness of the Holy Father be extended anew in protection of this Armenian nation, I prostrate myself to kiss the Holy Purple and with feelings of high esteem and great veneration I have the honor of reaffirming myself...

8

24 June 1918, Rome – handwritten draft from Gasparri to Dolci – ASV, *Guerra* [War], 1914–18, 244, 112, n⁰ 66827

Mi giunse a suo tempo insieme al relativo allegato il rapporto del 19 marzo, n⁰ 764, con cui V.S.Illma mi forniva un dettagliato ragguaglio circa l'intervista da lei avuta con cotesto Ambasciatore di Germania e col Ministro degli Esteri turco, relativamente alla protezione degli Armeni nei territori rioccupati dalle Truppe Ottomane.

Ringrazio V.S. di quanto Ella si compiacque di portare opportunamente a mia conoscenza circa l'importante argomento e nell'assicurarla che non mancai di farne parola all'Augusto Pontefice approfitto volentieri di questo ulteriore incontro per...

[Translation]

The report of March 19th, n⁰ 764, in which Y. M. Illus. furnished me with a detailed accounting of the interview you had with the Ambassador of Germany and with the Turkish Foreign Minister regarding the protection of the Armenians in the territories reoccupied by the Ottoman Troops, reached me in due course, together with its relative attachment.

I thank you for the extent to which you have seen fit to opportunely bring this important subject to my knowledge and, in assuring you that I did not fail to make mention of it to the August Pontiff, I will gladly take advantage of this latest communication in order to…

9

20 March 1918, Monaco – Schiappi to Gasparri – AAEESS, *Asia* 57, 2, n° 63502

Eminenza Reverendissima,

Appena ricevuto il cifrato di Vostra Eminenza reverendissima N. 86, Monsignor Nunzio si rivolse con ogni premura al Signor cancelliere dell'Impero con una Nota del 9 corrente, esponendogli con le più vive istanze il paterno desiderio di Sua Santità che i poveri Armeni sieno rispettati dai Turchi rioccupanti i territori attribuiti loro nel trattato di pace con la Russia.

Ora ho l'onore di inviare qui unita a Vostra Eminenza copia della lettera di risposta del Signor Cancelliere a Monsignor Nunzio insieme alla relativa traduzione italiana, che suona così:

> "Siccome con la conclusione dell'armistizio di Brest-Litowsk crebbe la possibilità di evacuare le Provincie anatoliche orientali, allora occupate dai Russi, il Governo Imperiale si mise ben presto in relazione col Governo imperiale Ottomano relativamente alla questione del trattamento della popolazione armena di queste Provincie. In tale occasione ci siamo potuti persuadere che il Governo turco è deciso a trattare gli Armeni con mitezza ed a fare tutto ciò che è possibile per facilitare in avvenire una pacifica comunanza di vita fra la popolazione cristiana e maomettana dell'Anatolia orientale. Quando le bande armene, che frattanto si erano stabilite nel territorio avacuato dalle truppe russe, menarono una terribile strage tra la popolazione maomettana, noi di nuovo ricevemmo dal Governo Turco la tranquillizzante assicurazione che esso non pensa a prendere misure contro la popolazione innocente e che la disciplina più severa sarà mantenuta fra le truppe turche che avanzano.
>
> Ma evidentemente il ritorno di uno stato pacifico è possibile soltanto allora, se gli Armeni si sottomettono al Governo Turco, se rinunziano alle loro aspirazioni politiche, ora completamente senza speranza di successo, se ritornano lealmente ai loro doveri civili. Sventuratamente anche al presente i Comitati rivoluzionari armeni in Svizzera sono all'opera, per stimolare all'estrema lotta gli Armeni contro la Turchia. In una riunione che ha avuto luogo

ultimamente a Ginevra sono stati inviati telegrammi in questo senso ai Comitati Armeni di Tiflis. In pari tempo si dice che Boghos Nubar Pascha, rappresentante dei Katholicos armeni in Parigi, sia stato richiesto di pregare il governo Inglese ad inviare ufficiali e soldati per proteggere gli Armeni che combattono. Secondo altre notizie, ufficiali francesi ed inglesi già si trovano nelle bande.

Se il Signor Cardinale Segretario di Stato trovasse mezzi e vie per resistere al procedere irresponsabile di quelli che spingono gli Armeni ad una vana resistenza, potrebbe così essere evitata una grave sventura alla popolazione cristiana, alla sorte della quale Sua Eminenza si interessa così vivamente."

Inchinato umilmente al bacio della Sacra Porpora,ecc.
firmato:
Lorenzo Schiappi
Incaricato d'affari int.

[Translation]
Most Reverend Eminence,

As soon as Your Most Reverend Eminence's encryption N. 86 was received, Monsignor Nuncio[221] addressed himself in all haste to the Lord Chancellor of the Empire[222] with a Note of the 9th of this month, putting before him, with the most urgent of requests, His Holiness's paternal desire that the poor Armenians be respected by the Turks reoccupying the territories attributed to them in the peace treaty with Russia.

Now I have the honor of sending to Your Eminence here enclosed a copy of the letter of reply of the Lord Chancellor to Monsignor Nuncio together with its relative Italian translation, which sounds like this:

> Since, with the conclusion of the Brest-Litowsk armistice, the possibility had increased of evacuating the eastern Anatolian Provinces, then occupied by the Russians, the Imperial Government quickly contacted the Imperial Ottoman Government regarding the question of the treatment of the Armenian population of these Provinces. In that occasion, we had the opportunity of being persuaded that the Turkish Government is determined to treat the Armenians with clemency and to do everything possible to facilitate a peaceful future communal life between the Christian population and the Mohammedans of eastern Anatolia. When Armenian bands, who in the meanwhile had established themselves in the territory

---

221 Eugenio Pacelli.
222 Michaelis.

evacuated by the Russian troops, conducted a terrible massacre amongst the Mohammedan population, we again received tranquilizing assurances from the Turkish Government that it is not thinking of taking measures against the innocent population and that the most severe discipline shall be maintained among the advancing Turkish troops.

But evidently the return of a peaceful state is possible only thus: if the Armenians submit themselves to the Turkish Government; if they renounce their political aspirations, now completely without hope of success; if they return loyally to their civic duties. Tragically, even at present the Armenian Revolutionary Committees in Switzerland are at work to incite the Armenians to the ultimate fight against Turkey. At a meeting that took place recently in Geneva, telegrams were sent to this effect to the Armenian Committees of Tiflis. At the same time, it is said that Boghos Nubar Pasha, representative of the Armenian Catholicos in Paris, has been asked to bid the English government to send officers and soldiers to protect the Armenians that are fighting. According to other news, French and English officers are already to be found among the bands.

If the Cardinal Secretary of State were to find ways and means to stand up against the irresponsible initiatives of those who are pushing the Armenians into a vain resistance, a grave misfortune could thus be avoided for the Christian population, in whose destiny Your Eminence is so keenly interested.

Bowing humbly to kiss the Holy Purple, etc.
signed:
Lorenzo Schiappi
Chargé d'affaires Int.

10

29 March 1918, Constantinople – Dolci to Gasparri – AAEESS, *Asia* 57, 2, n°
[…]520

Eminentissimo Principe,

Mentre intervenivo presso questo Governo per scongiurare, nel Nome Augusto del S. Padre, ogni rappresaglia contro gli Armeni, lo spavento di una nuova deportazione invadeva l'animo di quelli di Angora, e ne avevano ben ragione.

Il Commandante Militare, Muhid Hodja, ed il Presidente del Comitato locale Giovane Turco non solo insistevano presso il Vali, Kiani Bey, egregio funzionario, ma lottavano persino contro di lui che rifiutava loro la necessaria autorizzazione per procedere a tali rigori.

Nella generale trepidazione, gli abitanti di Angora m'inviarono secretamente un messo per informarmi della situazione in cui si trovavano e dell'imminente pericolo di deportazione. Il messo, sfuggendo alla vigilanza della Polizia, si presentava a me il 20 del corrente mese, quando già, nell'udienza del 18, avevo potuto conseguire, per l'intervento del S. Padre, da questo Sig. Ministro degli Esteri, le più ampie assicurazioni che verrebbe risparmiato agli Armeni tutti, e specialmente dell'Impero, ogni sorte di persecuzione con la speranza di una non lontana amnistia.

Per questa comunicazione, e specialmente al sentire che il Ministro degli Esteri mi aveva incaricato di assicurare il S. Padre che nessuna molestia si sarebbe recata agli Armeni dell'Impero, l'animo abbattuto di quel povero messaggero di Angora si confortò e sollevò. Egli si affrettò subito a tranquillizzare i suoi connazionali con quelle espressioni convenzionali che la sventura ha insegnato loro. Egli partito, mi sono recato subito dall'Ambasciatore di Germania per metterlo al corrente di quanto accadeva in Angora, e lo stesso giorno richiamavo su questo punto, con una Nota di urgenza, l'attenzione del Ministro degli Esteri.

Dalle comunicazioni pervenutemi dalla stessa città di Angora, apprendo con vivo piacere che il Governo, approvando la condotta del Valy, ha richiamato a Costantinopoli il comandante militare, il quale è qui giunto.

Considerata l'attuale situazione, mi permetto di sottoporre alla Sua alta saggezza che non sarebbe opportuno dare alla Stampa questi particolari, dai quali si potrebbe agevolmente qui comprendere la sorgente d'onde sono partiti.

Chinato al bacio ecc

[Translation]
Most Eminent Prince,

As I intervened with the Government here to prevent, in the August Name of the Holy Father, any reprisal against the Armenians, fear of a new deportation struck the hearts of those in Angora, and rightly so.

The Military Commander, Muhid Hodja, and the President of the local Young Turks Committee not only made demands of the Wâli, Kiani Bey, a distinguished functionary, but even fought against him as he refused them the necessary authorization to proceed with such severity.

In the midst of general trepidation, the inhabitants of Angora sent a secret messenger to inform me of the situation in which they found themselves, and of the imminent danger of deportation. The messenger, eluding the vigilance of the Police, presented himself to me on the 20th of this month, when previously, in the audience of the 18th, I had been able to garner from the Foreign Minister here, through the intervention of the Holy Father, the most ample assurances that all the Armenians, especially those of the Empire, shall be spared any sort of persecution, with hope of an amnesty not far in the future.

For this communication, and especially to hear the Foreign Minister had charged me with assuring the Holy Father that no harrassment would be borne by the Armenians of the Empire, the dejected soul of that poor messenger of Angora was comforted and relieved. He quickly rushed to calm his countrymen with those conventional expressions that misfortune has taught them. After he left, I went at once to the Ambassador of Germany to bring him up to date with what was happening in Angora, and the same day I recalled the attention of the Foreign Minister to this matter, with an urgent Note.

From the communications that have reached me from the very same city of Angora, I learn with keen pleasure that the Government, approving the conduct of the Wâli, recalled the military commander, who has now arrived here in Constantinople.

Considering the current situation, may I permit myself to submit to your eminent wisdom that it would not be opportune to give the Press these details, from which one might easily understand the source from which they came.

Bowed to the kiss etc.

11

15 May 1918, Constantinople – The sultan to the pope – ASV, *Guerra* [War], 1914–18, 244,112, n° 67801

Oltre all'originale in lingua turca la traduzione in francese:
[In addition to the Turkish language original, the translation into French:] [223]

Sainteté,

Nous avons reçu la lettre que Votre Sainteté a bien voulu Nous adresser, en date du 12 du mois de Mars 1918, par laquelle, dans Son sentiment de haute bonté, Elle nous fait part des inquiétudes que certaines informations tendancieuses qui sont parvenues jusqu'à Elle, Lui font éprouver au sujet des populations armeniennes se trouvant dans les territoires dont le sort a été prévu par le Traité de Paix de Brest-Litowsk.

Bien que ces territoires soient habités presque en totalité par des musulmans Nous sommes hereux de pouvoir renouveler à Votre Sainteté les assurances précédemment données dans Notre lettre du 10 du mois de Novembre 1915, relativement à la protection pleine et entière de la population arménienne. Le sentiment de haute sollicitude et de justice traditionnel de Nos Ancètres à l'égard de tous leurs sujets sans distinction de race ni de religion, ainsi que celui de tolérance et de respect pour les croyances des différentes

---

[223] Riccardi, *op. cit.*, summarizes the contents, but without giving the main points of the document (p. 116).

communautés dont le Tout-Puissant a daigné Nous confier la garde, constituent les principes immuable de Notre conduite souveraine.

Donc Votre Sainteté peut être assurée, que ceux qui ne devient pas di droit chemin et ne manquent pas à leurs devoirs envers leur pays continueront à jouir, à l'instar de tous Nos fidèles sujets, de toute Notre paternelle protection.

Bien que les armées russes aient évacué Nos provinces envahies, les bandes arméniennes se sont efforcées d'y opposer de la resistance à Nos troupes chargées de la réoccupation des dites provinces et elles se son livreées avec acharnement à leur ouvre de mort contre la population musulmane sans défense et n'ont laissé sur leur passage que ruine et désolation. Le district d'Erivan qui se trouve pourtant en dehors des limites fixées par le Traité de Brest-Litowsk n'a pas échappé à son tour aux horreurs commises par ces bandes qui se sont livrées, tout recemment encore, à un massacre qui a duré plus d'une semaine et dont le nombre des victimes s'élève à plus de cinq mille âmes, et plus de quarante mille personnes ont cherché refuge dans les montagnes et se trouvent exposées à des privations indescriptibles.

Nous éprouvons un grand chagrin devant ce déplorable égarement qui n'a pour tout résultat que d'ajouter d'autres maux à ceux que la guerre provoque et dont Nous tachons d'adoucir les cruelles conséquences.

Avec l'aide du Très-Haut Nous espérons que l'ordre et le calme seront bientôt rétablis dans ces territoires, et Notre plus vif désir de voir Nos sujets arméniens y vivre en paix et en plaine prosperité, côte à côte avec leurs concitoyens musulmans ne tardera pas à se réaliser entièrement.

Nous prions Votre Sainteté d'agréer, les meilleurs voex que Nous formons pour la conservation de Sa précieuse santé et pour Son bonheur.

Constantinople, le 15 Mai 1918
Signée:
Mohammed Réchad V.

12

14 June 1918, Constantinople – Dolci to Gasparri – *Ibid.*, n° 67801

Eminentissimo Principe,

Ho l'onore di trasmettere all'Eminenza Vostra l'Autografo di S. Maestà il Sultano, consegnatomi da questo Signor Ministro degli Esteri, nell'udienza di Lunedi 3 Giugno corr. colla copia d'uso.

Chinato al bacio della S. Porpora ecc.

[Translation]
Most Eminent Prince,

I have the honor of transmitting to Your Eminence the handwritten letter of His Majesty the Sultan, consigned to me by the Lord Foreign Minister here in the audience of Monday, June 3rd of this year, with its reference copy.

Bowed to the kiss of the Holy Purple, etc.

13

20 June 1918, Rome – handwritten draft from Gasparri to Dolci – *Ibid.*, n° 67801

Insieme all'Autografo di Sua Maestà il Sultano e la relativa copia d'uso, ho ricevuto regolarmente il rapporto di V.S.Illma del 4 Giugno n° 849.

Sono, ora, lieto di significarle che in conformità dell'espressomi desiderio non ho mancato di rassegnare nelle Auguste mani del S. Padre l'importante documento suaccennato; e mentre di ciò la rendo informata colgo...

[Translation]

Together with the handwritten letter of His Majesty the Sultan and the relative reference copy, I duly received the report of Y.M. Illus. of June 4th n° 849.

I am, now, happy to notify you that, in compliance with the desire expressed me, I did not fail to present the important aforementioned document into the August hands of the Holy Father; and as I keep you informed of that I will take...

14

21 June 1918, Tiflis (received in September) – Kalatosoff and Kapojan to Der Abramian – AAEESS, *Asia* 57, 2, n° 81691[224]

All'Illmo e Revmo Monsignore
Sergio Der Abramian,

Nonostante tutti gli sforzi adoperati da noi, non ci siamo riusciti ad entrare in relazione coll'Ecc. Vostra; abbiamo indirizzato parecchie lettere, un telegramma ed un radiotelegramma, ma non abbiamo ricevuto risposta alcuna, ed ormai son quattro o cinque mesi che non riceviamo istruzioni per continuare il governo della diocesi; causa n'è senza dubbio il disordine delle ferrovie di Russia e conseguentemente l'inerzia della posta. Ma Ella poteva benissimo farci arrivare qualche lettera per mezzo dei corrieri; senza dubbio, nelle circostanze attuali, il Vaticano avrà dei corrieri speciali, per parlare coi suoi nunzi presso le potenze europee, quindi per mezzo di questi si poteva trovare la maniera di mandarci qualche lettera o dispaccio; ma disgraziatamente noi restammo privi di tale consolazione.

Le sarà gia noto lo stato attuale della Russia e del Caucaso in generale, ed in particolare quello dei fedeli affidati alle nostre cure; stato peggiore e miseria

---

[224] F. Kalatosoff and F. Kapojan, Mekhitarists, were left by Der Abramian in Tiflis as his vicars.

maggiore di questa, non si poteva figurare, e proprio spettava a noi, d'esserne spettatori e governare la diocesi durante queste traversie storiche.

Artvin, Ardanuch, Kars, Batum, Alessandropoli, Axalzik, Akalkalak, Zori, coi rispettivi villagi occupati dai Turchi: ad Ardakan trucidati il prete Der Stepan Citrarian e tutti gli uomini al disopra dei duodici anni, senza distinzione di religione: le donne e le figlie violate e molte d'esse finora in servitù dei turchi.

Quelli poi, che si sono salvati dalla strage colla fuga, muojono di fame o per strada o qui a Tiflis; il padre separato dal figlio, lo sposo dalla sposa; le famiglie disperse parte rimasta nei paesi occupati e parti vagabonde ed affamate nelle città centrali: solamente per Tiflis sono passati quasi cinque mila fugiaschi armeni cattolici, tutti nello stato miserabile; dei ricconi, che erano assicurati per tutta la vita, oggi stendono per le vie la mano per domandare elemosina: alcuni poi si vergognano di stendere la mano per chieder soccorso e quindi finiscono la vita nei cantoni occulti. Insomma non ci regge il cuore, per descrivere queste scene strazianti: Kars e Batum totalmente evacuati dagli armeni cattolici: il parroco del primo scappato in Russia; quello del secondo per ora si trova a Tiflis, come pure il prete d'Erzerum, Eghianian; quello di Trebizonda P. Timoteo, e di Karacaci, Der Agop Mighirdician.

Per Tiflis pure vi sono stati parecchi giorni di panico, durante i quali sono fuggiti verso Vladicaucaso una cinquantina di mila ed anche adesso continuano ad emigrare; la panica [sic] fu si [sic] grande che un furgone da Tiflis a Vladicaucaso venne a costare duodici [sic] mila rubli, poiche [sic] di giorno in giorno s'aspettava l'arrivo dei Turchi; ma ora, grazie alla venuta di qualche mila [sic] soldati tedeschi, la gente alquanto s'è tranquillizzata; ma la è questa una tranquillità apparente, poiché s'aspetta una grandissima battaglia tra giorni fra i soldati tedeschi da una parte ed inglesi e russi dall'altra; questi ultimi s'avanzano, secondo le voci, dalla parte di Bacu e della Persia.

Quello poi che c'importa assai è il non aver relazione alcuna coi nostri fedeli, rimasti nei paesi occupati dall'armata turca. Soltanto ieri ricevemmo una lettera da Artvin dal revmo Dirlughian, in cui faceva noto ch'essi, ed i fedeli di Pchicur, Caeadel, e quei d'Ardanuak, che non aveano emigrato verso Ardakan, erano sani e salvi, grazie alla cura assidua e protezione d'un certo Ismael efendi, che s'era comportato verso dei nostri Armeni cattolici da benefattore ed esimio difensore.

Dietro il consiglio del rappresentante austriaco a Tiflis, che è un agente diplomatico ed ottimo cattolico e nostro grande amico, noi indirizzammo una petizione officiale al generalissimo dell'armata turca al fronte Caucaso, l'ecc. Vehib-Mehmed Pascia e mandammo una lista generale delle città e villagi [sic] occupati dai turchi ed abitati dagli armeni cattolici indicandone il numero dei fedeli ed i loro preti: la petizione scrivemmo in lingua francese e fra gli altri domandammo il permesso d'inviargli una delegazione d'armeni cattolici per esporgli i bisogni dei fedeli affidati alla nostra cura. Dopo quindici giorni per mano d'un officiale turco ricevemmo la risposta in francese, stampata e sottoscritta dallo stesso generalissimo, nella quale esso c'assicura [*sic*] che dove entrerà l'armata regolare turca, i nostri fedeli possono vivere tranquillamente e non aver paura di niente e tra le altre cose dice che egli è sempre pronto a ricevere ogni nostra delegazione, quando ci piacerà inviarla. Ora noi ci prepariamo d'inviare a Batum una delegazione composta da cinque persone: ciò è P. Dionigi, i signori Kamarian, Kaplanian, Pasinian Filip efendi e sig. Tactagian. Per ora s'è avuto il permesso del governo georgiano per passare i confini; tra qualche giorno s'otterrà pure il permesso del governo ottomano ed allora potrà partire la delegazione.

Ora ho sentito che signor Ferdinando Tactagian parte per Costantinopoli come membro della Delegazione armena, per trattative di pace; gli demmo una lettera officiale, sottoscritta da noi due membri dell'Amministrazione e da tre principali Kotorgiuresi, autorizzandolo d'esserne interprete dei nostri preghi davanti a Sua Beatitudine il Patriarca Mons. Terzian, e pregarla di dare qualche notizia delle famiglie cotorgiuresi, esiliate nei paesi interni della Turchia.

Vedendo che non si può avere nessuna relazione coll'Ecc. V. e colla S.Sede e coi nostri Decanati, per affari urgenti, probabilmente io stesso, verrò a Roma in qualità di delegato dalla parte degli armeni cattolici di Russia. Già sarei in viaggio verso l'eterna città; però per facilitare il viaggio il principe Schulemburg, Agente diplomatico della Germania a Tiflis, mi consigliò di munirsi anticipatamente dei documenti e passaporti necessari; quindi mi consigliò di scrivere una petizione in tre esemplari, per ottenere il permesso dalle rispettive autorità dei paesi belligeranti, il che l'ho fatto e gli [*sic*] presenterò insieme colla presente indirizzata all'Eccellenza Vostra; quindi prego V.Ecc. di darmi licenza di venire a Roma per esporre minuziosamente tutti i nostri desideri ed affari urgenti della diocesi e lo chieggono nello stesso tempo i fedeli cotorgiuresi. Mi faccia arrivare in qualche maniera una raccomandazione dell'Emmo Card. Gasparri e dell'autorità italiana, la quale ultima non farà, credo, difficoltà, giacché avrò delle commissioni dalla colonia italiana dimorante qui a Tiflis. [...]

[Translation]
To His Most Illustrious and Most Reverend Monsignor
Sergio Der Abramian,

Notwithstanding the efforts we have undertaken, we have not been able to make a connection with Your Exc.; we have addressed many letters, a telegram and a radiotelegram, but we have not received any reply, and by now it has been four or five months that we have not received instructions for continuing the government of the dioceses, due, no doubt, to the disorder of the Russian railroads and consequently the inertia of the mails. But Your Exc. could very well have gotten across some letter to us by courier; without a doubt the Vatican has special couriers, under the current circumstances, to communicate with its nuncios to the European powers so, by means of these, it should have been possible to find a way to send us some letter or dispatch, but unfortunately we remain deprived of such consolation.

You will already be aware of the current state of Russia and of the Caucasus in general, and in particular that of the faithful entrusted to our care; a worse state and greater misery than this would be impossible to imagine, and yet it is up to us to be the spectators to it, and to govern the diocese during these historic adversities.

Artvin, Ardanuch, Kars, Batum, Alexandroupolis, Akhaltsikhe, Akhalkalak, Zori, and their respective villages occupied by the Turks; at Ardakhan the priest Der Stepan Citrarian and all the men over twelve years of age slain, without distinction to religion; the women and daughters violated and many of these still in servitude to the Turks.

Then, those who were able to escape the massacres are dying of hunger, either along the way or here in Tiflis; father separated from son, husband from wife; families dispersed, a part remaining in the occupied towns and a part vagabond and hungry in the major cities; just by way of Tiflis nearly five thousand Armenian Catholic refugees have passed through, all in a miserable state; the well-to-do, who had been set for life, today hold out their hands in the street to beg for alms: some are embarrassed to hold out their hand and ask for help and so end their lives in hidden corners. In short, the heart cannot bear to describe these harrowing scenes: Kars and Batum completely evacuated by the Armenian Catholics; the parish priest of the former escaped to Russia; that of the latter is in Tiflis for now, as are also Eghianian, the priest of Erzerum, F. Timoteo of Trabizon, and Der Agop Mighirdician of Karakaci.

Around Tiflis there have been many days of panic as well, during which about fifty thousand fled towards Vladicaucasus, and even now they continue to emigrate; the panic was so great that a truck from Tiflis to Vladicaucasus came to cost twelve thousand rubles, seeing as the Turks were expected to arrive any day, but now, thanks to the arrival of several thousand German soldiers, people have calmed down somewhat. But this is an apparent calm, since a huge battle is expected within a matter of days between the German soldiers on one side and the English and Russians on the other; these latter have been advancing, according to rumors, from the direction of Baku and of Persia.

What matters a great deal to us is the lack of contact with our faithful remaining in the towns occupied by the Turkish army. Just yesterday we received a letter from Artvin, from the Most Rev. Dirlughian, in which he noted that they, along with the faithful from Pchicur, Caeadel, and those of Ardanuak, who hadn't emigrated towards Ardakhan, were safe and sound, thanks to the assiduous care and protection of a certain Ismael Effendi, who behaved towards Armenian Catholics as a benefactor and distinguished defender.

Following the advice of the Austrian representative to Tiflis, who is a diplomatic agent and a very good Catholic as well as our great friend, we addressed an official appeal to the *generalissimo* of the Turkish Army at the Caucasian front, his Exc. Vehib-Mehmed Pasha, and we sent an overall list of the cities and villages occupied by the Turks and inhabited by Armenian Catholics, indicating the number of the faithful and their priests; we wrote the petition in French and among other things we asked permission to send him a delegation of Armenian Catholics to explain the needs of the faithful entrusted to our care. After fifteen days, by hand from a Turkish officer, we received the response in French, stamped and undersigned by the same *generalissimo*, in which he assured us that wherever the Turkish regular army shall enter, our faithful can live peacefully and have nothing to fear and among other things he said that he was always ready to receive any delegation of ours, whenever it would please us to send it. Now we are preparing ourselves to send a delegation to Batum composed of five persons: that is, F. Dionigi, Misters Kamarian, Kaplanian, Pasinian Filip Effendi and Mr. Tactagian. For now, we have gotten permission to cross the borders from the Georgian government; within a few days we should also obtain the permission of the Ottoman government and then the delegation will be able to depart.

Now I have heard that Mr. Ferdinando Tactagian is leaving for peace talks in Constantinople, as a member of the Armenian Delegation; we gave him an official letter, signed by we two members of the Administration and by three Khodorciurese principals, authorizing him to be the interpreter of our prayers before His Beatitude the Patriarch Mons. Terzian, and to beg that he give us some news about the Khodorciurese families exiled in the interior towns of Turkey.

Seeing as we are unable to connect with Y. Exc. and with the Holy See and with our Deaconates, for urgent business, I will probably come to Rome myself, in the capacity of delegate on behalf of the Catholic Armenians of Russia. I would already be en route to the eternal city; however, to facilitate the trip, Prince Schulemburg, diplomatic agent of Germany in Tiflis, advised me to equip myself in advance with the documents and necessary passports; he then advised me to write a petition in three versions, to obtain permission from the respective authorities of the warring countries, which I have done, and I will present them together with the present [letter] addressed to Your Excellency; therefore I pray Y. Exc. give me leave to come to Rome in order to explain in detail all our wishes as well as the urgent business of the dioceses, and at the same time the Khodorciurese faithful do so ask. Have sent to me in some way a recommendation from the Most Em. Card. Gasparri and from the Italian authorities; these latter won't create any difficulties, I don't think, since I will have some errands from the Italian colony resident here in Tiflis. [...]

15

22 June 1918, Rome – Manna to Gasparri – ASV, *Guerra* [War], 1914–18, 244 K 12 c, 306, n° 66909

Eminence,

Le comité armenien en Engleterre pour le secours des armeniens, à ma demande par l'intermediaire du Père Ross, Secrétaire de la Propagation de la Foi, a bien accepté secouriir nos chretiens du Caucase et de la Perse; mai il ajoute que n'ayant pas, en ce moment, le moyeen d'envoiyer quelques secours dans ces contrées, les relations avec ses agents là, etant rompues, à cause des derniers événnements en Russie, il me prie de demander à Votre Eminence, si Elle a les moyens sûrs de faire parvenir, des secours, que le Comité voudrait bien mettre à la disposition, à tous les chretiens de ces Contrées et quels seraint ces moyens.

De plus ayant entendu que le Patriarche nestorien a été tué sans savoir le comment, nous sommes préoccupés pour le sort de nos chretiens. C'est pourquois je prierais Votre Eminence de télégraphier à Mgr Ratti pour savoir 1°)s'il a des nouvelles rassurant sur le sort del nos chretiens en Caucase et en Perse.2°) s'il a des moyens sûrs pour faire parvenir à ces contrées du Caucase et de la Perse des secours pour tous les Chretiens, armeniens et syro-chaldéans qui se trouvent dans ces Pays.

Prosterné au baiser...

Jacques Manna Eveque Chaldéen

16

25 June 1918, Rome – handwritten draft from Gasparri to Manna – ASV, *Guerra* [War], 1914–18, 244 K 12 c, 306, n° 66909

Monseigneur,

En réponse à votre lettre du 13 Juin cour. concernant la demande d'envoi de secours aux chrétiens armeniens et syri-chaldéens du Caucase et de la Perse, que le Comité Arménien d'Angleterre désirerait leur fair parveni, je m'empresse d'informer Votre Grandeur que la Secrétairerie d'Etat transmettra volontiers à Monseigneur Dolci, Délégué Apostolique à Constantinople, la somme d'argente que le dit Comité voudra bien leur destiner.

Je viens de télégraphier à Monseigneur Dolci, en le priant de s'enquerir sur le sort des chrétiens de ces régions si éprouvées, et de me communiquer des nouvelles à leur égard.

J'aurai soin de faire part à Votre Grandeur les renseignements qui me parviendront à ce sujet, et dans cette attente je saisis l'occasion de vous renouveler, Monseigneur, l'expression de mes sentiments dévoués en Notre Seigneur.

17

26 June 1918, Rome – handwritten draft of the encrypted telegr. from Gasparri to Mons. Maglione Rep. Holy See in Bern – *Ibid.*, n° 66909

Prego V.S. di trasmette il seguente telegramma a Mons. Dolci Delegato Ap. a Costantinopoli:

> Essendosi qui in grave apprensione a causa della voce che si è diffusa dell'uccisione del patriarca nestoriano, interesso V.S.I. a comunicarmi le notizie che Le sarà possibile avere sui cristiani dimoranti nella Persia e nel Caucaso

[Translation]

Please transmit the following telegram to Mons. Dolci Ap. Delegate in Constantinople:

> Being here in grave apprehension over the rumor that has spread of the slaying of the Nestorian patriarch, I would interest you in communicating to me whatever news you may have about the Christians living in Persia and in the Caucasus[225]

18

26 June 1918, Constantinople – Dolci to Gasparri – AAEESS, *Austria* 576, n° 69471

Eminentissimo Principe,

Stimo opportuno trascrivere all'Eminenza Vostra dal giornale officioso "L'HILAL" del 26 Giugno n. 1108 l'intervista di Ahmed Djevdet Bey sovra la formazione dei nuovi stati del Caucaso.

[Translation]

Most Eminent Prince,

I retain it opportune to transcribe for Your Eminence from the unofficial newspaper "L'HILAL" of June 26th n. 1108 the interview of Ahmed Djevdet Bey about the formation of the new Caucasian states.

> Les Nouveaux Etats du Caucase
> Interview d'Ahmed Djevdet Bey
> La délégation de l'Azerbaijan à la conférence de Constantinople est arrivé hier soir à notre ville par le bateau Gul Nihal et est descendue au Péra Palace. Comme l'Azerbaijan est des trois gouvernements nouvellement formés au Caucase, celui qui nous est

---

[225] It was not possible to find Dolci's response.

attaché au point de vue de la race et de la religion de ses habitants, un des rédacteurs de notre confrère le Tanine a été interviewer le chef de la Délégation Mehmed Emin Bey, pour se renseigner au sujet de la situation actuelle du Gouvernement de l'Azerbaijan.

Mehmed Emin Bey, devant sortir en ce moment pour faire une visite à S.A. le Grand Vizir chargea le premier secrétaire de la Délégation, Ahmed Djevdet Bey, de fournir les renseignements désirés.

Celui-ci déclara entre autres: Un traité d'amitié a été conclu à Batoum entre les Gouvernements Ottomans et le Gouvernement de l'Azerbaidjan, car les deux pays ne s'étant pas trouvés en état de guerre, il n'y avait aucun besoin pour eux de conclure un traité de paix. A Batoum on délimite d'une façon définitive les frontières entre l'Empire Ottoman et les trois nouveaux états formés au Caucase, et on laissa à la Turquie, les Sandjaks d'Ahelik et Alexandropol ainsi que la ligne ferrée située entre eux, une partie des sanjaks d'Etchmiatzine et Nahdjivan ainsi que tout le Sandjak de Sourmenek. Quant aux frontières entre l'Azerbaidjan, la Georgie et l'Arménie, elles seront fixées par la conférence de Constantinople. Seulement d'après l'accord préliminaire entre les Gouvernements de ces trois états, la superficie de l'Azerbaidjan sera de 90 000 klm carrés et sa population de 4 millions d'habitants dont les 3 millions 1/2 appartenant à la race turque et les 400 000 environ sont arméniens. La superficie de l'Arménie, est, d'après l'évaluation des délégués arméniens de 11.000 klm carrés et sa population d'environ un million d'habitants. Quant à la Georgie elle a une superficie de 70 000 klm carrés et une population de trois millions d'habitants.

Ahmed Djevdet Bey déclara que les relations entre les nouveaux gouvernements du Caucase sont amicales. Nos rapports avec les arméniens sont très bons et ils deviendront meilleurs et plus sincères à l'avenir.

L'Azerbaidjan possède une force militaire régulière et instruite. Quant à l'ancienne armée des Arméniens elle est maintenant dispersée. Actuellement, les arméniens possèdent une division et les Géorgiens deux division de troupes et encore celles-ci ne sont pas à effectifs complet.

Bakou qui est le véritable chef-lieu du Gouvernement de l'Azerbaidjan, se trouvant encore entre les mains des Bolchevikis pour le moment notre chef lieu est à Guendj. Dès que les Bolchevikis seront chassés de Bakou, nous y transporterons le siège de notre gouvernement. Je dois cependant ajouter qu'à part la ville de Bakou, dans aucune autre localité de l'Azerbaidjan il n'y a l'ombre d'un Bolchevikis.

Le gouvernement de l'Azerbaidjan est aujourd'hui constitué.

L'Assemblée nationale qui était composée de 45 déligueés, s'est dissoute après avoir formé un gouvernement de 12 membres. La présidence du Gouvernement de l'Azerbaidjan est assumée par Faih Ati Khan Khoisky.

La première tâche du Gouvernement est d'assurer la paix et la tranquillité à l'intérieur, et de défendre le pays contre les attaques extérieures.

Dans six mois, les élections pour la Constituante de l'Azerbaidjan commenceront. C'est cette assemblée qui donnera la forme définitive au Gouvernement de l'Azerbaidjan.

Nos cultures, nos productions sont d'une abondance sans pareille cette année.

Aujourd'hui il n'y a pas un gouvernement constitué en Arménie. Ceci provient des divergences entre les partis, tandis qu'en Géorgie il s'est formé un gouvernement composé des social-démocrates et des nationalistes."

Chinato al bacio ecc
[Bowed to the kiss etc.]

19
9 July 1918, Rome – telegram from Gasparri to Pacelli – ASV, *Guerra* [War], 1914–18, 244 K 12 c, 306, n° 68898

Monsignor Pacelli Nunzio Apostolico
Monaco

Voglia S.V. informarsi presso cotesto Governo se è possibile inviare urgenti soccorsi popolazioni armene e sirocaldee del Caucaso e della Persia i quali non si possono mandare per mezzo legazione Britannica e Costantinopoli

[Translation]
Monsignor Pacelli Apostolic Nuncio
Monaco

Would you inquire of the Government there whether it is possible to send urgent aid Armenian and Syro-Chaldean populations of the Caucasus and of Persia which cannot be sent by way of British legation and Constantinople

20
August 1918, Monaco – copy of the encrypted telegr. from Pacelli to Gasparri – *Ibid.*, n° 68898

In risposta al cifrato dell'E.V.R. n° 688, comunico che il governo Imperiale pur dichiarandosi disposto a trasmettere soccorsi alle popolazioni siro caldee ed armene, dice di dubitare che, specialmente per la Persia, il mezzo sia di pratica attuazione.

[Translation]

In response to Y.M.R.E.'s encryption n° 688, I relay that the Imperial government while declaring itself willing to send aid to the Syro-Chaldean and Armenian populations, says it doubts, especially as regards Persia, this route is practicable.

21

18 July 1918, Constantinople – Dolci to Gasparri – AAEESS, *Asia* 57, 2, n° […]61

Eminentissimo Principe,

Ieri Mercoledì 17 corrente, come mi era stato annunziato per telefono, i Delegati della Repubblica Armena vennero a visitarmi.

Sono tre, l'uno fù ritenuto all'Hotel per indisposizione, venne quindi il Presidente del Consiglio Nazionale con il Ministro degli Esteri. Sono due persone di condizione civile, sulla cinquantina, assai gentili e specialmente il Presidente che ha l'aria di essere molto intelligente e parla benissimo il francese L'altro parla poco e con qualche difficoltà.

Come è noto, essi sono qui per trattare col Governo Ottomano le varie questioni tra la Turchia e la loro piccola Repubblica.

Appena arrivati si affrettarono ad esprimere tutta la loro riconoscenza per l'opera del S. Padre a prò della loro Nazione, tanto tribolata, e m'incaricavano di presentarGli l'espressione di tutta la loro indelebile e più profonda gratitudine.

Ebbero parole amabili anche per me, ed io mi affrettai naturalmente a dire che io non avevo fatto che il mio dovere in ossequio ai venerati comandi del mio Augusto Capo, e li misi al corrente di quanti passi erano stati fatti per ordine di S.S. su questo affare. Essi però erano pienamente a conoscenza di tutto, avendolo appreso non solo dai giornali europei, ma dai notabili del Patriarcato Armeno scismatico.

Parlando della costituzione della nuova Repubblica, il Presidente mi ha detto confidenzialmente che essa, benché riconosciuta dal Governo Ottomano, non trova nessuna simpatia e nessun appoggio presso i rappresentanti delle Potenze cristiane; che la Germania protegge invece la repubblica giorgiana, ed è contraria al movimento dei Tartari che tendono a fare una politica, non tanto panislamica quanto panturca, il che altera le relazioni tra la Germania e l'Impero Ottomano. Durante la conversazione, accennando ai massacri degli Armeni in Turchia, il Presidente faceva la seguente insinuazione: Non so spiegarmi, Monsignore, come la Germania e l'Austria, queste due grandi potenze cristiane abbiano potuto, non dirò permettere, ma tollerare la strage degli Armeni; mentre una loro parola avrebbe potuto salvarli. Ed io a lui: Quello che di certo so', Signor Presidente... [manca la fine della lettera]

[Translation]

Most Eminent Prince,

Yesterday, Wednesday the 17th of this month, as had been announced to me by telephone, the Delegates of the Armenian Republic came to visit me.

They are three; one was indisposed and remained at the hotel; therefore the President of the National Council came with the Foreign Minister.[226] They are two civilians of polite degree, in their fifties, extremely courteous, especially the president who has the air of being very intelligent and who speaks quite good French. The other speaks little and with some difficulty.

As you know, they are here to negotiate the various questions between Turkey and their small Republic with the Ottoman Government.

As soon as they arrived they were quick to express all of their recognition of the Holy Father's work in favor of their greatly suffering Nation, and they charged me with presenting him the expression of all their deepest and indelible gratitude.

They also had kind words for me, and I naturally hastened to say that I had not done other than my duty in respect to my August Head's revered commands; I informed them how many steps had been taken by order of the Holy See in this affair. They, however, were fully aware of all of this, having learned of it not only from the European newspapers, but from notables of the Armenian schismatic Patriarchate.

Speaking about the formation of the new Republic, the President told me confidentially that, despite being recognized by the Ottoman Government, [Armenia] is not finding any sympathy or any support among the representatives of the Christian Powers; that Germany is instead protecting the Georgian republic, and is opposed to the movement of the Tartars who tend to have a policy that is not so much pan-Islamic as pan-Turkish, which alters the relationship between Germany and the Ottoman Empire. During the conversation, alluding to the massacres of Armenians in Turkey, the President made the following insinuation: I don't know how to explain to myself, Monsignor, how Germany and Austria, these two great Christian powers, were able to, I wouldn't say permit, but tolerate, the massacre of the Armenians, while one word from them would have been able to save them. And I to him: What I do know for certain, Mr. President, ... [the end of the letter is missing]

---

226 The president was Avetis Aharonian, future president of the Delegation of the Armenian Republic to the Conference of Paris; the Foreign Minister, Alexandre Khatissian; the third, absent due to indisposition, Mikayel Papagianian (Hovannisian, *op. cit.*, p. 52).

22

9 August 1918, Constantinople – Dolci to Gasparri – AAEESS, *Asia* 57, 2, n° 81286

Eminentissimo Principe,

Facendo seguito al mio Rapporto N° 890 del 18 Luglio mi reco a premura di portare a conoscenza di V. Eminenza Revma, che alcuni giorni dopo la visita fatta a me dai membri della Missione Armena del Caucaso, mi recai a restituirla, accompagnato dal mio Vicario, all'Hôtel Tokatlian, ove dimorano.

Avendoli prevenuti precedentemente per telefono, i delegati erano restati tutti all'Hôtel per ricevermi. Già sulla porta esterna stava un segretario ed un Colonnello dello Stato Maggiore armeno, insieme ad alcuni giovani valletti, vestiti dei pittoreschi costumi nazionali.

Fui tosto introdotto in un salone, ove il Presidente mi venne incontro e mi presentò tutti i membri della Missione. Essa, oltre i due già venuti alla Delegazione per visitarmi, si compone di un altro signore, già Deputato della Duma Russa, di un Generale, del Segretario e Colonnello già nominati.

Sono tutte persone colte e molto gentili, specialmente il Generale, già membro dello Stato Maggiore russo ed ora di quello della nuova Repubblica. Dicono che egli sia cattolico, ma non potrei affermarlo. So soltanto che sua madre era di Livorno.

La conversazione fu cordialissima e sempre improntata a sentimenti della più grande venerazione e riconoscenza per l'opera del S. Padre a favore dei loro connazionali.

Purtroppo, quando incidentalmente si parlò del loro Patriarcato di Esmiadzin e della situazione fatta qui a Mgr. Terzian, si capiva bene che si aveva da fare in genere a dei scismatici convinti.

Il presidente non mancò però di mostrare il desiderio di vedere un giorno sorgere la religione ?, sul terreno diplomatico, tra il suo paese e la Sta Sede.

La Missione volle anche offrirmi un thè durante la mia visita.

Colgo l'occasione ecc.

[Translation]
Most Eminent Prince,

Following up on my Report N° 890 of July 18th, I eagerly bring myself to inform Y. M. Rev. Eminence that several days after the visit made to me by the members of the Armenian Mission of the Caucasus I went to return it, accompanied by my Vicar, at the Hotel Tokatlian, where they were staying.

Since I had previously notified them by telephone, the delegates had all remained at the Hotel to receive me. Right at the front door were a secretary and a Colonel of the Greater Armenian State, together with several young valets, dressed in picturesque national costumes.

I was soon shown into a hall, where the President came up to me and introduced to me all the members of the Mission. This, besides the two who had already come to the Delegation to see me, is composed of another gentleman, formerly a member of the Russian Duma, of a General, and of the Secretary and Colonel mentioned above.

They are all very polite and cultured persons, especially the General, formerly a member of the Great Russian State and now of that of the new Republic. They say that he is Catholic, but I could not confirm that. I only know that his mother was from Livorno.

The conversation was very cordial and marked throughout with sentiments of the greatest veneration and recognition of the Holy Father's work in favor of their countrymen.

Unfortunately, when their Patriarchate of Etchmiadzin and the situation here with Mons. Terzian were discussed in passing, it was clear that they were, for the most part, convinced schismatics.

The president did not fail, however, to demonstrate the desire of seeing, one day, religion?[227] come up, on diplomatic terrain, between his country and the Holy See.

The Mission was also pleased to offer me tea during my visit.

I take the occasion, etc.

23

31 August 1918, Lugano – de Ritter a Gasparri – AAEESS,
Asia 57, 2, n° 81693

Légation de Bavière près le Saint Siège

Monsieur le Cardinal

Je suis chargé et j'ai l'honneur de remettre à Votre Eminence le pli ci-joint qui contient la réponse de Son Excellence Monsieur De Dandl, Président du Conseil des Ministres de Bavière, à la lettre que Votre Eminence a bien voulu lui adresser le 1 juillet du. au sujet des tristes souffrances des peuples chrétiens en Orient.

Veuillez agréer, Monsieur le Cardinal, en même temps les nouvelles assurances de ma plus haute et très respectueuse consideration

Baron de Ritter

allegati: l'originale in tedesco di von Dandl e la seguente traduzione italiana:

Attachments: von Dandl's original in German and the following Italian translation:

---

227 "?" applied by hand, perhaps by Gasparri, probably due to the theological divergences with the Armenian Apostolic Church. V. also note p. 114

24

29 August 1918, Monaco – von Dandl to Gasparri – AAEESS, *Asia* 57, 2, n° 81693

Il Ministro di Stato della
Real Casa e degli Esteri

Eminenza!

Ho avuto l'onore di ricevere la veneratissima lettera di Vostra Eminenza del 1° corrente, N° 66793. Ho grandemente apprezzata la fiducia, ivi espressa, che il Santo Padre ripone nell'interessamento col quale il Governo bavarese seconda le intenzioni Sue; ed io La prego di deporre ai Piedi di Sua Santità gli umilissimi e devotissimi ringraziamenti.

Le gravi sofferenze e le miserie, a cui i Cristiani in Oriente sono esposti particolarmente in questi tempi pieni di dolori e di miserie per tutti i popoli travolti dalla guerra mondiale, hanno formato oggetto di particolare cura del governo bavarese.

Io ho già altra volta ricevuto informazioni sulle condizioni dei Cristiani in Turchia e sul trattamento fatto alle popolazioni armene: esse mi hanno riempito di compassione e mi hanno dato motivo di mettermi in comunicazione col governo del Regno per ottenere un miglioramento di quel lamentevole stato di cose.

In base al Pro-Memoria benevolmente inviato da Vostra Eminenza e nel quale vengono confermate le notizie, che mi erano giunte, in adempimento del desiderio di Sua Santità, non ho mancato di mettermi nuovamente in relazione col Signor Cancelliere dell'Impero, al quale so che sta particolarmente a cuore tale questione. Con mia grande soddisfazione da una comunicazione, pervenutami da parte di lui, ho potuto rilevare quale viva parte il Governo prenda alla sorte dei Cristiani in Oriente; come esso miri con ogni premura a migliorarne le condizioni tristi in cui versano, specialmente degli Armeni, e come ad esso sia riuscito in questa via di ottenere già qualche successo.

Io La prego di star sicuro che il Governo bavarese, come finora ha fatto, continuerà per l'avvenire a considerare tale questione come un oggetto del suo speciale interessamento ed è deciso di promuovere ed incoraggiare, per quanto è possibile, ciò che è atto ad addolcire le sofferenze dei cristiani in Oriente.

Gradisca Vostra Eminenza anche in questa occasione l'assicurazione della mia profondissima venerazione con cui ho l'onore di essere

Di Vostra Eminenza

Devotissimo: von Dandl

[Translation]

The Minister of State of the
Royal House and for Foreign Affairs

Eminence!

I have had the honor of receiving Your Eminence's most venerated letter of the 1st of this month, N° 66793. I greatly appreciated the trust, expressed therein, that the Holy Father places in the interest with which the Bavarian Government should second His Holiness's intentions; and I bid you depose at His Holiness's Feet the most humble and devoted thanks.

The grave sufferings and misfortunes to which the Christians in the East are exposed, particularly in these times full of pain and misery for all the peoples overwhelmed by the world war, have been object of the Bavarian Government's particular attention.

I had already received news of the conditions of the Christians in Turkey and of the treatment given to the Armenian population: these filled me with compassion and gave me motive to put myself in communication with the government of the Realm to obtain an improvement in that lamentable state of affairs.

Based on the Memorandum kindly sent by Your Eminence and in which the news which had reached me came to be confirmed, in fulfillment of His Holiness's wish I did not fail to put myself once again in contact with the Lord Chancellor of the Empire who, I know, takes this matter particularly to heart. With great satisfaction, from a communication sent to me on his part, I was able to learn what an active role the Government takes in the fate of the Christians in the East; how it aims with all consideration to ameliorate the sad conditions in which they find themselves, especially the Armenians, and how it had been able in this way to obtain some success already.

I pray you to rest assured that the Bavarian Government, as it has done up until now, will continue in the future to consider this matter an object of its special interest and is decided in promoting and encouraging, as far as possible, that which is done to mitigate the sufferings of the Christians in the East.

That Your Eminence should enjoy, also in this occasion, the assurance of my most profound veneration with which I have the honor of being

    to Your Eminence
    Most Devoted: von Dandl

25

28 September 1918, Rome – handwritten draft from Gasparri to de Ritter – AAEESS, *Asia* 57, 2, n° 81693

Son Excellence
Mr. le Baron de Ritter
Envoyé Extraordinaire et
Ministre plénipotentiaire
de Bavière

J'ai eu l'honneur de recevoir la lettre en date du 31 août 1918 par laquelle Votre Excellence a bien voulu me transmettre la réponse de S.E.Monsieur de Dandl à la lettre que je lui avais adressée au sujets des tristes souffrances des peuples chrétiens en Orient.

En vous remerciant vivement je saisis bien volontier cette nouvelle occasione pour vous renouveler les assurances de ma très haute considération

26

28 September 1918, Rome – handwritten draft from Gasparri to Dolci – AAEESS, *Russia* 505, n° 81691

Notizie pervenute alla Santa Sede da fonte attendibile riferiscono che la situazione degli Armeni-Cattolici del Caucaso è quanto mai dolorosa e straziante.

Il Santo Padre pertanto mosso dalla Sua inesauribile carità e generosità m'incarica di trasmettere alla S.V. la qui acclusa somma di Franchi 10.000 affinché Ella la faccia pervenire sollecitamente ai due Vicari residenti in Tiflis Rev. Dionigi Kalatosoff e Rev. Antonio Kapoian. Detta somma dovrà essere distribuita tra i poveri Armeno-Cattolici di quella regione, particolarmente tra quelli che ora si trovano sotto la dominazione turca.

Inoltre Sua Santità desiderando porgere direttamente un aiuto ai due sullodati vicari ed al Parroco Giacomo Kirokonian si è compiaciuto affidare a ciascuno di essi la celebrazione di 200 Messe con la elemosina di L. 8,46. Anche questa somma ammontante a L. 5076,00 troverà V.S. qui acclusa e la trasmetterà come l'altra ai destinatari.

Interesso poi V.S. di far pratiche presso cotesto Governo affinché non soltanto le truppe turche ma anche le bande turche si astengano dal perseguitare e massacrare i poveri Armeni, segnatamente quelli delle Provincie di Batum, Artvin, Satlel, Ardaghan, Kars, Alessandropoli, Ardanousch, Akalzite, ecc. Si trovano in queste Provincie 54.000 cattolici, i quali sono stati e sono sudditi fedelissimi dei rispettivi Governi.

Procurerà inoltre V.S., d'intesa col Patriarca degli Armeni Cattolici, di mettersi in relazione con i Sacerdoti Armeni di Artvin, Batum, Akalzite,

Alessandropoli, ecc e far loro pervenire gli Olii Santi dei quali sono privi, rivolgendo loro nello stesso tempo parole di conforto e di incoraggiamento.

Approfitto dell'incontro ecc

[Translation]

News reaching the Holy See from reliable sources relate that the situation of the Armenian Catholics of the Caucasus is more painful and heartrending than ever.

The Holy Father insofar moved by his inexhaustible charity and generosity charges me to convey to you the enclosed sum of 10,000 francs such that you have it sent promptly to the two Vicars resident in Tiflis, Rev. Dionigi Kalatosoff and Rev. Antonio Kapojan. This sum should be distributed among the poor Armenian Catholics of that region, particularly among those who now find themselves under Turkish domination.

Moreover, His Holiness, desiring to directly offer aid to the two vicars commended above and to the parish priest Giacomo Kirokonian, was pleased to entrust to each one of these the celebration of 200 Masses with alms of L. 8.46. You shall find this sum also herein closed, totaling L. 5076.00, and send it along with the other to the recipients.

I then occupy you with interceding with the Government there such that not only the Turkish troops but also the Turkish bands abstain from persecuting and massacring the poor Armenians, signally those of the provinces of Batum, Artvin, Satlel, Ardakhan, Kars, Alexandroupolis, Ardanuch, Akalzite, etc. There are 54,000 Catholics in these Provinces who have been, and are, faithful subjects of their respective Governments.

Furthermore, you must try, in concert with the Patriarch of the Catholic Armenians, to contact the Armenian Priests of Artvin, Batum, Akalzite, Alexandroupolis, etc., have them receive the Holy Oils of which they are deprived, and at the same time send them words of comfort and encouragement.

I take advantage of the encounter etc.

27

24 October 1918, Constantinople – Dolci a Gasparri – AAEESS, *Russia* 540 bis, n° 85097

Eminentissimo Principe,

Sabato prossimo 26 Corrente, faranno ritorno ai loro rispettivi paesi le due Commissioni della Georgia e dell'Armenia, purché la speranza d'incontrarsi qui in Costantinopoli colle Autorità militari dell'Entente non li determini a differire la loro partenza. Prima di lasciare questa città, le due Prefate Commissioni si sono il 23 corrente fatte un gradito dovere di prendere congedo da questa Rappresentanza Pontificia, per rinnovare al S. Padre l'omaggio della loro ammirazione, e della loro perenne riconoscenza. Lascieranno qui in Costantinopoli due Incaricati d'Affari che mi hanno vivamente raccomandato di assistere presso la Sublime Porta.

Mi sono mostrato oltremodo cortese con loro; e durante la conversazione mi sono studiato di far loro rilevare quanto il S. Padre ha fatto in quest'immane conflitto, il Suo prestigio e la Sua forza morale di carattere mondiale, il consolidamento dei loro stati nascenti nell'unione col Pontificato Romano, e l'uguaglianza delle due religioni cattolica ed ortodossa, facendo loro osservare che i loro popoli potevano essere cattolici quasi senza accorgersene, poiché rimanevano nell'osservanza dei loro riti e delle loro pratiche religiose. Ed infine, aggiunsi che lo spirito del cattolicismo è pure quello di coltivare il sentimento nazionale ed il rispetto e l'obbedienza ai poteri costituiti, ciò che mi adoperai di illustrare con esempi pratici.

La Commissione Giorgiana insiste sempre nel riconoscimento, da parte della Sta Sede, del rito giorgiano cattolico, e sarebbe felice se potesse avere un capo religioso Cattolico di rito Giorgiano, insignito del carattere episcopale, promettendo assistenza e protezione. Quella Armena accoglieva con vera gioia e soddisfazione il contenuto del cifrato di Vostra Eminenza N. 31, intorno al desiderio del S. Padre che il Patriarcato Armeno Cattolico sia officialmente rappresentato sul luogo dal Patriarca stesso, ed in caso d'impossibilità, da personaggio che lo rappresenti. Il detto Cifrato mi giungeva nello stesso giorno ch'io riceveva la Commissione e poche ore prima di essa.

L'una e l'altra Commissione infine desidererebbero avere relazioni diplomatiche colla S.Sede, sulla protezione della quale contano molto per garantire la formazione e l'esistenza delle loro nazioni.

Tanto ho creduto opportuno di portare a conoscenza dell'Eminenza Vostra, e chinato al bacio ecc.

[Translation]
Most Eminent Prince,
Next Saturday, the 26th of this month, the two Commissions of Georgia and of Armenia shall return to their respective countries, provided that the hope of meeting with the military Authorities of the Entente here in Constantinople does not induce them to postpone their departure. Before leaving this city, on the 23rd of this month the two above-mentioned Commissions carried out the welcome duty of taking their leave from this Pontifical Delegation, to renew to the Holy Father the homage of their admiration and of their perennial recognition. They will leave two Chargés d'Affaires here in Constantinople, whom they urged me to assist at the Sublime Porte.[228]

---

228 The Armenian representative was Ferdinand Tahtagian (or Tactagian, v. doc. n° 14 cit.) Hovannisian, *op.cit.*, p. 55.

I showed myself to be extremely courteous with them; and during the conversation[229] I tried to point out to them how much the Holy Father has done in this terrible conflict, his reputation and his worldwide moral authority, the consolidation of their nascent states in union with the Roman Pontificate, and the sameness of the two religions, Catholic and Orthodox, having them observe that their peoples could be Catholics almost without being aware of it, even as they remained in observance of their rites and of their religious practices. And lastly, I added that the spirit of Catholicism is also that of fostering a national sentiment with respect for and obedience to the established powers, which I did my best to illustrate with practical examples.[230]

The Georgian Commission continues to insist on the recognition of the Georgian Catholic rite on the part of the Holy See, and would be happy if they could have a Catholic religious leader of the Georgian rite, conferred with an episcopal character, promising assistance and protection. That of the Armenians welcomed with true joy and satisfaction the contents of Your Eminence's encryption N. 31, regarding the Holy Father's wish that the Armenian Catholic Patriarchate be officially represented on site by the Patriarch himself, or should that be impossible then by someone representing him. Said Encryption reached me the same day in which I received the Commission, just a few hours beforehand.

In short, both one Commission and the other would wish to have diplomatic relations with the Holy See, on whose protection they are counting heavily in order to guarantee the formation and existence of their nations.

In any case, I believed it opportune to bring to Your Eminence's knowledge, and bowed to the kiss etc.

28

24 October 1918, Constantinople – Dolci to van Rossum – CO, 106, 4, 2, 3, n° 1191

All' Eminentissimo Principe
IL SIGNOR CARDINAL VAN ROSSUM
Prefetto di Propaganda
Roma

Eminentissimo Principe,

Sabato prossimo, 26 corrente, faranno ritorno ai rispettivi paesi le due Commissioni della Giorgia e dell'Armenia, purché la speranza d'incontrarsi qui, in Costantinopoli, colle Autorità militari dell'Entente, non li determini a differire la loro partenza. Prima di lasciare questa città, le due prefate

---

229 Doc. also cited and transcribed (beginning from this point, referring only to the Georgians) by Morozzo della Rocca, *op. cit.* p. 323.
230 Here Morozzo della Rocca's transcription ends.

Commissioni si sono, il 23 corrente, fatte un gradito dovere di prendere congedo da questa Rappresentanza Pontificia, per rinnovare al S. Padre l'omaggio della loro ammirazione, e della loro perenne riconoscenza. Lascieranno qui in Costantinopoli due Incaricati d'Affari che mi hanno vivamente raccomandato di assistere presso la Sublime Porta.

Mi sono mostrato oltremodo cortese con loro ; e, durante la conversazione, mi sono studiato di far loro rilevare quanto il S. Padre ha fatto in quest'immane conflitto, il Suo prestigio e la Sua forza morale di carattere mondiale, il consolidamento dei loro stati nascenti nell'unione col Pontificato Romano, e l'uguaglianza delle due religioni cattolica ed ortodossa, facendo loro osservare che i loro popoli potevano essere cattolici quasi senza accorgersene, poiché rimanevano nell'osservanza dei loro riti e delle loro pratiche religiose. Ed infine aggiunsi che lo spirito del cattolicismo è pure quello di coltivare il sentimento nazionale ed il rispetto e l'obbedienza ai poteri costituiti, ciò che mi adoperai di illustrare con esempi pratici.

La Commissione Giorgiana insiste sempre nel riconoscimento , da parte della Sta Sede, del rito giorgiano cattolico, e sarebbe felice se potesse avere un capo religioso Cattolico, di rito Giorgiano, promettendo assistenza e protezione. Quella Armena accoglieva con vera gioia e soddisfazione il contenuto del Cifrato di Vostra Eminenza N.31, intorno al desiderio del S. Padre che il Patriarcato armeno cattolico sia officialmente rappresentato sul luogo, dal Patriarca stesso, ed in caso d'impossibilità, da personaggio che lo rappresenti. Il detto cifrato mi giungeva nello stesso giorno ch'io riceveva la commissione, e poche ore prima di essa.

L'una e l'altra Commissione infine desidererebbero avere relazioni diplomatiche colla S. Sede, sulla protezione della quale contano molto per garantire la formazione e l'esistenza delle loro nazioni.

Tanto ho creduto opportuno di portare a conoscenza dell'E. Vostra, e chinato al bacio ecc

[Translation]

To His Most Eminent Prince
THE LORD CARDINAL VAN ROSSUM
Prefect of Propaganda
Rome

Most Eminent Prince,

Next Saturday, the 26th of this month, the two Commissions of Georgia and of Armenia shall return to their respective countries, provided that the hope of meeting with the military Authorities of the Entente here in Constantinople does not induce them to postpone their departure. Before leaving this city, on the 23rd of this month the two above-mentioned Commissions carried out the welcome duty of taking their leave from this Pontifical Delegation, to renew to the Holy Father the homage of their admiration and of their perennial recognition. They will leave two Chargés d'Affaires here in Constantinople, who they urged me to assist at the Sublime Porte.

I showed myself to be extremely courteous with them; and during the conversation I tried to point out to them how much the Holy Father has done in this terrible conflict, his reputation and his worldwide moral authority, the consolidation of their nascent states in union with the Roman Pontificate, and the sameness of the two religions, Catholic and Orthodox,[231] having them observe that their peoples could be Catholics almost without being aware of it, even as they remained in observance of their rites and of their religious practices. And lastly, I added that the spirit of Catholicism is also that of fostering a national sentiment with respect for and obedience to the established powers, which I did my best to illustrate with practical examples.

The Georgian Commission continues to insist on the recognition of the Georgian Catholic rite on the part of the Holy See, and would be happy if they could have a Catholic religious leader, of the Georgian rite, promising assistance and protection. That of the Armenians welcomed with true joy and satisfaction the contents of Your Eminence's encryption N. 31, regarding the Holy Father's wish that the Armenian Catholic Patriarchate be officially represented on site by the Patriarch himself, or should that be impossible then by someone representing him. Said Encryption reached me the same day in which I received the Commission, just a few hours beforehand.

In short, both one Commission and the other would wish to have diplomatic relations with the Holy See, on whose protection they are counting heavily in order to guarantee the formation and existence of their nations.

In any case, I believed it opportune to bring to Y. Emin.'s knowledge, and bowed to the kiss etc.

29

26 October 1918, Constantinople – Dolci to Gasparri – AAEESS, *Asia* 57, 2, n° [...]

Eminentissimo Principe,
Il giorno 23 avevo l'onore di ricevere il ven. cifrato dell'Eminenza Vostra:

> In seguito nuovi avvenimenti ed in previsione nuova organizzazione Armenia S.Padre desidera che Patriarcato armeno cattolico sia rappresentato officialmente sul luogo dal Patriarca stesso, in caso d'impossibilità da personaggio che lo rappresenti.

Poche ore dopo giungeva a questa Delegazione, in visita di congedo, la Commissione armena della quale fa parte lo stesso Ministro degli Esteri della

---

231 Underlined by hand (perhaps by van Rossum?). V. note p. 106.

nascente Repubblica. Alla lettura del citato cifrato, con la più grande soddisfazione del loro animo, ravvisarono nel desiderio espresso dal S. Padre una novella prova della sua sovrana benevolenza, verso la Nazione armena.

Il giorno appresso, comunicava personalmente l'Augusto desiderio a questo Eccmo Patriarca, Mons. Paolo Pietro XIII Terzian, il quale si affrettò a scrivermi la seguente lettera:

> Eccellenza Revma, Si prega caldamente V.E. Rma di aver la bontà di umiliare ai piedi del S. Padre il contenuto dei vivi sentimenti in risposta del Suo onorevole Dispaccio inviato ultimamente a V.E.Rma.
>
> Ammiro grandemente le alte concezioni delle sovrane sue idee, per la proposta fatta di rappresentare il nostro Patriarcato, nel centro stesso della Repubblica di Armenia, novellamente organizzata.
>
> Resto vivamente riconoscente io coi miei Vescovi suffraganei, col Clero e col popolo, per quella specialissima paterna cura che il S. Padre non cessa di dimostrare verso gli Armeni afflitti, in generale, ed in modo particolare per la nostra Comunità armena cattolica. Mi dichiaro in pari tempo prontissimo di eseguire io in persona il Suo desiderio, che per me è un ordine di sovrana Sua Autorità. Aspetto con impazienza le istruzioni necessarie in proposito.
>
> Mi affretto in pari tempo di presentare anche a V.E.Rma la mia sincera gratitudine anticipata per la sua gentilezza con cui si compiacerà di trasmettere a Sua Santità questi miei umilissimi sentimenti di filiale sottomissione.Intanto con sensi di vero ossequio ho l'onore di rassegnarmi ecc.

[Translation]

Most Eminent Prince,

On the 23rd I had the honor to receive Your Eminence's ven[erated] encryption:

> Following new events and with prevision new organization Armenia Holy Father wishes that Armenian Catholic Patriarchate be represented officially on site by the Patriarch himself, in case of impossibility by a figure that represents him.

A few hours later, the Armenian Commission of which the Foreign Minister of the nascent Republic is himself a member, visited this Delegation to take their leave. At the reading of the aforementioned encryption, to their heart's greatest satisfaction they recognized, in the wish expressed by the Holy Father, new proof of his supreme benevolence towards the Armenian Nation.

The following day, they personally communicated the August Wish to the Most Exc. Patriarch here, Mons. Paolo Pietro XIII Terzian,[232] who hastened to write me the following letter:

> Most Rev. Excellency, one prays heartily for Y.M.R. Exc. to have the goodness to humbly present at the feet of the Holy Father the content of these vivid sentiments in response to his honorable Dispatch recently sent to Y.M.R. Exc.
>
> I greatly admire the noble concepts of his sovereign ideas, for the proposal made to represent our Patriarchate in the very center of the newly organized Republic of Armenia.
>
> I remain vividly cognizant, I along with my supporting Bishops, with the Clergy and with the people, of that very special paternal care which the Holy Father never ceases to demonstrate towards the afflicted Armenians in general, and particularly towards our Armenian Catholic Community. At the same time I declare myself at the ready to carry out, in person, his desire, which for me is an order of his sovereign Authority. I await with impatience the necessary instructions in that regard.
>
> At the same time I also hasten to present to Y.M.R. Exc. my sincere gratitude in advance for the kindness with which you shall be pleased to convey to His Holiness these, my most humble sentiments of filial submission. Meanwhile with feelings of deepest respect I have the honor of presenting myself etc.

30

4 November 1918, Constantinople – Dolci to Gasparri – AAEESS, *Asia* 57, 2, n° [...]

Eminentissimo Principe,

L'augusto desiderio del S. Padre che il Patriarcato armeno cattolico sia rappresentato officialmente sul luogo dal Patriarca stesso ed in caso d'impossibilità da un suo Rappresentante, ha prodotto la più grata impressione non solo alla Delegazione della Repubblica armena, ma a tutta la stampa di questa Nazione.

Qualche giornale ha però travisato dal vero suo significato questo augusto desiderio del S. Padre come il giornale Giamanak del 30 Ottobre che pubblica:

[Translation]
Most Eminent Prince,

The Holy Father's august desire that the Armenian Catholic Patriarchate be officially represented on the spot by the Patriarch himself and in case of

---

232 Armenian Catholic patriarch of Cilicia.

impossibility by a Representative of his, has produced the most grateful of feelings not only in the Delegation of the Armenian Republic, but in all of this Nation's press.

A few newspapers, however, have distorted the Holy Father's august wish from its true meaning, like the newspaper *Jamanak* of October 30th which publishes:

> La République Arménienne.
>
> Sa Sainteté le Pape et la République Arménienne.
>
> Sa Saintaité le Pape ayant fait savoir à Mgr. Dolci qu'Il reconnaissait l'indépendance de la République Arménienne, invite S.E. d'engager Sa Grandeur le Catholicos des Arméniens catholiques à se faire représenter par un Délégué Apostolique spécial auprès de la République Arménienne.
>
> Du reste, au cours des multiples entretiens, que le Délégué Apostolique eut avec la Délégation Arménienne, celle-ci lui a déclaré que la République Arménienne ne mettait aucune différence entre les éléments constituant la population de la République et qu'aucune différence n'existait entre les Arméniens Grégoriens et les Arméniens Catholiques.
>
> Ainsi que notre journal l'a plus d'une fois relevé avec gratitude, Benoît XV a donné à notre Nation plus d'une preuve de sa sollicitude.
>
> Hier le Locum-tenens du Patriarcat, Mgr. Djévahindjian, s'est rendu chez le Délégué Apostolique pour le remercier de toutes les marques de sympathie envers la nation.
>
> Cette visite a été marquée de la plus grande cordialité. Nous ne pouvons nous empêcher de rappeler à cette occasion à nos lecteurs les multiples égards et les sentiments de bienveillance que Monseigneur Dolci avaient témoigne à Mgr. Zavène Patriarche des Arméniens pendant les jours malheureux de son exile.

Tanto ho creduto opportuno portare a conoscenza dell'Eminenza Vostra ed inchinato al bacio ecc.

[Translation]

At any rate, I believed it opportune to bring to Your Eminence's knowledge, and bowed to the kiss etc.

31

10 November 1918 – Memorandum[233] of the Armenian National Delegation for the U.S. ambassador to Rome – AAEESS, *Asia* 57, 2, n° 84492

Son Excellence Monsieur Nelson Page
Ambassadeur des Etats-Unis d'Amérique
à Rome

Monsieur l'Ambassadeur,

Nous soussignés, Mihran Damadian, représentant en Italie de la Délégation Nationale Arménienne accréditée auprès des Puissances Alliées, ayant son siège à Paris; Garbiss Dilsizian, président du Comité Central Arménien d'Italie; Dr. Nichan D. Stépanian, directeur politique de la périodique "Armenia" publiée à Turin, et secrétaire général du dit Comité, agissant en nos qualités respectives et en conformité des décisions prises au Congrès des organisations politiques arméniennes d'Italie, tenu à Rome les 29-30 et 31 octobre 1918, avons l'honneur de présenter à Votre Excellence le présent Memorandum, et vous serions infiniment obligés de vouloir bien le recommander à la bienveillante considération de Monsieur le Président Wilson.

Tous les Arméniens ont la ferme convinction que le Gouvernement des Etats-Unis d'Amérique - qui s'est si vivement intéréssé, dans le passé, au relevement moral et intellectuel du peuple armenien et qui a tant fait, pendant cette guerre, pour adoucir les souffrances matérielles de notre peuple si cruellement persécuté par la barbarie turque à cause de sa religion chretienne, de ses tendances européennes et de sa fidélité à la cause des Alliés, - voudra également, conformément aux nobles idéals de justice, de droit et de liberté proclamés par son grand Président, devenu l'idole des nations opprimées, prendre en main la cause de la régéneration politique de l'Armenie, sur la double base de la réalisation des legitimes revendications de la nation arménienne et de l'établissement dans le Proche-Orient d'une paix juste et durable.

L'organisation politique actuelle des Arméniens
et leurs porte-voix autorisés

Les Arméniens, qui ont toujours eu une organisation parfaite, sur des bases démocratiques, pour l'administration de leurs affaires nationales et religieuses, ayant proclamé, depuis la Guerre, l'union sacrée, se sont doués d'une

---

233 Copy probably given to Gasparri by Damadian in the audience conceded him on December 20th, 1918; v. doc. n° 36.

organisation d'un caractère essentiellement politique qui représente toute la nation et qui est constituée comme suit:

Les Arméniens du Caucase et les Arméniens de Turquie refugiés au Caucase ont formé leurs Conseils Nationaux respectifs qui s'occupent, de concert, de toutes questions politiques relatives aux destinées de l'Arménie turque et de l'Arménie russe. Les Arméniens de l'Etranger, à savoir, ceux de l'Egypte, des Etats-Unis d'Amérique, de la France, de l'Angleterre, de l'Italie, et de la Suisse - qui constituent d'importantes Colonies - ont formé des sections de l'Union National qui s'occupent également de la question politique de la nation et sont étroitement liées entre elles. A la tête de toute cette organisation des Arméniens de Turquie, de Russie et de l'Etranger, se trouve la Délégation Nationale Arménienne accréditée auprès des Puissances Alliées par S.S. le Patriarche Supreme de tous les Arméniens, qui siège à Paris et qui est présidée par S.E. Boghos Nubar. Cette Délégation étant aussi reconnue par toutes les organisations précitées, représente l'autorité politique par excellence de la nation arménienne: elle est, en quelque sorte, le Gouvernement Provisoire des Arméniens. La Délégation National a ses représentants dans les diverses capitales de l'Entente. Les représentants de la Délégation Nationale en Amérique sont M.M. Bastermadjian et Sevasly.

Les représentant de ladite Délégation en Italie et les représentant du Congrès des Comités arméniens d'Italie croient de leur devoir, dans cette période décisive de la question arménienne, de s'adresser à Votre Excellence qui représentez si dignement le gouvernement des Etats-Unis dans ce pays, pour vous soumettre respectiveusement leurs demandes nationales. Cette démarche, loin de contrecarrer celles qui sont faites directement soit par la Délégation Nationale soit par ses représentants en Amérique, vise au contraire à les appuyer et à leur adjoindre notre adhésion, servant en meme temps comme une preuve de la parfaite concordance de vues et de l'identité des aspirations nationales des Arméniens de tous les pays, ainsi que de la profonde admiration qu'ils ont tous pour la grande Démocratie américaine sur les sympathies et l'appui de laquelle ils mettent leur entière confiance et tout leur espoir.

[... a page is missing]

L'attitude des Arméniens pendant cette guerre

Dans le double but de rester fidèles aux idéals les plus sacrés de l'humanité et de se soustraire définitivement à la tyrannie barbare qui les opprimait depuis des siècles, les Arméniens, dès le début de la guerre, se sont rangés aux cotés des Alliés. Ils ont formé des corps de volontaires, voire meme une armée nationale. Ils se sont battus contre l'ennemi commun sur tous les fronts et plus particulièrement sur le front du Caucase. Leur bravoure, leur esprit d'abnégation, les services considérables rendus par eux à la cause alliée ont été reconnus et appréciés dans les déclarations des hommes d'Etat de l'Entente.

D'ailleurs, dans l'Ordre du jour ci-annexe, il y a une énumération détaillée de tous ces efforts déployés par le peuple arménien qui a ainsi doublement consacré sa cause, par le sang de ses martyrs et par le sang de se héros.

Les Arméniens du Caucase et de la Perse

Les Arméniens du Caucase, ayant combattu tant dans les rangs de l'armée russe qu'après la défection de la Russie bolchéviste, avec leurs propres forces nationales, et ayant souffert les horreurs de l'invasion turque; les arméniens de la Perse ayant partagé les mêmes luttes et les mêmes souffrances, leur cause est désormais indissolublement liée et unifiée à celle de leurs frères de l'Arménie turque. Des gouvernements qui oppriment et massacrent leurs sujets, des gouvernements qui, au lieu de protéger et de défendre leurs sujets dans leurs suprême détresse et dans leur agonie, les abandonnent à la merci de leurs pires ennemis, ces gouvernements perdent tous leurs droits de domination ou de souveraineté sur ces mêmes sujets.

Il convient de retenir aussi que les Arméniens du Caucase, suivant l'exemple des Géorgiens qui se sont déclarés indépendants, ont constitué depuis le mois de juin de l'année courant un Etat indépendant arménien dans la province d'Erivan et les régions adjacentes, et que, par conséguent, il existe déja *de facto* en ce moment un noyau d'Etat arménien constitué en Arménie russe.

Considérations générales sur l'opportunité
de la constitution d'un Etat Arménien

1º - La raison fondamentale des malheurs de l'Arménie git non seulement dans le fait qu'elle est sous une domination étrangère, mais aussi dans l'incapacité absolue du Turc de gouverner, et particulièrement de gouverner des population chrétiennes. Les rivalités des Puissances Européennes ont permis aux Turcs pendant une longue période de montre ce qu'ils peuvent faire en matière de gouvernement de races étrangères et des races chrétiennes, en particulier.

Le verdict de l'histoire est écrasant. Un développement autonome sous la Souveraineté turque a été essayé dans la Roumelie Orientale, en Grèce, en Macedoine. L'exspérience a conduit à la guerre dans chacun de ces cas, et a eu des conséquences désastreuses pour les populations en cause. Aussi longtemps que le Turc possedera et exercera la moindre autorité, il ne pourra pas y avoir de sécurité contre les fréquentes explosions d'une sauvagerie, qui est inhérente à sa nature. Il n'y a plus d'espoir de reformer le Gouvernement, car le Turc ne veut pas de réformes contraires à son esprit de domination par la violence; et lors même qu'il y consentirait, il est incapable de les mettre en exécution.

2º - L'importance stratégique des hauts plateaux arméniens, la connexion de la question arménienne avec la politique du "Berlin-Bagdad", et le fait aussi que l'Arménie marque le point de contact des sphères d'influence et de domination germano-turque et britannique en Orient, donnent à la question arménienne une importance qu'on ne saurait exagérer.

3º - Une Arménie indépendante servirait les intérets de la paix établissant un Etat-Tampon entre l'influence germanique au Nord-Ovest et l'influence britannique au Sud-Est. Elle éléverait une véritable barrière entre l'Asie Mineure et le Turkestan, et empecherait ainsi la réalisation du rêve pantouranien qui est une réelle et grande menace pour la paix du monde et la Civilisation.

4º - La chute du Tsarisme et l'entrée en guerre des Etats-Unis ont ouvert une porte à une solution de la question arménienne basée sur les principes de justice, d'honneur, de réparation et des droits des petites nationalités, proclamés par les Alliés et confirmés par le Président Wilson dans ses déclarations devenues historiques.

Toutes les transactions secrètes dont la politique impérialiste du Gouvernement Tsariste avait pris l'initiative et qui tendaient plus ou moins à des annexions, ont été écartées et il n'est plus question de partager l'Arménie entre deux sphères d'influence.

Les Revendications des Arméniens

Les revendications des Arméniens se résument comme suit:

1º - La libération définitive du joug étranger de tout le territoire historique de l'Arménie. Tout vestige de souveraineté turque sur l'Arménie doit être éliminé.

2º - La réconnaissance par les Puissances Alliées de l'Etat arménien de l'Ararat déjà constitue et son extension sur tout le territoire de l'Arménie russe.

3º - L'unification de l'Arménie turque et de l'Arménie russe ainsi libérées pour en constituer un Etat arménien unique, libre et indépendant, sous la garantie de la Société des Nations ou, à son défaut, sous la garantie collective des Puissances de l'Entente, y compris les Etats-Unis d'Amérique.

4º - La question de l'Armenie persane mettant en cause l'intégrité de la Perse, amie de l'Entente, et avec la quelle l'Arménie désire vivre en paix comme par le passé, les Arméniens s'en rettent à l'esprit de justice des Puissances alliées pour la solution à y être donnée.Et dehors de toute autre considération, les événements déplorables dont l'Azerbaidjan a été le théatre pendant la guerre, confèrent aux Arméniens le droit de poser cette question.

5º - L'unification et l'indépendance de l'Arménie une fois proclamées et sanctionnées par le Congrès de la Paix, il appartiendra aux Puissances Alliées d'établir les modalités de la reconstitution et de l'organisation du nouvel Etat; confermément aux voeux de la nation arménienne présentés par la Délégation Nationale. Les Puissances garantes pourront, par exemple, confier à une d'entre elles le mandat temporaire d'organiser l'Arménie sur des bases préetablies par toutes.

Delimitation de l'Arménie

L'Arménie comprend, suivant carte ci-annexée,[234] sauf délimitations précises à établir en son temps par la Délégation Nationale:

1º - L'Arménie Turque (les six vilayets d'Erzeroum, de Bitlis, de Van, de Kharpoot, de Diarbékir et de Sivas, avec une partie du vilayet de Trébizonde donnant accès à la Mer noire, ensemble avec la Cilicie (Petite-Arménie) se composant de parties des vilayets actuels d'Adana et d'Alep et comprenant tout le littoral méditerranéen à partir d'un point à l'Est de Séléfkè jusqu'à Djèbel Moussa).

2º - L'Arménie russe;

3º - L'Arménie persane (la partie nord-occidentale de la province d'Azerbaidjan).

Population, Ethnographie.

C'est le coté le plus discuté de la question arménienne; qu'il nous soit donc permis de traiter ce sujet avec un peu plus de détail.

L'Arménie, dans les limites désignées plus haut, renferme une population d'environ 5.000.000 d'habitants, dont environ 3.600.000 (o 2.600.000?) Arméniens répartis comme suit:

En Arménie russe, environ................ 1.400.000
En Arménie persane............................200.000
En Arménie Turque........................1.000.000 (1)
Totale..2.000.000 [sic]

(1) C'est le nombre probable des survivants et rescapés des massacres et déportations que l'on espère de retrouver, sur une population arménienne d'environ 1.800.000 que contenait l'Arménie turque avant la guerre.

Les Arméniens constituent, au point de vue intellectuel, commercial et économique, l'ame du pays et la creme de la population. Ils sont une race compacte, uniforme, homogène, ayant la meme religion, la meme langue, les memes traditions, les memes caractéristiques d'unité nationale. Il faut grouper à coté des Arméniens, les Nestoriens, les Chaldéens, les Grecs, les Syriens, les Juifs (ensemble, 300.000 ames); différents autres groupes ethniques, tels que les yézidis et les Kezelbaches (environ 400.000), les Fellahs dont la plupart de confession ansarieh (100.000). Tous ces éléments non-musulmans ou non-turcs vivent en meilleurs termes de voisinage et de solidarité avec les Arméniens et par conséquent accueilleraient avec joie la constitution d'une Arménie libre.

Dans l'Arménie russe, il existe 200.000 Tartares musulmans; ceux-ci étant des agricolteurs sont généralement paisibles; ce n'est que sous l'excitation et la provocation des Turcs qu'ils se brouillent avec les Arméniens. Viennent enfin les deux autres groupes musulmans, les Turcs (environ 700.000) et les Kurdes (également 700.000 environ). Ce double groupe turco-kurde ayant l'apparence d'un élément dont l'importance numérique viendrait aussitot après celle des Arméniens, il mérite de réduire cette prétendue importance à sa juste valeur. D'abord, les Turcs, et les Kurdes sont des races foncièrement

---

234 Not found.

différentes, parlant deux langues différentes, et qui n'ont d'autre lien que la religion musulmane; meme cette communanté de croyances n'est qu'apparente: les Kurdes ne sont musulmans que de nom. En second lieu, tant les Turcs que les Kurdes se subdivisent en une infinité de tribus et de peuplades artificiellement réunies sous les memes dénominations génériques de Turcs ou de Kurdes. La plupart de ceux qui sont classés sous le nom de Turcs sont des émigrés de Russie (Tcherkesses, Tchétchebes, etc.) des Arabes d'Algerie, de Tunisie, des Grecs convertis de Crete, des émigrés des pays balkanique (les Bosniaques, les nouhadjirs de Roumelie), ainsi que des musulmans non-turcs, comme les Yuruks, les Avchars, les Lazes, etc.), tous implantés à des dates relativement récentes en Arménie dans le but d'y augmenter artificiellement le nombre des éléments non-arméniens, tandis que, d'autre part, on tachait de diminuer le nombre des Arméniens par des persécutions, des massacres et des déportations. Il en est de meme des kurdes qui, loin de constituer un peuple unique et uniforme, sont divisés en un grand nombre de tribus et de clans, dont la plupart sont nomades, vivant dans un état primitif, perpétuellement en guerre les uns contre les autres et dont la principale occupation est le brigandage. Ils ont participé à toutes les sauvageries, à toutes les atrocités perpétrées par les Turcs sous les ordres du gouvernement ottoman.Il convient de noter cependant qu'une partie des Kurdes sédentaire sont d'origine arménienne, ayant embrassé l'islamisme pour se soustraire aux persécutions de Turcs; ceus-ci sont amis des Arméniens. D'une manière générale, les kurdes détestent les Turcs et ne s'associent avec eux que lorsqu'il s'agit de poursuivre impunement leurs méfaits sur les Arméniens paisibles et désarmés.

Dans l'ordre d'idées de la population future de l'Arménie, une autre consideration de la plus haute importance s'impose.

Le nombre total des Arméniens dans le monde dépasse les 4.500.000. Environ 2.600.000 Arméniens seuls habitant actuellement dans les limites de l'Arménie, il y a encore environ 2.000.000 d'Arméniens répartis comme suit:

Arméniens habitant les autres
provinces de Turquie(Constantinople,Thrace,Brousse,
Smyrne,Konia,Angora,Castemouni,Syrie,Bagdad), environ.........750.000
Armeniens de Russie, habitant pour la plupart
dans les provinces caucasiennes
limitrophes del'Arménie russe..600.000
Arméniens des autres provinces de la Perse............................. 50.000
Arméniens de l'Etranger, <u>dont la majorité réfugiés de Turquie</u>
(ceux de Bulgarie, Roumanie, Autriche, Hongrie, Pologne,
Egypte, Grèce, Suisse, Italie, France, Angleterre, Etats-unis,
Indes, etc...<u>500.000</u>
Total...1.900.000

Etant donné le patriotisme ardent des Arménies, il est évident qu'au bas mot la moitié de ces Arméniens, disons un million, ne tarderont pas à retourner dans leur pays natal dès qu'un Etat national libre y sera institué; par contre, la majorité des Turcs ne voulant vivre sous une administration non-turque, émigreront dans l'Anatolie turque; les Kurdes les plus remuants et d'ailleurs nomades, ne pouvant plus se livrer au pillage et d'ailleurs nomades, se retireront dans le Kurdistan. De sorte que, dans une dizaine d'années après son émancipation, l'Arménie, sous le rapport de la prépondérance numérique de la nation dont elle porte le nom, aura la meme configuration numerique ethnique que la Grèce, la Roumanie ou la Serbie.

En dernier lieu, il est à noter aussi que si le nombre des Arméniens a diminué dans ces dernières cinquante années par la faute des Turcs, et plus particulièrement par les massacres et déportation récentes, il en est de meme des populations turques et kurdes qui ont été plusieurs fois décimées par la guerre, par les epidémies; par la famine.

Le rôle des Arméniens

Le résulte de cette analyse, que, le seul élément qui représente en Arménie une superiorité numérique qui ira en croissant, une superiorité morale, intellectuelle et économique, ainsi qu'une homogénéité nationale incontestable, c'est le peuple arménien. L'Arménies à démontré ses capacités administratives en Turquie, en Russie, en Perse, en Egypte, où plusieurs représentants de cette race ont rempli les fonctios les plus élévées.

Il a donné, pendant cette guerre, les preuves de ses capacités militaires et de son héroisme. Non seulement il est capable de se gouverner, mais il a un rôle encore plus important à remplir: c'est grace à un gouvernement arménien, institué sur le bases de la civilisation et de la justice, que les Turcs et les Kurdes et les autres peuplades susnomées, commenceront à se départir de leurs instincts primitifs de sauvagerie et de brigandage et à entrer dans la voie de la civilisation et du progrès.En effet, le peuple arménien, par son passé historique, par son ancienne civilisation, par ses traditions démocratiques, par son caractère paisible et laborieux, par son esprit de tolérance exempt de toute velléité de vengeance et de répresailles, est appelé à jouer le rôle d'un élément d'harmonie, de concorde, de paix et de progrès parmi ces population si disparates et si divisées.

32

25 October 1918, Constantinople – Dolci to Gasparri – AAEESS, *Asia* 57, 1, n° 85098

Eminentissimo principe,

Facendo seguito al mio precedente Rapporto del 24 corrente N. 996, informo l'E. Vostra di un nuovo triste fatto di cui mi mise al corrente il Presidente della Commissione armena, il giorno stesso 23 corrente che egli e i colleghi vennero da me per congedarsi. Con animo profondamente addolorato, mi dava lettura e copia del Cifrato speditogli dal Rappresentante dell'Armenia in Tiflis, in data del 21 corrente, intorno ai recenti massacri degl'infelici armeni, in numero di 30.000, a Baku.

"Nell'amarezza del cordoglio, mi soggiunse, abbiamo subito pensato di ricorrere al Rappresentante Pontificio per invocare la protezione del S. Padre, che è stato sempre l'Angelo Tutelare della Nostra infelice nazione, e la cui imagine benefica resterà eternamente scolpita nel cuore di ogni armeno". Mi pregò quindi di trasmettere d'urgenza il seguente Dispaccio Cifrato, il che feci per il tramite della R. Legazione di Olanda.

N 63   24 ott.18

All'E. Card. Gasparri - Roma

Presidente Delegazione Armena recatosi da me con tutta la Commissione mi prega trasmettere E. Vostra dolorosa notizia che 30.000 armeni sono stati massacrati a Baku conforme Dispaccio telegrafico pervenutogli da Tiflis in data 21 Ottobre.

Presidente colla Commissione supplicano S. Padre, protettore insigne dell'Armenia, intervenire urgenza presso Governo Inglese per invio distaccamento truppe ententiste [*sic*], onde arrestare ulteriori ed imminenti massacri. Lo stesso presidente desidererebbe inoltre che questo atroce fatto fosse portato a conoscenza dell'opinione pubblica americana.

Presidente ha fatto energiche rimostranze Sublime Porta alle quali mi assocerò anch'io. Io ritengo però che numero 30.000 sia esagerato. Dolci.

Assicurai il Presidente che, mantenendo quanto aveva accennato nel testè trascritto telegramma, anch'io mi sarei recato alla Sublime Porta, per associarmi nel Nome Augusto del Santo Padre, alle rimostranze già fatte dalla Commissione per questo nuovo atroce misfatto, ed arrestare per sempre quelle scelleratezze che sconvolgono profondamente anche il cuore del selvaggio.

Per scolpire ancora una volta nella mente di questa Commissione Armena quanto il Santo Padre ha fatto per salvare dallo sterminio la loro Nazione in Turchia, ho creduto bene leggere ai membri il primo autografo del S. Padre al Sultano. Tutti ne ricevettero la più profonda impressione e non avevano parole per esprimere la gratitudine per questo documento Pontificio vibrante di apostolica energia. Io credo che il giorno che esso sia fatto di pubblica ragione non sia lontano, e lo ritengo necessario per il prestigio del Pontificato. Come pure sarei d'avviso di rendere popolare nella nuova Armenia, detto documento e la Nota per la pace ai Governi Belligeranti, nella quale si rivendica l'indipendenza della Nazione Armena. Debbo dirlo, e con mia meraviglia, lo stesso Ministro degli Esteri, facente anch'esso parte della Commissione, ignorava questo passaggio della Nota Pontificia sulla costituzione dell'Armenia. A sua richiesta mi sono affrettato di consegnargliene una copia. Da questa circostanza, come pure da altre, mi pare d'intravedere che l'opera del S. Padre è nota solamente agli Armeni di Turchia, e specialmente di Costantinopoli e non lo è invece per gli Armeni Russi.

Ed ora passo a trascrivere il Cifrato pervenuto al Presidente.

[Translation]
Most Eminent Prince,

Following up on my previous Report N. 996, of the 24th of this month, I inform Y. Emin. of a sad new fact which the President of the Armenian Commission related to me on the same day, the 23rd of this month, that he and his colleagues came to visit me to take their leave. With a profoundly distressed heart, he allowed me to read as well as gave me a copy of the Encryption sent to him by the Armenian Representative in Tiflis, dated the 21st of this month, regarding the recent massacres of the ill-fated Armenians, numbering 30,000, at Baku.

"In the bitterness of grief," he added, "we at once thought to appeal to the Pontifical Representative to invoke the protection of the Holy Father, who has always been the Guardian Angel of our unfortunate nation, and whose charitable image will remain carved for eternity in every Armenian's heart." He bid me then to urgently transmit the following Encrypted Dispatch, which he had made by way of the R. Legation of Holland.

N 63   Oct. 24 '18
To the E. Card. Gasparri - Rome

President Armenian Delegation come to me with all the Commission bids me transmit to Y. Emin. grievous news that 30,000 Armenians were massacred at Baku according to telegraphic Dispatch reached him from Tiflis dated October 21.

President and the Commission beg the Holy Father, distinguished protector of Armenia, to intervene urgently with the English Government such that they send detachment entente troops, in order to halt further and imminent massacres. The same president moreover would wish that this atrocious event be made known to the American public.

President made energetic remonstrances to the Sublime Porte to which I will associate myself as well. I retain that the number 30,000 is exaggerated. Dolci.

I assured the President that, maintaining what he had indicated in the telegram just transcribed, I would also go to the Sublime Porte, to join myself, in the August Name of the Holy Father, in the remonstrances already made by the Commission for this new atrocious misdeed, and arrest forever such wicked crimes as profoundly distress even the heart of a savage.

To engrave once again into the minds of this Armenian Commission how much the Holy Father has done to save their Nation in Turkey from extermination, I thought well to read to the members the first handwritten letter of the Holy Father to the Sultan. All of them received the deepest impression from it and had no words to express their gratitude for this Pontifical document vibrant with apostolic energy. I believe the day that this be made public is not far off, and I retain it necessary for the reputation of the Pontificate. As I would also advise to render public in the new Armenia said document and the Note for peace to the Belligerent Governments, in which independence for the Armenian Nation is demanded. I must say, to my surprise, the Foreign Minister[235] himself, also being part of the Commission, was unaware of this passage from the Papal Note on the constitution of Armenia. At his request I hastened to give him a copy. From this circumstance, as well as from others, I seem to sense that the work of the Holy Father is well-known only to the Armenians of Turkey, especially those of Constantinople, and yet is not to the Russian Armenians.

And now I will get on with transcribing the Encryption received by the President.

> Copie du telegramme date de Tiflis du 21 octobre 1918
>
> Nombre arméniens exterminés Bakou s'élève approximativement 30.000 hommes. Massacres affreux continuent trois jours. Troupes régulières Turques sont entrées dans la Ville par petits détachements et non seulement mesures n'étaient pas prises mais au contraire nombre de soldats ont pris part aux pillages et meurtres.Commandant turc était obligé après trois jours pendre quelques soldats. Ont été assassinés exclusivement arméniens. A présent les arméniens non assassinés surtout intellectuels par ordre du Gouvernement Azerbaidjian ....Autre part Gouvernement Azerbaidjian a envoyé Karabagh détachement turc pour entrer Coucha. Nouri pacha entra. Population arménienne partout est énervée par les horreurs de Bakou et de Noukhi, où tous le villages étaient également massacrés.Situation de notre Gouvernement devient pénible. Prions protester énergiquement auprès du Gouvernement ottoman afin cesser immédiatement arrestations par masses Bakou, permettre libre sortie de la Ville, aussi faire démarche d'urgence pour que les troupes quittent immédiatement Karabagh jusqu'à la solution de la question à la conférence, et que le

---

235 Khatissian, the future President of the Armenian Republic.

gouvernement Azerbaidjian admette la voie diplomatique pour régler paisiblement l'affaire sans intervention forces armée autrement les rescontres sanglantes et massacres sont inévitables. DJAMALIAN

Chinato al bacio ecc
[Bowed to the kiss etc.]

33

27 November 1918, Rome – handwritten draft from Gasparri to the Count de Salis – AAEESS, *Asia* 57, 2, n° 84211

S.E.M. Le Comte de Salis
Envoyé Extraordinaire
et Ministre Plénipotentiaire
de S.M. Britannique

Parmi les populations les plus éprouvées par la guerre, on peut sans doute compter les Arméniens, exposés depuis quatre ans aux plus cruelles souffrances.

Or, les Arméniens du Caucase, menacés par la famine, d'autant plus depuis que presque un demi-million de réfugiés a gagné leur pays, se sont adressés au Saint-Père en Le suppliant d'intervenir auprès des Puissances de l'Entente, afin de leur procurer les vivres absolument nécessaires à leur existence.

L'Auguste Pontife, douloureusement frappé par les prières de ces pauvres malheureux m'a chargé de faire appel aux sentiments charitables si justement appréciés de Votre Excellence, en Lui demandant de vouloir bien obtenir de Son Gouvernement si noblement humanitaire, et dans le plus bref délai possible, l'envoi de vivres que réclame leur pénible situation.

Dans la confiance que V. Exc. ne manquera pas de s'employer à ce sujet je saisis etc.

34

21 January 1919, Rome – de Salis to Gasparri – *Ibid.*, n° 84211

Monseigneur,

Par Sa Note No 84211 du 27 novembre dernier Votre Eminence s'est fait l'interprète d'un appel au Saint Père de la part des Arméniens du Caucase pour que les Puissances de l'Entente leur fournissent des vivres. J'en ai fait part au Gouvernement de Sa Majesté britannique par télégraphe.

Cette question, me répond-t-on, occupe l'attention sérieuse des Puissances et déjà les autorités militaires britanniques au Caucase font tout leur possible pour soulager la misère. Des détachements de troupes occupent Bakou et

Batoum. On estime que sous peu la tâche d'envoyer des secours aux arméniens sera rendue beaucoup plus facile.

Je saisis très volontiers cette occasion pour renouveler à Votre Eminence l'expression de ma très haute considération.

35

20 December 1918, Rome – Damadian to Gasparri – AAEESS, *Asia* 57, 2, n° [?]

Eminence,

La Délégation Nationale Arménienne présidée par Boghos Nubar Pacha, siegeant à Paris et que j'ai l'honneur de représenter en Italie, m'a chargé d'exprimer une nouvelle fois toute la profonde reccomaissance qu'elle doit au S. Siège pour la sollicitude paternelle que le Souverain Pontife n'a cessé de témoigner à la nation arménienne pendant la durée de cette guerre qui a constitué la plus dure épreuve de son histoire plusieurs fois séculaire.

La Délégation Nationale s'est adressée à diverses reprises pendant la guerre à S.S. le Pape Benoit XV pour solliciter, par l'entremise toujours empressée de Votre Eminence, sa haute intervention en faveur des victimes des massacres et des persécutions sans précédent auxquels étaient assujettis nos compatriotes en Turquie. Chaque fois sa demande fut favorablement accueillis, ou pour mieux dire, chaque fois que le situation exigeait une intervention énergique, le Saint-Père n'a point attendu nos supplications pour faire entendre sa voix pour la protection des vies, de l'honneur et des biens de nos connationaux. Si les Turcs n'ont pas été très disposés à entendre cette voix généreuse, s'ils ont quand même poursuivi leur oeuvre d'extermination, il n'en est pas moins vrai que beaucoup de maux furent adoucis, beaucoup de larmes furent séchées, beaucoup de sang innocent fut épargné grâce à cette intervention pontificale.

En outre, S.S. le Pape, dans son mémorable "cri de paix" adressé aux chefs des peuples bélligérents, a été le premier à reconnaître et à proclamer comme une des conditions d'une paix juste et durable, que la question de l'Arménie fût résolue dans le même esprit d'équité et de justice qui présidera la solution des autres questions territoriales et politiques et au même titre notamment que les questions des Etats balkaniques et de la Pologne.

Evoquant les relations inoubliables qui ont existé entre les Pontifes du Moyen-Age et le royame de la Petite-Arménie, évoquant ces souvenirs des temps chevaleresques où les Arméniens ont combattu côte à côte avec les Croisés pour la libération des Lieux-Saints du Christianisme, les Arméniens ont la plus grande confiance que le S. Siège qui a tant fait déjà pour le bien de nos frères d'Arménie, continuera à étendre sur la nations arménienne toute sa sollicitude et s'emploiera de toute son influence pour assurer aux Arméniens le rétablissement de leur indépendance dans les limites historiques de leur patrie, afin qu'ils puissent reprendre le rôle d'avant-gardes du christianisme et de la civilisation qui leur revient en Orient.

Le pays où l'arc-en-ciel a été le symbole de la réconciliation entre la Divinité et l'Humanité; le pays d'où est partie la colombe annonciatrice de la paix entre le Ciel et la Terre, ne peut, ne doit être laissé privé de justice, de tranquillité, et de prosperité au jour où une paix générale régnera enfin dans le monde.

Son Eminence,

Tous les Chrétiens arméniens, sans distinction de confession ni de classe, ont souffert du même martyre; ils ont tous démontré combien étaient inébranlebles leur foi chretienne et leur attachement à la civilisation occidentale; ils ont tous été l'objet d'une égale sollicitude de la part du Saint-Père; ils sont d'ailleurs indissolublement solidaires en tout ce qui concerne les intérêts suprêmes de la nation arménienne, une et indivisible. Il était donc naturel qu'ils fussent aussi unis dans leurs sentiments de reconnaissance envers leurs bienfaiteurs. Aussi, le représentant de la Délégation Nationale, dans cette démarche pour exsprimer au S. Siège la reconnaissance de tous les Arméniens, se sent-il heureux et honoré d'être présenté à Votre Eminence par S. Grandeur Monseigneur Koyounian, vicaire patriarcal-catholicossal des Arméniens catholiques, et d'être accompagné par le Rev. Père Ohannès Torossian, procureur général de la Congrégation Mekhitariste de Venise.

Unis ainsi dans la détresse et dans le martyre, les Arméniens resteront unis dans l'ère nouvelle de liberté qu'ils espèrent bientôt saluer, pour travailler ensemble au relévement politique, intellectuel et moral de leur pays, au rayonnement de la civilisation et de la fraternité chretienne, des bords de la Méditerranée jusqu'aux pieds du Caucase. Ils sont sûrs que cet esprit d'union et de solidarité dont sont animés les Arméniens impressionnera agreablement le bon coeur du Saint-Père qui en fera un titre de plus pour faire valoir leur droit à la liberté et à l'independance.

Veuillez agréer, Eminence, avec l'expression sincère de la gratitude de la Délégation nationale, l'hommage de ma profonde vénération.

[signed] Damadian

Représentant de la Dél. Nat. Arm.

36

3 January 1919, Rome – Damadian to Gasparri – AAEESS, *Asia* 57, 2, n° [?]

Eminence,

Me référant à l'audience que Votre Eminence a bien voulu m'accorder le 20 Décembre dr, au cours de laquelle j'ai eu l'honneur de Vous entretenir sur la situation diplomatique de la question arménienne, j'ai l'honneur de Vous soumettre quelques textes concernant les accords "secrets" relatifs à l'Arménie et à l'Asie-Mineur, intervenus en 1915-16 entre le gouvernement tzariste de Russie et les gouvernements anglais et français, dont a été question en cette audience.[236]

Ces accords qui étaient effectivement devenus caduques, après l'éntreée en guerre des Etats-Unis d'Amerique et la révolution russe - deux événements qui ont prêté à la guerre, en ce qui concerne le côté des Alliés, le caractère d'une croisade pour le triumph de la liberté du monde et du droit des nationalités de disposer librement de leur sort, - ces accords, dis-je, parais ont maintenant avoir été remis en vigueur et développés entre la France et l'Angleterre, - témoin la déclaration anglo-français du 8 Novembre dr, dont inclus également copie.[237]

Votre Eminence ne saurait ne pas se rendre compte combien ces accords, s'ils étaient appliqués comme bases du réglement du sort de la nation arménienne seraient préjudiciables aux intérêts de l'Arménie, qui réclame, à juste titre, <u>l'unification de tout son territoire historique, du Caucase à la Méditerranée</u>, baigné du sang de ses martyrs et de ses héros, <u>pour en constituer un Etat arménien libre et indépendant sous la garantie internationale des Puissances Alliés et des Etats-Unis d'Amérique ou de la Société des Nations, dès qu'elle serait réalisée.</u>

Eminence,

A l'occasion de la visite imminente au Saint-Siège du président Wilson,[238] permettez-moi de faire, par la présente, au nom de la Délégation Nationale Arménienne, un suprême appel auprès le S. Siège qui a tout fait pour le bien de notre nation martyre, en le suppliant d'interposer, auprès l'illustre Président Wilson, champion de la justice et des droits des peuples, grands et petits, ses bons offices et son influence d'autorité paternelle, impartiale, par excellence, afin que justice entière soit faite à notre nation par la reconnaissance de ses droits imprescriptibles et la réalisation de ses revendications nationales, telles quelles sont exposées plus haut.

Dans l'attente que cette démarche faite dans le moment le plus fatidique de notre histoire, trouvera un accueil favorable auprès de S.S. le Souverain Pontife, j'ai l'honneur de Vous présenter Eminence, l'hommage renouvelé de la reconnaissance de toute la nation arménienne ainsi que les nouvelles assurances de ma plus profonde vénération.

Allegati vari

[Various *attachments*]

---

236 These were articles from the magazine *Armenia* reporting correspondence from the Italian newspaper *La Nazione* [The Nation].
237 Not found.
238 This does not appear to have occurred.

37

28 January 1919, Rome – Dolci to Card. Marini – CO, *Armeni e Caucaso* [Armenians and Caucasus], 105, 3, 5, n° 1525

Eminentissimo Principe,

Ho potuto sapere in segreto, dal Segretario particolare di questo Eccmo Patriarca armeno, Mgr Terzian, che egli aveva rivolto una lettera a m. Clémenceau, al Presidente Wilson, al Re del Belgio e a Lloyd Georges. Di essa lettera ho avuto copia che invio a V. Eminenza Rev.ma.

Chinato al bacio ecc

[Translation]

Most Eminent Prince,

I found out in secret, from the private Secretary of the Most Exc. Armenian Patriarch, Mgr. Terzian, that he had addressed a letter to Mr. Clémenceau, to President Wilson, to the King of Belgium and to Lloyd George. Of this letter I obtained a copy which I send to Your Most Rev. Eminence.

Bowed to the kiss etc.

38

15 January 1919, Constantinople – copy of the letter from Terzian to Clémenceau, Wilson, the king of Belgium and Lloyd George[239] – CO, *Armeni e Caucaso* [Armenians and Caucasus], 105, 3, 5, n° 1525

La haute et entière justice, prix du sang mondial versé depuis plus de 4 années de guerre, est l'objet de l'aspiration présente de toute l'humanité et specialement des nations opprimées.

Parmi ces peuples, il est superflu de le dire, la Nation Arm. condamnée à l'extermination de la manière la plus atroce et la plus inhumaine, a, plus que tout autre besoin d'être soustraite au joug de l'esclavage et le de tyrannie.

Comme protecteur de la justice et des droits du plus faible au sein de cette nation opprimée, je me fais un devoir de faire appel au représentant de la Noble France dont les armées héroïques ont sauve la cause des peuples opprimés, afin que celle-ce daigne s'intéresser dans la mesure la plus juste, au sort de la Nat. Arm. et en obtenir la complète libération en assurant son indépendance dans les limites historiquement définies et réclamées par un droit imprescriptible, droit qui ne peut être jamais étouffé par la puissance et la préponderance de la tyrannie. L'Arménie majeure, l'Arménie mineure et la Cilicie forment le trépied sur lequel doit être replacé la nation Arménienne

---

239 Published by Naslian, *op. cit.*, vol. II. In a footnote (n° 150) he recounts that letters in the same terms, as far as Armenian requests are concerned, were sent by Terzian to Wilson, to the King of Belgium, to the British government and also to Orlando, pp. 943–944.

injustement depouillée, tyrannisée et menacée d'extermination durant de longs siècles.

De ce noble Pays de France qui garde encore les restes mortels de notre dernier Roi, du voisinage de ce tombeau, nous attendons M. le Prés., le décret de la Résurrection, de la libération définitive de la Nation, d'une manière telle qu'elle ne donne plus lieu à aucune aspiration traditionnelle. Telle est l'attente de toute notre Nation, telle est l'indemnité que réclame le sang innocent de nos martyrs; nous sommes persuadés que (la noble France) mettra en oeuvre dans ce but, toute sa haute influence, toujours généreuse dès qu'il s'agit d'actes humanitaires de si haute importance.

En adressant à V.E. cet appel nous entendons solliciter encore la tutelle et la protection dont aura besoin le nouvel Etat arménien. Qu'il nous soit permis à cette occasion d'attirer votre bienveillante attention sur trois points qui nous semblent particulièrement importants pour assurer l'unité, l'ordre et le développement normal de la nation.

Une, au point de vue national, la Nat. Arménienne se partage, au point de vue religieux en trois branches; les arméniens grégoriens qui sont les plus nombreux, les Arm. protestants. Afin que dans le nouvel état rien ne vienne troubler l'harmonie entre ces trois enfants d'une même famille il serait a désirer que dans les statuts du futur état arménien, aucune confession religieuse ne soit reconnue officiellement et qu'une large et loyale application du principe de la liberté de conscience soit accordée à chaque fraction pour se développer librement et concourir ainsi tous ensemble au bien général de la nation. Nous espérons que grâce à l'appui de la France une large et loyale application du principe de la liberté de conscience permettra à chaque fraction de se développer librement pour concourir tous ensemble au bien général de la Nation.

La situation nouvelle faite aux Arméniens au point de vue politique nécessitera aussi une nouvelle organisation ecclésiastique dans les provinces qui leur seront attribuées. Il serait donc grandement désirable qu'aucune entrave ne soit mise à une prompte réorganisation et que chaque branche de la famille arménienne puisse librement et rapidement se réconstituer suivant ses réglements et ses usages propres.

Enfin pendant la période des déportations et des massacres, les Arméniens, aussi bien les individus que les Communautès, ont subi des pertes matérielles considérables. Or pour que la jeune Nation Arm. dès le commencement de sa nouvelle vie, puisse se développer librement, il est indispensable qu'elle dispose de ressources qui seraient mises à sa disposition en compensation des dommages énormes qu'elle a éprouvées.

(omis dans les lettres à Wilson, roi de la Belgique et à Lloyd George)

Permettez-nous de vous rappeler Mr le P. que les Arméniens catholiques ont été toujours spécialement dévoués à la France. Ils ont toujours trouvé auprès de Ses Représentants une protection efficace et lui ont voué en retour une éternelle reconnaissance. C'est grâce aux subventions accordées par le Gouvernement de la République Française aux écoles Arm. Cath. grâce aux maisons d'éducation ouvertes par les religieux et les religieuses de France que presque toute notre population parle la belle langue française, aussi regardons-nous la France comme notre seconde patrie.

(finale pour Clémenceau)

C'est dans ce sentiment de profonde reconnaissance pour le passé et de ferme confiance pour l'avenir que nous vous prions de vouloir bien agréer M. le P. en notre nom, au nom de toute la Nation Arménienne et tout spécialement de la famille Arm. Catholique l'hommage de notre sincère et respectueux dévouement.

(finale pour Wilson George et Roi de la Belgique)

Dans la douce et ferme attente qu'il plaira à V.E. de réserver un accueil favorable à ma présente, prende en sérieuse considération la demande qui en fait l'objet et contribuer par Sa haute influence au succès complet de notre désir, je lui offre d'avance en notre nom, au nom de la nation Arménienne et de la famille arm. cath. nos plus vifs remerciements etc.

39

24 February 1919, Constantinople – Dolci a Marini – CO, *Armeni e Caucaso* [Armenians and Caucasus], 106, 4, 3, n° 1667

Eminentissimo Principe,

Trascrivo all'E.V.R.ma quanto ha pubblicato il giornale la Renaissance su l'opera del S. Padre per l'indipendenza Armena.

[Translation]

Most Eminent Prince,

I transcribe for Y.M.R. Emin. what the newspaper *La Renaissance* published about the Holy Father's work for Armenian independence.

En faveur dell'indépendance arménienne.

Nous apprenons de source autorisée que S.S. le Pape vient d'adresser au President Wilson une lettre autographe pour lui demander d'intervenir avec toute son autorité auprès du congrès, afin d'assurer définitivement le réglement de la question arménienne par l'indépendance de l'Arménie unie et intégrale. Un membre du Sacré collège a été chargé par S.S. de porter cette lettre à Mr Wilson.

Ce noble geste de SS. Benoit XV nous remet en mémoire la grande part prise par le Pape Célestin III à l'instauration de la dynastie des Roupénides dans le Royaume de Cilicie au XII Siècle, en récompense de l'assistance spontanée que les Croisées avaient trouvé auprès des princes et du peuple de la Cilicie, pendant toute la durée de leurs combats contre les Sarassins. Voici ce qu'écrit à ce sujet le Pape Grégoire XIII dans sa bulle Ecclesia Romana de l'an 1384. "Parmi les autres mérites de la Nation arménienne envers l'Eglise et la republique chrétienne, il en est un qui est éminent et digne de particulière mémoire c'est que, lorsque, autrefois les princes et les armées chretiennes allaient à la délivrance de la Terre Sainte, nulle nation et nul peuple plus promptement et avec plus de zèle que les arméniens ne leur prêta son aide en hommes, chevaux, en subsistances, en conseils avec toutes leurs forces et avec la plus grande bravoure et fidélité, ils aidèrent les chrétiens en ces saintes guerres.

Chinato al bacio ecc.

[Bowed to the kiss etc.]

40

[?] March 1919, Constantinople – Dolci to Gasparri – AAEESS, *Asia* 57, 1, n° [?]

Emo Principe,

In seguito degli attuali avvenimenti, il Locum-Tenens del Patriarcato Armeno Gregoriano, Mons. Djévahindjan, ha potuto compiere il vivo desiderio che da lungo tempo nutriva, di recarsi personalmente a questa Delegazione Apostolica, per ringraziare il S. Padre della Sua valida ed efficace protezione accordata alla nazione armena, durante tutto il tempo del suo dolore e della sua angoscia, come pure della continuata protezione verso i suoi figli superstiti, gli orfanelli.

Come è già ben noto all'Eminenza vostra, il Patriarca Armeno gregoriano non ha fatto ancora ritorno da Mossoul ove era stato deportato.

A proposito di questa visita il Giornale scismatico armeno NOR-GHIANH in data di ieri pubblicava:

[Translation]

Most Eminent Prince,

Owing to current events, the Locum-Tenens of the Armenian Gregorian Patriarchate, Mons. Djévahindjan, was able to fulfill the keen desire, which he had harbored for some time, to visit this Apostolic Delegation personally, to thank the Holy Father for his valuable and effective protection accorded the Armenian nation during the entire time of her suffering and anguish, as well as for the continued protection towards her surviving children, the orphans.

As Your Eminence is aware, the Armenian Gregorian Patriarch has not yet returned from Mosul where he had been deported.

Regarding this visit, the Armenian schismatic newspaper *NOR-GYANK* yesterday published:

C'est aujourd'hui que le Locum-Tenens Mgr. Djévahindjian rendra visite au nom de la Nation Arménienne au Délégué Apostolique Mgr. Dolci, pour remercier le Pape Benoit XV, par son entremise, de la bienveillance qu'Il a temoignée à plusiers réprises, à l'égard des Arméniens et principalement pour Sa sollecitude envers les orphélins et les veuves des exilés arméniens, retournés dans notre ville et dont le Vicaire du Pape a bien voulu assumer la protection.

Chinato al bacio ecc.
[Bowed to the kiss etc.]

41

6 March 1919, Constantinople – Dolci to Gasparri – AAEESS, *Asia* 57, 1, n° [?]

Eminentissimo Principe,

Di recente è giunto qui in città, ritornato dall'esilio, S.E. Mgr Zaven, patriarca armeno gregoriano. Una delle sue prime visite fu fatta a questa Delegazione. Egli era accompagnato dal suo vicario. Il Patriarca, dopo i primi convenevoli, entrò subito a parlare dell'opera del S. Padre in favore e per protezione della Nazione Armena, per la quale opera espresse i suoi sentimenti della più viva riconoscenza e mi pregò di trasmetterli al S. Padre. Cogliendo l'occasione, misi il patriarca al corrente di quanto fu fatto e che avrebbe potuto non giungere a conoscenza di lui, e credetti bene , giunto il momento opportuno, dargli lettura della prima Nota dalla Santità Sua rivolta a S.M. il Sultano.

Alla mia volta andai a restituirgli la visita. Fui ricevuto con somma deferenza ed onore, ed ebbi la consolazione di riudire da S. Beatitudine espressa la sua grande ammirazione per l'opera del S. Padre in questa guerra e la sua gratitudine in particolare per la parte che i suoi connazionali ne hanno goduto.

Chinato al bacio ecc.

[Translation]
Most Eminent Prince,

Recently H.E. Mgr. Zaven, the Gregorian Armenian patriarch,[240] arrived here in the city, returned from exile. One of his first visits was made to this Delegation. He was accompanied by his vicar. The Patriarch, after the initial pleasantries, quickly commenced speaking about the Holy Father's work in favor and for the protection of the Armenian Nation, in regard to which he expressed his feelings of deepest gratitude and prayed that I convey them to the

---

240 Another way of indicating the Armenian Apostolic Church.

Holy Father. Using the occasion, I made the patriarch aware of how much had been done of which he might not have been aware, and I thought it well, when an opportune moment had been reached, to read him the first Message from His Holiness addressed to H.M. the Sultan.

In turn, I went to repay the visit. I was received with all deference and honor, and I had the consolation of hearing once again H. Beatitude express his great admiration for the Holy Father's work during this war and his gratitude in particular for that part of it his countrymen had enjoyed.

Bowed to the kiss etc.

42

18 March 1919, Constantinople – Dolci to Gasparri – ASV, *Guerra* [War], 1914–18, 244, 69, n° 90014

Eminentissimo Principe,

Ho l'onore di rimettere all'Eminenza Vostra l'accluso giornale armeno "Erivan" n° 12 del 17 marzo 1919, dove si parla del S. Padre e della sua opera a vantaggio degli armeni.

Traduzione testuale:

Due grandi figure armenofile.

Con gran piacere pubblichiamo qui i ritratti di queste due grandi figure amiche e protettrici della nostra Nazione. Essi diedero prova che amano veramente noi altri armeni e son pieni di tenerezza per noi. Sfortunatamente le nostre colonne sono assai strette per raccontare quella larga parte ed influenza che essi ebbero all'occasione della deportazione degli armeni e dell'indipendenza dell'Armenia. S.E. Mons. Dolci, il cui cuore angosciava per le dolorose novelle delle vessazioni e stragi degli armeni, informava il Santo Papa dello stato orribile di questa nazione, e coi suoi personali ricorsi si sforzava di mitigare il gran male. Sua Santità scrisse al precedente Sultano tre [*sic*] lettere autografe durante la calamità armena, per far mettere un termine alla barbarie; ed è mercé questa sua mediazione che gli armeni di Angora furono salvati dalla seconda strage che era in procinto di eseguirsi. Il Santo Papa telegrafò a Kulmann, ministro degli affari esteri a Berlino, per impedire la deportazione, quando Talaat stesso si trovava a Brest-Litowsk. Questo suo efficace ricorso ebbe un effetto salutare. Al fronte del Caucaso era stato deciso d'impiccare numerosi armeni, accusati come spioni; appena avuto conoscenza di ciò S.S. Mons. Dolci corse da Enver, e ottenne la loro liberazione. Questi due terribili criminosi, Talaat e Enver, avevano uno speciale rispetto verso Mons. Dolci; e ciò soprattutto perché egli ispirava a loro una venerazione quale Delegato del Capo del Cattolicismo e della Germania e Austria cattoliche. In siffatta maniera, durante il corso della Guerra, si era più accentuata l'influenza e la parte civile del Trono Papale. Ma naturalmente, qui se ne sospettava, a tal punto che l'abitazione di Mons. Dolci era circondata di spioni. Sapevano essi (i turchi) che S. Eccza aveva a cuore la causa degli Armeni, faceva ricorsi per gli armeni ed amava la nostra sfortunata nazione.

Sua Santità mostrò pure grande simpatia alla Causa armena, e perciò mandò due speciali Delegati presso Mr. Wilson, per la formazione di un Armenia unita ed indipendente e grande, ed il Presidente dell'America ricevette con amore questo ricorso Papale. Gli sforzi e le cure infatigabili di Mgr Dolci per affrettare aiuto ai deportati ed affamati, superano ogni elogio. Egli fece colla stessa regolarità la distribuzione dei soccorsi venuti dall'estero; ed infatti all'invito del S. Papa è stato corrisposto inviando sovvenzioni straordinarie di grande importanza.

Qualora S.Santità sentì lo stato affamato del popolo nella repubblica armena, ricorse all'Europa ed al nuovo mondo, e furono inviati immediati soccorsi, ai nostri fratelli affamati del Caucaso.S.E.Mons. Dolci, aprì un orfanotrofio a nome del S. Papa, nel quale sono ricoverati ed educati orfani armeni di gran numero, godendovi tutte le cure e premure materne.

Con gratitudine dunque asseriamo la loro preziosa cooperazione ed opera per il successo della nostra causa e per l'alleviamento dei nostri dolori; e siamo sicuri che essi continueranno quest'opera soprattutto sino a quando i nostri bisogni saranno numerosi ed urgenti.

Chinato al bacio della S. Porpora, con sentimenti ecc...

[Translation]
Most Eminent Prince,
I have the honor of remitting to Your Eminence the enclosed Armenian newspaper "Erivan" n° 12 of March 17, 1919, which talks about the Holy Father and about his work on behalf of the Armenians.

Textual translation:

Two great Armenophile figures.

With great pleasure we publish here the portraits of these two great friends and protectors of our Nation. They gave proof that they truly love us Armenians and are full of affection for us. Unfortunately our columns are too narrow to fully recount the wide role and influence that they had on the occasion of the deportation of the Armenians and of Armenian independence. H.E. Mons.

Dolci, whose heart was tormented by the painful news of the oppressions and massacres of the Armenians, informed the Holy Pope of the horrible state of this nation, and with his personal appeals endeavored to mitigate the great evil. His Holiness wrote to the previous Sultan three [sic][241] handwritten letters during the Armenian calamities, in order to put an end to the barbarities; and it is thanks to this mediation of his that the Armenians of Angora were saved from the second massacre that was about to take place. The Holy Pope telegraphed to Ku[h]lmann, minister of foreign affairs in Berlin, to block the deportation, when Talaat himself was at Brest-Litowsk. This forceful appeal of his had a salutary effect. At the Caucasian front, it had been decided to hang numerous Armenians accused of being spies; as soon as he heard of this, H.H. [sic] Mons. Dolci rushed to see Enver and obtained their freedom. These two terrible criminals, Talaat and Enver, had a special respect for Mons. Dolci; above all because he inspired in them esteem as Delegate of the Head of Catholicism and of Catholic Germany and Austria. In such manner, during the course of the War, the influence and the advocacy of the Papal Throne became more accentuated. But naturally, here that was suspect, to the point that Mons. Dolci's residence was surrounded by spies. They (the Turks) knew that H. Exc. had the Armenian cause at heart, made appeals on behalf of the Armenians and loved our unfortunate nation.

His Holiness displayed great sympathy for the Armenian Cause, and therefore sent two special Delegates to Mr. Wilson, for the formation of a greater, independent, and united Armenia, and the President of America received this Papal appeal with love. Mons. Dolci's indefatigable efforts and care in rushing aid to those deported and hungry go beyond all praise. With the same regularity, he had the aid sent from abroad distributed; and in fact the Holy Pope's invitation was answered with the sending of extraordinary subsidies of great importance.

Whenever His Holiness heard of the hungry state of the people of the Armenian republic, he appealed to Europe and to the new world, and immediate aid was sent to our starving brothers in the Caucasus. H.E. Mons. Dolci opened an orphanage in the name of the Holy Pope, in which a great number of Armenian orphans are being sheltered and raised, enjoying there every maternal care and consideration.

---

241 Evidently, the papal Note to the Belligerant Powers became confused with another letter to the sultan.

Thus, with gratitude, we attest to their precious work and cooperation towards the success of our cause and towards the relief of our suffering; and we are sure that they will continue this work, especially so long as our needs continue to be numerous and urgent.

Bowed to the kiss of the Holy Purple, with feelings etc. ...

43

18 March 1919, Constantinople – Dolci to Gasparri – ASV, *Guerra* [War], 1914–18, 244, 69, nº 90034

Eminentissimo Principe,

Il giornale Armeno-Scismatico "Vercin Lur" (l'ultima novella), del 18 Marzo, 1919, N.1523, organo del defunto apostato Hormanian ex-patriarca, pubblica.

Traduzione dall'armeno.

Come i 61 Armeni furono liberati dal patibolo.

I fornai d'Aleppo sono ereditariamente Armeni di Sassun, erano essi che nel 1916 tenevano tutti i forni e meritavano la soddisfazione dell'intera popolazione. Questi uomini generalmente robusti, grandi ed operosi, non ostacolavano in checchessia gli interessi e le tendenze di altri, oltre il loro lavoro questi uomini attivi non si mischiavano di null'altro. Il governo turco che si è fissato per sistema d'essere assai condiscendente [*sic*] con simili persone, cominciò a ruminare che con qual mezzo potrebbe condannare all'annientamento questa gente umile... e, per arrivare a questo suo scopo, cominciò a perseguitarli.

Giusto a questo momento, 8 a 10 dei nostri Sansuniotti congetturando dove terminerebbero questi [*sic*] persecuzioni, avevano preso la deliberazione di passare segretamente i monti di Marache et per via di Sivas andare in Russia, per liberarsi dalle braccia distruttori [*sic*] dei Turchi.

Ed ecco che s'avviano essi per eseguire questo loro proposito. Ma essendo per sfortunio stato saputo in Aleppo che i fornai Sansuniotti s'erano fuggiti, si dà ordine , e gendarmi a cavallo mandati dal governo, li catturano a tre ore al di là di Marache e li torturano orribilmente sotto colpi di sferza. Il lettore può facilmente immaginare quali tormenti erano infatti si forti che da tutte le parti del loro corpo il sangue cominciò a sgorgare, e ciò che è il più terribile, quei mostri, una per una strapparono le loro unghie, e dalle dita cominciò a scorrere sangue in abbondanza. Il governo praticando questa barbarie, non intendeva che tirare dalla loro bocca i nomi di alcuni altri uomini, innocenti ai quali avea da dar la stessa lezione. E però uno dei poveri Sansuniotti, il quale era stato maltrattato più che gli altri, e che era già quasi in agonia, pronunziò i nomi di quei che conosceva. Avevano dunque ottenuto il desiderato.

V'era però una cosa che aveano fino a quest'ora trascurato. Si misero dunque a far minute ricerche sopra di loro, scoprirono sopra alcuni e nelle valigie di alcuni, certi pani (pidé) cotti nei forni e alcuni datteri. Ed ecco gran chiasso la sopra!... grande in verità, se come avessero scoperto rivoltelle cartuccie e...bombe! Appena fatta la scoperta, fecero arrestare i nostri fornai che avevano lasciato cuocere quei pani e due fruttivendoli i quali tra le altre frutta vendevano anche datteri! Gli arrestati sono interrogati sotto i colpi di bastone "se e chi avevano venduti pani e datteri"! Questi poi non sapendo di chi si trattasse, dicono d'averne venduti giorni fa a tale e a tale; tra di questi si trovavano pure D. Pasquale Malgian, del Collegio armeno di Roma, il quale era la più dotta ed amata persona del luogo, come pure il commerciante Agop Bassarian, David Godagian ed altri, di cui numero in tutto montava a 61. Questi 61 legati con manette di ferro insieme con i Sansuniotti, s'inviavano ad Aleppo, e là si gettarono in prigione. Nel processo quegli innocenti vengono condannati a prigione a uno, due e cinque anni, e la loro sentenza per essere confermata, si manda a Gemal Pacha, governatore della Siria. Gemal Pacha informa immediatamente la corte marziale di Aleppo di rivedere il processo e di condannarli ad ogni [sic] alla pena di patibolo. Il Tribunale comincia a pensare su questo crudele ordine, però ordine al quale non v'è forza da resistere. Dopo mille esitazioni, l'ordine dell'alta persona sitibonda di sangue viene eseguito, e subito la sentenza si comunica di nuovo a Sua...Barbarie. Ed ecco che S.E. Mons. Dolci indirettamente informatosi di queste misure di questa sentenza e delle immense torture subite da questi innocenti, alcuni giorni dopo manda una lettera del S. Papa al Sultano Mehmed Rechiad, un altra [sic] al Ministero degli Esteri, ed una terza ad Enver senza coscienza con le quali egli dimandava l'assoluzione di questi "delittuosi innocenti".

Il governo, di cui la politica, in queste circostanze, non ha altro merito che il temporeggiamento, tessando [sic] bellissime promesse s'inchina innanzi a Mons. Dolci dicendo: "Siamo noi pronti a contentare il vostro S.S.mo Sovrano. Ma questa questione dipendendo esclusivamente da Gemal Pacha, fummo obbligati a prendere il suo parere, considerando però che l'interesse del governo esige contentare il S. Papa, fù data istruzione che la sentenza sia inviata a Costantinopoli affinche [sic] essa venga attentamente esaminata qui nel Gran Quartiere.

Ecco la risposta secca e equivoca, che il Governo fece a Mons. Dolci, a questo pietoso infatigabile pastore; scorre un mese e nessuna risposta. Il misericordioso pastore, tremando che Gemal Pacha non eseguisse, al solito la sentenza, due o tre volte per settimana si recava alla Sublime Porta, per avere una risposta ed ogni volta gli dicevano: "Non abbiate timore, Eccellenza, vi contenteremo".

E un bel giorno, Monsignore Dolci, sente che Gemal Pacha, il carnefice della Siria, ha fatto un entrata trionfale a Cospoli,[242] ed intendeva recarsi a Berlino. Immantinente corse in automobile alla sua casa a Nichantache, ove Gemal Pacha lo riceve con onore e adulazione; ma quando Mons. Dolci apre la questione dei 61 armeni ecco quel che li risponde il Ministro sanguinario: Eccellenza, chiedete da me quel che volete, ma in pro degli Armeni non mi dite nulla, prego. Quanto a questi 61 armeni, tutti sono dei traditori, che hanno voluto tradire ai Russi i piani dell'armata, i segreti dell'armata. Se io perdonerò ad essi sappiate che la mia armata sarà disorganizzata. Io sono un soldato Monsignore; i soldati compiono pienamente i loro doveri. Ora debbo dirvi assolutamente, che io sono contro questi uomini. Allora il Delegato Apostolico istantemente supplicò, ma vedendo che i sentimenti umani non potevano influenzare questo tiranno, cominciò con la sua impeccabile diplomazia a dire, pretestando [sic] gl'interessi del governo turco.

"Eccellenza la tragedia armena ha eccitato tutta l'Europa contro la Turchia, la quale ormai si trova in uno stato assai difficile a causa delle stragi che organizzò e accompli. Se voi impiccate questi 61 armeni, malgrado l'intervento del S. Padre sappiate di certo che un altra [sic] volta inciterete contro la Turchia l'odio di tutta l'Europa. Io parlo soltanto per l'interesse del vostro Impero; interesse il quale impone questa volta ed in queste circostanze l'obbligo di comportarsi talmente, che non venga ravvivata, rinfiammata l'impressione degli inenarrabili massacri armeni. Dunque? Eccellenza, accordate grazia a questi 61 armeni in nome degli interessi della vostra patria? Il crudele, il maligno Gemal Pacha si prese a pensare e a meditare; poi con gran stento cominciò a pronunciare queste parole: "Mons. io sono un soldato: ma se il Ministro degli Esteri contempla un

---

242 Constantinople.

interesse nell'assolvere questi Armeni colpevoli, anch'io quanto a me, per contentarvi, non sarei contrario."

Così il loro principio di temporeggiamento si spuntava di nuovo con questa risposta di Gemal. Ma Mons. Dolci instancabile ed intrepido, corre subito dal Ministro degli Esteri, Ahmed Nessimi Bey, e ripetendo che gli interessi del Governo esigevano che questi 61 Armeni, venissero assoluti [sic], aggiunge pure, che se egli vi acconsentisse, pure Gemal Pacha avea dato parola di non opporvisi.

Il Ministro saltò in piedi, subito e caldamente serrando e scuotendo la mano di Mons. Dolci, gli disse sorridendo:

"È vero Mons. è vero che Hemal [sic] disse queste parole?

Mons. Dolci; replicò:

Ma sì, Sig. Ministro, posso anche dichiarare sotto firma che queste parole che Gemal disse, sono vere! " Allora il Ministro solennemente dichiara "Mons. Dolci, io mi congratulo con voi, sì, questi armeni sono già liberati, da oggi stesso essi hanno ottenuto il perdono".

Dopo una settimana, il governo fa sapere a Mons. Dolci che il Gov. Ottomano dando soddisfazione alla domanda del S. Papa, dalla sentenza del patibolo ha fatto degni del perdono quei 61 armeni, ma che essi per qualche tempo ancora resteranno in prigione:

Da queste 61 persone, 17 ultimamente morirono d'inanizione, ecc ed il Gov. d'Aleppo, seco trasportò il resto, quando l'armata inglese entrava vittoriosa in Aleppo. Attualmente non si sa nulla su di essi.

Ecco, così i 61 armeni furono liberati dal patibolo grazie a Mons. Dolci, buon Pastore, al quale offriamo i nostri sinceri e fervidi sensi di gratitudine.

firma Vahramian
Chinato al bacio ecc.

[Translation]
Most Eminent Prince,
The Armenian-Schismatic newspaper "Verchin Lur" (the Latest News), organ of the deceased ex-patriarch apostate Ormanian, of March 18, 1919, N. 1523, publishes:

Translation from the Armenian.
How the 61 Armenians were freed from the gallows.
The bakers of Aleppo are hereditarily Armenians from Sasun; it was they who in 1916 ran all the bakeries and merited the satisfaction of the entire population. These men, generally big,

robust and hard-working, were not disturbing the interests or the habits of others in any way whatsoever; beyond their labors these working men did not get themselves mixed up in anything else. The Turkish government, which had had the policy of being rather indulgent with such persons, started to ruminate over what means could be used to condemn these humble people to annihilation... and, to arrive at this end of theirs, began to persecute them.

Up until now, 8 to 10 of our Sasuntsis, imagining where these persecutions would end, had made the decision to go to Russia, traveling secretly over the mountains of Marash and by way of Sivas, in order to escape the destructive reach of the Turks.

And so, they set off to execute their plan. But, unfortunately, as it had been known around Aleppo that the Sasuntsi bakers had fled, an order was given, and the government sent mounted police who captured them three hours beyond Marash and tortured them horribly under the lash. The reader can easily imagine what torments there were: in fact so severe that blood began to gush from every part of their bodies, and what was most terrible, those monsters pulled out their fingernails one by one, and from their fingers blood began to run in abundance. The government, in carrying out these barbaric acts, intended nothing more than to pull out of their mouths the names of some other men, innocents to whom to teach the same lesson. And so one of the poor Sasuntsis, who had been mistreated worse than the others, and who was already almost dead, uttered the names of those he knew. Thus they obtained what they intended.

There was, though, one thing that they had overlooked up until now. They started, therefore, to make a detailed search of them; they discovered on the persons of some, and in the suitcases of others, some oven-cooked breads (pita) and some dates. And lo! What a big uproar over it!... truly huge, as though they had discovered revolvers, cartridges, and... bombs! As soon as the discovery was made, they had our bakers, who had cooked those breads, arrested along with two fruitsellers who, among other fruits, also sold dates! Those arrested were interrogated under the rod about "whether and to whom they had sold bread and dates"! They, then, not having any idea who it was about, say they have sold some days ago to so & so; among these were even d. Pasquale Malgian, of the Armenian College of Rome, who was the most educated and well-loved person in the area, even the businessman Agop Bassarian, David Godagian, and others, of whom the number came to 61 in all. These 61, bound with iron handcuffs together with the Sasuntsis, were sent to

Aleppo, and there they were thrown into prison. At trial, those innocents were condemned to prison for one, two, and five years, and to have their sentence confirmed they were sent to Gemal Pasha, governor of Syria. Gemal Pasha immediately instructs the military court of Aleppo to review the trial and to condemn each one to death. The Court began to consider this cruel order: an order, however, which there was no power to resist. After a thousand hesitations, the order of the bloodthirsty superior is carried out, and soon the sentence is once again communicated to His... Barbarity. And here it is that H.E. Mons. Dolci, having been indirectly informed of the measures of this sentence and of the immense tortures suffered by these innocents, a few days later sends a letter from the Holy Pope to Sultan Mehmed Reshad, another to the Foreign Minister, and a third to the conscienceless Enver with which he demanded the absolution of these "criminal innocents".

The government, whose policy in these circumstances has no merit other than that of buying time, weaving beautiful promises bows before Mons. Dolci saying: "We ourselves are ready to content your Most Holy Sovereign. But this matter depends exclusively on Gemal Pasha; we were obliged to adopt his opinion". Considering, however, that the interest of the government requires pleasing the Holy Pope, instruction was given that the sentence be sent to Constantinople so that it may be carefully examined here at headquarters.

Here is the dry and ambiguous response that the Government gave to Mons. Dolci, to this merciful, indefatigable shepherd: a month goes by and no response. The merciful pastor, trembling at the thought that Gemal Pacha might carry out the sentence as a matter of course, went two or three times a week to the Sublime Porte to get an answer and each time they told him: "Have no fear, Excellency, we shall satisfy you".

One day, Monsignor Dolci hears that Gemal Pasha, the executioner of Syria, has made a triumphal entry into Constantinople, and intends to travel on to Berlin. He rushes quickly by automobile to his house in Nishan Tash, where Gemal Pasha receives him with honor and adulation; but when Mons. Dolci brings up the question of the 61 Armenians this is how the bloodthirsty Minister replies: Excellency, ask of me what you will, but don't say anything to me in favor of the Armenians, please. As far as these 61 Armenians are concerned, they are all traitors, who wanted to betray army plans, army secrets, to the Russians. If I pardon them, know that my army will become disorganized. I am a soldier, Monsignor; soldiers carry out their duties in full. Now I must tell you absolutely, that I am against these men. The Apostolic Delegate begged right away, but seeing that human sentiments could not influence this tyrant, began employing his impeccable diplomacy to say, feigning the interests of the Turkish government:

"Excellency, the Armenian tragedy has roused all of Europe against Turkey, who now finds herself in a fairly difficult position, due to all the massacres that she organized and accomplished. If you hang these 61 Armenians in spite of the Holy Father's intervention, be aware that you will certainly incite the hatred of all Europe against Turkey. I'm speaking only in the interest of your Empire, an interest which, now and in these circumstances, imposes the obligation to behave in a such a way that the impression of the indescribable Armenian massacres is not revived, re-inflamed. Thus? Excellency, would you not concede a pardon to these 61 Armenians in the name of the interests of your country?" The cruel, the evil Gemal Pasha took to thinking and meditating; then with great difficulty began to pronounce these words: "Mons., I am a soldier, but if the Foreign Minister contemplates an interest in absolving these guilty Armenians, as for me, to please you, I would not be contrary to it either."

So, their principle of playing for time appeared once again with this response from Gemal. But Mons. Dolci, tireless and intrepid, rushed to the Foreign Minister Ahmed Nessimi Bey and, repeating that the interests of the Government demanded that these 61 Armenians be absolved, went on to add that, if he were to consent to it, even Gemal Pasha had given his word not to oppose it.

The Minister jumped to his feet and, quickly and warmly grasping and shaking Mons. Dolci's hand, said to him, smiling:

"Is it true, Mons.? Is it true that Gemal spoke these words?"

Mons. Dolci replied:

"But of course, Mr. Minister, I would sign my name to the fact that these words that Gemal spoke are true!" Then the Minister solemnly declared, "Mons. Dolci, I congratulate you, yes, these Armenians are already freed; as of today they have obtained a pardon."

After a week, the government let Mons. Dolci know that the Ottoman Gov., satisfying the Holy Pope's request, deigned to pardon those 61 Armenians from the sentence of death, but that they would still remain in prison for some time:

Of these 61 persons, 17 subsequently died from extreme malnutrition, etc. and the Gov. of Aleppo, transported the rest with them, when the English army entered victorious into Aleppo. Currently nothing is known of them.[243]

And, so, the 61 Armenians were liberated from the gallows thanks to Mons. Dolci, good Shepherd, to whom we offer our fervid and sincere feelings of gratitude.

signed Vahramian
Bowed to the kiss etc.

44

28 March 1919, Constantinople – Dolci to Gasparri – ASV, *Guerra* [War], 1914–18, 244, 69, n° 89948

Eminentissimo Principe,

Il NOR GHIANK, giornale armeno N.153 del 27 marzo 1919, ha pubblicato il discorso tenuto dal S. Padre nel Concistoro del 10 Corrente, intitolando l'articolo:

Il discorso del S Papa per l'Oriente.
Se Sua Santità non avesse fatto ricorso più
numerosi sarebbero stati i massacri armeni.

Vi aggiunge infine quest'osservazione:

Il Papa nella Sua allocuzione colle sue parole sulla Palestina ha voluto accennare a tre punti. 1° alle brame arabe, 2° ai programmi dei Sionnisti [*sic*], 3° alla propaganda protestante.

Io poi sto interessandomi per la pubblicazione di quest'importantissimo discorso in altri giornali e nel Bollettino del Vic.

Chinato ecc.

[Translation]
Most Eminent Prince,

The Armenian newspaper *NOR GYANK*, N.153 of March 27, 1919, published the speech made by the Holy Father during the Consistory of the 10th of this Month, entitling the article:

The Holy Pope's Speech for the East.
If His Holiness Had Not Made Recourse
the Armenian Massacres Would Have Been More Numerous.

At the end, this observation is added:

"The Pope in his speech, with his words on Palestine, wanted to mention three elements: 1° Arab desires, 2° Zionist plans, 3° Protestant propaganda."

---

243 They were freed by British forces after the armistice. Among them was also don Pasquale Malgian, Naslian, *op. cit.*, vol. I, p. 463.

Finally, I am taking care of getting this very important speech published in other newspapers and in the Newsletter of the Vic[ariate?].

Bowed etc.

45

16 May 1919, Constantinople – Dolci to Gasparri – AAEESS, *Russia* 505, n° 1120

Eminentissimo Principe,

In conformità del mio Rapporto del 9 Aprile N. 1099, onoro rimettere all'E. Vostra la ricevuta della somma di fr. sv. 12031,70 rilasciata dal P. Denys Kalatosoff allo stato maggiore inglese di Tiflis e trasmessomi per il tramite dell'Ambasciata con una lettera del Prefato Amministratore Apostolico che credo opportuno trascrivere.

[Translation]

Most Eminent Prince,

In accordance with my Report of April 9th, N. 1099, I am honored to send to Y.E. the receipt for the sum of SFr. 12,031.70 issued by F. Denys Kalatosoff to the English high command of Tiflis and passed on to me by way of the Embassy, with a letter from the aforementioned Apostolic Administrator that I believe it opportune to transcribe.

2 mars 1919

A S.E.Mons. Dolci D.A.

Excellence,

Avant hier j'ai reçu la lettre officielle de V.E. datée le 30 Mars 1919 N. 561, et le chèque y-inclus de la Banque Fédérale S.A. Zurigo n. 309338/1744, - 29 Mars 1919 - de la Valeur de frs Suisses 12031,70/00

Justement cet aide de S.S. le Pape nous arrive au moment d'une désolation générale du clergé arménien catholique et notre population. Mais plutôt le clergé est tombé dans une misère indescriptible, car la population devenue pauvre dans les pays dérobés par les soldats et les kurdes ne peuvent plus maintenir leurs prêtres, qui par plus sont restés privés de tout (avec leur familles, femmes, enfants) n'ayant plus de nourriture indispensable, des vêtements des chaussures etc.

Les prix sur les matières de première nécessité: pain, viande, vin pour la messe, cierges, bougies, allumettes, papier, médicaments, les aliments en général, les chaussures et les vêtements spécialement, augmentent chaque jour tellement qu'on ne sait plus ce qu'on doit faire, on perd la tête.

Par suite de cette chereté [*sic*] insupportable, la conduite exemplaire du clergé catholique fut ébranlée, et les plus faibles entre eux ont commencé ça et là de suivre le maintien du clergé acatholique du pays.

Pour dire la vérité, cette administration ecclésiastique d'un si vaste pays comme la Russie et tout le Caucase, se trouve dans de grands embarras par suite du manque de communications, ne pouvant pas arriver à temps nécessaire, par télégraphe ou par poste, même par le moyen de voyageurs. Ainsi le prestige et l'Autorité de cette administration va se diminuer de jour en jour, et ça et là la morale de quelque prêtre commence à laisser beaucoup à désirer.

Nous aussi quatre personnes: moi (1º membre) Don Antoine Kapazan (2º membre), le secrétaire et un courrier de cette administration, depuis septembre 1918 nous sommes privés de nos appointements que nous recevions auparavant du Gouvernement russe, ensuite du Gouvernement de Transcaucasie indépendante, et depuis le 26 Mai de 1918 du gouvernement de la Géorgie indépendante.

Nous avons fait plusiers recours à ce dernier gouvernement, mais pourtant tout est resté même sans réponse jusqu'aujourd'hui.

Ce ne serait pas inutile, si V. Excellence croirait possible d'en parler avec les Délégations de l'Arménie et de la Géorgie résidentes à Consple, en même temps que moi, je fais ici toutes les démarches nécessaires pour renouveler ces payements.

Le nom et l'office de V.E.Rev. ici et dans l'Arménie est pris en grande considération et respect. Je l'ai bien constaté et les Ministres de la Géorgie et ceux de l'Armenie. Ainsi une proposition de V.E. au Nom du St Père ne restera pas sans un résultat concret.

Cette administration fut toujours maintenue par le gouvernement depuis 1844, lors de son institution.

Notre administrateur Apostolique Mons. Serkis Der Abramian fut privé de son appartement depuis 1er Janvier de 1918 par suite de son absence à Rome.

A la Délégation de la Géorgie aspirant la reconnaissance de la part du St. Siège de Roma de l'indépendance de la Géorgie serait nécessaire de prévenir qu'il est nécessaire que les destitutions [sic] catholiques de leur pays soient respectées et maintenues comme le faisaient le gouvernement de la Russie.

Les S. huiles que j'ai déja reçues de la part de notre Patriarche à Consple, mais en quantité insuffisante, nous les avons déjà distribuées.

Nous sommes heureux d'avoir la Ste benédiction de Sa Sainteté le Pape, et celle de V.E. que je ne tarderai pas à la communiquer au clergé et à la population arménienne catholique et nous espérons bien que nous ne serons pas oubliés par le miséricordieux et grand coeur de S.Sainteté le Pape et de la bienveillante attention de V.E. dont je suis le très humble serviteur.

signé: P. Denys Kalatosoff

Chinato al bacio ecc
[Bowed to the kiss etc.]

46

27 June 1919, Constantinople – Dolci to Card. Marini – CO, Armeni e Caucaso [Armenians and Caucasus], 105, 3, 5, n° 2375

Eminentissimo Principe,

La stampa specialmente armena e greca, pubblica degli articoli sovra massacri di cristiani al Caucaso. Dal giornale la RENAISSANCE di oggi 27, N. 177 trascrivo il seguente articolo:

[Translation]
Most Eminent Prince,

The press, especially the Armenian and Greek press, is publishing articles about the massacres of Christians in the Caucasus. From the newspaper *The RENAISSANCE* of today the 27th, N. 177, I transcribe the following article:

AU CAUCASE

Le sang coule de nouveau…

Suivant les dernier journaux reçus du Caucase, les Tartares de la région de Kharabagh ont essayé d'organiser des massacres à Chouchi et ses environs. Le 4 Juin sur 50 ouvriers arméniens qui s'étaient rendus à leur travail dans le quartier musulman de la ville de Couchi, sept seulement sont rentrés, le reste a été massacré. Ce massacre a été, suivant certains indices, organisé par Soultanoff. En effet le 2 et 3 Juin, tout les musulmans habitant le quartier arménien ont été transférés dans le quartier Tartare. Le matin du 4, vers 10 heures, une forte fusillade a commencé dans la ville entre Tartares et Arméniens. Les premiers prépares d'avance envahissent rapidement la ville et s'emparent des positions stratégiques importantes, ils demandent l'expulsion immédiate hors de la ville, des membres de l'Union national arménienne. Les Arméniens ripostent [*sic*] à leur tour par les armes et perviennent à rejeter les Tartares de leurs positions.

Procédés habituels.

Une lettre reçue le 15 Juin de Couchi donne les détails suivants:

le 4 Juin à 10 heures du matin après une forte fusillade, les tartares attaquèrent les arméniens. Le lendemain des Kurdes attaquèrent à leur tour le village de Khaibali dont ils massacrèrent tous les hommes, et pillèrent les maisons. Ils dépouillèrent les femmes de leurs vêtements et 50 de celles-ci qu'ils avaient pris comme otage, furent exhibées toutes nues devant le gouverneur-général Sultanoff.

Les villageois pris à l'improviste, ne purent se défendre. Les villages de Dahloul, Tchamouchlou et Gargadjian eurent le même sort. Les fabriques de soie de M.K.Nersessian et G.Aharonian ont été pillées puis incendiées.

A Arèche.

Le 29 Mai, jour de l'anniversaire de la fondation de la République d'Azerbeidjan, le maire d'Arèche, e, par l'entremise d'une bande tartare, fait passer au fil de l'épée tous les émigrés arméniens qui se trouvaient dans son district. La même bande projetait également l'exterminatio des Arméniens des villages de Vartachène, Nij et Djalet.

Intervention.

Le Ministère des Affaires Etrangères de la République arménienne a remis au Gouvernement d'Azerbaidjian une protestation énergique contre ces massacres fromentés par le Gouverneur Sultanoff, et contre les prétions [sic] du gouvernement d'Azerbeidjian sur la partie arménienne du district de Kharabagh.

Le vice-président du conseil d'Erivan, M. Hadissian, a eu, à ce sujet, une entrevue avec le général Gossy, commandant les forces militaires anglises [sic] au Caucase.

Le journal arménien Achkhadavar de Tiflis est informé de source sûre, que les forces alliées ont opéré l'arrestation du gouverneur Général Sultanoff.[244]

Tanto ho creduto opportuno di portare a conoscenza dell'Eminenza Vostra, chinato al bacio ecc

[Translation]

As I believed it opportune to bring this to Your Eminence's knowledge, bowed to the kiss etc.

---

[244] In reality, Sultanoff was neither suspended from his post nor punished, but in fact returned soon afterwards to the Karabakh and ended up obtaining a definitive assignment to Azerbaijan (Hovannisian, *op. cit.*, pp. 181–185).

47

30 June 1919, Rome – Marini to Gasparri – AAEESS, *Russia* 540 bis, n° 97077

Il sottoscritto Cardinal Segretario della S.C. per la Chiesa orientale si permette di pregare l'Emo Signor Cardinale Segretario di Stato, affinché si compiaccia far avere il passaporto della S.Sede al Rmo P. Antonio Delpuch dei Padri Bianchi (Missionari d'Africa), che dovrà recarsi nelle provincie del Caucaso a compiervi una Missione affidata da questa S.C. con il titolo di Visitatore Apostolico.

In pari tempo lo scrivente Cardinale esprime anche il desiderio che cotesta Segreteria di Stato, in quanto crederà possibile, procuri d'interessare la Legazione d'Inghilterra presso la S. Sede, affinché solleciti il passaporto del R. Governo Inglese al sullodato Visitatore Apostolico, che dovrebbe partire quanto prima.

Intanto lo scrivente Cardinal Segretario si vale ben volentieri di questo incontro per baciargli con profondo ossequio umilissimamente le mani

[Translation]

The undersigned Cardinal Secretary of the S.C. for the Oriental Church permits himself to bid the Most Em. Lord Cardinal Secretary of State, that he might please obtain the passport of the Holy See for the Most Rev. F. Antonio Delpuch of the White Fathers (Missionaries of Africa), who will need to go to the provinces of the Caucasus to there carry out a Mission entrusted to this S.C. with the title of Visitor Apostolic.

At the same time, the Cardinal writing presently also expresses the desire that the Secretary of State, insofar as he deems possible, try to involve the Legation of England with the Holy See, in order that the passport of the R. English Government might be requested for the abovementioned Visitor Apostolic, who should leave as soon as possible.

Meanwhile the present writer Cardinal Secretary most willingly avails himself of this encounter to kiss, most humbly and with deep respect, the hands

48

1 July 1919, Rome – Der Abramian to Gasparri – AAEESS, *Russia* 540 bis, n° 92975

Eminenza Revma,

Per sottrarmi da qualunque responsabilità davanti alla S.Sede io mi ho creduto in dovere di esporre alla S. Cong. "Pro Ecclesia Orientali" il mio sommesso parere - di cui una copia accludo qui - ed ho voluto che la Segreteria di Stato sia al corrente di questi affari nelle attuali circostanze molto delicate, poiché io credo che in un molto vicino avvenire avrà Vostra Emminenza degli affari diplomatici con quelle neo-nate repubbliche giorgiana ed armena per il bene del cattolicismo e per l'incremento della fede cattolica.

Intanto chinato al bacio della Sacra Porpora ecc

[Translation]
Most Rev. Eminence,

To subtract myself from any responsibility whatever before the Holy See I felt it my duty to put before the S. Congr. "Pro Ecclesia Orientali" my humble opinion—a copy of which I enclose here—and I wanted the Secretariat of State to be abreast of these matters in the current, very delicate, circumstances, given that I believe that in a very near future Your Eminence will have diplomatic affairs with those new-born Georgian and Armenian republics, for the good of Catholicism and for the growth of the Catholic faith.

In the meantime, bowed to the kiss of the Holy Purple etc.

49

28 June 1919, Rome – Der Abramian to Assessor Mons. Papadopoulos – *Ibid.*, n° 92975

Eccellenza Reverendissima,

Nella privata Udienza che V.E. mi concesse in data 27 giugno 1919, fra le altre cose mi dichiarò che "andrà in Russia, nel Caucaso, un Visitatore Apostolico per gli affari degli Armeni e dei Georgiani etc.". Per sottrarmi a qualunque responsabilità davanti alla S.Sede, mi credo in dovere d'esporre alla S. Congregazione il mio umile e sommesso parere.

Se questo Visitatore Apostolico va unicamente per gli affari degli Armeni Cattolici e dei Georgiani e non ha nessun altro scopo politico, io umilmente dichiaro che per conservare il prestigio dei principi cattolici non è spediente che esso vada e porti tale titolo, facendo inoltre spese enormi inutili.

1º Non v'è nessuna discordia fra i detti georgiani Cattolici e gli Armeni cattolici. I detti georgiani Cattolici di rito armeno da oltre 25 o 30 anni desiderano d'abbracciare il rito latino, eccitati a ciò dai Padri del monastero di Ferykey di Costantinopoli, lasciando il rito armeno: diverse volte hanno fatto ricorso alla S.Sede e sempre hanno avuto risposta negativa. Al mio tempo, dal 1909, di nuovo hanno insistito ed io ho esposto alla S.Sede che un tale passo sarebbe stato un insulto al rito orientale armeno e che, se la S.Sede avesse voluto permetter loro di cambiare il rito, imponesse loro il rito giorgiano orientale guadagnando così anche le simpatie dei giorgiani scismatici verso la Chiesa Cattolica e rendendo più facile la loro unione alla Cattedra di S. Pietro. Anche l'anno scorso nel mese di agosto dietro richiesta della S.C. protocollo N.677 ho esposto il mio parere ripetendo sempre la stessa cosa. Quindi, secondo me, non rimane altro che scrivere al Vescovo di Tiraspoli di mettere in esecuzione il comando della S. Congregazione, senza dare un aspetto troppo solenne. Inoltre, in questi giorni, ho ricevuto una lettera dal mio Vicario P. Dionigi Kalatossoff in cui mi dice che i detti Georgiani cattolici hanno scelto un prete e due secolari per mandarli come delegati a Roma per tale questione e che il Governo Georgiano ha loro concesso 60.000 rubli per sostenere le spese del viaggio.

2º Mandando un Visitatore Apostolico per gli Armeni Cattolici di Russia, si supporrà una colpa e un colpevole,e così un rappresentante della S.Sede in persona mia sarà pubblicamente diffamato per aver difeso i principi della Chiesa Cattolica e perciò perseguitato da un ceto plebeio che s'è profittato delle circostanze rivoluzionarie russe e con questo passo la S.Sede offenderà i sentimenti cattolici della sana parte della popolazione cattolica; perché i Cattolici sono persuasi che la Santa Sede non avrebbe dato nessuna importanza al plebeo ed insieme quei poveri ribaldi avranno più coraggio di ripetere la stessa cosa, data occasione, se non altro almeno per diffamare il loro Capo spirituale e per cagionargli disgusto.

3º Se però la S.Sede mandando un Visitatore Apostolico ha altri scopi oltre che gli affari degli Armeni Cattolici, sarebbe meglio, secondo il mio parere, che non porti il nome di Visitatore Apostolico degli Armeni cattolici del Caucaso ma piuttosto per gli affari georgiani che è una questione più o meno grave e non v'è nessuno di mezzo che possa essere diffamato; ciò però non impedisce che indirettamente, senza dare un aspetto solenne, esso Visitatore Apostolico vede e studi gli affari armeni per l'organizzazione presente e futura ed anche prenda informazione sulla mia persona.

Ecco, eccellenza Revma, il mio sommesso parere in questa materia che ho brevemente esposto per sottrarmi a qualunque responsabilità nello avvenire, senza alcun mio interesse individuale. del resto lascio tutto al savio giudizio della S. Congregazione.

Chinato al bacio ecc

[Translation]
Most Reverend Excellency,

In the private Audience which Y.E. conceded me on June 27, 1919, among other things you stated to me that "to see to the affairs of the Armenians and the Georgians, etc., a Visitor Apostolic will go to Russia, to the Caucasus." To subtract myself from all responsibility before the Holy See, I believe myself obliged to put before the S. Congregation my humble and subdued opinion.

If this Visitor Apostolic goes solely for the affairs of the Armenian and Georgian Catholics, and has no other political scope, I humbly declare that to conserve the prestige of Catholic principles it is not expedient that he go and bear that title, incurring enormous pointless expenses besides.

1º There is no discord between the so-called Georgian Catholics and the Armenian Catholics. For 25 or 30 years, the so-called Armenian-rite Georgian Catholics have wished to embrace the Latin rite, stimulated to this by the

Fathers of the monastery of Ferikoy of Constantinople, leaving the Armenian rite: various times they have made recourse to the Holy See and they have always had a negative response. In my time, since 1909, again they insisted and I told the Holy See that such a step would have been an insult to the Armenian eastern rite and that, if the Holy See had wanted to permit them to change the rite, it would have imposed on them the Georgian eastern rite thus also gaining the sympathies of the Georgian schismatics towards the Catholic Church and rendering their union to the Cathedra of St. Peter easier. Also, last year in the month of August, following a request by the S.C., protocol N.677, I laid out my view, repeating the same thing still. Therefore, to my mind, nothing remains but to write to the Bishop of Tiraspol to put into execution the order of the S. Congregation, without giving it too solemn an aspect. Moreover, I recently received a letter from my vicar F. Dionigi Kalatosoff in which he tells me that the so-called Georgian Catholics have chosen a priest and two secular clergymen to send as delegates to Rome about this matter and that the Georgian Government has conceded them 60,000 rubles to cover their travel expenses.

2º Sending a Visitor Apostolic for the Armenian Catholics of Russia will suggest guilt and a guilty party, and so a representative of the Holy See in my person will be publicly defamed for having defended the principles of the Catholic Church and hence persecuted by a plebean class who has profited from the Russian revolutionary circumstances, and with this step the Holy See will offend Catholic sentiments of the healthy part of the Catholic population; because Catholics are persuaded that the Holy See would not have given any importance to the common people and together those poor rascals will be further encouraged to repeat the same thing, given the occasion, if for no other reason than to defame their spiritual Leader and to cause him disgust.

3º If, however, the Holy See has other purposes besides the affairs of the Armenian Catholics in sending a Visitor Apostolic, it would be better, in my opinion, that he not bear the name of Visitor Apostolic to the Catholic Armenians of the Caucasus, but rather for Georgian affairs, which is a more or less serious question and there is no one in the midst of it who might be defamed; that, however, doesn't impede, indirectly, without being too official, this Visitor Apostolic observing and studying Armenian affairs with an eye towards present and future organization, and also collecting information about my person.

Here, Most Rev. Excellency, is my most humble opinion on this matter, that I have briefly expounded upon in order to subtract myself from any future responsibility, without any individual stake in the matter. After all, I leave everything to the wise judgment of the S. Congregation.

Bowed to the kiss etc.

50

10 February 1919, Constantinople – Dolci a Gasparri – AAEESS,
Asia 117, n° 10228[245]

Eminentissimo Principe,

Quando il 17 Settembre faceva ritorno a questa città Monsignor Cesarano, per favore singolare dell'Ammiraglio Mortola che sospendeva la partenza di un ufficiale per dargli un posto sul piroscafo, la cura di Fiuggi era già tardiva. Ciononostante, avrei desiderato di valermi della licenza così benignamente accordatami, per fare quella dei fanghi ai ginocchi che il medico mi consigliava. Non ho giudicato però opportuno di allontanarmi a causa del timore dei cristiani dell'interno dell'Impero, sulla loro sicurezza personale, cagionata dalla situazione anormalissima dell'Anatolia. Essa trovasi sotto l'Impero di Mustaffa Kemal Pacha, che ha radunato sotto il suo comando un forte esercito e si è reso assolutamente indipendente dal Governo Centrale di Costantinopoli. L'allarme poi è andato sempre crescendo per la rottura di comunicazione fra l'Anatolia ed il governo centrale. Questo, fino ad oggi, non può estendere i suoi ordini al di là di Ismidt e di alcune altre città del litorale del Mar di Marmara.

L'E. Vostra può quindi immaginare il panico dei cristiani dell'interno e le loro insistenze, specialmente da parte dei nostri 4 mila cattolici di Angora e del loro Vescovo Mons. Bahabian, affinché fossi intervenuto presso le Alte Autorità dell'Intesa per tutelare e garantire la loro vita. Mons. Vescovo a causa di questi incidenti non ha ancora potuto far ritorno alla sua sede.

Il mio apprezzamento su questo allarme dei cristiani è che esso sia esageratissimo, dacché non posso convincermi che Mustafa Kemal Pacha abbia da provocare l'opinione pubblica europea, rinnovando massacri di cristiani, il che darebbe il colpo di grazia all'Impero turco.

Nonostante questo mio parere personale, credetti dovere intervenire. Un primo raggio di luce mi fece intravedere la situazione oscurissima dell'Anatolia, sotto il punto di vista politico; esso mi venne da un personaggio autorevole che mi disse: Il Governo rivoluzionario di Kemal Pacha è più simpatico del Governo Centrale, per la ragione che ha un programma <u>definito e preciso</u>; la lotta per l'integrità territoriale dell'Anatolia".

Fra le interviste avute cogli alti Commissarii, interessante fu quella coll'Alto Commissario Inglese, gentilissimo, franco e vero soldato marinaro, L'ammiraglio Robert. Essa durò un'ora e mezzo e la riassumo concisamente.

Egli disse:

---

[245] A copy of this document was found in the Archives of the [Sacred Congregation for] Extraordinary Ecclesiastical Affairs (AAEESS), *Asia* 117, by Riccardi, *op. cit.*, note 139, p. 128.

a) Che la situazione in Anatolia era gravissima sotto il punto di vista politico ma non destava nessuna inquietudine seria sotto quella della sicurezza essendo stata a lui garantita la vita dei cristiani e degli stranieri. La rottura dei ponti ferroviari e delle communicazioni telegrafiche erano fatti, senza dubbio, fuori d'ordine, da occasionare, ma non da giustificare un vero allarme di persecuzione. Su questo oggetto l'Ammiraglio concludeva: "la vita dei cristiani è oggi più sicura di quello che fosse due mesi fa".

b) Che questa situazione politica dell'Anatolia, indipendente dell'Amministrazione centrale, non poteva tollerarsi e che egli desiderava un governo responsabile degli avvenimenti del paese.

Le mie impressioni sono state:

a) Che il Gabinetto Damad Ferid Pacha era alla vigilia della sua caduta.

b) Che la situazione in Anatolia, creata da questo movimento rivoluzionario in armi per l'integrità nazionale, può fornire al Congresso della Pace un ripiego politico per arrestarsi sullo smembramento e quella regione, qualora tale smembramento non convenisse alle nazioni interessate. Per sottomettere oggi l'Anatolia, che i turchi difenderebbero col metodo delle guerriglie occorrerebbe una penetrazione armata con forze abbastanza considerevoli, il che richiederebbe un'azione concorde delle grandi Nazioni. La Francia e l'Italia non si mostrano presentemente proclivi a farlo, e l'Inghilterra non si scosterà, su questo punto, dalla condotta delle sue alleate.

c) Che, se non accade qualche grande avvenimento politico, non vi è assolutamente nessun pericolo, almeno imminente, per la vita dei cristiani in Anatolia. È il mio convincimento personale pur riconoscendo che, fino a quando questo falso allarme dei cristiani non cessi non è opportuno allontanarmi dal posto.

Durante la conversazione poi con l'Ammiraglio inglese, si parlò pure dell'indipendenza dell'Ucraina, della Georgia e dell'Armenia. Le mie impressioni furono che si desidera nuovamente una grande Russia e non sembrano ben disposti per l'indipendenza di quelli stati specialmente della Georgia e dell'Ucraina. La ragione politica che si adduce è che questi piccoli stati potrebbero esser facilmente soggiogati dall'influenza tedesca. Io ho energicamente difeso la loro indipendenza, dimostrando che la risurrezione della Grande Russia sarebbe il più grave errore che l'Europa commetterebbe. Fui indotto a prendere questa difesa perché ritengo che sarebbe un gravissimo danno per i nostri alti interessi religiosi la ricostituzione del colosso moscovita.

Chinato al bacio ecc

[Translation]

Most Eminent Prince,

When Monsignor Cesarano returned to this city on September 17th, thanks to the singular favor of Admiral Mortola, who held up an official's departure in order to give him a place on the steamer, the Fiuggi cure[246] was already belated. That notwithstanding, I would have liked to take advantage of the leave, so kindly accorded me, to undergo the mud treatments to my knees that the doctor recommended. I did not think it appropriate to leave my place, however, because of the Christians' fear for their personal security in the interior of the Empire, provoked by the most abnormal situation in Anatolia. She finds herself under the Empire of Mustafa Kemal Pasha, who has gathered a powerful army under his command and who has made himself absolutely independent from the Central Government of Constantinople. Alarm has been growing due to the breakdown in communications between Anatolia and the central government which, up until now, has not been able to extend its orders beyond Izmit and a few other cities along the Marmaran coastline.

Y. Emin. can thus imagine the panic of the Christians of the interior and their insistences, especially on the part of our 4 thousand Catholics of Angora and of their Bishop Mons. Bahabian, that I intervene with the High Authorities of the Entente to safeguard and guarantee their lives. Because of these incidents Mons. Bishop has not yet been able to return to his see.

My evaluation of the Christians' alarm is that it is quite exaggerated, since I cannot convince myself that Mustafa Kemal Pasha would provoke European public opinion by renewing the massacres of Christians, which would be a deathblow to the Turkish Empire.

Notwithstanding this personal opinion of mine, I believed I must intervene. I was allowed to glimpse an early ray of light on the dark situation in Anatolia, from a political point of view; this came to me by way of a influential personage who told me: "The revolutionary Government of Kemal Pasha is preferable to the Central Government because it has a <u>definite and precise</u> program: the battle for territorial integrity of Anatolia".

Among the interviews held with the high Commissioners, most interesting was that with the English High Commissioner Admiral Robert, who is very kind, straightforward and a true seafaring soldier. This lasted an hour and a half, and I summarize it briefly.

He said:

a.) That the situation in Anatolia was very grave from a political point of view, but did not arouse any serious anxiety from a security point of view, having, himself, been vouchsafed with the lives of Christians and of foreigners. The destruction of the railroad bridges and the breaking-off of telegraphic communications were doubtlessly done outside of orders, occasioning, but not justifying, true alarm over persecution. On this subject the Admiral concluded: "<u>Christians' lives are safer today than</u> they were two months ago."

---

246 Translator's Note: Fiuggi is an Italian town known for its healing spa waters.

b.) That the current political situation in Anatolia, independent of the central Administration, could not endure, and that he wished for a government responsible for the happenings in the country.

My impressions were:

a.) That the Damad Ferid Pasha Cabinet was on the eve of its fall.

b.) That the situation in Anatolia, created by this armed revolutionary movement for national integrity, could furnish the Peace Congress with a political expedient to stop the dismantling of that region, in the case that such a breakup not be convenient for the nations concerned. To subdue Anatolia today, what with the Turks defending her using guerrilla methods, an armed penetration with quite considerable forces would be needed, requiring a joint action by the great Nations. France and Italy currently do not show themselves to be so inclined, and England will not deviate, on this point, from the conduct of her allies.

c.) That, barring some great political event, there is absolutely no danger, at least imminently, to Christians' lives in Anatolia. That is my personal conviction, while recognizing that, until this false alarm on the part of the Christians ceases, it is not opportune for me to leave my post.

During the conversation with the English Admiral, we also spoke about the independence of the Ukraine, of Georgia and of Armenia. My impressions were that a greater Russia is once again desired, and that they do not seem very well-disposed towards the independence of those states, especially of Georgia and of the Ukraine. The political reason one adduces is that these small states could easily be subject to German influence. I energetically defended their independence, demonstrating that the resurrection of Greater Russia would be the worst mistake that Europe could commit. I was predisposed towards taking this line of defense since I retain that the reconstitution of the Muscovite colossus would be a great detriment to our deeper religious interests.

Bowed to the kiss etc.

51

21 October 1919, Erevan – Delpuch to the president and Armenian foreign minister Khatissian – AAEESS, *Asia* 126, n° 3643

Monsieur le Président,

Vous connaissez tout l'intérêt que Sa Sainteté le Pape porte à la nation Arménienne. Il désire ardemment que ce noble peuple le plus éprouvé de la terre ait enfin le bonheur de retrouver dans la paix et la liberté une patrie au sein de laquelle il pourra développer tranquillement ses admirables qualités de travail et d'organisation. Il a été heureux, dans le passé, de lui donner l'appui de sa puissance morale et d'élever, le premier, la voix en sa faveur; il sera toujours prêt à entretenir, avec le gouvernement arménien, les relations les plus amicales.

Sur le territoire qui bientot, il faut l'ésperer, sera donné à votre nation, Sa Sainteté compte de nombreux fidèles qui tout en conservant les rites, la discipline et les usages nationaux, professent la doctrine catholique dont Elle a la garde et dont Elle détient le Suprême Pontificat. Le Saint Père, espère fermement que les Arméniens Catholiques jouiront toujours, au sein de leur patrie retrouvée, de la liberté la plus grande pour professer leur croyance et se développer. Il fera tous ses efforts pour que, de leur côté, ils contribuent à assurer le bien être de leur pays et à renforcer l'unité nationale qui seule fait les peuples forts.

Dans ce but Sa Sainteté le Pape a besoin de pouvoir exercer librement auprès d'eux toutes les prérogatives de son ministère apostolique. Il a besoin notamment:

1º De pouvoir étendre librement par lui même et par ses représentants sa vigilance pastorale et son autorité sur l'ensemble des arméniens catholiques.

2º De pouvoir fonder des établissements de bienfaisance (hopitaux, orphelinats, etc.) et surtout des écoles dans lesquelles les jeunes générations viendront puiser, avec une solide éducation morale, les enseignements qui leur permettront d'être plus tard des citoyens vertueux et utiles à leur pays.

3º Il a besoin que le Patriarcat catholique, les evéchés, les eglises et les établissements de bienfaisance puissent acquérir la propriété de leurs meubles et immeubles suffisants pour assurer leur entretien et leur developpement normal.

Je tiens à noter que, pour ce qui concerne les écoles, (écoles d'enseignement classique, d'enseignement professionel et écoles élémentaires) tout en initiant leurs élèves à la connaissance des langues et de la culture occidentales, la place principale sera toujours donné à l'enseignement de la langue et de l'histoire nationales.

Toutes ces questions pourront faire l'objet de pourparler et d'accords ultérieurs. Je n'ai, pour ce qui mi concerne, qu'à remplir un rôle d'informateur; à mon retour à Rome je devrai faire connaître à Sa Sainteté les dispositions du gouvernement Arménien; rien ne me serait plus agréable que d'apporter les meilleurs renseignements.

Je ne doute pas, Monsieur le Président, que, dans leur haute équité, le gouvernement et le peuple Arméniens si justement épris de liberté ne veuillent donner toute facilité à Celui qui est investi de la plus haute autorité morale et qui, le premier, a élevé sa voix en faveur de tous les Arméniens persécutés sans distinction de croyance.

Veuillez agréer, Monsieur le président, les sentiments de profond respect avec lesquels je reste ecc

52

3 November 1919, Erevan – Alkhatissian and der Akopian to Delpuch – AAEESS, *Asia* 126, nº 3643

Mon très Révérend Père,

J'ai l'honneur de vous accuser réception de Votre lettre du 22 Octobre écoulé relative à l'exercice du Ministère apostolique du St Siège en Arménie.

Ainsi que Vous le savez, la liberté de conscience étant admise en Arménie toutes les confessions y sont librement exercées. Le Gouvernement de la République se fera un devoir de donner toutes les facilités voulues aux Autorités Réligieuses Catholiques dans l'exercice de leur Ministère apostolique, et prêtera tout son assistance dans l'accomplissement de leur tâche.

Saisissant l'occasion, je Vous prie, Mon très Révérend Père, d'être auprès le St Père, l'interprête de notre profonde gratitude et de notre infinie reconnaissance, pour Sa haute intervention en faveur des Arméniens, et de le prier d'élever Sa haute et juste voix au moment décisif de notre cause.

Veuillez agréer, Mon très Révérend Père, l'assurance de ma plus haute consideration

53

21 November 1919, Tiflis – Delpuch's report to Papadopoulos – AAEESS, *Asia* 126, n° 3643[247]

[pp. 3–5 from the report]

A Erivan, la réception n'a été ni moins cordiale ni moins respectueuse qu'ailleurs. J'ai été à la gare par le Sous secrétaire d'Etat aux Affaires Etrangères, et un Délégué du Commandant de la place. J'ai été ensuite invité à un thé à la Résidence avec le Haut Commissaire Allié. Le lendemain, le Président de la République m'a reçu en audience privée et m'a chargé de transmettre ses hommages respectueux au St. Père et ses remerciments pour tout ce qu'il a fait en faveur des Arméniens. Son Excellence connaissait la lettre si ferme, écrite jadis par le St. Père au Sultan de Turquie, au sujet des massacres. Il m'a dit combien cet acte avait été au coeur du peuple Arménien. Il m'a ensuite donné l'assurance que l'Eglise Catholique aurait toute liberté pour la fondation des oeuvres d'Apostolat, leur direction et pour l'établissement de la hiérarchie catholique. Le Gouvernement Arménien serait tout heureux, si le siège du Patriarcat Catholique était fondé sur le territoire de la République. Pour donner un caractère plus authentique à ses déclarations Monsieur Khatissian m'a dit de lui laisser une note écrite. Votre Excellence en trouvera une copie ci jointe avec la réponse officielle si cordiale que je viens de recevoir. De vive voix, le Président a insisté sur la création d'une Délégation Apostolique partageant sa résidence entre Tiflis et Erivan.

Dans un grand diner qui a été ensuite donné le Président a voulu me céder sa propre place. Il était à ma gauche, j'avais à ma droite le Général Nazarbékof généralissime des troupes Arméniennes. Cet illustre soldat était jadis un des principaux Généraux de l'Armée Russe. Il s'est illustré à Ourmiah, à Van et à Tiflis. Après la débacle russe, il était commandant en chef du front du Caucase

---

[247] A copy of this document was found in AAEESS, *Asia* 126, by Riccardi, *op. cit.*, note 23, p. 122.

et a défendu son pays avec une indomptable énergie. A l'armistice le Général en chef Turc a voulu par respect pour ce héros lui faire le premier la visite. A ce diner le Président a porté un toast au St. Père en termes très élevés. Avant de quitter Erivan j'ai été reçu par le Catholicos[248] qui se trouvait dans cette ville. Le Patriarche ne savait comment exprimer son admiration pour le St. Père et pour son inepuisable charité. L'Archevêque d'Erivan m'a même dit que si les circostances le permettent, le Catholicos a l'intention d'envoyer une Délégation à Rome pour remercier Sa Sainteté. A Edmiadzin ou je me suis rendu ensuite, le chancelier du Catholicosat, l'Evêque Tyraire et Mgr. Mesrop l'ancien Archevêque de Tiflis m'ont fait visiter cet antique siège de la nation Arménienne et m'ont comblé d'égards. A mon départ, le Gouvernement a mis un train spécial à ma disposition pour me faire visiter la région de Kars où le commandant de la place a mis un officier à ma disposition pour me faire visiter la place et me faire rendre les honneurs. [...]

[pp. 5–6]

Je donne tous ces détails à Votre Excellence, pour que la S. Congrégation se rende un compte exact de l'immense prestige dont le Souverain Pontife jouit dans ces région du Caucase. Ce n'est certes pas pour faire valoir ma personne: tout autre à ma place aurait eu les mêmes succès.

Ici tout le monde qui pense a les yeux tournés vers Rome. Tout le monde reconnait la superiorité incontestée du Catholicisme, l'intensité de sa vie religieuse, sa culture élévée, son empire sur les âmes, sa vertu éminnemment moralisatrice. Ce ne sont pas seulement les hautes classes sociales qui pensent ainsi. Ce sentiment est bien plus profond. Lors de ma visite à Achaldzich, au moment de mon arrivée, les cloches de l'Eglise Orthodoxe joignaient leurs sons, aux carillons de l'Eglise Catholique. A Gori, en l'absence de l'Evêque, le clergé orthodoxe de la ville decida de venir en corps me saluer à la gare et me recevoir. A ma descente du train, le Doyen, devant une foule considerable qui écoutait silencieuse, me pria en son nom et au nom du peuple, de transmettre l'hommage de son respect au Pontife Romain. Il fit ensuite un magnifique éloge de l'Eglise Catholique, de sa vie religieuse, de ses bienfaits. Dans la région d'Alexandropol, alors que je me rendais dans des villages Catholiques, je devais traverser deux villages Grégoriens. Avant d'arriver à la première localité, ma voiture avançait au milieu d'un cortège de cavaliers. A l'entrée du bourg je vis avec surprise tout le peuple massé pour me recevoir. Les enfants des écoles étaient alignés sur les deux bords de la route et le clergé schismatique en ornements sacrés m'attendait et chantait les hymnes liturgiques. Les cloches sonnaient à toute volée. Un peu embarassé, je descendis de voiture et baisai la

---

248 The patriarch (or Catholicos) of Etchmiadzin, the Armenian religious center close to Erevan, is considered the head of the Armenian Apostolic church. Naslian, *op cit.*, vol. II, p.445.

croix qu'on me présentait, pour ne pas heurter ces pauvres gens. Pour ne pas me rendre à l'Eglise je prétextai la hâte où j'étais d'arriver de bonne heure, pour pouvoir rentrer immédiatement à Alexandropol. Je laissai une offrande pour payer des friandises aux enfants des écoles et tout le monde fut enchanté. Au second village schismatique, même réception et même acceuil.

Partout on savit que je n'étais qu'un simple prêtre. Ma qualité seule de Visiteur Apostolique et d'envoyé du St. Siège suffisait seule pour qu'on m'accorde ces honneurs qu'on ne donne même pas aux Evêques. [...]

54

27 November 1919, Tiflis – Delpuch to Khatissian – CO, 106, 2, 3, n° 3228

Monsieur le Président,

Au moment de laisser Tiflis, pour rentrer à Rome, je me fais un devoir de venir Vous redire toute ma reconnaissance pour l'acceuil si bienveillant et si cordial que j'ai trouvé partout le territoire de la République Arménienne.

Je Vous remercie de tout coeur pour la lettre si délicate et d'une inspiration si élevée que Votre Excellence a bien voulu m'écrire. Le St Père sera profondément touché des sentiments qu'elle exprime pour Sa personne et de la liberté accordée à Son Ministère Apostolique.

Soyez assuré, Monsieur le Président, que Sa Saintete garde toujours à Votre pays et à son noble peuple, les sentiments de l'amitié la plus grande et la plus dévouée. Elle s'efforcera toujours de contribuer, dans la mesure de ses moyens, à la réalisation des nobles et légitimes aspirations du peuple Arménien. Elle sait combien par son passé héroïque, sa fermeté dans la conservation de ses traditions et ses qualités, la nation Arménienne mérite de prendre sa place au milieu des peuples libres.

J'emporte pour ma part, le souvenir ému de tout ce que j'ai vu en Arménie de souffrances indicibles héroiquement supportées.

Veuillez agréer, Monsieur le Président, avec mes meilleurs voeux pour Votre personne, l'expression des sentiments de profond respect avec lesquels je reste de Votre Excellence ecc.

55

[? perhaps January 1920] – Report of Delpuch to the S. C. for the Oriental Church – CO, 106, 2, 3, n° 3516

[pp. 6–13]

par. 8 La République Arménienne se déclara indépendente en même temps que celle des Géorgiens et des Tartares. Elle choisit Erivan comme capitale au moins provisoire de l'Etat et y installa tous les organes gouvernementaux. Les deux anciennes provinces russes et d'Erivan, sauf pour cette dernière, les districts orientaux occupés par les Tartares, forment son territoire provisoire, en attendant que la Conférence de la Paix décide du sort des provinces de l'Empire Turc, que les Arméniens revendiquent.

Dans tous leurs actes, le Gouvernement et le Parlement de la République Armenienne s'inspirent des principes d'un libéralisme très large sans aller toutefois jusqu'à la sécularisation des biens de l'Eglise Arménienne Grégorienne. Tout le monde officiel appartient au parti révolutionnaire "Tachnagtzoution" à tendances socialistes très prononcées, mais poursuivant plutôt des buts politiques. Beaucoup de membres du clergé arménien grégorien de tous les degrés de la hiérarchie, ont donné leur nom et prêtent leur activité à ce parti.L'unité de vues est loin de régner entre ceux qui le composent, aussi se subdivise-t-il entre plusieurs fractions assez opposées entre elles, ce qui ne saurait être pour cette malheureuse nation un gage de stabilité nien assurée. Tous cependant sont unis entre eux, dans un sentiment de haine profonde contre leurs voisins immédiats, les mussulmans turc et tartares qui restent toujours à leurs yeux les ennemis héréditaires, parce que toujours ils ont été les oppresseurs abhorrés de leur race.

par. 9

[...]

3° *Relations mutuelles de ces nationalités*. A cause des dangereux voisins qui les entourent, de leur faiblesse numérique comme population, et de la dépendance mutuelle dans laquelle ils se trouvent pour leurs voies de communication, ces trois petits états auraient tout intérêt à s'unir étroitement entre eux et à s'entendre pour former une sorte de confédération.La Géorgie e l'Azarbaidjan l'ont compris: aussi depuis le mois de Juin 1919 les deux républiques sont-elles liées entre elles par un traité d'alliance défensive et d'union économique.Les relations les plus amicales règnent entre Tiflis et Bakou ainsi qu'entre les peuples qui en dépendent.Les musulmans, tenus toujours systématiquement à l'écart par la Russie, manquent d'hommes instruits et habitués aux affaires; aussi non seulement le gouvernement de Bakou, mais encore ceux du Kouban et du Daghestan recourent-ils volontiers aux bons offices des Géorgiens pour l'organisation de leur états respectifs. Les Géorgiens en effet ont l'esprit très ouvert et sont très intellectuels par tempérament. Durant les dernières années surtout, ils ont pris une part très active aux luttes intérieures de la Russie, aussi comptent-ils, parmi eux, un bon nombre d'hommes politiques de valeur.

En Arménie quelques hommes intelligents sentent le même besoin d'union avec les deux autres états, et s'efforcent d'y tendre mais trop de haine séparent les Arméniens des deux autres peuples, pour que l'unité puisse encore se faire avec eux. Ces haines nationales remontent aux temps les plus anciens; elles sont encore trop vivaces. Aussi les hommes qui travailleront à propager les lumières de la foi catholique dans ces contrées, devront-ils avoir toujours cette situation présente à l'esprit pour ne pas faire de faux pas et pour ne pas compromettre irrémédiablement leur ministère auprès de chacun des adversaires.

Les Géorgiens nourrissent une aversion profonde pour les Arméniens et volontiers les accusent de tous leurs maux. Dans le passé le plus lointain, ils ont été en lutte les uns contre les autres. A une époque plus récente, alors que la Russie dominait, les Arméniens ont toujours eu les préférences du gouvernement russe à cause de leur habilité dans les affaires administratives, tandis que les Géorgiens étaient tenus en suspicion. A ces causes générales s'en joignent d'autres plus immédiates encore.

par.10 Essentiellement hommes d'affaires, les Arméniens sont partout où il y a à gagner. En Géorgie ils forment des centres très nombreux et très prospères, soit dans les campagnes, soit dans les villes. Le Géorgien moins positif, moins travailleur, plus ami du mouvement, de la gaîté a toujours été un assez médiocre administrateur. Il dépense beaucoup pour ses plaisirs et se ruine facilement. L'Arménien au contraire, plus attentif et souvent aussi, il faut le dire, peu scrupuleux, acquiert facilement ce que l'autre gaspille, et prend peu à peu sa place. C'est ainsi qu'à Tiflis, sur une population de près 450000 habitants, les Arméniens forment presque la moitié, et occupent les positions les plus importantes. Les banques, le commerce le plus lucratif sont entre leurs mains. Les quartiers les plus riches, les maisons les plus belles sont leur propriété. Ils ont la fortune entre leurs mains tandis qu'à côté la noblesse et la bourgeoisie Géorgiennes n'occupent que des situations médiocres et voient souvent leurs biens de famille passer aux mains des Arméniens. Aussi n'est-il pas rare d'entendre les Géorgiens accuser les Arméniens de tout accaparer, de les ruiner "de boir leur sang!" selon leur expression, de les opprimer. Si à ces causes on ajoute les querelles religieuses du passé, des conflits récents et profondément regrettables au moment de la dissolution de la confederation transcaucasienne, et surtout le caractère entier, tenace et rancunier de chacun de ces deux peuples, on pourra se faire une idée des divisions qui les séparent, en les opposant l'un à l'autre.

par.11 Aussi les mariages sont-ils très rares même entre les catholiques des deux nationalités. Les Géorgiens catholique semblent même plus acharnés encore que les orthodoxes contre les Arméniens en général. La question du rite d'une part dont il sera parlé plus loin, les maladresses aussi de Mgr Der Abrahamian n'ont fait que les rendre plus aigues, en ces derniers temps. Ainsi que je l'ai dit dans mes précédents rapports, le clergé latin, lui-même par ses imprudences, son étroitesse de vues attise ses haines et les excite. Détail significatif: lors de mon arrivée à Tiflis, au début de Septembre, le clergé Arménien-Catholique fut systématiquement exclu, par les catholiques géorgiens, de la réception solennelle qui me fut faite à l'Eglise Géorgienne et du banquet qui la suivit, alors que les représentats du Catholicos orthodoxe avaient reçu une invitation et étaient présents. Il n'y a presqu'aucune relation entre les deux clergés catholiques. Je dois dire pour être juste que les Arméniens catholiques, pour ce qui les concerne, et en particulier le clergé, cherchent à atténuer ces contrastes, mais sans grand espoir de succès.

par.12 Des haines encore plus profondes divisent les Arméniens et les Tartares. Il y a d'abord la haine de race et de religion entre le musulman et le chrétien, entre l'oppresseur et l'opprimé. Ces haines sont encore excitées par la situation politique présente. J'ai indiqué plus haut la situation géographique des populations arméniennes, disséminées au milieu des tribus musulmanes. Entre les deux Républiques de Bakou et d'Erivan il n'y a pas de frontière ethnographique. Dans la majeure partie de la Province d'Erivan, les populations sont très mêlées et les Arméniens y sont trop souvent en minorité. C'est surtout vrai dans les districts orientaux. Les population tartares en appellent à leur frères de la République voisine et se soulèvent. Les Arméniens en font autant vers leurs frères. De là proviennent des conflits souvent sanglants où les infortunés arméniens ont souvent le dessous. Durant mon séjour des combats acharnés ont été livrés dans ces régions, où la République d'Azerbaidjan cherchait à s'implanter par la ruse et la violence. Toutes ces causes font que la paix est loin de régner dans ces contrées si éprouvées. Il faut reconnaître toutefois que l'Arménie ne fait que défendre ses droits en s'opposant à l'envahissemment toujour croissant de régions qui sont le berceau de sa race. Il faut aussi reconnaître à la Géorgie le mérite de n'être qu'un agent de paix entre les deux races rivales. Elle ne cesse en effet de s'interposer entre les Tartares et les Arméniens, pour les amener à des accords pacifiques et à une paix durable, qui permettront aux trois états de s'unir de nouveau, en une confédération assez puissant, pour se défendre contre leurs ennemis du dehors.

par. 13- [...] 4º *Situation juridique internationale des trois Etats du Caucase*. L'indépendance que se sont données les trois Républiques Transcaucasiennes n'a été que fort précaire jusques à ces derniers temps. La Conférence de la Paix de Paris s'est abstenue de la reconnaître. Ces dernier jours seulement, sous la pression des événements, elle a consenti à reconnaître une indépendance "de fait" à la Géorgie et à l'Azerbaidjan. Il en sera de même dit-on, de l'Arménie dans un delai assez court.

Je n'ai pas à rechercher ici les causes qui ont fait retarder jusques à ce jour cette reconnaissance tant désirée.

Je noterai simplement que ces retards irritent profondément ces populations, désireuses à juste titre, de ne pas retomber sous le joug moscovite. Aussi les trois gouvernements acceptent-ils avec faveur tout ce qui peut apparaître comme un acte de reconnaissance même indirecte. C'est ce sentiment joint à la conception très élevée qu'on se fait de l'autorité morale du Pontife Romain, qui a fait accueillir avec tant d'égards le Visiteur Apostolique envoyé en Transcaucasie. Bien que ma mission n'eut qu'un caractère essentiellement ecclésiastique, ma venue dans ces contrées a prouvé à tous que le Souverain Pontife les estimait et voulait la réalisation de leurs désirs.

par. 14 Le Gouvernement Géorgien et le Gouvernement Arménien ont un ardent désir de voir le Saint Père, leur accorder cette reconnaissance au moins "de facto", par la présence d'un Representant Pontifical permanent en Transcaucasie.

A Erivan, M. Khatissof, le chef du Gouvernement me l'a dit formellement, et avec insistance. Je lui ai fait observer que le nombre relativement restreint des Catholiques sur le territoire de la République Arménienne et l'etat rudimentaire de leur organisation, ne permettrait probablement pas d'instituer un Délégué spécial pour Erivan et y résidant en permanence; mais que le St Père ne ferait sans doute pas de difficulté d'envoyer un Prélat en Transcaucasie pour gouverner les Catholiques latins comme cela ce fait ailleurs, pour préparer l'organisation ecclésiastique et pour traiter avec les divers gouvernements locaux. L'envoyé pourrait avoir sa résidence à Tiflis à cause de l'importance et de la situation centrale de cette ville, avec une résidence secondaire dans Erivan où il pourrait venir aux moments voulus pour traiter les affaires. M. Khatissof a reconnu le bien fondé de ces remarques et a déclaré qu'il accepterait avec faveur, cette combinaison.

par. 15 Le Gouvernement Géorgien ne désire pas avec moins d'ardeur un acte analogue du St. Père en sa faveur. J'ai, dans mon rapport du 25 Septembre fait le récit de l'accueil si chaleureux que me fit le Gouvernement, à mon arrivée à Tiflis. On lui avait dit que je venais avec une Mission officielle. Même après que ce malentendu eut été dissipé, il ne changea rien à ses dispositions bienveillantes. Il comprit très bien que le St Père voulait étudier la situation avant de faire des actes. Durant mon séjour, par écrit (Voir la lettre du ministre des Affaires Etrangères de Géorgie) et de vive voix, le Gouvernement n'a cessé de me promettre le meilleur accueil au Représentat Pontifical qui viendrit à Tiflis.

par. 16 A mon départ de Tiflis, j'envoyai une lettre au President Jordania pour le remercier des attentions qu'on avait eues pour moi. A mon arrivée à Batoum, le Consul, M. Tchinidjef vint me prier de la part du Président d'intercéder auprès du St. Père pour qu'il fasse un acte en faveur de la reconnaissace de la Géorgie. Je lui répondit que les sentiments d'affection du Souverain Pontife envers la Géorgie et son désir formel de voir reconnue l'indépendance et les autres droits de toutes les nationalités étaint trop connus, pour douter de ses sentiments. J'ajoutai que les traditions du St-Siège étaient de ne pas devancer la décision des grandes puissances dans la reconnaissance officielle des nouveaux Etats et des nouveaux gouvernements, mais que préoccupé du bien des âmes, il n'hésitait pas à traiter avec eux les questions qui intéressent l'Eglise.Il consentirait probablement à envoyer un Prélat, en Géorgie, qui, tout en administrant les Catholiques, aurait mission de traiter les questions qui pourraient surgir avec le Gouvernrment. Sa présence et la

Mission dont il serait chargé ce Prélat, seraient comme un acte de reconnaissance "de fait" de l'indépendance du pays. M. Tchinidjef profondément touché me dit sa pleine satisfaction.

Dans l'exposé que je ferai plus loin des mesures à prendre, je soumettrai respectueusement ma manière de voir à Votre Eminence, sur l'utilité de repondre à ces désirs et sur les moyens d'y faire droit pour autant que la chose sera possible.

II - Situation Religieuse du Caucase

par.17 Dans cette second partie de mon Rapport je donnerai des indications précises et objectives 1º sur l'état religieux et moral des populations non catholiques et de leurs dispositions par rapport à l'Union; 2º Je ferai connaître l'état des Catholiques.

Pour plus de clarté je laisserai de côté ici tout ce qui a trait aux Arméniens soit catholiques soit grégoriens. L'examen de ce côté de la question compliquerait trop mon exposé. Le group arménien est trop important et trop particulier: il mérite d'être étudieé dans une relation subsidiaire qui fera l'objet d'un rapport spécial qui sera joint immédiatement à celui-ci.

[...]

[pp. 49–51]

par 77 De l'ensemble des données qui composent tout ce rapport, et de celles que j'ai consignées dans mes relations précédentes, appairaissent déjà quelles devront être les mesures d'ordre pratique qui devront être prises pour assurer les fruits de la Visite faite et procurer l'extension du royaume de N.S.

Pur obéir au désir exprimé formellement par Sa Sinteté et après avoir mûrement réfléchi devant Dieu, je vais, dans ce qui va suivre, faire l'exposé de ces mesures d'ordre pratique.

IV - Mesures d'ordre pratique à prendre.

par.78 Dans ma relation du 25 Novembre,[249] j'ai insisté plus spécialement sur la nécessité de faire voir d'une façon tangible l'organisation véritable de la Ste Eglise Catholique à ces orthodoxes du Caucase, qui ne l'ont vue jusques à ces jour que dans la présence de quelques prêtres plus ou moins abandonnés à eux-mêmes. Pour miex les attirer à nous, il faut autant que possible satisfaire leurs aspirations *dans ce qu'elles ont de juste* et éviter tout ce qui peut froisser une susceptibilité toujours en éveil entretenue en eux par leurs rivalités nationales. Il faut enfin dans la mesure du possible donner une organisation ecclésiastique convenable aux nombreux catholiques des divers rites qui habitent ces contrées.

par.79 1º A mon humble avis, il faut avant tout établir un *Représentant permanent* du Souverain Pontife dans ces régions et plus spécialement dans le

---

249 Not found, not even by Riccardi, unless Delpuch is referring instead to document nº 53, cit., of November 21st.

deux Républiques chrétiennes, quoique dissidentes, de Géorgie et d'Arménie. Il doit être investi d'une dignité et de pouvoirs suffisants pour s'imposer au respect et aux égards de tous. Dans les pays orthodoxes où le mariage du bas clergé est la règle générale, le caractère épiscopal est le seul considéré: le représentant du Souverain Pontife, doit, semble-t-il en être revêtu.

par.80 a) *Son titre officiel* pourra être momentanément celui de Visiteur Apostolique, tant que ces contrées n'auront pas reçu une organisation plus complète et moins rudimentaire. Je crois devoir noter toutefois que ce titre de Visiteur n'a pas là-bas un sens très précis. Le terme qui a toujours été employé par tous, pour désigner le Visiteur, était celui de "Délégué Apostolique" ou "Délégué du Pape".

par.81 b) *Le territoire* sur lequel devra s'étendre le pouvoir du Visiteur Apostolique semble devoir être non seulement la Transcaucasie que j'ai déjà décrite, mais toute l'ancienne Vice-Royauté du Caucase dont le Gouvernement Russe avait tracé les limites, en tenant compte du caractère similaire des population. Outre les provinces de la Transcaucasie, la Vice-Royauté comprenait, au Nord du Caucase les 4 gouvernorats du Kouban, de Stavropol, du Terek et du Daghestan. Ces provinces forment aujourd'hui les deux Républiques indépendantes du Kouban et du Daghestan dite encore "des Montagnards". Ces régions sont habitées en grande partie par des populations musulmanes et ne contiennent que peu de centres chrétiens comme Ekaterinondar, Novo-Rossik, Vladicaucase et Mosdog habitées, comme le sud du Caucase par des Polonais, des Géorgiens et des Arméniens avec des russes. Les Catholiques sont très éloignés de Saratov, le siège de l'Evêché; ils se rattachent plutôt à Tiflis dont ils ont toujours dépendu civilement.

A ces districts on pourrait joindre le Gouvernement de Crimée ou Symphéropol peuple des mêmes éléments avec de nombreux Arméniens catholics qui relèvent de Tiflis.

par.82 c) *La Résidence principale* doit être Tiflis à cause de l'importance de cette ville considérable et de sa situation centrale. Mais pour répondre au désir exprimé par le Gouvernement Arménie, le Représantant pontifical devra avoir une résidence secondaire dans la capitale de cette République et y séjourner de temps à autre, en attendant que cet Etat puisse recevoir un représentant spécial. La capitale actuelle est Erivan reliée à Tiflis par une ligne de chemin de fer. Dans les autres république musulmanes de la région, des relations suivies ne semblent pas nécessaires; grâce au prestige dont jouit le Souverain Pontife dans tous les Etats musulmans, les Gouvernements se montrent ordinairement très libéraux à l'égard des catholiques. Lorsque des nécessités obligeront à des relations, le Visiteur trouvera toujours auprès d'eux le meilleur accueil.

par.83 d) *Les facultés et les pouvoirs les plus amples* devront être concédées au Visiteur Apostolique afin qu'il puisse au plus tôt organiser ces régions et mettre à profit les éléments catholiques qu'elles renferment, tout en restant en relations étroites evec le Siège Apostolique.

par.84 2º *La séparation des territoires de l'ancienne Vice-Royauté russe du Caucase* (Transcaucasie et républiques du Nord du Caucase) *avec ceux de la Crimée*, de la juridiction eccésiastique de l'Evêque de Tiraspol et leur *érection en juridiction ecclesiastique indépendante* me semble une mesure indispensable qui doit être prise au plus tôt. Les populations catholiques qui les habitent sont trop abandonnées [...]

56

[n.d.] – Relation of Card. van Rossum on the Delpuch report – CO, 106, 2, 3, nº 3825

[...] [pp. 6–8 della relazione]

par.12 - Ciò premesso, il primo passo che sembrerebbe necessario di fare sarebbe l'invio di un *incaricato permanente* della Santa Sede (V. *Rapporto del P. Delpuch,* nº 79) che, munito delle qualità e dei poteri convenienti, possa nel Caucaso gettare le basi di una organizzazione ecclesiastica seria, disciplinata ed efficace, seguendo le direttive che si compiaceranno di stabilire gli E.mi Cardinali, secondo quanto qui subordinatamente si propone al Loro illuminato parere.

par.13 - In via ordinaria la Santa Sede per sopraintendere all'organizzazione ecclesiastica nei paesi orientali suole designare un Delegato Apostolico con territorio e competenze determinate. Anche per il Caucaso l'istituzione di una nuova Delegazione Apostolica potrà in massima riconoscersi come un provvedimento efficace ed opportuno, se non necessario, tanto più che le nuove Repubbliche lo considererebbero quale un ambito atto di benevolenza e di riconoscimento della loro esistenza da parte della S. Sede (V. *Rapporto del P. Delpuch,* nn. 13,14, 15, 16).

Vi sono però alcune considerazioni che, pur salvando la massima di istituire fin da ora un incaricato permanente della S. Sede nel Caucaso, potrebbero consigliare *per ora* non l'invio di un Delegato Apostolico, bensì il ritorno di un Visitatore Apostolico, come un espediente per stabilire nel Caucaso le prime basi dell'organizzazione dell'apostolato cattolico e predisporvi l'istituzione di una Delegazione Apostolica non appena la situazione religiosa e politica del paese sarà meglio determinata.

par.14 - Dal punto di vista religioso, infatti, è da considerare che nel Caucaso vi è da dare un assetto diverso e migliore del presente tanto agli affari religiosi dei cattolici armeni quanto a quelli dei georgiani, come si esporrà anche in altra ponenza, e in questo assetto vi saranno dei problemi da risolvere non scevri di difficoltà e per i quali l'incaricato della S. Sede dovrà esercitare per qualche tempo dei poteri straordinarî e discrezionali, che non sono di competenza ordinaria dei Delegati Apostolici. Si proporrebbe perciò per il momento l'invio di un Visitatore Apostolico; che, se mai, o per mancanza di tatto o per la natura stessa di certi problemi scottanti venisse ad urtare troppo l'ambiente del popolo orientale georgiano e armeno, così propensi agli eccessi, sarebbe certamente più facile alla Santa Sede il ritirare un tal Visitatore rappresentante un Ufficio transitorio, anziché il Delegato Apostolico che importa il carattere di un ufficio stabile.

par.15 - Dal punto di vista politico poi è da considerare come non sarebbe ancora possibile determinare nel Caucaso i confini ecclesiastici di una Delegazione Apostolica (subordinati in genere a quelli politici di uno o più stati), dal momento che ancora la Conferenza non ha determinati i confini precisi delle tre Repubbliche della Georgia, dell'Azerbeidjan e dell'Armenia, né le circostanze ancora sanno indicare se a tutte e tre queste repubbliche converrà dare lo stesso Delegato Apostolico o se converrà proporre altre combinazioni territoriali con le Delegazioni Apostoliche limitrofe.

par.16 - Del resto anche lo stesso P. Delpuch, mentre propone l'invio di un incaricato della S. Sede con residenza a Tiflis (V. *Rapporto* n. 79) è di parere che esso abbia il titolo transitorio di Visitatore Apostolico, fino a che quelle regioni non avranno ricevuta una organizzazione più completa e più regolare (V. *Rapporto* n° 80).

par.17 - Dato pertanto che gli E.mi Padri abbiano a decidere di inviare nuovamente e subito nel Caucaso un Rappresentante permanente della Santa Sede con il titolo provvisorio di Visitatore Apostolico, converrà anzitutto determinare in particolare modo a quali territorî dovrà estendersi almeno provvisoriamente la sua missione. Il P. Delpuch proporrebbe che al Visitatore Apostolico fosse per ora affidata tutta la regione compresa nell'antico Vicereame russo del Caucaso (V. *Rapporto* dal n. 1 al n. 5 e nn. 81, 83), tenendo conto del carattere affine delle popolazioni, e aggiungervi di più la provincia di Crimea.

par.18 - Tale proposta può risultare opportuna almeno per il momento, in attesa che sia possibile inviare nella Russia del nord un altro Visitatore, oltre quello inviato ora dalla S. Congregazione per l'Ucraina, per conoscere e provvedere intanto ai bisogni dei cristiani posti a nord e in prossimità della catena del Caucaso tra i quali si sa che vi sono notevoli nuclei di cattolici di diverso rito privi di ogni assistenza, senza contare altri cristiani ed infedeli. Avere presto delle informazioni precise sulla situazione religiosa di quelle regioni sarà certamente molto utile alla S. Sede e per questo si potrebbe dare al Visitatore Apostolico del Caucaso, oltre l'incarico di visitarle, anche quello di provvedere provvisoriamente con giurisdizione di Ordinario a quanto urge per l'assistenza religiosa dei cattolici ivi dimoranti, considerato che il loro Vescovo, Monsignor Kessler, da oltre un anno non si sa dove si trovi rifugiato, cercato a morte dai bolscevichi.

Anche per la Crimea si potrebbe dare al Visitatore Apostolico, se si crede, l'incarico provvisorio di riferire sulla situazione religiosa locale e di provvedere ai bisogni più urgenti dei cattolici.

[Translation]

[…] [pp. 6–8 of the report]

para. 12 - That stated, the first step that it would seem necessary to take would be to send a *permanent envoy* of the Holy See (v. *Report of F. Delpuch*, n° 79), equipped with suitable qualities and powers, who can lay the foundation for a serious, disciplined and effective ecclesiastical organization in the Caucasus, following the directives that the Most Emin. Cardinals shall please themselves to establish, according to that which is here humbly proposed to their illuminated opinion.

para. 13 – Normally, the Holy See, in supervising the ecclesiastical organization in the eastern countries, is used to designating an Apostolic Delegate with a determined territory and responsibilities. As regards the Caucasus as well, the institution of a new Apostolic Delegation could be recognized on the whole as an effective and opportune, if not necessary, measure, all the more so since the new Republics would consider it a desirable act of benevolence and of recognition of their existence on the part of the Holy See (v. *Report of F. Delpuch*, nn. 13, 14, 15, 16).

There are, however, some considerations that, while still maintaining the principle of immediately appointing a permanent envoy of the Holy See to the Caucasus, might suggest *for now* not the dispatch of an Apostolic Delegate but rather the return of a Visitor Apostolic, as an expedient for establishing the initial foundations of the organization of the Catholic apostolate in the Caucasus and the establishment of the institution of an Apostolic Delegation there just as soon as the religious and political situation of the country is better determined.

para. 14 – From the religious point of view, in fact, it should be considered that in the Caucasus there needs to be given a different and better structure than there is currently, as much in regard to the religious affairs of the Armenian Catholics as to those of the Georgian, as will be expounded upon in a separate proposal; in this arrangement there will be problems of no small difficulty to resolve, for which the envoy of the Holy See will have to occasionally exercise extraordinary and discretionary powers that are beyond the ordinary scope of Apostolic Delegates. Therefore, for the moment, it would be proposed to send an Visitor Apostolic; if ever, whether for lack of tact or whether due to the very nature of certain hot issues, he were to come to be too much at odds with the environment of the eastern Georgian and Armenian people, so prone to excesses, it would certainly be easier for the Holy See to recall such a Visitor, representing a transitory Office, rather than an Apostolic Delegate who conveys the character of a permanent office.

para. 15 – From a political point of view, it should be considered that in the Caucasus it would not yet be possible to determine the ecclesiastical boundaries of an Apostolic Delegation (in general subordinate to the political [boundaries] of one or more states), since the Conference still has not determined the precise borders of the three Republics of Georgia, Azerbaijan and Armenia, nor are the circumstances yet able to indicate whether it will be suitable to give the same Apostolic Delegate to all three of these republics, or whether it will be more advantageous to propose other territorial combinations with the surrounding Apostolic Delegations.

para. 16 – For that matter, even F. Delpuch, while he proposed dispatching an envoy of the Holy See with headquarters in Tiflis (v. *Report* n° 79), is of the opinion that he have the transitory title of Visitor Apostolic, until these regions have gotten a more complete and more regular organization (v. *Report* n° 80).

para. 17 – Given, therefore, that the Most Emin. Fathers have to decide whether to send a permanent Representative of the Holy See with the provisory title of Visitor Apostolic once again, quickly, to the Caucasus, first of all it would be best to determine to which territories in particular his mission should extend itself, at least provisionally. F. Delpuch would propose that the Visitor Apostolic be, for now, entrusted with all the area included in the old Russian Viceroyalty of the Caucasus (v. *Report* from n° 1 to n° 5 and nn. 81, 83), keeping in mind the similar character of the populations, and adding to that the province of the Crimea.

para. 18 – Such a proposal could turn out to be appropriate at least for the meantime, while waiting for the possibility of sending another Visitor to northern Russia, besides the one sent now from the S. Congregation for the Ukraine, to learn of and at the same time provide for the needs of the Christians situated north of and in proximity to the Caucasus range, in which there are known to be considerable groups of Catholics of different rites deprived of all assistance, not counting other Christians and infidels. Having some precise information soon on the religious situation of those regions will certainly be very useful to the Holy See, and for this reason the Visitor Apostolic of the Caucasus, beyond the task of visiting them, could be given also that of providing provisionally with jurisdiction of Ordinary for whatever is urgently needed for the religious assistance of the Catholics living there, considering that for over a year it's been unknown where their Bishop, Monsignor Kessler, has taken refuge, as his life is sought by the Bolsheviks.[250]

Even in the Crimea, the Visitor Apostolic could be given, optionally, the temporary duty of reporting on the local religious situation and of providing for the Catholics' most urgent needs.

---

[250] He had taken refuge first in Odessa and then in Romania, from which he managed to send news of himself. Morozzo della Rocca, *op. cit.*, pp. 190–191.

57

13 January 1920, Constantinople – Dolci to Marini – CO, 106, 2, 3, n° 3172

Eminentissimo principe,

Il Visitatore Apostolico del Caucaso Rev. P. Delpuch in data del 12 Nov. p.p. mi scrive da Tiflis:

[Translation]

Most Eminent Prince,

The Visitor Apostolic of the Caucasus Rev. F. Delpuch writes me from Tiflis dated Nov. 12th last:

> Je suis harassé de fatigue. Demain je part pour Bakou, fin de visiter les catholiques de cette ville.
>
> Je suis toujour ici dans les meilleurs termes avec le gouvernement Georgian. Selon le sage conseil que m'avait donné V. Excellence, avant mon départ de Constantinople, je me suis toujour tenu avec lui, sans rien sacrifier sur les principes. J'ai aussi les meilleurs relations avec la haute societé et j'y ai fait des connaissances précieuses qui seront utiles en son temps.
>
> En Arménie, j'ai eu le même accueil qu'en Géorgie. Le Président M. Khatisoff est un homme excellent qui m'a donné les assurances le plus formelles pour la liberté de l'eglise et pour l'Apostolat catholique.
>
> La situation de ce malheureux pays est lamentable. 30000 orphelins sont privés de tout secours. Le nombre des réfugies prives de tout abri est aussi très grand et l'hiver arrive.
>
> Les orphelinats américains donnent le couvert et des vivres à 30000 autres enfants. Mais la situation morale de ces infortunés est lamentable. Il n'y a aucune vie religieuse parmi eux. Le sectarisme protestant fait gage, sauf à Erivan où le Catholicos a protesté énergiquement.
>
> Les enfants des deux sexes âgés souvent de 15 et 16 ans, vivent dans la promiscuité la plus grande. Les dortoirs eux-mêmes sont communs dans beaucoup d'endroits. Votre Excellence peut juger des suites de cette promiscuité.
>
> On s'étonne partout de ne voir que l'Amérique et les Américains au Caucase: on se demande ce que fait la charité catholique. Elle ne peut être partout helas, mais il pourrait cependant quel chose à faire. Le Souverain Pontife est vénéré et aimé partout. Partout j'ai reçu les marques du plus grand respect. Jusque dans les villages Grégorians, le clergé, les écoles et la population sont venus à ma rencontre avec les ornements sacrés. Dans les villages catholiques la population était au comble de la joie. Des escortes de cavaliers venaient à ma rencontre. Dans les villages catholiques j'etais accueilli par des vivas, des cris, des

hourras poussés par l'honneur du Souverain Pontife et de son envoyé.

Un champ immense s'ouvre à l'Apostolat. Tout le monde attend qu'on fasse quelque chose. Si la visite devait rester stérile les conséquences seraient desastreuses. Les dissidents eux-mêmes insistent.

J'ai vu notamment l'ancien sous-secrétaire pour les Affaires du Caucase à Pétrograd[251] qui promet tout son appui et demande qu'on aille de l'avant sans se laisser arrêter par le péril russe. La Russie même si elle revient ne saurait être la Russie d'autrefois.

J'ai pu recueillir des enseignements précieux sur la Perse et les difficultés surgies entre la Mission et les Chaldéens. J'en entretiendrai V. Excellence à mon passage à Consple à la fin de ce mois.

Chinato al bacio della S. Porpora ecc...
[Bowed to the kiss of the Holy Purple etc. ...]

58

15 January 1920, Rome – handwritten draft from Gasparri to the Armenian president Khatissian – AAEESS, *Asia* 126, n° 3643

Monsieur le Ministre,

Le Saint Père a accueilli avec une vive satisfaction les sentiments que Votre Gouvernement a bien voulu exprimer à Son égard lors de la mission confié au R.P. Delpuch et Il a été profondément touché de la réception cordiale qui lui a été faite aussi bien de la part des autorités que des populations arméniennes.

Ayant toujours suivi avec le plus paternel intérêt les douloureuses vicissitudes de la noble et généreuse nation Arménienne et ayant donné de nombreux et éclatants témoignages de Sa constante sollicitude en faveur de Son indépendance, Sa Sainteté aime à espérer que Votre Gouvernement voudra bien assurer à l'Eglise Catholique dans Votre pays toute la liberté qui est conforme à sa divine institution et qui lui permette de déplayer sa bienfaisante activité au profit des particuliers et de l'Etat.

Aussi est ce avec une effusion de coeur tout particulière que le Souverain Pontife, en joignant ses prières a celles des Arméniens catholiques implore des bénédictions celestes sur leur noble et chère patrie et forme des voeut ardents pour sa prospérité morale et matérielle.

En joignant mes sentiments personnels à ces voeut du Saint Père, je prie Votre Excellence de vouloir bien agréer l'assurance de ma plus haute considération

---

[251] Gregorio Evangouloff, Undersecretary for the Caucasus of the tzarist government, was Commissioner of Education in the communist government in 1922; v. doc. n° 82 and doc. n° 119.

59

20 January 1920, Constantinople – encr. telegr. from Cesarano to Gasparri – AAEESS, *Asia* 57, 2, n° 1066

Patriarca Armeno Gregoriano ha deciso di recarsi a Parigi per favorire causa armena ed ha pure invitato Luogotenente Sayeghian ad andarvi oppure inviare vescovo patriarcato armeno cattolico rappresentante. Al Luogotenente sembra che proposta gioverebbe interessi cattolici e prestigio patriarcato. Se Santa Sede trova proposta accettabile, si implora autorizzazione per partire con risposta telegrafica

[Translation]
Armenian Gregorian Patriarch has decided to go to Paris to promote Armenian cause and has even invited Lieutenant[252] Sayeghian to go otherwise send bishop representative Armenian Catholic patriarchate. To the Lieutenant seems proposal would be good for Catholic interests and prestige patriarchate. If Holy See finds proposal acceptable, authorization to leave begged with telegraphic reply

60

28 January 1920, Rome – Gasparri to Cesarano – AAEESS, *Asia* 57, 2, n° 1066

In risposta suo cifrato N. 83 le significo che Santo Padre permette a Monsignor Giovanni Naslian di fare parte missione armena Parigi, quale rappresentante patriarcato armeno cattolico. Se detto Prelato è già in viaggio per Roma si recherà poi a Parigi di qui

[Translation]
In reply your encryption N. 83 I inform you that Holy Father permits Monsignor Giovanni Naslian[253] to take part Armenian mission Paris, as representative Armenian Catholic patriarchate. If said Prelate is already en route to Rome he will then go to Paris from here

---

252 *Locum Tenens* (i.e., Vicar of the Patriarch of Constantinople).
253 Bishop of Trabizon.

61

29 February 1920 – article in *La Croix* about Delpuch's trip – CO, 106, 2, 3, n° [?]

Le Saint-Siège
et les
Républiques Transcaucasiennes
L'accueil qu'elles ont fait au T.R.P.Delpuch
visiteur apostolique[...]

Les 25,26 et 27 de ce mois de février, s'est tenu à Genève le "Congrès des oeuvres de secours aux enfants des pays éprouvés par la guerre"

Il était organisé par l'Union internationale de secours aux enfants, qui se proposait d'y "dresser en quelque sorte le bilan des ravages exercés par la guerre dans les générations les plus jeunes" et aussi d'y "fixer les grandes ligne de l'action international de secours". Ce sont les termes mêmes du Bulletin de l'Union, "Sauvez les enfant", qui se publie à Genève.[...] Commissions dont les travaux ont commencé le Congrès[...] par ordre alphabetique: Allemagne, Arménie, Autriche, Etats de la Baltique (Esthonie, Lituanie, Russie du Nord), Belgique, France, Hongrie, Italie, Pologne, Roumanie, Russie du Sud (Crimée, Ukraine).

On sait la part décisive qu'a eue dans la fondation de cette Union international, la généreuse intervention du Souverain Pontife, qui a ouvert la souscription par un don de 100.000 lires. Nous avons dit aussi les hommages significatifs qu'ont rendus à l'auguste charité du Pape les dirigeants de l'Union dans leur assemblée constitutive des 6, 7 et 8 janvier dernier, dont le représentant pontifical, Mgr Maglione, a présidé la première séance. Les sommes envoyées directement au Saint-Père pour cette grande croisade de charité, dépassent actuellement 4 million de lires.

Au Congres [...]participera, outre Mgr Maglione, représentant du Saint-Siège, le T.R.P. Delpuch, des Pères Blancs, visiteur apostolique de la Géorgie, de l'Arménie et du reste du Caucase.

Nos lecteurs aimeront à trouver ici, à cette occasion, d'interessants détails sur l'accueil fait au R.P. Delpuch par le gouvernement de la Géorgie, de l'Arménie et de l'Azerbeidjan.

[...] Il y a la un group intéressant de catholiques: 25 000 en Gèorgie et 40 000 en Arménie. Le souvenir des oevres catholiques, specialement des écoles, y est toujours vivant: c'est en 1845 que le tsar Nicolas I expulsa de Géorgie nos missionnaires - des Frères Mineur Capucins - contre le voeu des populations et cette mesure brutale d'intolerance religieuse est restée liée, dans la memoire des Transcaucasiens, à tout le reste du régime qui s'appliqua à étouffer leurs liberés civiles. Musulmans de l'Azerbeidjan, Arméniens grégoriens (ceux-ci depuis les dernières grandes épreuves où leur nation fallit sombrer tout entière dans le sang), orthodoxes géorgiens surtout, y manifestent à l'Eglise catholique la même courtoise sympathie.Lorsque, voici deux ans, eut lieu l'élection du nouveau patriarche ou "catholicos"géorgien, celui-ci, en une lettre d'une belle inspiration chretienne, fit part à S.S. Benoit XV de sa nomination: il ne put l'expedier lui-même, ayant été emporté, peu de jours après, par une mort inopinée, mais les évêques georgiens qui l'avaient élu tinrent à faire parvenir au Souverain Pontife ce document qui devenait comme une sort de testament: ils ajoutèrent que les sentiments du défunt "catholicos" étaient les leurs à eux aussi

[...] l'arrivée de l'envoyé pontifical en Transcaucasie a occasionné des manifestations fort impressionnantes de le part des autorités politiques en Géorgie, en Arménie et dans l'Azerbeidjan.

[...] Même acceuil à Erivan, vers le milieu d'octobre. Là, les réceptions eurent moins d'eclat comme il convenait dans la capitale d'une nation qui était, tout entière, en deuil de millions de ses fils. La situation économique de l'Arménie était d'allieurs affreuse. Des multitudes de réfugiés, rescapés des massacres, campaent dans les rues et autour de la ville. Dans la ville même, 13 à 14 000 orphelins avaient cherché un refuge. La moitié d'entres eux avaient trouvé des abris de fortune. Les autres errant sans gite. Il n'avait été possible de pourvoir suffisamment à la subsistance ni des uns ni des autres. Détail navrant: l'hiver derniers, tous les matins, des chariots passaient dans les rues pour recueillir les corps des enfant, morts d'inanition et de froid durant la nuit.

L'attitude des autorités arméniennes n'en fut pas moins significative. Le sous-secrétaire d'Etat aux Affaires étrangères attendait, à la gare, l'envoyé pontifical que le président du Conseil s'empressa de recevoir officiellement. Le "catholicos" (patriarche) arménien qui se trouvait dans la capitale reçut, lui aussi, le T.R.P. Delpuch avec les plus grands égards, et le chargea de dire sa reconnaissance à S.S.Benoit XV pour le bien que le Pontife avait fait aux Arméniens. Le visiteur apostolique s'entendit exprimer les même sentiments, quelques jours après, par les évêques arméniens réunis en synode à Etzmiadzin (à 18 chilomètres d'Erivan), et le "catholicos" s'y plut à lui faire visiter l'antique monastère qui est sa résidence habituelle, et qui date du V siècle[...]

[...] Il n'y eut pas que ces égards extérieurs. Des sentiments furent exprimés qui sont plus éloquents encore. A Erivan le gouvernement arménien promit la plus grande liberté aux oevres catholiques. Et le Président de la République (comme l'avait fait aussi , on l'a vu, le "catholicos" grégorien) avait tenu à redire à l'envoyé pontifical la reconnaissance de tout son peuple et de toute sa race envers S.S. Benoit XV, connaissait le texte de la lettre très forte que le Pape avait envoyée au sultan pour conjurer celui-ci d'imposer un terme aux massacres des Arméniens. *Cette lettre*, déclara-t-il, *nous a été au coeur.*

[...]

62

6 March 1920, Rome – Papadopulos to Mons. Cerretti[254]– AAEESS, *Asia* 126, n° 3643

Il sottoscritto Assessore della Sacra Congregazione per la Chiesa Orientale, avendone già fatta parola con il S. Padre nell'ultima Udienza, sottopone alla decisione di cotesta S. Cong.ne per gli Affari Ecclesiastici Straordinari le tre note qui compiegate con i relativi allegati, con le quali si è creduto opportuno proporre l'invio di una lettera distinta di felicitazioni e di voti da parte della S. Sede alle tre nuove repubbliche Georgiana, Armena e Tartara, che ebbero recentemente il riconoscimento, sebbene non definitivo, dalla Conferenza

Intanto lo scrivente Assessore profitta ben volentieri dell'occasione per rinnovarLe ecc.

[Translation]

The undersigned Assessor of the Sacred Congregation for the Oriental Church, having already spoken of the matter with the Holy Father in the latest Audience, submits to the decision of the S. Cong.n for Extraordinary Ecclesiastical Affairs the three notes here enclosed with their relative attachments, with which it was believed opportune to propose the sending of a letter of congratulations and of best wishes on the part of the Holy See to each of the three new Georgian, Armenian and Tartar republics, who recently received recognition, even if not definitive, by the Conference

In the meantime, the undersigned Assessor gladly profits from this occasion in order to renew to you etc.

63

12 March 1920, Paris – Naslian to French Catholic public opinion[255] – AAEESS, *Asia* 57, 2, n° [?]

Appel à la France Catholique.

En ce moment suprême où la Conférence de la Paix décidera du sort de la Turquie, la mission Patriarcale Nazionale Armenienne est venue à Paris pour faire entendre son dernier cri de détresse et d'engoisse et attirer la compassion du monde chrétien sur une Nation qui gît encore sous l'oppression de la tyrannie musulmane.

Tous les arméniens catholiques et non-catholiques sans distinction ayant souffert ensemble de terribles persécutions et subi d'atroces massacres, autorisés par le gouvernement ottoman, organisés par les jeunes turcs et

---

254 Secretary of the Sacred Congregation for Extraordinary Ecclesiastical Affairs.
255 Published by Naslian, *op cit.*, vol. II, pp. 539–542.

exécutés par les musulmans, avec un raffinement de cruauté rebutant, se trouvent en commun accord d'être délivrés du joug islsmique.

Le Patriarcat Arménien-Catholique, que le soussigné Evêque présente en sa qualité de Délégué, sûr de trouver en France l'appui moral dont il a grandement besoin pour obtenir le salut de son peuple, s'adresse avec pleine confiance à la haute autorité de l'Episcopat Français et aux nobles sentiments de la France catholique, sa protectrice séculaire, pour qu'ils portent leur concours efficace à la cause arménienne. Le sang d'un peuple infortuné crie justice et pitié. De centaines de milliers des martyrs se sont vaillamment offert à la mort pour conserver intacte jusqu'au bout leur Foi de chrétiens. C'est au nom de ce sang abondamment répandu que nous venons faire appel aux plus nobles sentiments de charité chrétienne qui élèvent l'homme au dessus de lui - même. Quelle qu'elle soit la valeur que les intérêts politiques donnent parfois aux raisons sentimentales on ne saurait nier le prix du sang. Voir une Nation, qui veut vivre, lutter sans cesse en prise avec la mort et ne pas compatir à sa douleur, à sa misère, c'est renier tout sentiment humain. Pareil à ces épaves qui, poussées par la furie des flots, viennent jusqu'au rivage pour annoncer une catastrophe arrivée quelque part sur mer, nous les survivants à un désastre inouï, nous venons faire entendre qu'une nation presqu'entière a sombré dans les flots de son propre sang. Dix évêques arméniens catholiques, centvingt prêtres et centmille arméniens-catholiques; trentesept évêques arménien-grégoriens, sept cents prêtres et septcent cinquante mille arméniens-grégoriens furent impitoyablement égorgés en haine de religion; deux cent mille orphelins restent sans abri à la charge d'une nation, elle même dépouillée, appauvrie, réduite à l'extrême misère. Les squelettes et les cadavres de centaines de milliers des chrétiens jonchent le désert de la Mésopotamie et de l'Arabie où les avait poussés la haine phanatique de l'Islam. Telles furent les terribles conséquences du "Djihad" (guerre religieuse) que les turcs avaient déclarée contre les chrétiens, ayant pour visée d'exterminer un peuple qui n'a jamais voulu se rendre au intimidations de changer sa foi contre la religion de Mahomet. Alors que la France était en prise avec ses ennemis et que son territoire était livré à toutes les horreurs de l'invasion, le moment paru propice aux turcs pour assouvir leur haine contre le christianisme, et l'ont fait ; et ils le feront toutes les fois que l'occasion se présentera, ainsi que les Délégués turcs à la Conférence de la Paix l'ont fait entendre en montrant le sceptre hideux du fanatisme musulman pour influer sur les décisiones du Conseil Suprême; les récents massacres de la Cilicie prouvent leur instinct sanguinaire.

Nous sommes sûrs de la sympatie que la France a toujours eu pour l'Arménie, comme l'a si noblement déclaré Mr. le Président Poincaré dans une de ses lettres adressées aux Patriarche des Arm-Catholiques:" L'Arménie n'a jamais douté de la France, comme la France n'a jamais douté de l'Arménie";[256] et il ajouté:"Après avoir supporté ensemble les mêmes souffrances pour le triomphe du Droit et de la justice, les deux Pays peuvent aujourd'hui communier dans la même allegresse et la même fierté". Ah que nous serions heureux d'être en état de sentir cette allegresse qui paraît encore bien loin de nous! Tandis que d'autres Nations se réjouissent de leur délivrance, l'Arménie se noie encore dans son propre sang. Après les amères déceptions qui ont suivi les différents massacres, tant de fois répétés, ne serait-il pas lamentables notre sort si nous retournions de nouveau aux conditions insupportables du passé? Notre meilleur espoir repose sur la France; elle peut nous sauver, si Elle le veut. Combien sont réconfortantes pour nous les déclarations faites au nom de la France par le même Président de la République dans sa lettre susmentionnée: "Il sait le concours que l'Arménie et plus particulièrement le noble Pays de la Cilicie attendent de lui pour jouir en sécurité des bienfaits de la Paix et de la Liberté et je puis assurer Votre Béatitude que la France répondra à la confiance que lui a témoignée à cet égard".

Nous ne demandons que de voir au plus tôt réalisées ces promesse si consolantes et si douces. Nous ne sommes pas trop exigents dans notre revandications; nous ne demandons que le droit qu'a tout homme de vivre. Sur les ruines encore fumantes se dressera, avec le concours de la France, une Arménie toute jeune, pleine de forces et de vitalité, pour reprendre la place digne qu'elle a toujaours occupée, d'être l'avant garde du christianisme en Orient et que lui réservent ses qualités intellectuelles et morales.

Nous ne demandons que notre patrimoine usurpé, mille fois scellé par le sang de nos aieux, de nos pères, de nos frères et de nos fils, que de voir notre foyer qui seul pourra garantir la sécurité de notre vie, de notre honneur et de notre bien; et les service que nous rendrons au Regne du Christ et à l'humanité dans ces pays arriérés soit compté comme un faible tribut de notre vive reconnaissance et de profonde gratitude envers ceux qui auront défendu notre cause, et nous serons particulièrement redevables au Vénéré Episcopat Français et à la France Catholique qui a toute l'Autorité voulue pour obtenir de la Conférance de la Paix la délivrance définitive d'un peuple martyr.

Nos revandications déjà présentée à la Conférance de la Paix se résument ainsi:

I. Délivrance définitive de la Nation Arménienne du joug musulman, en lui reconnaissant une indépandance et en la constituant en état libre.

II. Récupération des territoires historiques de l'Arménie dans les limites aussi larges que possible.a) avec un débouché sur mer, indispensable pour sa vie économique. b) Frontières limitrophes à la zone d'occupation française, ce qui nous garantirait la sécurité et nous préserverait de toute attaque éventuelle.

III. Retour à leur religion chrétienne des arméniens convertis de force à l'Islamisme.

---

256 Letter from Poincaré to Terzian of February 16th, 1919, in Naslian, *op. cit.*, vol. II, p. 946.

IV. Délivrance de nos orphelins, de nos filles et de nos mères retenus encore par les musulmans.

V. Moyens pour faciliter le rapatriement des épaves de la Nation Arménienne dispersées dans l'Asie mineure, la Mésopotamie, la Syrie, l'Arabie et ailleurs.

VI. Désarmement des turcs et mesures éfficaces pour assurer la vie des chrétiens arméniens se trouvant en Arménie et hors des territoires qui formeraient l'Arménie.

VII. Restitution des biens usurpés et retenus par les turcs. 1º. Restitution aux propriétaires survivans des biens qui leur reviennent de droit. 2º Restitution aux autorité religieuses respectives de tous les biens tombés en déshérence.

VIII. Indemnité à accorder à chaque propriétaire et communauté laisser pour réparer les pertes et les dommages de toute nature occasionnés pendant la guerre.

La lettre ci-incluse,[257] conforme à l'original, adressée par son Eminence le Cardinal Secrétaire d'Etat de Sa Sainteté, à Son Eminence le Cardinal Amette Archevêque de Paris, prouve la Paternelle sollicitude de Notre S.P. le Pape pour la Nation Arménienne.

Dans le ferme espoir que notre présent appel adressé à l'Episcopat français trouverait auprès de Votre.............le bienveillant accueil qu'il mérite, m nous la prions afin qu'elle daigne nous donner son adhesion de la manière qu'elle le jugera à propos, en nous prêtant ainsi son efficace appui auprès de la Conférence de la Paix.

Le Délégué du Patriarcat Arménien Catholique

+ Jean Nazlian Evêque de Trébizonde

64

13 March 1920, Paris – Naslian to the French foreign minister – AAEESS, *Asia* 57, 2, nº [?]

Après l'Audience que Son Excellence Mr. le président du Conseil et Ministre des Affaires Etrangères de France a daigné lui accorder, le soussigné Représentant du Patriarcat Arménien-Catholique auprèes de la Délégation Nationale Arménienne, se permet de lui exposer par cette note le but de sa mission.

Le but commun de la Mission Patriarcale nationale Arménienne, formée des trois fractions de la Nation, est d'agir, de concert avec la Délégation nationale Arménienne auprès de la Conférence de la Paix pour faire valoir ses revendications et défendre ses intérêts qui peuvent être résumé ainsi.

---

257 Not found.

Revendications communes.

I. Délivrance définitive de la Nation Arménienne du joug musulman, en lui reconnaissant une indépendance et en la constituant en Etat libre.

II. Récuperation des territoires historiques de l'Arménie dans des limites aussi larges que possible. 1º . Avec un débauché sur mer, indispensable pour sa vie economique; 2º . Frontières limitrophes de la zone d'occupation française ce qui nous garantirait la sécurité et nous préserverait de toute attaque éventuelle.

III. Moyens pour faciliter le repatriement des épaves de la Nation Arménienne dispersées dans l'Asie Mineure, la Mésopotamie, la Syrie et ailleurs.

IV. Délivrance de nos orphelins, de nos filles, et de nos mères retenus encore par les musulmans.

V. Désarmement des Turcs et mesures pour assurer la vie des Arméniens se trouvant hors des territoires qui formeraient l'Arménie

VI. Restitution des biens usurpés et retenus par les turcs: 1º Restitution au propriétaires survivants des biens qui leur reviennent de droit. 2º Restitution de tous les biens "Mahlul" (en déshérence).

VII Indemnité à accorder à chaque propriétaire et Communauté lésés de toutes les pertes et dommages occasionnés pendant la guerre.

Revendications et désirs particuliers

Le but spécial de la Délégation du Patriarcat Arménien-Catholique est de coordonner ses intérêts nationaux à ceux de la France dont il veut faire valoir la bienfaisante influence en Armenie.

Aussi le soussigné implore l'assistance et le patronat du Gouvernement Français dans ses réclamations à la Turquie et dans sa réorganisation des Etablissements et Instituts du Patriarcat en Arménie, en Cilicie et partout ailleurs.

Le Patriarcat Arm-Catholique désire:

I. Que la France continue à garder son Protectorat séculaire sur les Arméniens-Catholiques, comme en ce moment l'Angleterre voudrait l'avoir pour le non-catholiques.

II. Que les Etablissements scolaires et même Universitaires, à l'instar de l'Université de Beyrouth soient fondés en Arménie, comme se propose de le faire le Gouvernement des Etats Unis d'Amérique.

III. Que des bourses soient accordées en France pour la jeunesse arménienne de deux sexes, qui voudrait parfaire ses études et se former dans la culture française sur la base d'un programme dont les détails seront plus tard arrêtés par le Patriarcat.

IV. Que la France aide le Patriarcat à relever ses ruines à restaurer son organisation dissoute pendant la guerre.

V. Que le Gouvernement Français aie la bienveillance de prendre la charge d'assurer aux arméniens catholiques la récuperation des biens privés et publiques ainsi que la part des indemnités qui leur sont dûes par la Turquie, surtout dans les provinces qui ne feront pas partie de l'Arménie.

Le Patriarcat Arm-Catholique a à reconstituer douze diocèses entièrement dévastés au cours des atroces événements de 1915-1916, pendant lesquels sont tombés victimes d'une barbarie incalifiable [sic]

dix évêques catholiques arméniens, cent quarante prêtres, un grand nombre de religieuses et plus de cent mille de nos fidèles catholiques.

Les pertes totales de la Nation Arménienne comprennent cinquante évêques, et vicaires Patriarcaux, huit cent prêtres et une population d'à peu près un million.

Les cent mille orphelins de la bas âge abrités actuellement par la Nation et les cent autre mille gradés encore par les musulmans, sans compter ceux qui ont déjà peri, peuvent servir de mesure pour évaluer le nombre incroyable des victimes de la Nation Arménienne.

Le Délégué prie instamment S.Exc. M. le Ministre des Affaires Etrangères de France d'intéresser le Gouvernement de la République afin qu'il veuille soutenir auprès du Conseil Suprême la première partie de la présente note et en accueillir favorablement la deuxième que le soussigné est prêt à détailler et à préciser davantage, si Son Excellence juge à propos.

65

3 April 1920, London – Aharonian to Gasparri – AAEESS, *Asia* 57, 2, n° 4764

Eminence,

J'ai l'honneur, comme Président de la Délégation de la République Arménienne auprès de la Conférence de la Paix, de présenter a Votre Eminence Révérendissime deux exemplaires de l'Atlas historique de l'Arménie que je désire offrir par la gracieuse entremise de votre Eminence l'un à la Bibliotheque du Vatican et l'autre à l'Institut Oriental.

Il s'agit d'un document qui a servi de base aux aspirations et revendications de la nation Arménienne proposées à la Conférence de la Paix; et connaissant bien l'intérêt que le Saint Siège et tout particulièrement Sa Sainteté le Souverain Pontife portent au sort et au succès de la cause arménienne, j'espère que ce document sera bien accueilli.

A cette occasion que Votre Eminence veuille présenter a Sa Sainteté le Souverain Pontife les sentiments de profonde gratitude pour tous Ses bienfaits auxquels vint s'ajouter tout recémment la généreuse donation en faveur des victimes des récents terribles événements de la Cilicie que nous déplorons encore.

Que Votre Excellence daigne agréer l'expression de mes sentiments respectueux et de vive reconnaissance

66

[?] April 1920, Rome – Gasparri to Aharonian – AAEESS, *Asia* 57, 2, n° 4764

Monsieur le Président,

Je n'ai pas manqué de transmettre au Saint Père l'expression des nobles sentiments que Votre Excellence a bien voulu formuler dans sa lettre du 3 Avril courant.

Sa Sainteté, vivement touché, m'a chargé de Vous confirmer encore une fois la sollicitude toute paternelle avec laquelle Elle suit les questions se rattachant au sort de la généreuse nation arménienne et Elle Vous remercie en même temps de grand coeur de l'envoi des deux exemplaires de l'Atlas Historique de l'Arménie dont Elle a pris connaissance avec un vif intérêt.

En m'associant à ces Augustes sentiments, je profite de cette occasion pour Vous assurer, Monsieur le Président, de ma plus haute considération.

67

5 April 1920, Paris – Naslian to Gasparri – AAEESS, *Asia* 57, 2, n° 5288

Eminenza R.ma

La Delegazione Armena mi affidò a Londra confidenzialmente un importante documento, che mi credo in dovere di portare a conoscenza di Vostra Eminenza. Tale documento facendo parte del trattato per l'Armenia, la Conferenza di Londra avea voluto communicare alla Delegazione medesima per averne le osservazioni. Questa in una delle sue riunioni, ove eravamo presenti anche noi, discusse questo progetto e l'approvò quasi integralmente manifestando il desiderio che all'art. 5 soltanto si opponesse una clausola, con cui si riservasse al Governo Armeno il diritto di controllo sopra gli Istituti contemplativi. Nell'insieme, come vedrà Vostra Eminenza, sono molto liberali e larghe le disposizioni prese, le quali ci gioveranno assai nelle istituzioni che la Chiesa Cattolica vorrà creare e fondare in Armenia.

Per aver maggiore e più esplicita dichiarazione della libertà promessa dai nostri stessi Delegati, feci un osservazione sull'inciso del medesimo articolo nelle prime linee: *à des minorités ethniques <u>de religion ou de langue</u>* e proposi che tale inciso fosse sopresso nella parte doppiamente sottolineata, poiché osservai che dicendovisi: *de religion ou de langue* in senso diviso e non *de religion et de langue* in senso composto, potrebbe contemplare fra *les minorités* anche noi cattolici, ed in questo caso si manterebbe nel trattato stesso una distinzione ad uso turco nel seno della medesima nazione a base di religione, mentre la religione non dovea essere riguardata base di distinzione e di disparità di diritti. Mi fu risposto che parlandovisi di <u>ressortissants arméniens</u> e non di <u>Arméniens</u> semplicemente, non vi si alludeva agli armeni cattolici o protestanti, i quali doveano essere compresi nel rango della maggioranza come armeni; del resto la religione di Stato non essendo che la Cristiana in genere, non si potevano considerare per frazioni distinte le communita dei Cattolici e protestanti armeni.

Trovai in fondo che erano ben disposti per il principio della libertà assoluta di Religione e di culto e che non s'intendeva nella clausola proposta alla Conferenza riservare al governo se non un'assicurazione contro mene politiche possibili a crearsi per abuso delle libertà concesse in quell'articolo ai non-armeni, o meglio ai musulmani. Qualora Vostra Eminenza avesse altre osservazioni da suggerirmi potrei ancora presentarle come mie al Consiglio supremo della Conferenza.

L'attitudine dei Delegati e della Colonia armena fu più espansiva per noi a Londra che qui, anzi fu questa che sostenne le spese nostre di albergo. Però quella del Patriarca non mi ispirò affidamento. Come già mi costava [sic] da Costantinopoli Mons. Zaven è molto *chauvin* e lavora concentrare intorno al suo patriarcato tutta l'azione nazionale, ed a ciò contribuì disgraziatamente di molto la situazione interna del Patriarcato nostro a Costantinopoli. Questo Patriarca adunque per quanto benevolo all'esteriore, non poté sostenere l'indipendenza dell'azione nostra nei circoli cattolici, e quando questi si mossero a favore della questione nazionale con dimostrazioni indirizzate al Delegato del Patriarcato Cattolico, non nascose il risentimento di gelosia. Non poté però escluderci dai consigli, come volle tentare, né dall'attenzione dei Delegati armeni e da quella della Colonia armena. Dimodo che tutti questi compresero l'importanza della missione nostra e ne apprezzarono l'azione. I cattolici inglesi poi vi contribuirono molto con speciali riguardi per noi, si distinsero in ciò [......]

D'altronde l'indipendenza da desiderarsi per noi per la parte finanziaria ci avrebbe anche meglio sostenuto in posizione superiore e ci avrebbe dato modo di intrattenerci anche più a Londra sino al giorno del ritorno della Delegazione Armena a Parigi. Ciò poteva essere utile poiché si avrebbe continuato a prendere parte nelle discussioni e riunioni. Però i nostri mezzi non erano sufficienti per affrontare le spese a Londra, e la Delegazione fece sottintendere che non poteva arrivare a tutte le spese, tanto più che altri pure arrivavano ad aumentarne l'onere.

Qualora però si prolungasse la permanenza dei Delegati Armeni a Londra pel rinvio possibile degli affari, una seconda nostra visita colà in condizioni più indipendenti e con raccomandazioni speciali ai Vescovi ed a qualche Istituto Religioso, potrebbe essere utile.

Quanto alle persone dei Delegati summenzionati devo notare che Noubar Pascià, per quanto nobile e colto e liberale, ci si è sembrato sotto soggezione del Patriarca Zaven e meno indipendente che l'altro Delegato della Repubblica di Erivan, il quale anche nel metodo di azione ha saputo dare una sistemazione meglio conforme ad una vera Legazione Governativa ed ha per collaboratori un generale, un Consigliere finanziario molto competente ed altri. L'organizzazione della Delegazione di Nubar Pascià ha una forma più popolare e democratica, per cui ci è sembrato meno seria e gli addetti non presentano una serietà da affidarsi; non vi è che la persona di Nubar Pacha stesso che salva e sostiene l'importanza di questa Delegazione. Con tutto ciò l'azione concorde nelle richieste nazionali d'avanti [*sic*] al Consiglio Supremo ed ai Governi scongiura il pericolo di divisione nell'insieme della questione nazionale nonostante l'antagonismo nei dettagli, per cui continuano ad avere sedi distinte e gli sforzi di fusione delle due Delegazioni in una non riuscirono.

La Delegazione della Repubblica Armena, giova dirlo, fu più esplicita a favore del Cattolicismo in Armenia e nelle sue assicurazioni sempre più larga e liberale.

Venne nel frattempo a Parigi e poi a Londra il Vescovo scismatico di Erivan, allo scopo, come disse lui, di ottenere la fusione delle due Delegazioni. M'intrattenni con lui due volte lungamente, malgrado la sua riserva e ne potei rilevare, che la Missione sua era più tosto per assicurarsi la posizione del clero Gregoriano sia per la parte finanziaria sia politica. Esso per riuscirvi si vale principalmente di tre proposizioni, come di assiomi: 1º la libertà di religione e di culto in Armenia riconosciuta dallo Stato per cui la religione officiale sarà puramente <u>la cristiana</u> senz'altra aggiunta, è pienamente conforme alla <u>Regola di Fede</u> professata *ab antiquo* [*sic*] dalla Chiesa Gregoriana; 2º la Chiesa Gregoriana e quindi la Sede di Ecimiazin è la più antica ed anteriore alla cattolica-armena e protestante, quindi più indigena, più nazionale, più germana; 3º il Clero Gregoriano ha vissuto e vive tuttora più da vicino della vita del popolo armeno condividendone sempre tutti i sentimenti, tutte le sofferenze durante le secolari peripezie e vicende; perciò questo clero non deve essere privato dei suoi mezzi di sostentamento e di azione.

Di questi ed analoghi assiomi, che hanno la speciosità di forma per attirare le masse popolari, si serve quel Vescovo delegato *ad hoc* dal Patriarca di Ecimiazin per visitare a guadagnarsi le colonie armene d'Europa e deve recarsi anche in America. L'influenza sua potrebbe essere pregiudizievole al cattolicismo nel senso che mancando un azione [*sic*] cattolico-armena nel movimento nazionale non vi figurerebbe interessato se non il clero gregoriano. E la Repubblica armena sembra adottare per norma d'azione di assistere finanziariamente e moralmente tutti quelli Istituti, che hanno contribuito alla vita ed indipendenza nazionale. Guidata da tale norma la Repubblica armena tende a sovvenzionare il Patriarcato e gli Istituti di Ecimiazin, e già nella nuova Università Armena istituita ad Alessandropoli sono invitati ad insegnare alcuni del clero di Ecimiazin. Non converrebbe forse affrettare ad occupare fin d'ora una posizione conveniente nella nuova Repubblica Armena e precisamente a Erivan, che ne è e resterà credo la Capitale, creandovi un centro di rappresentanza officiale e creando pure un altro centro di azione dipendente dal primo ad Alessandropoli medesima? Poiché, deve sapere Vostra Eminenza che nella delimitazione dei confini della nuova Armenia sembra deciso dal Supremo Consiglio che all'Armenia Russa saranno aggiunte dalla Turchia tre provincie soltanto, quelle di Van tutta sino ai confini della Persia, quella di Bitlis e quella di Erzerum; Trebizonda, Erzingian, Kharput ne sarebbero escluse, però il litorale tra Batum e Trebizonda sarà annesso all'Armenia con esclusione di Artvin. Così una parte soltanto della Diocesi di Trebizonda ed una parte di quella di Kharput vi sarà compresa. Quindi nell'Armenia nuova non entrano queste due Diocesi che molto parzialmente, mentre quelle di Musc e di Erzerum vi si comprendono intieramente. In questo caso un rappresentante cattolico a Erivan sarebbe forse necessario per seguire da vicino tutto l'andamento delle cose e quindi preparare la riorganizzazione della Chiesa Cattolica in Armenia. Tanto più che una Associazione di Cattolici Khodorciuriotti si è costituita nel Caucaso per rifare e riprendere quel quartiere cattolico di Erzerum e dispone già di mezzi forti. Non si potrebbe utilizzare fin d'ora quest'associazione?

Sono dell'umile avviso, Eminenza, e mi voglia perdonare la libertà d'interloquire in materia, che il sistema dello *statu quo* pel nostro Patriarcato d'avanti [*sic*] alle vertenze attuali è rovinoso, invece è il tempo opportuno di approfittare 1º del dissesto del clero scismatico, 2º delle necessità che risente il governo armeno dell'azione ed opera nostra; 3º della transizione in cui vanno prendendo conformazioni e direttive altre confessioni religiose ed associazioni.

Devo dire per aggiunta che la Delegazione Armena ha fatto ricorsi ad un Comitato Americano ad intraprendere le medesime opere che questo si è già in procinto di fare nei paesi balcanici e cioè di prendersi alcune zone del territorio per ricostruirlo e rialzare dalle rovine. Egualmente la medesima Delegazione ha domandato al Consiglio Supremo che nel trattato per la Turchia s'inserisse un articolo per assicurare e mantenere i privilegii dei Patriarcati Armeni (scismatico e cattolico). Il Patriarca Scismatico Zaven voleva in ciò specificare lo statuto del loro patriarcato, e ciò potendo essere a svantaggio del nostro ho insistito ed ottenuto che si formulasse la domanda in forma generica per i privilegi dei nostri Patriarcati senza altra aggiunta. Voleva inoltre firmare lui solo a quella domanda il medesimo Patriarca per tutti i Patriarcati, ho insistito ed ottenuto che si presentasse quella domanda sotto firma dei Delegati soli.

Tutto ciò può rilevare meglio la necessità per nostro Patriarcato di occupare fin d'ora posizione in Armenia e di risolvere almeno in forma provvisoria la questione [*sic*] patriarcale abolendo il regime di tre capi, come lo è attualmente.

Quanto a me, attenderò qui il ritorno da Londra della Delegazione Armena e quindi assisterò alla riunione dell'Assemblea Nazionale che si era annunziata per Parigi, quindi mi approfitterò della circostanza per assistere alle feste di Canonizzazione a Roma, per quindi conformarmi alle istruzioni che mi si vorrà dare costì.

Tutto ciò dovrò subordinare anche all'eventualità di dover riandare a Londra, qualora gli affari vi si protraessero di molto ed esigessero una ricognizione per me di quanto hanno fatto i nostri Delegati.

Mi perdoni Vostra Eminenza di essere stato troppo prolisso e mentre mi prostro ecc

Allegato al doc. n° 67, p. 256: Londra - La Conferenza di Londra alla Delegazione Armena - Schema di Trattato

[Translation]

Most Rev. Eminence

In London, the Armenian Delegation confidentially entrusted to me an important document,[258] that I believe is my duty to bring to Your Eminence's knowledge. The Conference of London wanted to communicate said document to the very same Delegation in order to have their observations, it being part of the treaty for Armenia. The Conference, in one of their meetings where we were also present, discussed this project and approved it almost entirely, displaying only the desire that a clause be added to art. 5 which would reserve to the Armenian Government the right to control the contemplative Institutions. Overall, as Your Eminence will see, the arrangements that were made are very liberal and tolerant, and will be extremely good for the institutions that the Catholic Church would like to create and found in Armenia.

To have a greater and more explicit declaration of the freedom promised by our own Delegates, I made an observation about a phrase of the same article in the first lines: *à des minorités ethniques de réligion ou de langue*; I proposed that the underlined part of that phrase be cancelled, because I noted that saying *de réligion ou de langue* in a divided sense and not *de réligion et de langue* in a composite sense, could consider also us Catholics among *les minorités*, in which case a Turkish-style distinction in the heart of the very nation would be maintained within the treaty itself, on the basis of religion, while religion should not be regarded as a basis for distinction and for disparity of rights. It was replied to me that in speaking of *ressortissants arméniens* and not of simply *Arméniens*, no allusion was made to the Armenians Catholics or Protestants, who should be included in the majority as Armenians; besides, the State religion not being, in general, other than Christian, they could not consider the communities of Armenian Catholics and Protestants as distinct fractions.

I found, basically, that they were well-disposed towards the principle of absolute freedom of Religion and of worship and that, in the clause proposed

---

258 V. *Attachment.*

at the Conference, it was not intended to reserve to the government anything more than an insurance against political problems that might possibly arise from abuse of the freedoms conceded in that article to non-Armenians, or rather, to Muslims. In the case that Your Eminence should have other observations to suggest me, I could still present them as my own to the Supreme Council of the Conference.

The attitude of the Delegates and of the Armenian Community was more expansive towards us in London than here, in fact it was the community that paid our hotel expenses. However, the attitude of the Patriarch did not inspire confidence in me. As I already knew from Constantinople, Mons. Zaven is very *chauvin* and works to concentrate all of the national efforts around his patriarchate, and the internal situation of our Patriarchate in Constantinople unfortunately contributes much to this. This Patriarch, therefore, however benevolent on the exterior, cannot bear our independence of action in Catholic circles, and when these moved in favor of the national question with demonstrations addressed to the Delegate of the Catholic Patriarchate, he did not hide his jealous resentment. He could not, however, exclude us from the councils, as he wanted to attempt, nor from the attention of the Armenian Delegates and the Armenian Community. So, in the end, all of them understood the importance of our mission and appreciated its work. The English Catholics, moreover, contributed greatly to it, with special regards for us; they distinguished themselves in this [...]

However, the independence we would like on the financial side would have also better maintained us in a superior position and would have given us the possibility of staying in London even longer, up until the day of the Armenian Delegation's return to Paris. That would have been useful since we could have continued to take part in the discussions and meetings. However, our means were not sufficient to cover the expenses in London, and the Delegation made the implication that it could not meet all the expenses, all the more so as even others were arriving to add to the burden.

If, however, the Armenian Delegates in London were to prolong their stay due to a possible postponement of business, a second visit of ours there, under more independent conditions and with special recommendations to the Bishops and to some Religious Institutes, could be useful.

As to the figures of the abovementioned Delegates I must note that Nubar Pasha, however noble and educated and liberal, seemed to us to be under subjection to the Patriarch Zaven and less independent than the other Delegate from the Republic of Erevan who, in his approach, has been able to create an arrangement more consistent with a true Governmental Legation and has as collaborators a general, a very competent financial Counsel, and others. The organization of Nubar Pasha's Delegation had a more popular and democratic form, for which it seemed to us less serious, and the attachés don't present a sense of trustworthy reliability; there is naught other than the figure of Nubar Pasha himself that preserves and sustains the importance of this Delegation. Even with all that, their concordant action in the national requests before the Supreme Council and before the Governments dispels the danger of division over the larger national question notwithstanding their antagonism over details, for which they continue to have separate headquarters and for which efforts to fuse the two Delegations into one have not been successful.

The Delegation of the Armenian Republic, it pleases me to say, was most explicit in favor of Catholicism in Armenia and in its ever more ample and liberal assurances.

In the meantime, the schismatic Bishop of Erevan came to Paris and then to London, in order, as he said, to accomplish the fusion of the two Delegations. I had two long meetings with him, despite his reserve, and I can reveal that his Mission was instead that of securing the position of the Gregorian clergy both in its financial as well as its political aspects. To succeed in this, he avails himself principally of three propositions, or axioms, as it were: 1º the freedom of religion and of worship in Armenia recognized by the State according to which the official religion will be Christianity, pure and simple; it fully conforms to the Rule of Faith professed *ab antiquo* [*sic*] by the Gregorian Church; 2º the Gregorian Church and therefore the See of Etchmiadzin is the oldest, predating the Catholic-Armenian and protestant, therefore more indigenous, more national, more germane; 3º the Gregorian Clergy has lived, and lives still now, closer to the lives of the Armenian people, always sharing all their feelings, all their sufferings over centuries of incidents and misadventures; that is why this clergy should not be deprived of its means of support and of operation.

This Bishop delegate *ad hoc* from the Patriarch of Etchmiadzin is using these and analogous axioms, which have the speciousness of form that attracts the popular masses, in order to visit and win over the Armenian communities of Europe and he is also supposed to be going to America. His influence could be prejudicial to Catholicism in the sense that, lacking a Catholic-Armenian action group within the national movement, there is no interested party represented if not the Gregorian clergy. And the Armenian Republic seems to adopt the operational norm of assisting, financially and morally, all those Institutions that have contributed to national life and independence. Guided by this norm, the Armenian Republic tends to subsidize the Patriarchate and the Institutes of Etchmiadzin, and some of the clergy of Etchmiadzin have already been invited to teach in the new Armenian University instituted in Alexandroupolis. Would it not perhaps be better to hasten to occupy in advance an advantageous position in the new Armenian Republic and precisely in Erevan, which is, and I believe will remain, the Capital, creating there a center of official representation and also creating another center of activity subordinate to the first in Alexandroupolis itself? Since, Your Eminence should know, in delimiting the borders of the new Armenia it seems to have been decided by the Supreme Council that only three provinces from Turkey will be added to Russian Armenia: that of all of Van up to the borders of Persia, that of Bitlis and that of Erzerum. Trabizon, Erzingian, and Kharput would be excluded; however, the coast between Batum and Trabizon will be annexed to Armenia with the exclusion of Artvin. Thus only a part of the Diocese of Trabizon and a part of that of Kharput will be included therein. Therefore, these two Dioceses do not enter into the new Armenia except very partially, while those of Mush and of Erzerum will be entirely included. In this case, a Catholic representative in Erevan might be necessary in order to closely follow the entire process of things and then make preparations for the reorganization of the Catholic Church in Armenia. All the more so now that an Association of Khodorciur Catholics has formed in the Caucasus to take back and rebuild the Catholic quarter of Erzerum and they already have serious means at their disposal. Couldn't use be made of this association here and now?

I am of the humble opinion, Eminence, and please pardon my liberty in commenting on the matter, that in light of current disputes the system of the *statu quo* is ruinous for our Patriarchate; instead, it is the opportune time to profit 1° from the disorder of the schismatic clergy, 2° from the need that the Armenian government feels for our work and efforts; 3° from the transition during which other religious denominations and associations are taking shape and directive.

I must add that the Armenian Delegation has made appeals to an American Committee to undertake the same efforts that they are already in the process of carrying out in the Balkan countries, and that is to seize some areas of the territory in order to reconstruct it and raise it up from the ruins. Similarly, the same Delegation asked the Supreme Council that an article be inserted into the Turkish treaty to assure and maintain the privileges of the Armenian Patriarchates (schismatic and Catholic). In this [article], the Schismatic Patriarch Zaven wanted to specify the statute of their patriarchate, and that possibly being to the disadvantage of our own, I insisted on and obtained that the request be expressed in a generic form: for the privileges of our Patriarchates, period. He wanted, besides, to sign the request just he alone, this Patriarch himself for all the Patriarchates; I insisted on and obtained that the request be presented under the signatures of the Delegates only.

All this should better highlight the need for our Patriarchate to take up a position in Armenia at once, and to resolve, at least in a provisory fashion, the patriarchal question abolishing the three-headed regime, as it is currently.

As far as concerns me, I will wait here for the return of the Armenian Delegation from London and then attend the meeting of the National Assembly that was announced for Paris, then I will take advantage of that circumstance to attend the Canonization celebrations in Rome, to then comply with the instructions that will be given me there.

All of this will also depend on the eventuality of having to go back to London, in the case that affairs there protract themselves exceedingly and require a reconnaissance on my part of how much our Delegates have gotten done.

Your Eminence will pardon me for having been too prolix and while I bow etc

Attachment to doc. n° 67, p. 256: London – The Conference of London to the Armenian Delegation – Outline of Treaty.

Chapitre I

Article I

L'Arménie s'engage à ce que les stipulations contenues dans les articles 2 à 8 du présent chapitre soient reconnues comme lois fondamentales, à ce qu'aucune loi, aucun reglement , m'aucune action officielle ne soient en contradition ou en opposition avec ces stipulations et à ce qu'aucune loi, aucune réglement m'aucune action officielle ne prévalent contre elles.

Article 2

L'Arménie s'engage à accorder à tous les habitants pleine et entière protection de leur vie et de leur liberté sans distinction de naissance, de nationalité, de langage, de race ou de réligion:

Tous les habitants de l'Arménie auront droit au libre exercice, tant public que privé, de tout foi, réligion ou croyance, dont la pratique ne sera pas incompatible avec l'ordre publique et les bonnes moeurs.

Les atteintes au libre exercice de cultes seront punies des même peines quelque soit le culte intéressé.

Article 3

L'Arménie s'engage à reconnaitre les dispositions que les Puissances Alliées jugeront opportunes relativement à l'emigration réciproque et volontaire des individus appartenant aux minorités ethniques.

Article 4

Tous les resortissants Arméniens seront égaux devont la loi et jouiront des mêmes droits civils et politiques sans distinction de race, de langage ou de réligion.

La différence de réligion, de croyance ou de confession ne devra nuire à aucun resortissant Arménien en ce qui concerne la jouissance des droits civils et politiques, notamment pour l'admission aux emplois publics, fonctions et honneurs ou l'exercice des différentes professions et industries.

Le Gouvernement Arménien présentera dans un délai de deux ans après la mise en vigueur du présent traité, aux principales puissances alliées un projet d'organisation d'un systéme électoral tenant compte des droits des minorité ethniques.

Il ne sera edicté aucune restriction contre le libre usage par tout ressortissant Arménièn d'une langue quelconque, soit dans les rélations priveés ou de commerce soit en matière de réligion, de presse, ou de publications de toute nature, soit dans les reunions publiques.

Nonobstante l'établissement par le Gouvernement Arménièn d'une langue officielle, des facilités approprieés seront données aux ressortissants Arménièns de langue autre que l'Arménièn pour l'usage de leur langue soit oralement, soit par ecrit devant les tribunaux.

Article 5

Les resortissantes Arménièns appartenants à des minorités ethniques, de réligion ou de langue, jouiront du même traitement et des mêmes garanties en droit et en fait que les autres resortissants Arménièns. Ils auront notammente un droit égal à créer, diriger et controler à leur frais des institutions charitables, réligieuses ou sociales, des écoles et autres établissements d'éducation avec le droit d'y faire librement usage de leur propre langue et d'y exercer librement leur réligion.

Article 6

En matière d'enseignement public, le gouvernement Arménièn accordera dans le villes et districts où réside une proportion considérable des resortissants de langue autre que la langue Arméniènne, des facilités appropriées pour assurer que dans les écoles primaires, l'instruction sera donnée, dans leur propre langue aux enfants de ces resortissants Arménièn de rendre obligatoire l'enseignement de la langue Arméniènne dans les dites écoles.

Dans les villes et districts, où réside une proportion considérable de resortissants Arménièns appartenant à des mindités ethniques, de réligion au de langue des minorités se verront assurer une part équitable dans le bénéfice et l'affectation des sommes, qui pourraient être attribuées sur le fonds publics pour la budget de l'Etat les budgets municipaux du autres, dans en but d'éducation, de réligion, ou de charité.

Article 7

L'Arménie agrée de prendre à l'egard des Musulmans et en ce qui concerne leurs etatus familiaux et personnels, toutes dispositions permettants de regler ces questios selon les usages musulmans.

Le Gouvernement Arménièn provoquera egalement la nomination d'un Réis-ul-ulemà.

L'Arménie s'engage à accorder protection aux mosqueés, cimitières et autre etablissements réligieux musulmans. Toute autorisation et facilité seront assureés aux fondations pieuses (vakoures), et aux etablissements musulmans réligieux et charitables actuellement existant, et l'Arménie ne refusera, pour la création de nouveaux établissements réligieux et charitables, aucune des facilités nécessaires garanties aux autres établissements privés de ce genre.

Article 8

L'Arménie convient que, dans la mesure où les stipulations des articles précédents affestent des persones appartenent à des minoritée de race, de réligion ou de langue, ces stipulations constituent des obligations d'intérêt international et seront placées sous la garantie de la Société des Nations. Elles ne pourront être modifiées sous [sic] l'assentiment de la majorité du Conseil de la Societé des Nations. Les Etats-Unis d'Amerique, l'Empire brittannique, la France, l'Italie et le Japon s'engagent à ne pas refuser leur assentiment à toute modification des dits articles, qui serait consentie en due forme par une majorité du Conseil de la Société des Nations.

L'Arménie agrée que tout membre du Conseil de la Société des Nations aura le droit de signaler à l'attention du Conseil toute infraction ou danger d'infraction à l'une quelconque de ces obligations, et que le Conseil pourra procéder de telle facon et donner telles instructions qui paraitrent appropriées et efficaces dans la circostance.

L'Arménie agrée en outre qui en cas de divergence d'opinion, sur des questions de droit ou de fait concernant ces articles, entre l'Arménie et l'une quelconque des Principales Puissances Alliées et associées ou toute autre Puissance, membre du Conseil de la Société des Nations, cette divergence sera considérée comme un différend ayant un caractére international, selon les termes de l'article 14 du Pacte de la Société des Nations.

L'Arménie agrée que tout differend de ce genre sera, si l'autre partie le demande, déféré à la Cour Permanente de justice internationale. La décision de la Cour permanente sera sous appel et aura la même force et valeur qu'une décision rendus en vertu de l'article 13 du Pacte.

Chapitre II

Article 9

L'Armenie s'engage à ne conclure aucun Traité, Convention ou accord, et à ne prendre aucune mesure qui l'empécherair de participer à toute convention générale qui pourrait être conclus sous les auspices de la Société des Nations en une de traitement équitable du commerce des autres Etats, au cours d'une période de cinq années à partir de la mise en rigueur du présent Traité.

L'Arménie s'engage également à étendre à tous les Etats alliés ou associés toute faveur ou privilège qu'elle pourrait, au cours de la même periode de cinq ans, accorder en matière donanière [sic], à l'un quelconque des Etats avec les quels, depuis le mois d'août 1914, les Etats alliés ou associés ont été en guerre, ou à tout autre Etat qui, en vertu de l'article 322, du Traité de paix avec l'Autriche, aurait avec ces mêmes Etats des arrangements douaniers spéciaux.

Article 10

Jusqu'à la conclusion de la convention génerale ci dessus vissé l'Arménie s'engage à accorder le même traitement qu'aux navires nationaux ou aux navires de la Nation la plus favorisée, aux navires de tous les Etats alliés et associés qui accordent un traitement analogue aux navires Arméniens.

Par exception à cette disposition le droit est expressement reconnu à l'Arménie et à tout autre Etat allié ou associé de réserver son trafic de cabotage aux navires nationaux.

Article 11

En attendant la conclusion sous les auspices de la Société des Nations, d'une Convention générale destinée à assurer et à maintenir la liberté des communications et du transit, l'Arménie s'engage à accorder, sur le territoire Arménien, y compris les eaux territoriales, la liberté de transit aux personnes, marchandises , navires, voitures, wagons et courriers postaux transitant en provenance ou à destination de l'un quelconque des Etats alliés ou associé, et à leur accorder en ce qui concerne les facilités, charge, restrictions on toutes autres matières, un traitement au moins aussi favorable qu'aux personnes, marchandises, navires, voitures, wagons, et courriers postaux de l'Arménie ou de toute autre nationalité, origine; importation ou proprieté qui jouirait d'un régime plus favorable.

Toutes les charge imposées en Arménie sur ce trafic en transit devront être raisonnables eu égard aux conditions de ce trafic. Des marchandises en transit seront exemptes de tous droit de douanes ou autres. Des tarifs communs pour le trafic en transit à travers l'Arménie et des tarifs communs entre l'Arménie et un Etat allié ou associé quelconque comportant des billets ou lettres de voiture directs, seront établis si cette Puissance alliés ou associés en fait la demande.

La liberté de transit s'éendra [sic] aux services postaux, télégraphiques ou téléphoniques.

Il est entendu qu'aucun Etat allié ou associé n'aura le droit de réclamer le bénéfice de ces dispositions pour une partie quelconque de son territoire dans la quelle un traitement réciproque ne serait pas accordé en ce qui concerne le même objet.

Si, en cours d'une période de cinq ans, à partir de la mise en riguer [sic] du présent Traité, la Convention générale ci-dessus prévus n'a pas été conclus sous les auspices de la Société de Nations, l'Arménie aura, à quelque moment que ce soit, le droit de mettre fin aux dispositions du présent article, à condition de donner un préavis de douze mois au Secrétaire général de la Société des Nations.

Article 12

Tous les droits et privilèges accordés pour les articles précedents aux Puissances alliées et associées seront également acquis à tout les Etats membres de la Société des Nations

68

6 April 1920, Paris – Ahmed Riza[259] to the pope – AAEESS, *Asia* 57, 1 , n° [?]

Très Saint Père,

Souffrez qu'un Turc, qui a respectuesement conservér un souvenir impérissable de l'audience que Votre Sainteté a bien voulu lui accorder à son passage à Rome, vienne vous suggérer une idée dont la réalisation contribuera à rehausser encore davantage votre prestige personnel et constituera dans l'histoire de l'Eglise une page unique et glorieuse.

Le Saint-Siège, dont la politique fût, durant la guerre, humaine et généreuse, voudra attacher à cette idée l'importance qu'elle mérite, et prouvera ainsi à l'univers entier et à toute la chrétienté réunie que le désir suprême du Saint Père est d'appliquer sur terre les propres paroles de l'Evangile qui recommande aux hommes de bonne volonté d'aimer leurs prochains, de ne leur faire aucun mal et de ne pas porter sur eux des jugements téméraires.

Or il est infiniment regrettable qu'aujourd'hui, dans les affaires turques, la religion serve d'instrument en Europe à quelques hommes ambitieux pour faire aboutir leurs desseins politiques. Ces politiciens poussent même leur haine jusqu'à calomnier injustement une nation qui est fière d'avoir donné l'hospitalité et montré une large tolérance envers les catholiques depuis des siecles. Par contre dans les pays des Balkans, dernièrement détachés de la Turquie et passés dans les mains des Etats orthodoxes, l'Eglise et les congrégations catholiques ont perdu leurs privilèges.

Il est injuste aussi d'invoquer la différence de croyance pour priver un peuple de ses droits légitimes, de sa liberté et de son indépendance. J'ai la certitude que Votre Sainteté désapprouve complètement cette façon d'agir.

Je me permets de faire appel à ses sentiments de loyauté et de lui soumettre l'idée de prendre l'initiative de conseiller aux Puissances alliées et associés la formation et l'envoi sur les lieux d'une commission mixte à laquelle se joindraient des représentants du Sait-Siège. Cette commission impartiale et équitable serait chargée d'effectuer une enquête minutieuse et de rechercher les

---

259 Ahmed Riza Bey, one of the first two leaders of the Young Turks movement when it was formed in Paris. He represented the more moderate and liberal wing (Sidari, *op. cit.*, pp. 43–47). No response to his letter was found.

causes et les responsabilitée des prétendus massacres dont on accuse les turcs à l'égard des arméniens.

La Croix ne fera que rehausser son éclat et son prestige en prenant la défense du Croissant dans un but de justice et de pure vérité.

Sa Sainteté connait les rapports d'amitié qui ont uni vos illustres prédécesseurs avec toute la lignée des Khalifs. Elle sait aussi avec quelle tolérance, alors qu'ils étaient tout puissants, les Khalifs ont laissé à la Papauté sa domination spirituelle et à certains égards temporelle sur les catholiques d'Orient.

Ce que les Turcs musulmans par la voie de leur Khalif accordaient aux Catholiques, je vous demande que les catholiques, par votre organe vénéré, contribuent à le faire obtenir aux musulmans turcs: je veux dire un traitement équitable et humain.

On a représenté les Turcs comme des massacreurs au moment de la guerre balkanique. La grande enquêt de Carnégie a démontré que les coupables étaient dans le camp adverse. On les a accablé de la même accusation sur les populations orthodoxes de la région de Smyrne et vous connaissez les résultats si favorables aux Turcs de la grande enquête internationale qui a eu lieu il y'a quelques mois.

Pourquoi au point de vue de cette malheureuse question arménienne dont les ennemis de la Turquie veulent faire le glaive meurtrier de mon pays, pourquoi ne constitue-t-on pas une pareille enquête!

Je vous demande Très Sain Père, puisque vous êtes la plus haute et la plus juste puissance spirituelle du monde, de vouloir bien intercéder en notre faveur pour que cette oevre de justice soit acceptée.

Je suis convaincu que la Papauté, qui a sans cesse deployé, depuis le commencement du conflit mondial, tous ses nobles efforts pour le rétablissement de la paix et de la justice, voudra profiter de cette occasion pour prouver au monde son impartialité et ses sentiments vraiment humains.

Je prie le Très Saint Père de bien vouloir agréer les hommages de mon profond respect.

69

13 April 1920, Rome – Tigran Nazarian to the pope – AAEESS, *Asia* 57, 1, n° 5293

Beatissimo Padre,

Vengo con la presente con profonda venerazione e distinto ossequio a umiliare a vostra Santità come sommo Pontefice e padre Clemente l'omaggio e la gratitudine dell'Armenia del popolo armeno desolato. Si Padre Santo, dal popolo armeno perseguitato, deportato , massacrato per l'amore della Religione di Cristo e della Patria.

Il popolo armeno per la libertà sua e delle Nazioni ha perduto nei massacri e nella guerra coi soldati degli alleati più di un milione di anime. Con tutto ciò oggi gli alleati vittoriosi prima di liberarci dal duro giuogo di islam della turchia, hanno voluto creare nel Caucaso un'altra questione Balcanica conoscendo una Repubblica detta Adrberjan. Da 1600 anni la provincia di Karabach l'istorico Aguank e Arzak, hanno ceduto alla Repubblica detta Adrberjan che è di nazione turca e alleata coi turchi. Perché ciò Santissimo Padre e con quale ragione?

Io in qualità di delegato degli Armeni di Karabach e di Zanguezur protesto contro questo atto ingiusto e supplico in nome di tutti gli armeni l'augusta intercessione di vostra santità presso la conferenza della Pace che si radunerà in questo corrente mese a S. Remo per decidere definitivamente i confini dell'Armenia, che la Provincia Karabach sia legata all'Armenia come è stata considerata sempre come una parte dell'Armenia. Deh Padre Santo, Voi che con sovrano gesto e clemenza avete asciugato tante lacrime ai fedeli e desolati abbiate pietà ai miei compatrioti desolati, non vogliamo che le nostre Chiese i Conventi Cristiani e le tombe dei nostri martiri siano contaminate dai barbari turchi nemici giurati del cristianesimo, non vogliamo che centinaia di migliaia dei cristiani armeni rimangano sotto il duro giogo islamico.

Prostrando con profonda venerazione al bacio ecc

[Translation]

Most Holy Father,

With the present, I come with profound veneration and distinct respect to humbly offer to your Holiness as supreme Pontiff and Clement father the homage and the gratitude of the Armenia of the desolate Armenian people. Yes, Holy Father, of the Armenian people persecuted, deported, massacred for the love of Christ's Religion and of the Country.

The Armenian people, for their liberty and for that of Nations, has lost in the massacres and in the war alongside the allied soldiers more than a million souls. With all this, today the victorious allies, before liberating us from the severe yoke of Turkish Islam, decided to create another Balkan question in the Caucasus, recognizing a Republic called Azerbaijan. The province of Karabakh, for 1600 years the historical Aghuank and Artsakh, they ceded to the Republic called Azerbaijan, which is of Turkish nationality and is allied with the Turks. Why so, Most Holy Father, and with what reason?

I, in quality of delegate of the Armenians of Karabakh and of Zanguezur, protest against this unjust act and I implore in the name of all Armenians the august intercession of Your Holiness with the Peace conference which will meet this month in San Remo to definitively decide the borders of Armenia, that the Province of Karabakh be united to Armenia as it has always been considered a part of Armenia. Oh Holy Father, you who with mercifulness and with sovereign gesture have dried so many of the tears of the faithful and desolate, take pity on my distressed compatriots: we do not want our Churches and Christian Convents and the tombs of our martyrs contaminated by the barbarous Turks, sworn enemies of Christianity; we do not want hundreds of thousands of Armenian Christians to remain under the harsh Islamic yoke.

Prostrating with profound veneration to kiss etc

70

27 May 1920, Paris – Naslian to Mons. [Papadopulos?] – CO, 106, 2, 3, n° 4363

Ill.mo e Rev.mo Monsignore,

Mons. Derabrahamian mi significava da parte sua che mi adoprassi presso la Delegazione Armena per prevenirla contro certi malintesi a svantaggio della S. Sede possibili per l'astensione di Padre Giovanni Torossian dalla partecipazione alle riunioni dell'Assemblea Nazionale, a cui è stato invitato: non se ne prenda pena che io saprò far comprendere tutto a chi di dovere senza compromettere nulla e nessuno. Deve sapere per altro che il sullodato Padre non farebbe parte della Delegazione ma bensì dell'Assemblea Nazionale in cui fin dall'anno scorso si era voluto avere un rappresentante dei mechitaristi di Venezia. Inoltre sia il Delegato del Caucaso sia altri membri della Delegazione medesima mi hanno spesso posto delle quesrioni [sic] sulla natura e condizioni dell'intervento della S. Sede negli affari dei Mechitaristi, ed ho notato che simili quesrioni [sic] erano formulate da insinuazioni e notizie date dai Padri medesimi a questi laici; per l'intervento ho detto che sarà stato invocato dai Padri medesimi per ragioni di richieste interne, sarà stato motivato dall'avanzata età dell'Abbate, dalla situazione anormale creata anche per quel Convento dalla guerra; in tutti i casi quell'intervento sarà provvisorio e non farà che del bene; ho spiegato che non vi poteva essere pericolo di latinizzazione, e che tutte le insinuazioni in questo senso erano certamente maliziose e non degne di attenzione. Anzi al Signor Aharonian che ultimamente aveva visitato l'Isola di San Lazaro ed aveva inteso lagnanze contro l'ingerenza della S.Sede, come pure contro l'attuale amministrazione e le disposizioni prese, ho spiegato anche meglio come provenissero da questioni personali tra Padri e che non si doveva supporre nelle disposizioni della S. Sede la più lontana intenzione di latinizzazione od accaparramento di beni ed inoltre dimostrai come l'intervento della S. Sede soltanto poteva salvarli dall'impaccio in cui si trova detto Convento; ha ben penetrato quanto gli ho esposto ed ha dato ragione all'azione della S. Sede. Devo far rilevare pertanto che il movimento d'opposizione vuol presentare lo stato attuale di cose sotto un aspetto sfavorevole ai bisogni attuali della Nazione, come se fosse con ciò vincolata la loro attività e fossero impediti o ritenuti i Padri dal far il bene che avrebbero potuto fare in queste condizioni critiche della nazione; e non potendo rimproverarne apertamente la S. Sede, né rigettarne la responsabilità sopra altri, tendono a insospettire l'opinione pubblica a sfavore delle misure prese da cotesta S. Congne. Deve sapere in proposito che fin da quando stavo a

Cospoli in un Giornale Armeno era comparso quale un estratto di una lettera pervenuta da Venezia che il Vaticano [*sic*] volendo servirsi dei Mechitaristi in Armenia, quali ben visti dagli Armeni, avea preso misure aliene dalle tradizioni di quel Convento per formarne i nuovi soggetti sul modello del Clero Collegiale (dei Collegii di Roma), il quale non godeva la fiducia della nazione; inoltre il Senatore [...]am Effendi parlando a me stesso in proposito si era scagliato contro Mons. Sardi, quale autore di tali misure ed avea detto che esso stesso personalmente menerebbe una campagna sui giornali se persistesse tale stato di cose. Oggi vengo a ricevere il Giornale "Voce del Popolo", il quale sotto il titolo "Vogliamo una risposta dalla Congregazione Mechitarista" fa un articolo di fondo rilevando l'ininazine [*sic*] non giustificata per loro dei Mechitaristi e termina in queste proposizioni: Noi esigiamo dai PP. Mechitaristi due cose e lo esigiamo con diritto: primieramente lavorare in Italia per la Causa Armena e secondariamente assumersi la cura di qualche migliaja di orfani. I Mechitaristi tacciono; direste che la loro bocca è chiusa a catenaccio d'oro etc etc. Devo notare che prima di quest'ultimo inciso vi si vede uno spazio di 9 linee sopresse [*sic*] dalla censura. E [*sic*] facile travedere in queste proposizioni e nell'insieme dell'articolo che tale silenzio sia imposto ai Padri da riguardi per autorità contro cui essi non oserebbero parlare. Non si preoccupi Lei per la Delegazione che io cerchero [*sic*] assicurare contro possibili insinuazioni a sfavore della S. Sede.

Voglia consentire che lo trattenga anche di un altra queszione [*sic*]: si dice che a Costantinopoli si oppongano i nostri alla vendita dell'Hotel Bristol; non è impossibile che a capo di quella opposizione trovandosi il famoso Terzibasian ed altri abituati a tirarsene profitti personali in simili atti, cerchino di trasferire a Costantinopoli medesima le trattative di tale vendita; inoltre il nostro Locum-Tenens, che niente vuol sia fatto durante la sua geszione [*sic*] degli affari communali [*sic*] nostri il che possa comparire contrario pur lontanamente ai diritti nazionali, può aver anche le sue ragioni e riguardi ingiustificabili per opporsi alla medesima vendita. Quindi io sarei del parere che la S. Congregazione verificasse bene se realmente c'è un offerta [*sic*] cosi superiore a quella di Roma; poiche [*sic*] per impedire l'operazione facilmente esagerano, se poi si venisse ai fatti di procedere alla vendita a quel prezzo, quelli stessi che oggi presentano prezzi favolosi sotto un pretesto od altro ne possono rilevare l'esorbitanza e tener le parti del compratore, contro chi sa quali rimunerazioni; non è che esagero o faccio giudizii temerarii, ho assistito ad analoghe scene in queszioni [*sic*] amministrative, Io sarei del desiderio di vedere quell'Immobile messo a salvo un giorno prima contro ogni possibile malversazione e pretensioni e dopo verificato se realmente esiste una offerta superiore senz'altro vorrei si passasse alla sua alienazione , poiché non avremo in apresso [*sic*] tempo più opportuno da evitare l'intervento laico.

Gli affari dell'Armenia non sono consolanti: nel Caucaso si minaccia l'esterminio definitivo di tutti i superstiti armeni, i mezzi di difesa mancano ed i Tartari d'accordo con i Turchi sono decisi di schiacciarli e forse già stanno in opera, cosi [*sic*] che prima della soluzione diplomatica della queszione [*sic*] si deplorerà forse la soluzione a la turca: il Capitano Poidebard, Gesuita, che è di ritorno da Erivan mi diceva è imminente una vera catastrofe finale specialmente dopo l'invasione bolscivista e quindi mi consigliava prevenire la S. Sede onde voglia in qualche modo prevenire il disastro intervenendo energicamente ove le è possibile. Attendo in proposito un rapporto da quel Capitano, e quindi esporrò il caso al Santo Padre.

Anche a Trebizonda e Samsoun sembra precaria la situazione cosi che non so quali istruzioni abbia da dare ai miei Sacerdoti, i quali pure sembrano molto preoccupati. Mi scrivono da Costantinopoli che i Turchi avrebbero fatto delle minaccie per mio conto, non so quale importanza annetervi ma certo non sarebbe prudente ritornar in Diocesi nelle condizioni attuali; ne parleremo costi. [*sic*]

Il Sacerdote, che mi accompagnava, da Pasqua in poi sotto mille pretesti voleva separarsi da me ed andar in altri alberghi per essere più indipendente, non ho consentito finche [*sic*] ho potuto, finalmente approfittando di una mia assenza, si è partito senza lasciarmi indirizzo; devo dire che nella sua condotta avea fin da Londra notato un attitudine d'indipendenza e di disprezzo, di modo che spesso mi ha abbandonato solo nelle strade e non ha voluto accompagnarmi, come pure ajutarmi nelle scritture da fare etc. etc. Con mia sorpresa trovai che si era perfino preparato una carta da visita attribuendosi il titolo di "Repprésentant du Patriarcat Arménien Catholique", tengo ancora uno di quei biglietti; ciò spiega tutto e mi son pentito mille volte di aver consentito alla sua venuta con me sotto nome di Segretario che gli è sembrato umiliante. Malgrado questa penosa difficoltà mi è riuscito tener celato lo scandalo alla Delegazione ed esso stesso non ha osato servirsi del preteso suo titolo apertamente e quindi non riuscendogli farsi dare l'importanza che si voleva abusivamente dare si è allontanato dopo d'aver fatto molti dispetti; per amore della delicata posizione e per evitare ogni scandalo ho sopportato tutto in silenzio; oggi però avendo quest'occasione di scriverle ho voluto metterla a corrente del fatto a scanso anche d'ogni responsabilità. Mi è stato detto dopo sua partenza che esso passerà per Roma, il che mi sorprende poiche l'ho sentito esprimersi molto male della Curia Romana in diverse occasioni e malgrado le osservazioni che ho dovuto fargli non mi è riuscito cambiargli i sentimenti. In tutto anche in materie serie non solo disciplinari ma dottrinali pure mi si è rivelato di una mentalità troppo independente per non dir altro. Mi è stata questa una sorpresa assai penosa poiche [*sic*] personalmente lo stimavo e non avrei supposto tali disposizioni di animo in lui, essendo esso ritenuto a Costantinopoli uno dei migliori sacerdoti. E [*sic*] stata una vera croce per me d'averlo avuto in compagnia ed ho molto penato per disimpegnarmi con onore della delicata mia missione senza dar sentore ai scismatici dell'abbandono in cui mi ha voluto lasciare e delle difficoltà che ha tentato crearmi. Mi son tirato grazie a Dio dall'imbarazzo ed a cio [*sic*] ha contribuito molto utilmente anche la venuta del Patriarca, accolto onorevolmente dalla Delegazione e dal Governo Francese. Di tutto cio faro [*sic*] un raporto [*sic*] quando saro [*sic*] a Roma, il che non ritarderà.

Una notizia pure communicatami da Costantinopoli mi sorprende che cioè Mons. Sayeghian accompagnato da Mons. Terzibascian voglia venire a Roma. Mentre il Patriarca Zaven ritorna a Costantinopoli, e fatti non indifferenti si attendono colà per la nazione e nel seno stesso della communità nostra, mi sorprenderebbe realmente tale assenza del Locum-Tenens e la venuta di Terzibascian a Roma interpretata ogni volta sfavorevolmente da tutta la nazione a scapito stesso del prestigio e dell'azione della S. Sede, mi sembra ed è molto pregiudizievole, specialmente in queste circostanze, quindi sarei dell'avviso di impedire tale progetto inopportuno, il quale creerebbe molte difficoltà e darebbe luogo ad increscievoli polemiche e nuove eccitazioni a Costantinopoli. Termino con ossequiosa riserva di ulteriori rapporti officiali. Pertanto mi voglia credere di Vostra Signoria ecc
firmato
Giov. Naslian
Vescovo di Trabzon

[Translation]
Most Illustr. and Most Rev. Monsignor,

Mons. Der Abrahamian emphasized, for his part, that I should to do my best with the Armenian Delegation to forewarn them against certain possible misunderstandings to the disadvantage of the Holy See regarding Father Giovanni Torossian's abstention from participation in the meetings of the National Assembly, to which he was invited: do not worry about it, as I know how to make everything understood to those concerned without compromising anything or anyone. What's more, you must know that the abovementioned Father would not be part of the Delegation but rather of the National Assembly, in which they have wanted to have a representative of the Mekhitarists of Venice since last year. Moreover, the Delegate of the Caucasus, as well as other members of the same Delegation, often asked me questions about the nature and conditions of the Holy See's intervention in the affairs of the Mekhitarists, and I noted that such questions were formulated from insinuations and information given by the Fathers themselves to these laymen; regarding the intervention I said that it might have been requested by the Fathers themselves for reasons of internal policy, it could have been motivated by the advanced age of the Abbot, by the abnormal situation created also for that Convent by the war; in any case, that intervention will be provisory and will do nothing but good; I explained that there would be no danger of latinization, and that all the insinuations to this effect were certainly malicious and unworthy of attention. In fact, to Mister Aharonian, who had recently visited the Island of San Lazzaro and had heard complaints against the interference of the Holy See, and likewise against the current administration and the regulations established, I explained even further how they arose from personal issues between Fathers and that in the dispositions of the Holy See should not be suspected the furthest intention of latinization or of the securing of assets and moreover I demonstrated how only the intervention of the Holy See could save them from the predicament in which said Convent found itself; everything I set forth sunk in well and he approved of the actions of the Holy See. I must point out further that the opposition movement would like to present the current state of things in a light that is unfavorable to the present needs of the Nation, as though with this their activity were constrained and the Fathers were impeded or held back from doing what good they could have done in these critical conditions of the nation; not being able to reproach the Holy See openly, nor throw the responsibility back onto others, they tend to make the public suspicious, in disfavor of the measures taken by your S. Congn. On this subject, you should know that since I arrived in Constantinople an Armenian Newspaper published an excerpt from a letter arrived from Venice, that the Vatican, wanting to make use of the Mekhitarists in Armenia since they were well-regarded by the Armenians, had taken measures alien to the traditions of that Convent in order to cultivate new ones subject to the model of the Collegial Clergy (of the Colleges of Rome), which does not enjoy the confidence of the nation; moreover, the Senator [...]am Effendi, speaking to me personally about the matter, lashed out at Mons. Sardi as author of these measures, and said that he himself would personally lead a campaign in the newspapers should such a state of things persist. Today I come to receive the Newspaper "Voice of the People" which, under the title "We Want an Answer from the Mekhitarist Congregation," has an editorial pointing out the unjustified, for them, inaction of the Mekhitarists and ends with these sentences: We demand two things from the Mekhitarist Fathers and we demand them by right: first, that they work in Italy for the Armenian Cause and, second, that they assume the care of several thousand orphans. The Mekhitarists are silent; you might say that their mouths are closed with a golden chain etc etc. I must note that before this last phrase a space of 9 lines can be seen, suppressed by the censors. It is easy to discern in these sentences and in the overall article that this silence is imposed on the Fathers by a regard for authorities against whom they dare not speak. You should not worry about the Delegation as I will try to ensure against possible insinuations unfavorable to the Holy See.

Please allow me to detain you with another question as well: it is said in Constantinople that we are opposed to the sale of the Hotel Bristol; it is not impossible that, at the head of this opposition being the famous Terzibasian along with others used to extracting personal profits for themselves in similar proceedings, they seek to transfer the negotiations of such sale to Constantinople itself; also, our *Locum-Tenens*, who does not want anything done during his management of our community affairs which could appear even faintly contrary to national interests, may also have his own unjustifiable reasons and concerns for opposing said sale. Therefore I would be of the opinion that the S. Congregation should verify thoroughly whether there really is an offer so much higher than that of Rome, since in obstructing the operation they could easily exaggerate: if then it were to come to the facts and to proceed with the sale at that price, the very same who today present fabulous prices under one pretext or another could point out the exorbitance and take the side of the buyer, in the face of who knows what remuneration. It's not that I am exaggerating or making rash judgments; I have been witness to analogous scenes in administrative matters. I would be desirous of seeing that Building rescued as soon as possible from all potential misappropriation and claim and, after having verified whether a superior offer really exists, I would certainly like for it to enter into conveyance, since later on we will not have a more opportune occasion to avoid secular intervention.

The affairs in Armenia are not comforting: in the Caucasus the definitive extermination of all the surviving Armenians threatens; means of defense are lacking and the Tartars in league with the Turks are decided to crush them, and perhaps they are already at work, so that before the diplomatic solution to the question arrives perhaps we shall bemoan the Turkish idea of solution. Captain Poidebard, Jesuit, who is on his way back from Erevan, told me a true final catastrophe is imminent, especially after the Bolshevik invasion, and thus he advised me to warn the Holy See so that it might in some way avert this disaster by intervening energetically wherever possible. I am waiting for a report from the Captain on the subject, and then I will lay out the case to the Holy Father.

In Trabizon and Samsun as well the situation seems so precarious that I don't know what instructions to give to my Priests, who also seem very worried. They write to me from Constantinople that the Turks have made threats against me; I don't know how much importance to attach to it but it certainly would not be prudent to return to the Diocese under the current conditions; we will talk about this there.

From Easter onward, the Priest who accompanied me, using a thousand pretexts, wanted to separate himself from me and go to other hotels to be more independent; I withheld my consent as long as I could; finally, taking advantage of one of my absences, he left without leaving a forwarding address. I must say that, in his conduct since London, I had noted an attitude of independence and of scorn, in that he often abandoned me alone in the streets and did not want to accompany me, nor even help me with the paperwork that needed doing, etc. etc. To my surprise, I found that he had even prepared himself a visiting card ascribing to himself the title of "*Repprésentant du Patriarcat Arménien Catholique*"; I still have one of those cards. That explains everything, and I have repented a thousand times for having consented to his coming with me in the role of Secretary, which seemed humiliating to him. Despite this painful difficulty, I have been able keep the scandal concealed from the Delegation and he himself has not dared to openly use his assumed title and therefore, not being able to get the unauthorized importance he wanted to give himself, he went away after having caused many vexations; for the sake of the delicate position and to avoid any hint of scandal I bore it all in silence; today, however, having this occasion to write to you, I wanted to keep you informed of the fact, also to avoid any responsibility. After his departure, I was told that he will pass through Rome, which surprises me since I have heard him express very negative opinions of the Roman Curia on various occasions and despite the observations that I was obliged to make to him I was not able to change his feelings. In everything, also in serious matters not only disciplinary but even doctrinal, he revealed himself to have too independent a mentality to say the least. This was a very painful surprise to me, since personally I esteemed him and I would not have supposed him to have such a frame of mind, his being considered one of the best priests in Constantinople. It was a true cross for me to bear, to have had him in my company, and I struggled greatly to fulfill my delicate mission with honor without giving the schismatics an inkling of the state of abandonment in which he chose to leave me, or of the difficulties that he tried to create for me. I avoided embarrassment, thank God, and contributing to this very advantageously was also the arrival of the Patriarch, received with honor by the Delegation and by the French Government. Of all of that I will make a report when I am in Rome, which shall be soon.

Another piece of news communicated to me from Constantinople surprises me, which is that Mons. Sayeghian wants to come to Rome accompanied by Mons. Terzibashian. While the Patriarch Zaven returns to Constantinople, and important matters are waiting there, for the nation as well as in the very heart of our community, such an absence of the *Locum-Tenens* would really surprise me and the coming of Terzibashian to Rome is always interpreted unfavorably by the whole nation to the very detriment of the prestige and efforts of the Holy See, it seems to me, and it is very prejudicial, especially in these circumstances, therefore I would advise preventing that inopportune project, which would create many difficulties and would give place to annoying polemics and new

agitation in Constantinople. I close in respectful reservation of further official reports. Meanwhile please believe that I am of Your Lordship etc
  signed
  Giov. Naslian
  Bishop of Trabizon

71

1 June 1920, Constantinople – Dolci to Gasparri – AAEESS, Austria 576, n° 7232

            Eminentissimo Principe,

Con lettera del 30 p.p. qui compiegata, fui invitato dal Gran Vezir, Damad Ferid Pacha, a recarmi il giorno susseguente al suo Konak per avere con lui un'intervista. L'oggetto di essa fu quello di richiedere:

a) il mio parere sul Trattato di pace di S. Remo e, se questo fosse favorevole alla sovranità ed indipendenza dello Stato Ottomano, autorizzare il Gran Vezir a rendere questo mio parere di pubblica ragione.

b) l'intervento del S. Padre presso le grandi Potenze firmatarie del Trattato per modificarne le condizioni.

Alla prima dimanda risposi: ch'ero ben dolente di non poterlo secondare per l'ordine categorico de' miei Superiori. La S. Sede aveva, durante il conflitto europeo, assolutamente vietato ai suoi Rappresentanti all'estero di accordare interviste e di esternare pubblicamente un giudizio qualsiasi sovra ogni sorta di avvenimenti politici.

Alla seconda, che io ritenevo con sicurezza che il S. Padre, per il principio di neutralità da Lui scrupolosamente osservato, e per la grave offesa di essere stata esclusa la Sua altissima autorità dalla Conferenza della Pace, si trovava nell'impossibilità di aderire alla sua preghiera.

Il Gran Vezir mi soggiunse allora che, per il bene comune dell'Impero Ottomano e per quello della Chiesa Cattolica, avessi fatto presente alla S. Sede che là ove penetrava la Grecia doveva esulare il turco ed il cattolico: che le Croissant et la Croix erano sempre andati d'accordo [*sic*]: che i cattolici in modo particolare furono sempre amati e beneficati dal Sultano e che in ogni tempo(!) godettero della più ampia libertà nell'esercizio del loro culto.

Lungo la conversazione mi feci ardito di domandargli se Egli fosse disposto a sottoscrivere il trattato di pace. N'ebbi questa ingegnosa risposta: "Monsignore, per dirle questo, dovrei pensarlo, ma mi trovo nell'impossibilità di farlo, come colui che ha ricevuto un colpo sulla testa.

Nonostante questa sua evasiva, la mia impressione è ch'egli, cognato di Sua Maestà, firmerà il trattato, se, rifiutandovisi, vedesse per sempre perduta Costantinopoli e la Corona.

La persona del Gran Vezir, non solo è odiata, ma detestata dai Nazionalisti. Già si è scoperta una congiura contro la sua vita e gli arresti de' cospiranti continuano ancora. Essi l'accusano di alto tradimento per il suo indirizzo politico, che, suscitando la guerra civile, fiacca le forze vive di resistenza contro la Grecia, loro aborrita nemica. Si dice che Adrianopoli opporrà accanita resistenza alle truppe greche che si avvanzeranno fra qualche giorno per occuparla e che i Nazionalisti dispongono in Anatolia di un forte esercito bene armato ed equipaggiato. Le speranze del trionfo della loro causa nazionalista sono anche riposte nel collegamento di queste forze con quelle tartare e bolcheviche [*sic*].

Di tanto ho creduto opportuno ragguagliare l'Eminenza Vostra e con sensi di somma stima ecc

[Translation]
Most Eminent Prince,

With the letter of the 30th last here enclosed, I was invited to visit the Grand Vizier, Damad Ferid Pasha, to go the following day to his *Konak*[260] to have an interview with him. The object of this was that of requesting:

a.) my opinion on the Peace Treaty of San Remo and, should this be favorable to the sovereignty and independence of the Ottoman State, to authorize the Grand Vizier to render public this opinion of mine.

b.) the intervention of the Holy Father with the Great Powers signatory to the Treaty so as to modify its conditions.

To the first question I answered: that I deeply regretted being unable to indulge him, by categorical order of my Superiors. The Holy See had, during the European conflict, absolutely forbidden its Representatives abroad to grant interviews or to publicly express any judgment whatsoever upon any sort of political event.

To the second, that I confidently believed that the Holy Father, for the principle of neutrality scrupulously observed by him, and for the grave offense of his Most High authority's having been excluded from the Peace Conference, would find it impossible to assent to his request.

The Grand Vizier added to me then, that, for the common good of the Ottoman Empire and of the Catholic Church, I should remind the Holy See that there where Greece enters the Turk and the Catholic should exit: that the Crescent and the Cross had always gotten along: that the Catholics in particular were always loved and assisted by the Sultan and that they always(!) enjoyed the most ample freedom in the practice of their religious worship.

Further along in the conversation I made so bold as to ask him if he were disposed to subscribe to the peace treaty. He made this clever response:

---

260 Translator's Note: *Konak*. In Turkish, an important private, or often official, residence.

"Monsignor, to tell you this, I would have to think it, but I find myself unable to do so," as if he had received a blow to the head.

Notwithstanding this evasion of his, my impression is that he, His Majesty's brother-in-law, will sign the treaty if, in refusing, he were to see Constantinople and the Crown lost forever.

The figure of the Grand Vizier is not merely hated, but detested, by the Nationalists. A plot against his life has already been uncovered and arrests of the conspirators continue still. They accuse him of high treason for his policies, which, in instigating the civil war, weakened the active forces of resistance against Greece, their abhorred enemy. It is said that Adrianopolis will put up a fierce resistance to the Greek troops who will be advancing to occupy her within a few days, and that the Nationalists in Anatolia have at their disposal a powerful army, well-armed and well-equipped. Hopes for the triumph of their nationalist cause are also placed in the liaison of these forces with those of the Tartars and Bolsheviks.

I believed it opportune to inform Your Eminence of this, and with feelings of highest esteem etc

72

18 June 1920, Rome – handwritten draft of Gasparri's reply to Dolci
– *Ibid.*, n° 7232

Accuso regolare ricevimento del Rapporto 1266, in data 1 giugno corrente, nel quale V.S.Revma mi trasmetteva il resoconto di una intervista col Gran Vizir Damad Ferid Pacha.

Nell'approvare la riservatezza delle sue risposte, profitto ecc

[Translation]

I acknowledge the timely receipt of Report 1266, dated June 1st of this month, in which Your Most Rev. conveyed to me the account of an interview with the Grand Vizier Damad Ferid Pasha.

In approving of the discretion of your responses, I profit etc

73

8 June 1920, Paris – Boghos Nubar to the pope – AAEESS, *Asia* 57, 1, n° 8131

Très Saint Père,

Le sort indécis de la cause arménienne, qui a été jusqu'ici et est certainement encore le sujet de la sollicitude particulière de Votre Sainteté, me fournit l'heureuse occasion de présenter à Votre Auguste Personne, au nom de toute la nation arménienne, une instante requête digne de la plus bienveillante attention du Siège Apostolique.

Aucune cause en effet ne peut être plus justement déférée à la haute Mission de Justice, qui donne à Votre Pouvoir Suprême une influence morale supérieure à tous les intérêts et points de vue humains, que la cause de l'Arménie martyre; martyre précisément parce qu'elle est chrétienne; opprimée, parce qu'elle est fidèle à ses traditions; menacée d'extermination, parce qu'elle peut élever une forte barrière contre les invasions antichrétiennes et barbares.

L'inqualifiable persécution, dont l'Arménie a été victime de la part du Gouvernement et du peuple Turc, en a fait une Cause de lèse humanité, à laquelle la justice mondiale s'intéresse pour réclamer une satisfaction complète. Malheureusement le monde politique, trop préoccupé d'intérêts personnels ne veut point prendre le parti de résoudre cette grave question par un acte qui soit en harmonie avec les promesses solennellement faites et les principes si hautement proclamés des droit des peuples.

La voix autorisée de Votre Sainteté, qui déjà s'est fait entendre d'une façon efficace en faveur de l'Arménie, peut certainement intervenir de nouveau pour déterminer les Puissances à accomplir à l'égard de la nation Arménienne l'acte de pleine justice, sans lequel la victoire ne peut assurer la paix du monde, pas plus que celui des intérêts ne peut prévaloir sur la justice.

Restreindre et enfermer notre territoire comme dans un cercle et par là l'exposer de toute part au péril d'invasion des ennemis séculaires du nom chrétien, c'est consacrer la loi de la force brutale, en justifiant ainsi les actes anti-humanitaires qui consistent à massacrer les populations pour s'emparer de leurs biens. Abandonner en outre à ses propres moyens de défense et celà pour sauvegarder quelqu'avantage matériel, une nation victime exposée à des races sanguinaires décidées à l'exterminer, n'est-ce point santionner la loi de l'égoisme et des intérêts injustes?

Très Saint Père, Votre Sainteté qui, en qualité de Père commun de la famille morale de l'humanité, embrasse dans un même amour toutes les Nations, est l'unique autorité sur terre qui puisse efficacement intéresser les Grandes Nations en faveur des faibles menacées d'oppression et de mort.

C'est pourquoi, au nom de la nation que je représente, j'ose faire appel aux généreux sentiments de Votre Sainteté et la supplier de vouloir bien interposer son autorité pour conjurer le péril d'extermination des Arméniens, obtenir des Nations civilisées en faveur de l'Arménie, un secours moral et matériel à l'abri de tout péril, et enfin assurer ses droits territoriaux, financiers et civils.

Sa Grandeur Monseigneur Jean Nazlian, Evêque de Trébizonde, qui a apporté sa collaboration à notre Délégation, aura bientôt l'occasion d'exposer en détail à Votre Sainteté la situation actuelle de l'Arménie; c'est pourquoi je me tiens à des généralités.

Avec la confiance que Votre Sainteté daigne accueillir favorablement ma pressante requête que j'ai l'honneur de déposer à ses pieds, je suis ecc

74

8 July 1920, Rome – handwritten draft from Gasparri to the Count de Salis – AAEESS, *Asia* 57, 1, n° 8131

Son Excellence M. le Comte de Salis
Envoyé Extraordinaire et Ministre Plénipotentiaire
de S.M. Britannique près le Saint Siège

Le Président de la Délégation Nationale Arménienne auprès de la Conférence de Paix, vient d'adresser au Saint Père une lettre dans laquelle il expose le dangers qui menaceraient de nouveau ce peuple, déjà si cruellement éprouvé au cours de sa douloureuse histoire, si le pays qui lui est assigné était restreint dans ces limits et enfermé comme dans un cercle par des pays à population non chrétiennes, ennemies seculaires de la nation arménienne.

D'ordre de Souverain Pontife, le Cardinal Secrétaire d'Etat de Sa Sainteté en informant de ce qui précède Votre Excellence, a l'honneur de La prier de vouloir bien attirer là dessus la bienveillante attention de Gouvernement de S.M. Britannique afin que, fidèle à sa traditionnelle politique de protection accordée aux arméniens, il prenne en sérieuse considération les désastreuses conséquences qui pourraient découler pour cette Nation du fait d'une tracé de frontières qui la tiendrait éloignée de ses amis d'Europe et empêcherait l'exercice efficace de toute action protectrice en sa faveur.

Confiant que cet appel trouvera un sympathique accueil auprès de Votre Gouvernement, qui voudra bien user de son influence pour conjurer de nouvelle douloureuses complications dans l'avenir, le Cardinal soussigné profite de cette occasion pour Vous renouveler, Monsieur le Ministre, les assurance de plus haute consideration

75

9 July 1920, Rome – handwritten draft from Gasparri to Nubar – AAEESS, *Asia* 57, 1 n° 8132

Monsieur le Président,

D'ordre du Saint Père je n'ai pas manqué de communiquer le contenu de Votre lettre du 8 Juin dernier à S.E. le Ministre d'Angleterre en le priant de vouloir bien attirer l'attention de son Gouvernement sur les dangers qui menaceraient la noble et généreuse nation arménienne du fait des limites politiques qu'on se propose de lui assigner.

En espérant que cet appel du Saint Siège trouvera un sympathique écho chez tous les amis du peuple arménien, le Saint Père me charge de Vous Transmettre les Augustes remerciements des sentiments que Vous avez exprimés et de Vous assurer en même temps qu'Il ne cesse pas d'implorer le

Seigneur de mettre un terme aux souffrances de Votre peuple et de le diriger dans les voies d'un avenir heureux et prospère.

Veuillez recevoir, Monsieur le Président, l'expression ecc

76

10 October 1920, Paris – Historical commentary by Nubar – AAEESS, *Asia* 57, 1, n° 1350

En 1916, à la suite des Conventions tripartites de Londres, où le sort de l'empire ottoman fut décidé, la France s'inspirant de ses traditions chevaleresques, promit aux arméniens une large autonomie en Cilicie et dans les provinces de Sivas, Kharpout et de Diarbékir, en reconnaissance de leurs droits historiques et ethnographiques sur ces régions.

Et il fut convenu que pour mériter leur libération du joug turc dans cette partie de l'empire ottoman, les Arméniens apporteraient leur concours aux Alliés en se battant contre les Turcs dans une expédition française en Cilicie. C'est ainsi que la Légion d'Orient devenue plus tard Légion Arménienne, fut crée. Ce geste généreux de la France provoqua un enthousiasme indescriptible dans tous les milieux arméniens et de toutes parts les volontaires accoururent par milliers. La Légion arménienne ne se fit pas attendre pour se distinguer. Elle gagna en 1918 la bataille d'Arara, considérée par les officiers français qui la commandaient, comme le pivot des opérations militaires en Palestine et qui valut à nos volontaires non seulement les félicitations de leurs Chefs, mais aussi celles, très chaleureuses, du général Allenby, Commandant en Chef des forces britanniques en Orient.

Après l'armistice, le Gouvernement de la République, fidèle à sa promesse, fit occuper la Cilicie par les troupes arméniennes et ordonna le rapatriement aux frais de l'Etat de la plupart des survivants des massacres, déportés en Syrie.

Ainsi, grâce aux sacrifices du Gouvernement de la République et au dévouement des autorités françaises en Syie et en Cilicie, environ 170.000 Arméniens Cilicies furent rapatriés dans leurs foyers.

Mais peu après l'occupation de cette région par les Français les kémalistes les attaquaent de toutes parts et essayaient de les en chasser. Pour arriver plus facilement à leurs fins ceux-ci avaient vainement cherché sinon la collaboration active, tout au moins la neutralité des populations arméniennes de la Cilicie; mais ces dernières, repoussant avec indignation les avances des Turcs firent partout cause commune avec les Français.

Ainsi à Marache, les Arméniens se battirent côte à côte avec les Français, ce qui leur coûta, après la retraite de ces derniers, environ 12.000 victimes.

A Hadjine, malgré les exhortations des Français d'abandonner la ville, les Arméniens ont repoussé jusqu'ici vingt huit attaques des Turcs et les tiennent encore en respect.

Zeitoun a mis en échec toutes les attaques kémalistes et le drapeau tricolore flotte toujours sur les hauteurs de la cittadelle arménienne.

A Aintab, nonobstant le manque de ravitaillement et malgré toutes sortes de privations, la défense héroïque des Arméniens a provoqué l'admiration des Officiers de l'Etat-Major Français.

Partout ailleurs, à Sis, à Ourfa, à Hassan-Beyli, à Kurt-kalé, etc etc les forces françaises ont été très efficacement secondées par les Arméniens, dont la bravoure et la loyauté sont devenue proverbiales.

Mais malgré tout leur dévouement et en dépit de tant de sacrifices qu'ils s'étaient imposés, les Arméniens devaient se préparer à une déception pénible.

Le bruit, devenu de plus en plus persistant, de l'abandon de la Cilicie aux Turcs produisit l'effet d'un coup de massue sur la tête des malheureuses populations chrétiennes qui, à peine libérées des plus terribles persécutions se refusainet d'être mises à nouveau sous le joug odieux des Turcs. Aussi, à deux reprises, en Avril et en Mai 1920, les Chrétiens de la Cilicie protestèrent-ils avec la dernière énergie contre l'abandon de cette région à la Turquie. Ce fut peine perdue. En désespoir de cause, ceux-ci tentèrent un dernier et suprême effort, en proclamant, par un manifeste di 1 Août, leur libération du joug turc et leur détermination de lutter jusqu'à la mort pour échapper à l'oppression de leurs bourreaux.

Mais ce manifeste n'eut pas plus d'effet que les précédentes protestations, et le Traité de Sèvres n'en tenant aucun compte fit abandon de la majeure partie de la Cilicie aux Turcs.

La Délégation Nationale Arménienne qui, par son acte en date du 14 Août 1920 adressé au Conseil Suprême, a protesté contre cette injustice, est la première à reconnaitre qu'une fois le Traité signé, l'on ne saurait plus échapper à ses conséquences. Aussi, tout en regrettant que le Conseil Suprême n'ait pas tenu compte des légitimes aspirations de nos compatriotes au sujet de la Cilicie, la Délégation propose-t-elle de garantir la vie et la sécurité des 270.000 Chrétiens de ce pays en leur octroyant une autonomie administrative sous le contrôle ou la protection de la France, tout en conservant, d'après les termes du Traité, la souveraineté turque sur cette région. La Cilicie deviendrait ainsi une province privilégiés de la Turquie et son autonomie administrative lui serait octroyée par iradé de S.M. le Sultan, sans que cela pût en aucune façon donner lieu à des difficultés internationales.

D'autre-part, la Délégation apprend avec en profond regret que les troupes françaises seraient sur le point de se retirer de la Cilicie et procéderaient à l'expatriation, sous le nom de réfugiés, de plus de 20.000 Arméniens originaires de Marache, Hadjine, Sis, etc. abrités provisoirement à Adana après la retraite des troupes françaises des localités susdites. Cette mesure, si elle était mise à execution, ferait la ruine complète de nos maiheureux compatriotes déjà si cruellement éprouvés.

Aussi, confiante en la justice française, la Délégation espère que cette mesure, que rien ne justifie d'ailleurs, sera contremandée. Elle a également le ferme espoir que la France, protectrice séculaire des chrétiens en Orient, n'évacuera pas la Cilicie, et n'abandonnera pas à leur triste sort les malheureuses populations chrétiennes de cette région.

77

20 October 1920, Paris – handwritten letter from Terzian to Gasparri – AAEESS, *Asia* 57, 1, n° 19169

Eminenza Re.ma,

Prendo la rispettosa libertà di mandare qui inclusa la lettera di S.Ec. Boghos Nubar Pacha e prego di aver la bontà di communicarla al Santo Padre.

In questi tristi giorni siamo assai dolenti per i recenti avvenimenti dall'Asia Minore e di Cilicia, che i giornali celano. In questa stagione migliaia di armeni si mandano dalla loro città ai paesi lontani per mezzo dei kemalisti, da Kutahia, da Eskischir, da Bilegin, ecc. ecc. e dall'altra parte si cede in Cilicia ai turchi. Questa povera nazione armena si avvicina alla sua ultima rovina e sterminio.

Qui il sullodato Boghos Pacha, Presidente della Delegazione nazionale armena, mi ha pregato di ricorrere a chi di diritto; insieme abbiamo fatto molti ricorsi: ma che giova tutto ciò. Il Santo Padre ch'è stato nostro vero Padre e Liberatore per tanti Atti magnanimi, può solo salvare il resto degli armeni colla Sua Potente ed autorevole voce. Prostrato davanti l'Augusto Trono supplico umilmente la Sua pronta Intervenzione.

Chinato al bacio ecc.

[Translation]
Most Rev. Eminence,

I take the respectful liberty of sending here enclosed the letter of H. Exc. Boghos Nubar Pasha[261] and I pray you to have the goodness to communicate it to the Holy Father.

In these sad days we are very sorrowful for the recent events in Asia Minor and in Cilicia, that the newspapers suppress. In this period thousands of Armenians are driven from their cities to far-off countries by the Kemalists, from Kutahia, from Eskisehir, from Bilegin, etc. etc. and at the same time Cilicia is being ceded to the Turks. This poor Armenian nation is nearing its final ruin and extermination.

Here the above-mentioned Boghos Pasha, President of the National Armenian Delegation, begged me to appeal to those concerned; together we have made many appeals: but what good is all that. The Holy Father who has

---

261 Not found.

been our true Father and Liberator by so many magnanimous Acts, can only rescue the rest of the Armenians with His Powerful and authoritative voice. Prostrate before the August Throne I humbly beg his rapid Intervention.

Bowed to the kiss etc.

78

6 November 1920, Rome – handwritten draft from Gasparri to Nubar – AAEESS, *Asia* 57, 1, n° 13138

Monsieur le Président,

En me référant à Votre lettre du 18 Octobre dr,[262] je m'empresse de Vous informer que le Saint-Père, avant même que la susdite lettre ne Lui fût parvenue, avait daigné faire des démarches opportunes en signalant les nouveaux dangers qui allaient menacer Votre cher pays.

Profondément ému par les nouvelles alarmantes qui se propagent ces derniers jours sur la situation de la glorieuse nation arménienne devenue encore une fois victime d'une agression, le Souverain Pontife vient de réitérer ses instances afin de prévenir si possible des calamités ultérieures.

En donnant cette nouvelles preuve de Son affection paternelle pour Votre patrie, le Saint Père me charge Excellence de Vous exprimer en même temps les voeux chaleureux qu'Il forme aux pieds du Seigneur tout puissant en faveur de l'Arménie et de ses populations

En Vous faisant part de ce qui précéde et en joignant l'expression de mes sentiments personnels de profonde sympathie, je profite de cette occasion pour Vous renouveler, Monsieur le Président, l'assurance de la très haute consideration

79

21 November 1920, Rome – Naslian to Cerretti – AAEESS, *Asia* 57, 1 , n° 13508

Eccellenza,

In attesa dell'imminente arrivo di S.E. Mons. Patriarca Terzian ho rimandato la nota suggeritami da Vostra Eccellenza per l'insieme delle richieste Armene, per cui s'implora l'alto interessamento ed intervento della Santa Sede facendovi valere la potente sua influenza.

Il prelodato Patriarca è arrivato ieri 20 corrente, e siccome notizie sempre più incalzanti ci desolano, mi permetto d'accordo col medesimo presentare in fretta la succinta nota, che qui accludo, riservandoci un più completo esposto

---

262 Not found.

di tutte le richieste per gli interessi nazionali in genere e per i cattolici in specie a base anche del Trattato di Sèvres.

In Cilicia i cristiani sono minacciati di oppressione in seguito all'abbandono di quella regione da parte della Francia; a Marasc più particolarmente e nei paesi occupati dai Kemalisti, i Cristiani ed in specie i cattolici, quali protetti francesi, sono perseguitati: per necessità rinchiusi in recinti pubblici delle chiese, presbiterii e scuole a migliaia, vi restano condannati a perire senza poter sortire, e sottoposti alle più barbare prove con ogni sorta di attentati all'onore ed alla fede delle famiglie cristiane.

Un telegramma da Erivan pubblicato soltanto oggi dell'11 del mese corr. annunzia la disastrosa situazione creata nell'Arménia del Caucaso, di cui il Governo e popolo sinti [sic] in una guerra fatale ed impegnati a sostenerla ad oltranza d'avanti [sic] all'alternativa di vita e di morte, spiega tutta la decisiva gravità del momento per gli armeni.

S'impone quindi un efficace intervento dell'Augusto Pontefice di cui la voce autorevole commoverebbe opportunamente il mondo civile a favore di questa nazione e suo neonato Governo, così ingiustamente aggrediti da bande congiurate nell'odio anticristiano ed antieuropeo contro ogni elemento d'ordine e di cristiane convinzioni.

Eppero [sic] si supplica la S.Sede di fare d'urgenza tutto quello che le è possibile per salvare questa nazione in Armenia, in Cilicia ed in Turchia. Tale intervento avrebbe l'alto significato morale della paternità mondiale dell'Augusto Pontefice, unico Vindice della giustizia per tutti e specialmente per i deboli sopraffatti dalla prepotenza.

Pertanto ho l'alto onore di rassegnarmi ecc

Allegato al doc.n° 79 p. 291:

Appunti di Naslian per l'intervento della S. Sede a favore dell'Armenia.

1. Si richiede l'intervento della S.Sede presso le Potenze dell'Intesa per sollecitarne gli ajuti necessarii a scongiurare l'annientamento dell'Armenia.

2. Intervento se è possibile presso i Kemalisti per invitarli alla moderazione.

3. Presso il Partito Popolare Italiano presentare la causa armena degna di far oggetto della loro azione presso il Governo Italiano che sembra ben visto dai Kemalisti.

4. Interessare Sua Eminenza il Card. Mercier perché si adoperi presso il suo Governo e popolo a favore della medesima causa e trovi modo di sollecitare l'opera della Società delle Nazioni.

5. Interessare l'opinione del mondo cattolico a favore della povera Armenia per sua indole e tradizioni profondamente cristiani vittima del

fanatismo mussulmano, per cui dopo la Polonia è il baluardo più convinto contro l'invasione anticristiana del Bolscevismo e panislamismo.

6. Interessare più particolarmente la Francia della sorte dei cristiani in genere e degli armeni in specie nella Cilicia che a) non può e non deve essere riguardata regione maomettana come l'Algeria e Marocco; la Cilicia è per tradizione cristiana ed i 270.000 cristiani superstiti dei massacri, invitati dal Governo stesso francese a rientrarvi dopo l'armistizio del 1918, hanno diritti più che i maomettani a vedervi assicurata la loro vita e libertà; b) la Francia vi è impegnata per suo onore e per gli interessi suoi rimanervi a protettrice dei cristiani; c) è nell'interesse della Francia di ritenere la Cilicia non solo per semplice zona d'influenza, ma bensi [sic] costituirvi una autonomia amministrativa per i Cristiani, che non sarebbe contrario all'applicazione stessa del Trattato di Sèvres, potendo mantenervi la sovranità turca come in provincia privilegiata della Turchia medesima; d) non deve la Francia fare la consegna della Cilicia ai Kemalisti i quali non possono rappresentare la Turchia firmataria del trattato di Sèvres; e) non deve consegnarla neanche al Governo di Costantinopoli prima che questo abbia puntualmente e pienamente eseguito tutte le clausole del Trattato suddetto; f) deve la Francia rispettare in Cilicia le tradizioni armene e relativi diritti anche per la collaborazione degli armeni nell'occupazione di quella regione, prezzo di sacrifizii e di sangue armeni; (V. Allegato A.

7. Interessare Sua Eminenza il Card. Dubois per intervenire presso il suo Governo nel senso esposto ed adoperarvisi onde vengano risparmiati agli armeni i maltrattamenti inesplicabili di cui son oggetto principalmente gli armeni dalla parte del Governo e Comando Francese di Cilicia (V. Allegato B)

8. Modi e misure di obbligare la Turchia ed i Kemalisti ad accettare il Trattato e conformarvisi eseguendone le clausole specialmente per riguardo dell'Armenia, non mancherebbero alle Potenze se avessero volontà decisa in proposito: potrebbero essi e dovrebbero a) estendere le zone d'occupazione ed a ciò non occorrerebbero nuove spedizioni militari, i cristiani indigeni e specialmente gli armeni vi si presterebbero; b) mandare alcune delle corazzate stazionarie a Costantinopoli in numero più che sufficiente a fermarsi nei porti di Samsun, di Trebizonda , di Batum;la presenza di queste navi come impressiona Costantinopoli e tiene in guardia a Costantinopoli, lo farebbe meglio in quelle provincie che non sarebbero state occupate dai Kemalisti se già vi fossero presenti alcune di quelle navi; c) serie pressioni sulla Sublime Porte con minaccie contemplate nel Trattato indurrebbero questa, che è certamente in secreto accordo con i Kemalisti, a consigliar a questi ultimi un attitudine [sic] meno pretenziosa ed audace. Accademiche dichiarazioni della Società delle Nazioni non bastano, ci vogliono atti pronti ed efficaci.

9. Si obbjetterà per la mobilizzazione dei cristiani contro i Kemalisti, come ci è stato fatto specialmente dai Francesi, che i Maomettani sarebbero

eccitati e provocati per rappresaglie in cui potrebbero eccedere i cristiani particolarmente gli Armeni pieni di animo vendicativo; ma si può loro osservare che a) i Maomettani di Turchia non possono essere concitati più di quello che lo sono attualmente; b) la responsabilità di misure energiche contro i Turchi potendo facilmente far ricadere sopra i Kemalisti, l'eccitazione maomettana vi convergerebbe da se [sic] e non sognerebbero la possibilità di riuscire nel progetto panislamico di quelle bande avventuriere; c) l'animosità poi dei cristiani contro i giovani turchi è precisamente quella disposizione che ci vorrebbe per determinare questi ad un azione militare, bisognerà adunque sfruttarla, che del resto non è stato difficile né lo è di soffocarla o moderarla come e quando lo vorranno i Comandi militari; d) ma poi perché essere tanto teneri di una razza sanguinaria che appena si crede libera e fuori d'attenzione o di mano europea, rinnova gli atti i più atroci contro i cristiani che hanno giurato di esterminare? e) e la pace del mondo non si avrà, anzi non è difficile prevedere complicazioni già annunziate da alleanza di Bolscevichi e maomettani, se non si vorrà mettere sotto freno le mosse dei Kemalisti, dei Turchi cioè liberi da controllo ed armati.

[Translation]

Excellency,

While waiting for the imminent arrival of H. E. Mons. Patriarch Terzian I sent once again the note suggested me by Your Excellency for the collection of Armenian requests, for which is begged the deep interest and intervention of the Holy See asserting its powerful influence.

The abovementioned Patriarch arrived yesterday, the 20th of this month, and since ever more pressing news distresses us, I permit myself, in accord with the same, to quickly present the succinct note which I enclose here, reserving for ourselves a more complete exposition of all the requests for the national interests in general and for the Catholics in particular based on the Treaty of Sèvres as well.

In Cilicia the Christians are threatened with oppression following the abandonment of that region on the part of France; in Marash most particularly and in the towns occupied by the Kemalists, the Christians and in particular the Catholics, as French protectees, are persecuted: of necessity penned up by the thousands in the public enclosures of the churches, presbyteries and schools, they remain condemned to die without being able to come out, and are subjected to the most barbarous trials with every type of attempt upon the honor and the faith of the Christian families.

A telegram from Erevan, of the 11th of the current month but published just today, announces the disastrous situation created in Caucasian Armenia, whose Government and people ... in a fatal war and committed to sustaining it to the end in front of the alternative of life and of death, [and] explains all the critical gravity of the moment for the Armenians.

Required, then, is an effective intervention of the August Pontiff, whose authoritative voice should suitably move the civil world in favor of this nation and her newborn Government, so unjustly assailed by bands sworn to anti-Christian and anti-European hatred of every element of order and of Christian convictions.

However, the Holy See is entreated to urgently do all that is possible to rescue this nation in Armenia, in Cilicia and in Turkey. Such an intervention would have the high moral significance of the worldwide paternity of the August Pontiff, singular Vindicator of justice for all and especially for the weak overpowered by arrogance.

Meanwhile, I have the high honor of presenting myself etc

Attached to doc. n° 79 p. 291:
Naslian's notes about the intervention of the Holy See in favor of Armenia.

1. The intervention of the Holy See with the Entente Powers is requested to solicit from them the assistance necessary to prevent the annihilation of Armenia.

2. Intervention if possible with the Kemalists to invite them to moderation.

3. To the Italian Popular Party, present the Armenian cause as worthy of being object of their action with the Italian Government, which seems well-regarded by the Kemalists.

4. Interest His Eminence Card. Mercier[263] such that he do all he can with his Government and people in favor of the same cause, and try to solicit the action of the League of Nations.

5. Interest the opinion of the Catholic world in favor of poor Armenia, because of her nature and profoundly Christian traditions the victim of Muslim fanaticism, and who, after Poland, is the most staunch bulwark against the anti-Christian invasion of Bolshevism and pan-Islamism.

6. Interest France more particularly in the fate of the Christians in general and of the Armenians in particular in Cilicia which a.) can not and should not be regarded a Mohammedan region as are Algeria and Morocco; Cilicia is traditionally Christian, and the 270,000 Christian survivors of the massacres, invited by the very same French Government to return there after the armistice of 1918, have more rights than do the Mohammedans to see their lives and liberty guaranteed there; b.) France is committed by her honor and by her interests to remain there a protector of the Christians; c.) it is in the interest of France to hold Cilicia not just as a simple zone of influence, but rather to

---

263 Archbishop Primate of Belgium.

establish an administrative autonomy there for the Christians, which would not be contrary to the application itself of the Treaty of Sèvres, being able to maintain Turkish sovereignty there as in a province privileged by Turkey herself; d.) France must not consign Cilicia to the Kemalists, who cannot represent Turkey signatory to the Treaty of Sèvres; e.) must not consign her, either, to the Government of Constantinople before this has fully and punctually executed all the clauses of the above-mentioned Treaty; f.) France must respect Armenian traditions and respective rights in Cilicia, especially given the collaboration of the Armenians in the occupation of that region at the cost of Armenian sacrifices and blood; (v. Attachment A).[264]

7. Interest His Eminence Card. Dubois[265] in intervening with his Government in the sense set forward, and in doing his utmost such that the Armenians be spared on the part of the Government and French Command of Cilicia the inexplicable abuses to which principally the Armenians are subject (v. Attachment B).[266]

8. If they were to have decisive will in the matter, the Powers have no lack of ways and measures to oblige Turkey and the Kemalists to accept the Treaty and conform to it, executing its clauses especially with regard to Armenia: they could and should a.) extend the zone of occupation, and for that new military expeditions would not be necessary—the indigenous Christians and especially the Armenians would lend themselves; b.) send some of the battleships stationed at Constantinople in more than sufficient number, to stop in the ports of Samsun, of Trabizon, of Batum; the presence of these ships, as it does impress Constantinople and keeps Constantinople on its guard, would do so better in those provinces which would not have been occupied by the Kemalists if some of those ships had already been present there; c.) serious pressure on the Sublime Porte with threats contemplated in the Treaty would induce that court, which is certainly in secret accord with the Kemalists, to recommend to the latter a less pretentious and audacious attitude. Academic declarations by the League of Nations are not enough; ready and effective action is needed.

9. Some will object to the mobilization of the Christians against the Kemalists, as has been done especially by the French, since the Mohammedans would be agitated and provoked by reprisals in which the Christians might go too far, particularly the Armenians full of vindictive spirit; but let them observe that a.) the Mohammedans of Turkey cannot be more agitated than they are currently; b.) the responsibility of energetic measures against the Turks potentially falling easily back onto the Kemalists, the Mohammedan agitation would converge on itself and they could not dream of the possibility of

---

264 Not found.
265 Archbishop of Paris after Amette.
266 Not found.

succeeding in the pan-Islamic project of those bands of adventurers; c.) the animosity, then, of the Christians against the Young Turks is precisely the disposition that is needed to resolve them to military action, it needs therefore to be exploited, which was not difficult, after all, nor is it to stifle or moderate when and how the military Commands should want; d.) but then why be so tender to a bloodthirsty race who, as soon as they believe themselves free from European attention or out of the Europeans' way, renew the most atrocious acts against the Christians, whom they have sworn to exterminate? e.) and the peace of the world shall not be had; on the contrary, it is not hard to preview complications already announced by the alliance of Bolsheviks and Mohammedans if no one puts a stop to the moves of the Kemalists, of the Turks that is, uncontrolled and armed.

80

28 November 1920, Rome – Gasparri to Terzian – AAEESS, *Asia* 57, 1, n° 13163

Mi è giunta la pregiata lettera di V. E. Rma, in data del 20 ottobre scorso, circa i pericoli che minacciano la Nazione Armena in Cilicia.

Posso assicurarLa che la Santa Sede si è ripetutamente e caldamente interessata nel senso desiderato da V.E. e non manca di tener presente il gran argomento.

Nell'esprimere la fiducia che il Signore benedirà queste premure e risparmierà a cotesta nobile nazione, già così crudelmente provata, nuovi dolori, profitto dell'incontro ecc

[Translation]

I received the esteemed letter of Y.M.Rev.E., dated last October 20th, about the dangers that threaten the Armenian Nation in Cilicia.

I can assure you that the Holy See has repeatedly and whole-heartedly taken interest in the sense desired by Y.E. and does not fail to bear in mind the great topic.

In expressing faith that the Lord will bless these attentions and will spare this noble nation, already so cruelly proven, new pains, I profit from the encounter etc

81

18 December 1920, Tiflis – Moriondo[267] to Card. [Marini?] – CO, 106, 2, 3, n° 4999

Voglio sperare che Le sia giunto il rapporto, inviatoLe in data 12 scors. Novembre nel quale riferivo particolareggiatamente la situazione oltremodo

---

[267] Natale Gabriele Moriondo, Bishop of Cuneo, envoy to the Caucasus as Visitor Apostolic. His report of November 12th was not found.

critica della regione affidata alle mie cure di Visitatore Apost. e la condizione non meno critica in cui io stesso mi trovo.

Riferendosi a detto rapporto, credo ora opportuno fare noto all'Eminenza Vostra, quanto di rilevante è avvenuto in seguito.

1. La situazione politica è di molto peggiorata, causa i gravi avvenimenti politici, che pure saranno noti all'Eminenza Vostra: voglio dire, la disfatta dell'Armenia, per opera dei Kiemalisti, e la caduta di essa in mano d'un governo bolscevico; la vittoria dell'armata bolscevica sulle truppe del Gen. Wrangel in Crimea, e il fallimento completo della rivolta, che i partiti avversi tentarono contro il regime bolscevico, nel Kuban e nel Daghestan.

Fatti, che costituiscono un pieno successo del governo bolscevico di Mosca, che è ormai padrone di tutta la Russia del sud, fino all'antico confine dell'Asia Minore. Non rimane, fuori del suo dominio, che la Repubblica della Georgia, la quale difficilmente potrà sfuggire alla sorte comune.

Le persone competenti e ben informate ritengono ciò come certo, solo dissentono sulla data. Vi è chi crede che il fatto avverrà fra qualche mese, quando il terreno sarà meglio preparato, e vi è chi pensa che potrebbe verificarsi a breve scadenza, con un colpo di scena improvviso. Tutti però sono di parere che ciò si farà in modo pacifico, senza strepito d'armi, né spargimento di sangue; come già avvenne nelle Repubbliche dell'Azerbedjan e dell'Armenia.

È pure sentimento comune delle personalità politiche, che tutte queste regioni del Caucaso ritorneranno sotto il dominio di un regime Russo, che le potrà forse governare con altra forma politica da quella della autocrazia ora tramontata, ma che ben difficilmente concederà ai popoli la necessaria libertà religiosa, specie riguardo al Cattolicismo.

E quando simili fatti avvengano, che potrò io fare ancora in queste regioni? È vero che anche al presente sono pressoché nell'impossibilità di far qualche cosa di quanto era scopo della mia missione, ma sotto un regime bolscevico sarà certo più difficile ancora la mia permanenza, se pure non diverrà pericolosa.

2. La situazione economica va parimenti peggiorando ogni dì più. Il costo della vita è aumentato dell'ottanta per cento circa, sui prezzi che davo nell'ultimo rapporto. La miseria pubblica è indescrivibile. L'inverno è molto rigido e dal principio di Novembre cadono copiose nevicate.

3. La situazione religiosa soffre naturalmente di tutti questi mali, i quali non solo impediscono di migliorarla, ma la rendono ognor più critica e fan temere che per lungo tempo ancora queste regioni abbiano a rimanere nello stato di desolazione religiosa, in cui furono sotto la tirannia dello czarismo.

4. L'attuale Governo Giorgiano intanto comincia a metter la mano sui beni religiosi. Giorni fa dichiarò proprietà dello stato quattro dei più importanti Monasteri con rispettive Chiese, considerandoli come monumenti

d'arte. E avendo trovato a mancare un calice di valore, ne chiese ragione al Patriarca, il quale rispose, esser stato venduto pel mantenimento del Clero, che più non ha di che vivere. Ne seguì un vivace conflitto fra Governo e Patriarca, che ebbe come risultato, la citazione di questi ai tribunali. Intanto la stampa mena una campagna piena d'insulti e d'accuse contro il clero.

4. Riferivo nel precedente rapporto di aver sottratto alla giurisdizione eccl. Armena e sottomesso all'Amministrazione dei Giorgiani i paesi del distretto di Akaldzike, che avevo visitati in persona, e mi avevano espresso il lor volere esplicito in proposito. Dicevo pure d'aver promosso un referendum, dello stesso tenore, nei paesi del distretto di Akalkalaki. Il risultato di esso fu, che il paese di Tursk chiese di rimanere sotto la giurisdizione Armena, e quelli di Bavra, Kulgumo e Kartikam, quasi all'unanimità, dimandarono di passare alla giurisdizione dell'Amministrazione Giorgiana. A giorni, quando avrò terminate alcune formalità necessarie a farsi, deciderò secondo i voleri espressimi.

5. Seppi, per via indiretta, che sono giunti a Cospoli i Missionarii Gesuiti, che erano destinati a Tiflis. La notizia mi fé specie, non avendo io ricevuto avviso alcuno in riguardo, sia dalla S. Congregazione, sia dai detti Missionarii. Telegrafai subito loro di non proseguire e di attender ordini a Cospoli. Poiché, come già scrissi nel precedente rapporto, io son persuaso che non sia questo il momento di far venir Missionarii. Essi sarebbero nell'impossibilità di lavorare, avrebbero davanti a se una situazione economica disastrosa e un avvenire scoraggiante e pieno d'incertezze. Non sarebbe forse neppur possibile trovar loro un'abitazione.

Prego quindi l'Eminenza vostra di volerm'inviare subito ordini riguardo a questi Missionarii, o meglio ancora comunicarli loro direttamente, per mezzo del Delegato Apostolico di Cospoli.

6. Avendo saputo che l'armata turca dei Kiemalisti maltratta le popolazioni dei paesi armeni ultimamente occupati, credetti cosa utile intervenire presso il Comando di essa, raccomandando, a nome del Sommo pontefice, le popolazioni cristiane e specialmente i cattolici. Mi fu risposto che si userà loro ogni riguardo. Voglio sperare che non saranno semplici parole.

Questa è, Eminenza, la situazione in cui mi trovo: e, come già dissi altra volta, io penso che ormai la mia permanenza quì sia del tutto inutile, e per lungo tempo ancora non potrà raggiungere alcuno degli scopi che da essa si speravano. Questo pure è il parere delle personalità politiche e diplomatiche che quì si trovano.

Se questa S. Congregazione ancor non ha preso determinazioni in riguardo, prego l'Eminenza Vostra a voler disporre che lo si faccia quanto prima, poiché il ritardo non fa che sempre più compromettere le cose.

Qualora l'Eminenza Vostra avesse ordini urgenti da comunicarmi, lo potrà fare per radiotelegrafia del Ministero degli Esteri, che ogni dì comunica colla Missione Italiana di quì. Il corriere postale viene molto irregolarmente e con grandissimo ritardo.

Voglia, Eminenza, ricordarmi nelle sue preghiere, e gradisca i sensi della mia filiale obbedienza, mentre con ossequio le bacio il sacro anello.ecc.

[Translation]

I would like to hope that you received the report sent to you on this past 12th of November, in which I related in detail the extremely critical situation of the region entrusted to my care as Visitor Apost. and the condition, not less critical, in which I find myself.

In reference to said report, I believe it is now opportune to notify Your Eminence of how many important things have happened subsequently.

1. The political situation is greatly worsened, due to the serious political events, which shall be known to Your Eminence, by which I mean: the unmaking of Armenia by the Kemalists, and her fall into the hands of a Bolshevik government; the victory of the Bolshevik army over the troops of Gen. Wrangel in the Crimea, and the complete failure of the revolt that the opposing parties attempted against the Bolshevik regime in Kuban and in Daghestan.

Facts which constitute an ample success for the Bolshevik government of Moscow, by now master of all of southern Russia, up to the former boundary of Asia Minor. Nothing remains outside its dominion but the Republic of Georgia, who shall succeed in escaping the common fate with difficulty.

Qualified and well-informed persons hold that to be certain, only disagreeing on the date. There are those who believe the event will come to pass a few months from now, when the ground shall be better prepared, and those who think that it could happen in the shorter term, with a sudden *coup de théâtre*. All, however, are of the opinion that this will take place in a peaceful way, without the clamor of arms, or the spilling of blood; as has already occurred in the Republics of Azerbaijan and of Armenia.

It is also the common feeling among political figures that all these regions of the Caucasus will return under the dominion of a Russian regime, that will perhaps be able to govern them with a political form different from that of the autocracy upon which the sun has already set, but which is very unlikely to concede to the peoples the necessary religious freedom, particularly with regard to Catholicism.

And should similar events come to pass, what more will I be able to do in these regions? It is true that even at present it is nearly impossible for me to do any of the things that were the aim of my mission, but under a Bolshevik regime my stay will certainly be more difficult still, if it doesn't become outright dangerous.

2. The economic situation goes along equally, worsening more every day. The cost of living has risen by about eighty percent over the prices I gave in the

last report. The people's poverty is indescribable. Winter is very harsh and from the beginning of November snow falls copiously.

3. The religious situation naturally suffers from all of these ills, which not only impede its improvement but render it every hour more critical and make one fear that for a long while to come these regions must remain in the state of religious desolation in which they were under the tyranny of tzarism.

4. The current Georgian Government, meanwhile, has begun to put their hands on religious assets. Days ago it declared four of the most important Monasteries, with their respective Churches, property of the state, deeming them art monuments. And having found a valuable chalice missing asked an account of it of the Patriarch, who responded that it had been sold for the maintenance of the Clergy, who have nothing else to live on. Thereby ensued a spirited dispute between the Government and Patriarch, which resulted in the Patriarch's being called into court. In the meantime, the press is leading a campaign full of insults and accusations against the clergy.

4. [sic] I referred in the preceding report to having subtracted from Armenian eccles. jurisdiction and submitted to the Administration of the Georgians the towns of the district of Akhaltsikhe, which I had personally visited; they had expressed to me their explicit desire in that regard. I also spoke of having promoted a referendum, in the same vein, in the towns of the district of Akhalkalaki. The result of this was, that the town of Tursk[268] asked to remain under Armenian jurisdiction, and the towns of Bavra, Khulgumo and Kartikam, almost unanimously, asked to pass to the jurisdiction of the Georgian Administration. In a few days, when I will have completed some formalities necessary to doing so, I will decide according to the wishes expressed to me.

5. I found out, indirectly, that the Jesuit Missionaries who were destined for Tiflis have reached Constantinople. The news surprised me, not having received, myself, any notice in that regard, either from the S. Congregation, or from said Missionaries. I quickly telegraphed them to not proceed onward and to wait for orders in Constantinople. Since, as I already wrote in the preceding report, I am persuaded that this is not the moment to have Missionaries come. They would find it impossible to work; they would have before themselves a disastrous economic situation and a discouraging future full of uncertainties. It might not even be possible to find them lodging.

I pray, then, that Your Eminence send me immediate instructions regarding these Missionaries or, better yet, communicate with them directly, by means of the Apostolic Delegate of Constantinople.

6. Having heard that the Turkish army of the Kemalists ill-treat the populations of the recently occupied Armenian towns, I believed it useful to intervene with their Command, entrusting them, in the name of the Supreme

---

268 Translator's Note: Tursk is probably Turtshki, now in Georgia.

Pontiff, with the Christian populations and especially the Catholics. It was replied to me that every consideration will be shown. I want to hope that these won't be mere words.

This is, Eminence, the situation in which I find myself: and, as I already said before, I think that my sojourn here now is utterly futile, and for a long time to come shall not reach any of the ends that were hoped for from it. This is also the opinion of the political and diplomatic figures here.

If this S. Congregation has still not made a determination in this regard, I pray that Your Eminence would arrange that it be made as soon as possible, since the delay does nothing but compromise things even more.

Should Your Eminence have urgent orders to communicate to me, you may do so via the radiotelegraph of the Foreign Ministry, that each day communicates with the Italian Mission here. The postal courier comes very irregularly and with enormous delay.

Would that Eminence remember me in his prayers, and appreciate the sentiments of my filial obedience, as with deep respect I kiss the holy ring, etc.

82

23 January 1921, Rome – Delpuch to Marini – CO, *Armeni in genere e Caucaso* [Armenians in general and Caucasus], 1921–22, 106, 3, 5, 2, n° 5145

Eminentissime Seigneur,

Je me fais un plaisir et un devoir de transmettre la lettre çi-jointe que j'ai reçue durant le récent séjour que j'ai fait à Constantinople. Elle émane d'une des plus hautes personnalités du monde Arménien du Caucase. L'auteur est ce même M. Grégoire Evengouloff, ancien ministre à Petrograd pour les Affaires du Caucase et membre du Conseil impérial de Russie,[269] dont j'ai longuement rapporté le témoignage dans mes rapports sur ma mission au Caucase. Votre Eminence y trouvera la confirmation de tout ce que j'ai dit sur l'état et la nature d'esprit du monde Arménien grégorien. Ce qu'il dit de ces compatriotes de l'Arménie russe, s'applique également à ceux de Turquie.

Il est à noter que l'auteur de cette lettre n'est pas catholique lui-même, mais nourrit des sentiments de profonde vénération pour l'Eglise catholique.

Je reste toujours etc.

83

23 October 1920, Tiflis – Evangouloff to Delpuch – CO, 106, 3, 5, 2 n° 5145

Reverendissimo ed Illustrissimo Padre!

Forse nella sua tenace memoria è rimasto ancora vivo il ricordo del nostro abboccamento di qualche ora, nella casa del mio compianto fratello, il Rappresentante Diplomatico della Repubblica d'Armenia in Georgia, sign, Leone Evangouloff, presso cui Lei una sera favorir volle per il "the".

---

269 V. note n° 251.

Io ho saputo che dalla mia sincera conversazione d'allora Lei ha formato favorevole opinione su quelle disposizioni e provvedimenti che io aveva insistito essere necessario studiar quanto prima ed affidare a mani esperte e sicure.

Avendo fiducia che per Lei non sarà noioso il sentirmi un'altra volta; mentre ardentemente desidero cooperare con animo e cuore alla Sua summenzionata opera e portarvi ogni facilitazione secondo le mie deboli forze; m'approfitto della venuta di P. Dionigi a Constantinopoli per vedere Vostra Paternità, e mi permetto sinceramente e amichevolmente di scrivere ciò che segue, in rimenbranza di ciò che lungamente parlammo insieme.

È ben noto a Lei, Reverendissimo Padre, come ad illustre orientalista e storico, come gli Armeni, in seguito a disaccordi sul concilio di Calcedonia separarono la loro chiesa da quella greca, e siccome essi, come nazione, erano continuamente circondati da nemici e senza tregua in mezzo a rovine e pericoli guerreschi, per guisa tale isolarono la loro chiesa ed allontanarono ogni intromissione straniera; che questa divenne una cittadella di autodifesa per l'intiera nazione armena. Per conseguenza venne formandosi questa profonda persuasione,- come in tutto l'oriente del resto - che: chi apparteneva alla chiesa armena, era armeno, e che chi era fuori della chiesa nazionale, quegli non era armeno.

Quindi il cattolico, il riformato, benchè per nascita armeni, essendo eterodossi, non erano più armeni. In Oriente, è certo ben noto a Lei, un greco non ortodosso non è greco, ma invece appartiene a quella nazione, la religione della quale professa. Così anche la nazione Serba, secondo le varie professioni religiose, si divide in tre nazionalità: chiamansi Serbi (ortodossi), Croati (cattolici) e Bosniaci (maomettani). In Georgia, poi, si considerano come giorgiani solo gli ortodossi, e i giorgiani-cattolici sono chiamati "Frachi"; come pure tutti i cattolici di Oriente; mentre in Pologna un polacco non cattolico non era chiamato polacco.

Ed ecco mutua neutralità, isolamento, divisione e sfiducia fra persone e communità appartenenti alla medesima nazione, ma di diverse religioni. In breve, in Oriente e per gli orientali, la professione religiosa e la nazionalità, sono idee inseparabili e causa di molta confusione ed imbrogli. E questo fatto è più chiaro a Lei, che per lunghi anni ha lavorato in Oriente che ad altri non esperti dell'Oriente.

È questo ecco la principale ragione, che, nonostante che la Chiesa Cattolica sia tanto rigogliosa, e disponga di pronti ed illuminati operai, pur tuttavia non abbia dato prove di larghi successi per quanto riguarda la chiesa armena, il suo clero e perfino il suo popolo; come invece ne ha avute in altri luoghi in Occidente.

Per la chiesa, clero e popolo armeno, in seguito all'isolamento di autodifesa della medesima chiesa, è straniero chiunque non professa ciò che essa professa; e quindi un cattolico, sebbene pure armeno di nascita, non è armeno; egli è cattolico, è straniero.

La chiesa armena, come centro e suprema protettrice d'ogni armeno, anche fuori dell'Armenia, era divenuta una forza congiungente, centripeta, senza di cui non si poteva comprendere la nazione armena. La chiesa nazionale armena fuse in uno tutta l'armenità del mondo, rendendo indivisibili le idee: la nazionalità e la religione nazionale.

Questa neutralità, questo separatismo autodifesico della chiesa armena, era sì un grande fonte d'energia; ma bisogna dire, che allo stesso tempo ne era la causa principale di debolezza. Ed ecco dov'era il principio della presente dolorosa situazione della chiesa armena.

Dopo la caduta del regno d'Armenia signora e protettrice dell'abandonata nazione armena, divenne la chiesa nazionale armena, nella persona dei Catholicos e della gerarchia ad essi sommessa. E così le molteplici necessità della nazione armena, la soluzione di questioni sia pure oltre l'ambito del campo ecclesiastico, divennero oggetto incontestabile delle cure e premure dei capi della chiesa e degli ordinari diocesani. La liberazione degli schiavi, la cura delle vedove ed orfani, l'istruzione dei fanciulli e fanciulle, l'amministrazione delle scuole, il collocamento e provvedimento degli emigranti, fugiti [sic] e sottrati [sic] dagli straggi [sic], protezione politica contro le persecuzioni del proprio popolo, ecc., ecc.; fin anche l'organizzazione d'autodifesa, invitando volontari, provvedendo ad essi le occorrenze belliche; il fare dei passi diplomatici, degli appelli e domande; il mandare dei deputati e rappresentanti presso i governi d'Europa: come al Congresso di Berlino. Di questo abbiamo un'altra prova più recente: la missione politica di Boghos Nubar Pascià presso le potenze europee, come legato e rappresentante del Catholicos degli armeni, avente per credenziali l'enciclica del medesimo Catholicos, come di Capo responsabile e supremo della nazione armena.

Stando le cose in questo modo, la chiesa nazionale armena, pure politicamente forte, era assorbita completamente da lotte politiche, e per conseguenza anche d'intrighi dei partiti, e da sottigliezze e minuzie diplomatiche per poter difendere la nazione armena dalle supercherie dei governi stranieri; ed i ministri della medesima, cioè la gerarchia della chiesa nazionale, dal primo all'ultimo, essendo scelti unicamente per le loro attitudini in questo campo nazionale, e non come ferventi e pii ecclesiastici, col volger dei secoli si ebbe una schiera d'alto clero, d'individui capaci e strenui operatori politici, ma inetti e non corrispondenti alla loro propria vocazione, che era di Padri in spirito, di veri ecclesiastici. Eccoci la vera e propria ragione dell'attuale debolezza ed impotenza della chiesa nazionale armena; e questo fin a tal punto, che a me sono note persone, le quali per trovare consolazione spirituale, durante varie sfortune e dispiaceri personali, si rivolgono a conventi o chiese straniere, collo scopo di rimettersi e confortarsi spiritualmente; chiedendo a ministri di chiese straniere la soluzione di dubbi che li travagliano internamente.

Lo scopo di tutte le premure della gerarchia armena e l'unica linea direttiva d'azione, era risollevare la nazione armena dalla sua caduta, e di vederla quanto prima, in possesso e dotato di organizzazione politica, come le altre nazioni. Ed ecco questo suo desiderio si è realizzato, le sue incessanti fatiche sono state coronati di successo, si ricostituì lo Stato armeno; il quale immediatamente prese nelle sue mani tutti quei rami d'operosità, che d'indole loro rispettavano alle autorità civili, ma che per necessità di fatto erano stati compiuti dalla chiesa nazionale armena, per mancanza dello Stato indipendente armeno. Ma questo cambio di ruoli, pure liberando il clero armeno da occupazioni civili, che lo sopraccaricavano, nondimeno divenne la causa dell'attuale dolorosa situazione della chiesa armena. La gerarchia, benché da una parte soddisfatta del fatto della realizzazione dello Stato armeno, dall'altra vide se stessa allontanata dallo splendido campo di operosità d'una volta. E questo non è tutto. Essa si avvide che la primiera sua attività politica, compiuta per necessità, aveva spento in se lo spirito ecclesiastico e disabituato dall'adempimento dei doveri d'ecclesiastico.

In questo ecco consiste la propria tragedia! La gerarchia armena essendo, da una parte, affievolita nello spirito ecclesiastico, sentendo in se poco ardore per le attitudini della vocazione ecclesiastica; dall'altra, le vennero sottratte tutte quelle occupazioni e opere di politica, d'istruzione, di provvedimento, ecc., tutta quella che insomma formavano l'ogetto de cure dello Stato.

La nazione armena che tanto soffrese, che per tanti secoli fu tribolata, abbisogna, come tutte le altre nazioni, d'efficace e reale conforto, di rifocillamento spirituale, specialmente perché il suo martirologio non è ancora finito; le sue vedove e le sue orfane non sono consolate; ai suoi malati, ai mutilati e affamati rimasti senza occupazione, non è stato ancora provveduto; le sue necessità vaste quanto il mare, esigono grandi cure, incoraggiamento ed aiuto. Ma per riuscire a tutto questo, per apportarvi un rimedio morale e spirituale, per ispirare pazienza e costanza, forza e corragio [sic], la Chiesa e la gerarchia armena non trovano più in se [sic] del vigore sufficiente per far fronte a tanti bisogni in seguito di quei secolari avventurosi [sic] prove ed interminabili persecuzioni; a cui sempre, insieme a tutta la nazione, vennero esse sottoposte, che le fecero affievolire in se medesimi, rendendole bisognose di energica riforma, di nuovo rifiorimento per diventarsi vitali e sorgenti di vita spirituale-morale per la gregge.

L'avvenire mostrerà quale via d'uscita troverà per se, in questi difficili condizioni, e con quali direttive incomincierà ad agire l'antica chiesa armena e la sua gerarchia. Secondo noi, questo deve formare l'oggetto delle più vive preoccupazioni dei migliori e più assennati ecclesiastici armeni.

La questione è questa: nella presente difficile situazione della nostra nazione, quando ogni ora, ogni giorno è prezioso per curare le ferite morali e spirituali del popolo armeno, per confortarlo, consolarlo, incoraggiarlo ed animarlo, può forse essa e le sue necessità aspettare lungamente per la ricerca di quei rimedi efficaci su cui essa deve porre le sue speranze di rinascenza morale?

L'esperimento della storia del passato nostro e delle altre nazioni, ci ha dimostrato, come in circostanze simili di sfacimento comune, quale salutare ed amorevole ruolo si sono assunte le istituzioni ecclesiastiche;i monasteri, i religiosi, le monache; che si sono trasformati in ospedali, orfanotrofi, scuole e case di rifugione, ecc., ecc.

Dunque , anche ora che i nostri sono distrutti, saccheggiati, dispersi o ridotti a miseria, in seguito della tirania [sic] dei nemici, è mai possibile che quella rigogliosa ed organizzata chiesa che ha sempre nutrito in se amore ed affetto verso tutta la nostra nazione armena,-benchè una parte sola di essa si sia ricoverata sotto il di Lei manto,- è possibile, dico, ch'Essa resti indifferente in faccia di tanta miseria?

Non si affretterà Essa con tutte le sue forze, autorità e cristiana compassione ad accorrere in ajuto della nazione armena: tribolata, stanca ed oppressa?

C'è bisogno forse di ricordare quale prezioso aiuto apportò alla tribolata nazione armena la Grande Chiesa Romana durante l'ultima dinastia dei nostri re di Cilicia, dopo le incursioni e depredamento dei barbari? Non era forse Essa che incoraggiò e promosse l'aiuto dell'Europa nella persona delle Repubbliche di Venezia, Genova, Livorno, ecc., d'onde vennero in Cilicia sia ecclesiastici, sia uomini esperti e dotti, sia commercianti, ed ajutarono a riedificare, rifiorire e far rivivere la nostra nazione, ed a stringere durature relazioni coll'Europa?

Certo, ora con questo ragionamento, noi non osiamo permetterci neppure l'ombra di esagerate pretese; ma non è egli vero che non si possono dimenticare le vive e parlanti prove ed i vincoli storici, cominciando dalla stirpe reale dei Lusignani, rè dell'Armenia, fino a Caterina Cornaro? Non vorrà forse la Santa Cattedra, - sempre rigoliosa e forte, - dei successori di Celestino III, porgere una mano d'ajuto almeno in misura tale, perché l'Armenia almeno questa volta si rialzi definitivamente dalla secolare caduta;senta in quest'ora un appoggio palpabile da parte d'Essa medesima, e rivolga i suoi sguardi verso quella cultura di mente e di spirito , che brilla in Occidente di bagliori inestinguibili.

Discendendo più al pratico, noi riteniamo assolutamente necessario mandare, quanto prima, persone prudenti ed esperimentate; ma riteniamo insieme necessario che questi siano di nazione e di cuore armeni; e che loro capi responsabili siano di tali uomini da essere ben visti ed accettati alla massa armena; senza indisporla ed irritarla.Quì ripetiamo quel che già fu detto sopra: cioè: in Oriente chi non è della medesima nazione, egli è stimato straniero.

Siccome quelli che verranno certo non saranno di religione gregoriana ma cattolici, è necessarissimo che essi appartengano ad una tale istituzione, dell'armenità e del patriotismo di cui il popolo, la massa armena, non possa dubitare; e che questa abbia prove palpabili della loro operosità in pro della nazione, mostrando un precedente che colpisca gli occhi di tutti.

Queste persone e questa istituzione, - per nostra profonda convinzione,- è la casa di Mechitar Sebastese: Venezia e Vienna, ed i figli di Lui ed allievi: R.R.P.P. Mechitariani. Da questi non fugge la nazione armena, essa è digià sodisfatta [*sic*] dalla loro operosità di più di due secoli, ne è riconoscente. Essa li riceverà con piacere e li ascolterà, come sempre anche allora, quando il soggetto della loro conversazione non sia semplicemente scientifico, mappure [*sic*] religioso.

Non solo la scuola, ma anche la chiesa dei P.P. Mechitaristi saranno frequentati dagli armeni, senza timore; perché sanno, per convinzione, che essi non condurranno il popolo armeno alla mania dello straniero, ad estinguere il patriottismo, al cambio della propria nazione. Come con esempio può servire la chiesa degli Mechitaristi di Vienna. In quella città non esiste una chiesa armeno-gregoriana, per conseguenza tutti gli armeni ivi abitanti od altri di passagio, senza distinzione di professione religiosa, vanno, frequentano quella modesta chiesa armena, preferendola ad altre splendide degli stranieri.

Mi spiegherò meglio.

Ormai sono passati due secoli dacche, in seguito alle persecuzioni del Turco, l'Abbate Mechitar portò e fondò la sua Congregazione a San Lazzaro. Similmente è un secolo dacché l'altro ramo di essa si è trapiantato a Vienna per fiorirvi là.

I tempi esigevano così: andare, allontanarsi dai luoghi delle persecuzioni, dalla terra avventurosa di Madre Armenia; e in terra straniera, in tranquilla sicurezza: istruirsi, fiorire, e da lungi rendersi utile all'amata nazione.

Ma non è egli vero che ormai è arrivato anche per la nostra infelice e dispersa, istorica nazione armena, l'ora di raccogliersi in uno? Quindi è necessario che ogniuno [*sic*], specialmente quegli che sono consapevoli e dotati d'energia e di pronta erudizione d'attività, s'affrettino a ritornare nell'Armenia; ove tutti, a proporzione della propria capacità, ciascuno, lavorino all'edificazione della casa politica morale pel nuovo Stato Armeno.

Noi siamo partigiani del trasferimento in madre patria perfino delle colonie armene trovantesi vicino all'Armenia; tanto più per quelle che sono sì lontane, e nel tempo stesso sì utili per la patria; come quelle di Venezia e Vienna, ecc.. Non volendo io rendere deserto l'incantevole isola di San Lazzaro ed il monastero pieno di reminiscenze gloriose e storici, e ritenendo più convenevole che la Casa Madre dei Mechitaristi rimanga al medesimo posto; desideriamo che formi in Armenia, per così dire, una seconda casa centrale dei Mechitaristi, con tutti i rami della sua molteplice operosità.

Così si fonderà a Alessandropoli, - presunto centro della loro futura attività, come centro del cattolicismo, - un *Monastero* degli P.P.Mechitaristi di Venezia, con annessa bella *chiesa*. Una *scuola* per maschi, un altra per figlie; queste colle sezioni tecniche adatte a ciascun sesso. Una *stamperia*, una *libreria*, una *biblioteca*; tutto ciò con i debiti accessorj, come sapranno far meglio persone munite d'educazione europea e ben esperti nel loro mestiere religioso-scientifico, avendo l'unico scopo l'utilità morale-intellettuale ed il progresso del nostro popolo.

Mi spiego: il monastero servirà di dimora e asilo tranquillo per studiosi e modesti religiosi. La chiesa rispecchierà la purezza di rito e cerimonie, la dignità del canto sacro; vi si ascolterà predicazioni edificanti, sode ed erudite. La loro scuola oltre le scienze solite, sarà segnalata d'insegnamento della pura lingua nazionale armena: vecchia e nuova, e d'altre lingue europee si ricercate ora presso di noi Quanto alla stamperia Mechitarista, chi può da noi gareggiare con loro: sono già purtroppo [*sic*] note le edizioni di gran valore e lusso ed arte. Questo è loro specialità incontestabile. La libreria sarà ricca d'assortimenti d'edizioni armene ed europee, piuttosto di tutto ciò che riguarda l'Armenia e le novità scientifiche. Va senza dire che i P. P. Mechitaristi pubblicheranno un loro organo periodico scientifico-religioso, rilevante i più freschi ed interessanti prodotti della mente in Europa. Avranno loro fra altri anche una biblioteca ricca di libri, per facilitare ai studiosi loro ricerche scientifiche; essa sarà l'unico compendio d'edizioni almeno nazionali. In tal modo essi diverranno in Armenia, e prima che altrove, in Alessandropoli, un centro, intorno al cui s'aggrupperà la parte più intelligente del popolo. Così poco la volta si estenderanno per tutta l'Armenia partecipando la nazione alla provvisione scientifico-morale ramassato da loro in corso di più di due secoli.

Devo dire che questa mia proposta, a prima vista, pare debba aprire la porta a molte spese; ma in realtà non è così. La costruzione d'un monastero, e piuttosto d'una chiesa, in principio certamente richiede una forte somma; ma non è forse vero , che ogni chiesa poi ha le sue rendite? Accanto alla chiesa, indispensabilmente occorre aprire una cereria ed un magazzino di arredi sacri: paramenti, vasi sacri, biancheria, libri, vetrami, ecc.; la di cui necessità è più che evidente, sia dall'attuale stato di devastazione dell'Armenia, sia d'ora in avanti per agevolare il fornimento delle chiese in generale, anche non cattoliche. Fino ad oggi tutto ciò si riceveva dalla Russia, ed era tutto improntato d'ortodossia: le forme, le stoffe marcate di croce storta, ecc.; il nuovo magazzino deve essere non solo per le chiese cattoliche, ma pur anco per le eterodosse un centro di rifornimento avezzando tutti a forme nobili usati fra i cattolici. Ed al tempo stesso sarà una fonte di rendite.

Il rimpianto [*sic*] d'una stamperia, con l'annessa libreria e biblioteca, richiede certo delle spese; ma una tale impresa, nell'ora attuale, è opera commerciale di prima classe; una stamperia ben messa ora in Armenia godrà enormi lucri. I vecchi storchi e macchine delle stamperie mechitariane di Venezia e Vienna, trasportati in Armenia colla loro risparmio di carte, porterà d'immensi guadagni nel tempo di tanta crisi di simili materie.

Più di tutt'altro dev'essere costosa la pubblicazione del pensiero scientifico-religioso; giacché per anco ci manca l'amore per la lettura, fors'anche la capacità; siccome la massa dei contadini armeni non sa leggere. Ma i P.P.Mechitaristi sono abbituati a simili onorevoli ed utilissimi spese. Né la nazione armena si mostrerà indifferente.

I P.P.Mechitaristi sono anche buoni ed esemplari rifioritori d'economia rurale, cioè dell'agricoltura, nel vasto senso di questo ramo di scienza pratica. Ne fan fede le varie medaglie d'oro e d'argento e diplomi d'onore da essi meritate.

A quest'operosità di religiosi cattolici, noi riteniamo necessario che vada congiunta l'apertura di un monastero di monache cattoliche. L'unico monastero di donne presso gli armeni gregoriani del Caucaso, è quello di Tiflis; e l'opera di aprire un monastero di monache in Armenia, sarà un atto troppo grata ed all'uopo, fin anche indispensabile. Ed eccone la ragione. In Armenia ci sono innumerevoli madri che hanno disgraziatamente perduto i loro figli ed anche figlie; ci sono ancor non meno di consorti che hanno perduto i loro mariti. Addolorate madri, addolorate consorti hanno altrettanto bisogno di conforto e consolazione quanto di pane e d'acqua; e non v'è nessuno che loro dia consolazione; e questa manca ad essi. Non c'è una communita [*sic*] di istruite e spiritualmente forti donzelle, che le richiami dalla disperazione, che le riconforti abbattute; che asciughi le loro lagrime, porti e attiri le dolorose fissazioni delle loro mente a Dio, a vitali occupazioni. Roma tiene la sua disposizione, le Suore dell'Immacolata Concezione di Costantinopoli; le quali sono provviste sia di scienza, sia di una lunga esperienza nell'opera educatrice pia e religiosa, sia di conoscenza di varie lingue, unita ad esimie arti manuali, ricami, ecc. Ecco che importante lustro possono esse portare alla giovine generazione d'ambo i sessi nella nuova Armenia; specialmente alle diligenti ragazze, preparandone delle madri e consorti pie e forti di spirito per la nazione armena. Un gruppo d'esse, avendo a capo una esperta ed intelligente Superiora, bisogna mandare ad Alessandropoli, che deve diventare il centro del cattolicismo; un altro gruppo pure ad Erivan. All'arrivo di queste a destinazione, la loro principale opera deve essere la cura degli orfani, e più in là, designare alcune d'esse per l'intendenza degli ospedali. In Russia in genere e in specie nell'Armenia Russa c'erano e ci sono attualmente sorelle di carità, non religiose, le cui difetti sono abbastanza noti; era quindi evidente la mancanza di suore di carità religiose, che in modo così utile ed edificante operano in Europa. In tal maniera anche questo vuoto sarà colmato per opere delle suore armene a grande conforto delle sofferenti.

Reverendissimo Padre Visitatore,
avendo fiducia nella vostra longanimità, mi sono permesso di spiegare le mie buone proposte, afermandomi [sic] un po' più su alcuni punti di vista; ma a Lei quante altre specie di opere più utili sono note, con cui la chiesa cattolica, in questa ora di molteplici difficoltà, potrà arrecare aiuto, conforto e luce al nostro desolato popolo e goderne l'immensa gratitudine. Io devo dire che questo sarà l'unica via di rimediare ai dominanti pregiudizi, che chi non appartiene alla chiesa nazionale armena, egli non è armeno, è straniero e quindi persona da sospettarsi. Al contrario: avvicinandosi al rinascimento del popolo armeno con nobile ed illuminata operosità e recando, senza ombra d'interesse materiale, rimedio e medicina ai suoi mille mali e necessità, si dimostrerà chiaramente al bravo armeno qual'è in realtà il vero spirito del cristianesimo, e che "l'amore del prossimo" non è la mera e semplice parola o frase nella bocca dell'ecclesiastico, ma la realizzazione pratica di alti ideali d'uomini di principi vivificanti di verità, bontà e nobiltà.

Essendo ben noti a Lei i sentimenti del mio cuore, concetti della mia mente, aventi per lo scopo unico il vero utile della mia nazione, il suo nobilitamento spirituale e morale elevamento; spero che Lei non lascierà senza attenzione questo mio manifestato desiderio, - per tradurre il quale in pratica metto a sua disposizione le mie deboli forze,- e si impegnerà colla Sua alta influenza di intervenire dove e come occorrerà, per affrettarne la realizzazione. A proposito come saremmo avventurati se nella prossima quaresima, ad Alessandropoli ci fosse concesso d'ascoltare una serie di prediche pie ed imponenti che attiri i cittadini sotto le volte della chiesa armeno cattolica.

Raccomandandomi alle Sue pie preghiere mi segno con rispetto e sincerità di Vostra Paternità Revma Illma amico e servo, l'ex sotto-segretario del Consiglio Imperiale di Russia Grégoire Evangouloff

P.S. Pour vous faire parvenir à temps et rédiger en italien tout ce que aurez lu ci-dessus, je me sais servi du concours aimable du P Denis Kalatosoff et Don François Aghadjanian. Le même.

[Translation]
Most Reverend and Most Illustrious Father!

Perhaps, in your tenacious memory, the recollection still remains alive of our few hours' talk at the house of my late lamented brother, the Diplomatic Representative of the Republic of Armenia in Georgia, Mr. Leone Evangouloff, where one evening you did us the honor of having "tea".

I learned that, from my sincere conversation of that time, you formed a favorable opinion of those arrangements and provisions that I had insisted were necessary to study as soon as possible, and to entrust to secure and expert hands.

Having faith that it will not be tiresome for you to hear from me once again, while I ardently wish to co-operate with heart and soul to your abovementioned work and to bring to it every facilitation according to my feeble powers, I profit from the coming of F. Dionigi[270] to Constantinople to see Your Fatherhood, and I permit myself sincerely and amicably to write the following, in memory of that which we long talked about together.

It is well-known to you, Most Reverend Father, as a distinguished orientalist and historian, how the Armenians, following disagreements over the council of Chalcedony, separated their church from the Greeks', and given that they, as a nation, were continually surrounded by enemies and relentlessly in the midst of the ruins and dangers of war, in such a guise they isolated their church and warded off all foreign intrusion, such that this became a citadel of self-defense for the entire Armenian nation. In consequence, this profound conviction came to be formed—as in all of the orient, for that matter—that who belonged to the Armenian church, was Armenian, and that whosoever was outside of the national church, they were not Armenian.

Hence the Catholic, the reformed, although Armenians by birth, being heterodox, were no longer Armenians. In the Orient, as is certainly well-known to you, a non-orthodox Greek is not Greek, but instead belongs to that nation the religion of which he professes. So also the Serbian nation, according to the various religious professions, is divided into three nationalities: called Serbs (orthodox), Croats (Catholics) and Bosniacs (Mohammedans). In Georgia, besides, only the orthodox are considered as Georgians, and the Georgian-Catholics are called "Frachi", as are, too, all the Catholics of the Orient, while in Poland a non-Catholic Pole was not called Polish.

So here we have mutual neutrality, isolation, division and mistrust among persons and communities belonging to the same nation, but to different religions. In brief, in the Orient and for the orientals, religious profession and nationality are inseparable ideas, and the cause of much muddling and confusion. And this fact is clearer to you, who for long years worked in the Orient, than to others not experts of the Orient.

It is this, here, the principle reason that, notwithstanding the fact that the Catholic Church is so thriving and has ready and enlightened workers at her disposal, nevertheless she has still not given evidence of extensive successes where the Armenian church, her clergy, and even her people are concerned, as instead have been had in other places in the West.

For the Armenian church, clergy and people, owing to the self-defensive isolation of this same church, whoever does not profess that which she professes is a foreigner; therefore a Catholic, even though Armenian by birth, is not Armenian: he is Catholic, he is a foreigner.

The Armenian church, as center and supreme protector of every Armenian, even outside of Armenia, had become a conjoining force, centripetal, without

---

270 F. Dionigi Kalatosoff.

which one could not understand the Armenian nation. The national Armenian church fuses into one all the Armenity of the world, rendering indivisible the ideas: nationality and the national religion.

This neutrality, this self-defending separatism of the Armenian church, was indeed a great source of energy but, it must be said that, at the same time, it was its principal cause of weakness. And it's here where the beginnings are of the Armenian church's present painful situation.

After the fall of the kingdom of Armenia, the Armenian national church became, in the figure of the Catholicos and of the hierarchy subdued to her, queen and protectress of the abandoned Armenian nation. And so the manifold needs of the Armenian nation, the solution even to issues far beyond the sphere of the ecclesiastical, became incontestable objects of the cares and considerations of the leaders of the church and of the diocesan ordinaries. The liberation of the slaves, the care of widows and orphans, the instruction of the young boys and girls, the administration of the schools, the employment and provision for emigrants, refugees and those saved from massacres, political protection against the persecutions of their people, etc., etc.; even to the organization of self-defense, inviting volunteers, providing them with military necessities; the making of diplomatic moves, of appeals and demands; the sending of deputies and representatives to the governments of Europe: like to the Congress of Berlin. Of this we have another more recent demonstration: the political mission of Boghos Nubar Pasha to the European powers, as legate and representative of the Catholicos of the Armenians, having by way of credentials the encyclical of the very same Catholicos, as supreme and responsible Leader of the Armenian nation.

Things being as they are, the Armenian national church, while politically strong, has been completely absorbed by political struggles, and consequently also by partisan intrigues and by diplomatic subtleties and minutiae, [too much so] to be able to defend the Armenian nation from the oppression of foreign governments; and the ministers of the same, that is, the hierarchy of the national church, from the first to the last, having been chosen solely for their aptitudes in this national arena, and not as fervent and pious ecclesiastics, with the passing of the centuries a host of high clergy was obtained, of capable individuals and strenuous political operators, but unsuited and not correspondent to their own vocation, which was of Fathers in spirit, of true ecclesiastics. Here is the real and true reason for the current weakness and impotence of the Armenian national church, and this to the point where persons are known to me who, to find spiritual consolation during various personal sorrows and misfortunes, turn to foreign convents or churches, with the aim of recovering and comforting themselves spiritually, asking ministers of foreign churches the solutions to doubts that afflict them internally.

The purpose of all the attentions of the Armenian hierarchy, and the sole directive line of action, was to raise the Armenian nation up again from her fall and to see her as before, endowed with and in possession of a political organization, like the other nations. And here this wish of hers came true; her incessant efforts were crowned by success; the Armenian State was reconstituted, which immediately took into its hands all those branches of industry that, by their nature, appertain to the civil authorities but that, by practical necessity, had been carried out by the Armenian national church in the absence of the independent Armenian State. But this exchange of roles, even while freeing the Armenian clergy from the civil occupations that overloaded them, nevertheless became the cause of the current distressing situation of the Armenian church. The hierarchy, though on the one hand satisfied by the fact of the realization of the Armenian State, on the other hand saw itself turned away from the splendid field of activity of yore. And that's not all. They realized that their primary activity of politics, performed out of necessity, had extinguished their ecclesiastical spirit and left them unaccustomed to fulfilling the duties of a cleric.

Of this, here, consists the real tragedy! The Armenian hierarchy being, on one side, dampened in ecclesiastical spirit, feeling in themselves little ardor for the aptitudes of the ecclesiastical vocation; on the other, seeing all those occupations and works of politics, of instruction, of provisioning, etc., in short, all that constitutes the object of the State's attention, being taken from them.

The Armenian nation that suffered so much, that for so many centuries was troubled, has need, as do all the other nations, of effective and authentic comfort, of spiritual refreshment, especially because her martyrology is not yet finished; her widows and her orphans are not consoled; for her sick, for the mutilated and hungry remaining without work, there has yet been made no provision; her needs, as vast as the sea, demand great cures, encouragement and aid. But to succeed in this, to bring about a moral and spiritual remediation, to inspire patience and constancy, strength and courage, the Armenian Church and its hierarchy no longer find in themselves sufficient vigor to affront so many needs, following those centuries-old hazardous trials and interminable persecutions to which, together with all the nation, they were always subjected, that made them diminished within themselves, rendering them needful of energetic reform, of new reflourishing to become vital, and sources of moral-spiritual life for the flock.

The future will show what way out she will find for herself, in these difficult conditions, and with what directives the old Armenian church and her hierarchy will commence acting. In our opinion, this must form the object of the most vivid preoccupations of the best and wisest Armenian ecclesiastics.

The question is this: in the present difficult situation of our nation, when every hour, every day, is precious to tending the moral and spiritual wounds of the Armenian people, to comforting them, consoling them, encouraging them and animating them, can she and her needs perhaps wait at length for the search for those effective remedies on which she must rest her hopes of moral revival?

The experiment of our past history, and that of the other nations, has shown us, in similar circumstances of shared undoing, what a salutary and loving role the ecclesiastical institutions have assumed: the monasteries, the monks, the nuns, that transformed themselves into hospitals, orphanages, schools and houses of refuge, etc., etc.

Thus, even now that ours are destroyed, sacked, dispersed or reduced to poverty following enemy tyranny, is it ever possible that the thriving and organized church that has always harbored love and affection towards all of our Armenian nation—despite the fact that only a part of her is sheltered under its mantle—is it possible, I ask, that the Church remain indifferent in the face of so much misery?

Won't the Church hasten with all of its efforts, authority and Christian compassion to run to the aid of the Armenian nation: suffering, tired and oppressed?

Is there, perhaps, a need to remind what precious assistance the Great Roman Church brought to the troubled Armenian nation during the last dynasty of our kings of Cilicia, after the incursions and depredations of the barbarians? Was it not, perhaps, the Church that encouraged and promoted the aid of Europe, represented by the Republics of Venice, Genoa, Livorno, etc., so that not only ecclesiastics, but learned men, experts, and businessmen came to Cilicia, and they helped to rebuild, reflourish and revive our nation, and to seal lasting relations with Europe?

Certainly, now, with this reasoning, we do not dare to permit ourselves even the mere shadow of exaggerated claims, but isn't it true that one cannot forget the living and speaking evidence and the historical ties, beginning with the royal stock of the Lusignani, kings of Armenia, up until Caterina Cornaro? Would not the Holy Seat—always flourishing and strong—of the successors of Celestine III want to offer a helping hand, at least in such measure that Armenia, at least this time, rises up definitively from her age-old decline, feels in this hour a palpable support on the part of the same, and directs her gaze towards that culture of mind and of spirit that shines in the West with an inextinguishable glow.

Descending more to the practical, we retain it absolutely necessary to send, as soon as possible, prudent and experienced persons, but we also retain it necessary that these be Armenians in nationality and at heart, and that their leaders be the sort of men to be well-regarded and accepted by the Armenian public, without angering and irritating them. Here we repeat that which was stated above: that is, in the Orient, he who is not of the same nation is judged a foreigner. Since those who will come will certainly not be of the Gregorian religion, but Catholics, it is extremely necessary that they belong to such an institution whose Armenity and whose patriotism the people, the Armenian masses, cannot doubt, and that this have palpable evidence of its activity on behalf of the nation, displaying a precedent that is obvious to everyone's eyes.

These persons and this institution—it is our profound conviction—is the house of Mekhitar of Sebaste in Venice and Vienna, and the sons of him and his students: the Reverend Mekhitarist Fathers. From them the Armenian nation would not flee; she is already satisfied by their activity of over two centuries and she is grateful for it. She will receive them with pleasure, and will listen to them, then as always, when the subject of their conversation is not simply scientific, but religious as well.

Not only the school, but also the church of the Mekhitarist Fathers will be attended by the Armenians, without fear, because they know, out of conviction, that they will not lead the Armenian people into foreign fads, to extinguish their patriotism, to the change of their own nation. The Mekhitarist church in Vienna can serve as an example. In that city an Armenian-Gregorian church does not exist; consequently, all the Armenians living there or others traveling through, without distinction for religious profession, go there; they attend that modest Armenian church, preferring it to the foreigners' more splendid ones.

I will explain myself better.

By now two centuries have passed since, following the persecutions of the Turk, the Abbot Mekhitar brought to and founded his Congregation on San Lazzaro. Similarly, it has been a century since its other branch transplanted itself in Vienna to flourish there.

The times required this: to go, to remove themselves from the scene of the persecutions, from the hazardous ground of Mother Armenia, and on foreign soil, in peaceful security: educate themselves, flourish, and render themselves useful to the beloved nation from afar.

But is it not true that, by now, the hour has arrived for our unhappy and dispersed historic Armenian nation to collect herself into one? Therefore it is necessary that everyone, especially those who are self-aware, energetic, and with ready practical knowledge, hasten to return to Armenia, where everyone, in proportion to his own capacity, each one, should work at the building of the moral-political home for the new Armenian State.

We are partial to the relocation to the mother country even of those Armenian communities found close by to Armenia, more so those who are far away, and at the same time so useful to the country, like those of Venice and Vienna, etc. Not wanting to render deserted the enchanting island of San Lazzaro and the monastery full of glorious and historic reminiscences, and retaining it more suitable that the Mekhitarists' Mother House remain in the same place, we desire that in Armenia be formed, in a manner of speaking, a second headquarters of the Mekhitarists, with all the branches of their manifold activity.

Thus would be founded in Alexandroupolis—presumed center of their future activity, as a center of Catholicism—a *Monastery* of the Mekhitarist Fathers of Venice, with a beautiful annexed *church*. *A school* for boys, another for girls, these with the technical sections appropriate for each sex. A *printing house*, a *bookstore*, a *library*, all these with the necessary accessories, as will know best people equipped with a European education and fully expert in their religio-scientific profession, and having the single purpose of moral-intellectual utility and the progress our people.

I'll explain myself: the monastery will serve as residence and peaceful asylum for scholars and modest religious. The church will reflect the purity of rite and ceremonies, the dignity of the holy *canto*; edifying, solid and erudite sermons will be heard there. Their school, beyond the usual subjects, will be distinguished by the teaching of the pure national Armenian tongue, old and new, and of other European languages in demand now hereabouts. As for the Mekhitarist printing house, who among us can compete with them; they are already ... renowned for their editions of great value, opulence and art. This is their incontestable specialty. The bookstore will be rich with assortments of Armenian and European editions, along with all that which concerns Armenia and scientific news. It goes without saying that the Mekhitarist Fathers will publish a religio-scientific periodical of their own, featuring the most fresh and interesting intellectual products of Europe. They will have also a library rich in books, to facilitate the scholars' scientific research; this will be an unequalled compendium of, at least, national editions. In such a way, they will become, in Armenia, and before anywhere else, in Alexandroupolis, a center around which the most intelligent segment of the people will assemble. So, little by little, they will extend over all Armenia: the nation participating in the scientific-moral provender amassed by them over the course of more than two centuries.

I must say that this proposal of mine, at first sight, would seem to open the door to many expenses, but in reality that is not so. The construction of a monastery and, in addition, of a church, certainly requires a hefty sum at the outset, but is it not perhaps true that every church then has its revenues? Next to the church, indispensably, it will be necessary to open a wax factory and a store of sacramental furnishings: paraments, holy vessels, linens, books, glassware, etc., the necessity of which is more than evident, as from the current state of devastation of Armenia, as from now on, to facilitate the supply of the churches in general, even non-Catholic ones. Up until now all of this material arrived from Russia, and was all marked by orthodoxy: the shapes, the cloth marked with crooked crosses, etc.; the new store should be a supply center not only for the Catholic churches but also for the heterodox, accustoming everyone to the noble forms used among the Catholics. And at the same time it will be a source of income.

The setting up of a printing house, with annexed bookstore and library, certainly requires some expenditure, but such an enterprise, at the current time, would be a first-class commercial concern; a well-set-up printing house today in Armenia would enjoy enormous profits. The old presses and machines of the Mekhitaran print houses of Venice and Vienna, transported to Armenia with their stores of paper, will bring immense earnings in the time of crisis over such materials.

More costly than anything else might be the publication of scientific-religious opinion, because for now the love for reading is lacking, maybe also the capacity, since the masses of Armenian peasants do not know how to read. But the Mekhitarist Fathers are habituated to similar honorable and extremely useful expenditures. Nor will the Armenian nation show herself indifferent.

The Mekhitarist Fathers are also good and exemplary stewards of rural economy, that is, of agriculture, in the vast sense of this branch of practical science. The various gold and silver medals and honorary diplomas they have merited attest to this.

To this activity of Catholic monks, we retain it necessary that the opening of a monastery of Catholic nuns be added. The only monastery of women among the Gregorian Armenians of the Caucasus is that of Tiflis, and the work of opening a monastery of nuns in Armenia will be all too welcome an act and purposeful, practically indispensable. And here is the reason why. In Armenia there are countless mothers who have unfortunately lost their sons and also daughters; there are no fewer a number of wives who have lost their husbands. Grieving mothers, grieving wives have as much need of comfort and consolation as of bread and water; there is no one to give them consolation; and they need this. There isn't a community of educated and spiritually strong ladies to call them back from desperation, to comfort them when they are disheartened, to dry their tears, bring and attract the painful fixations of their minds to God, to vital occupations. Rome has at its disposition the Sisters of the Immaculate Conception of Constantinople, who are equipped with learning, with a long experience in the work of pious and religious education, with the knowledge of various languages, together with distinguished manual arts, embroidery, etc. Here is what important polish they can bring to the younger generation of both sexes in the new Armenia, especially to the diligent girls: preparing them as mothers and wives who are pious and strong in spirit for the Armenian nation. A group of these sisters, headed by an expert and intelligent Mother Superior, should be sent to Alexandroupolis, that should become the center of Catholicism; another group also to Erevan. Upon arrival at their destination, their principal work should be the care of the orphans, and later on, some of [the sisters] designated for the intendancy of the hospitals. In Russia in general, and especially in Russian Armenia, there have been and there are currently sisters of charity, non-religious, whose defects are rather well-known; the lack of religious sisters of charity, that in such a useful and edifying way operate in Europe, was therefore evident. In such a manner, this vacuum will be filled as well by the works of the Armenian sisters to the great comfort of the suffering.

Most Reverend Father Visitor,

having faith in your forbearance, I have permitted myself to explain my good proposals, imposing myself a bit more on certain points of view, but how many other types of more useful works are known to you, with which the Catholic church, in this time of numerous difficulties, will be able to bring aid, comfort and light to our desolate people and enjoy their immense gratitude? I must say that this will be the only way to redress the predominant prejudice that he who does not belong to the Armenian national church is not Armenian, is a foreigner and thus a person of whom to be suspicious. On the contrary, by approaching the rebirth of the Armenian people with noble and illuminated industry and by bringing, without a shadow of material interest, remedy and medicine for her thousand ills and necessities, it will be clearly shown to the good Armenian what is in reality the true spirit of Christianity, and that "love thy neighbor" are not the mere and simple words or phrases in the mouth of the churchman, but the practical realization of high ideals of principled men giving life to truth, goodness and nobility.

The feelings of my heart and concepts of my mind being well-known to you, having the single goal of the true profit of my nation, her spiritual ennoblement and moral elevation, I hope that you will not leave unattended this, my expressed wish—for the translation of which into practice I put at your disposition my humble abilities—and will commit yourself with your high influence to intervene wherever and however needed, to hasten its realization. Speaking of which, we might venture that, during the next Lent, in Alexandroupolis we should be allowed to hear a series of pious and commanding sermons that attract the citizens under the vaults of the Armenian Catholic church.

Entrusting myself to your pious prayers I sign myself with respect and sincerity, friend and servant of your Most Rev. and Most Ill. Fatherhood, the ex under-secretary of the Imperial Council of Russia Grégoire Evangouloff

P.S. Pour vous faire parvenir à temps et rédiger en italien tout ce que aurez lu ci-dessus, je me sais servi du concours aimable du P Denis Kalatosoff et Don François Aghadjanian.[271] Le même

84

25 January 1921, Rome – Naslian, notes commenting on the Treaty of Sèvres – AAEESS, *Asia* 57, 1, n° 16169

Si avrebbe voluto estendere un esposto di osservazioni su tutto il contesto del Trattato di Sèvres, ma data la precipitazione di complicazioni

---

271 The future patriarch and cardinal.

sopravvenute, che non lasciano veder chiara la situazione dell'Armenia e l'attitudine dei Governi per essa come pure per la Turchia stessa, mi limiterò a tre punti soltanto i quali insieme agli interessi nazionali implicano anche quelli religiosi e vorrei interessarne in particolar modo cotesta Segreteria di Stato, già tanto sollecita per questa medesima causa.

Questi punti si possono ridurre a tre:

1 Situazione dell'Armenia e degli Armeni in genere;

2 Indennità per i danni e restituzione di beni dovuta dalla Turchia;

3 Interessi religioso-politici;

I Situazione dell'Armenia e degli armeni in genere

1 L'Armenia si trova oggi in stato d'invasione, e ne subisce le tristi e disastrose conseguenze, analoghe a quelle del tempo di guerra; le popolazioni rifugiatevi, che insieme a quelle del paese formavano un considerevolissimo numero di armeni, sono in via d'esterminazione un altra volta; la gioventù in specie è implacabilmente condannata a morte dai Turchi invasori con i medesimi artifici dei passati massacri: altri passati a fil di spada addirittura, altri messi fuori d'abitazione nudi e senza ristoro, gelano vivi sotto l'intemperie del freddo intenso di 24° gradi sotto il 0°; altri, relegati nei centri turchi dell'Anatolia, è facile supporre come possano essere trattati. Le poche notizie pervenute confermano ciò.

2 - I Bolscevichi padroni del paese, non vi rimediano; russi in spirito, giudei nelle ultime loro intenzioni, facilmente tollerano l'esterminio di questo popolo troppo in vista.

3 - Del Sovietismo poi imposto al Governo armeno, non se ne devono attribuire agli Armeni le responsabilità pregiudizievoli ai diritti dell'Armenia sinora riconosciuti.

4 - Tale invasione ha subito l'Armenia per la tenace sua fedeltà alle potenze dell'Intesa, da cui nel Trattato di Sèvres è considerata quale una delle Alleate contraenti.

5 - Quindi in una eventuale revisione del Trattato si deve migliorarne le condizioni per l'Armenia e non peggiorarle, e si dovrà tener ferme le disposizioni almeno prese negli art. 88-93.

6 - La formula adottata oggi in alcuni ambienti politici, di regolare le cose a base della realtà, è ingiusta nel senso del fatto compiuto della forza sul debole; quella realtà deve essere la giustizia dovuta agli oppressi;

7 - Quindi all'Armenia bisogna riconoscere:

1) il diritto all'esistenza da assicurare contro l'ingiusta determinazione dei nemici suoi inumani di annientarla;

2) il diritto all'indipendenza in stato libero;

3) il suo territorio nel Caucaso e nelle Provincie dell'Asia Minore con accesso al mare (88-93)

8 - Il Curdistan che storicamente non ha esistito, non devesi costituire a pregiudizio dell'Armenia e dei suoi territoriali diritti, rendendoli più esposti anche da quel lato ad una cerchia di altra razza sanguinaria e nemica per odio anche anticristiano.

9 - In Cilicia, che ingiustamente si rilascia alla Turchia, si deve creare condizioni di sicuro domicilio per tutti i Cristiani ed una posizione privilegiata agli Armeni, che vi hanno titoli di diritti imprescrittibili.

10 - La scaltra divisione del Governo Ottomano in due Governi irresponsabili degli atti reciproci, in quello di Kemalisti ribelle ed in quello del Sultano impotente ha fatto veder chiaro che il Turco non vorrà mai sottostare a nessuna delle condizioni del Trattato, come non è stata a nessuna delle clausole dell'armistizio impunemente.

11 - La sola sanzione post all'art. 36 per riguardo dell'occupazione di Costantinopoli non può essere sufficiente, ai Turchi più importa l'esterminio degli armeni che la perdita di Costantinopoli, temendo più crearsi alle spalle un forte nemico che un concentramento per la restrizione di territorio, che la gelosia di Governi potrà rendere ricuperabile sempre.

12 - Le restituzioni di territorii occupati a sfavore della Turchia, le si dovranno, nel caso di eventuale restituzione, ritornarle dopo e contro l'adempimento da sua parte di tutte le clausole dei doveri imposti ad essa per l'Armenia e gli armeni in genere.

13 - Anche le disposizioni militari prese nel Trattato saranno insufficienti a garantire la tranquillità in Turchia e la pace con i paesi limitrofi:

a) Come potranno smobilitare i Turchi dopo che si lasceranno padroni di se, mentre non hanno potuto fare quando questi erano battuti? (153)

b) I Kemalisti tradirono il segreto di una smobilitazione apparente, congedando i soldati forniti di tutte le loro armi e munizioni, dichiarando soldati tutti i Turchi capaci di portare le armi, così il divieto (art. 164) sarà inefficace.

c) Questo pericolo è anche maggiore con arruolamento di volontarii di cui all'art. 165.

d) I cristiani, i quali sembrerebbero non esclusi dal far parte dell'armata (idem) non avendo ufficiali di carriera, quali vuole l'art. 167, si troveranno effettivamente esclusi.

e) I prigionieri turchi di guerra restituiti prima della ratificazione del Trattato, sono stati arruolati nelle truppe dei kemalisti; a che dunque valgono gli articoli 208-209 ?

f) I Kemalisti oggi hanno reclutato anche gli armeni superstiti rientrati nel loro paese e li fanno morire impunemente; chi se ne prende pensiero di compassione almeno?

14 - Non sono le academiche declamazioni della Società delle Nazioni che potranno rimediare al male deplorato, il vero germe del male inoculato nel

Trattato stesso si trova nelle disposizioni opportunistiche ed utilitaristiche dei Governi e nella gelosia reciproca.

15 - Le disposizioni per riformare e render tollerabile il sistema giudiziario in Turchia sono nulle, quindi bisognerebbe almeno contemplarlo nella riforma giudiziaria che si vuol creare in regime a sostituzione del regime delle capitolazioni;l'essere cristiani è una pregiudiziale contro i cristiani (136)

16 - Quanto agli armeni in genere

a) Non bisognerà trattarli da sudditi ottomani in tutti quelli articoli, in cui quei sudditi sono riguardati come nemici, p.e. agli art. 239,283,284,289,291, etc

b) al contrario bisognerà riconoscerli in tutto sudditi di potenza alleata nel senso dell'art. 290,293 comma 2/308 etc, anche se all'epoca della ratificazione del Trattato non avesse ancora avuto luogo l'opzione.

c) Le condizioni di opzione di sudditanza devono essere più chiare e larghe:

•vi sarà una maggioranza di armeni, che non saranno dai o nei territorii separati o da separare dalla Turchia, quindi non è quale ci vorrebbe la disposizione degli art. 123,125.

•il doversi trasferire entro i dodici mesi dello stato d'opzione (art. 126) sarebbe per gli armeni un nuovo genere di deportazione, se non si concedesse loro tempo e modo di assicurare i loro interessi.

d) Per gli armeni che dovranno rimanere sudditi ottomani si dovrà anche rendere sostenibile il sistema giudiziario in Turchia (V.N° Osser.15), il servizio militare (V.N° Osserv. 13) come pure tutta la vita civile.

e) I Kemalisti nell'ultima invasione uccidono senz'altro gli armeni prigionieri di guerra, che fossero sudditi ottomani; questo potranno fare anche in Cilicia ed altrove, se non si prenderanno misure efficaci nel Trattato;

f) Tuttora restano centinaja di migliaja di orfani e donne armeni nelle mani dei Turchi; gli alleati non vollero continuare l'assistenza cominciata sulle commissioni armene di ricerche; perchè adunque non formulerebbero almeno l'art. 147 con più efficaci sanzioni come almeno all'art. 215.

g) Le spese del rimpatrio degli armeni detenuti che vennero messi fuori dei loro paesi e domicilii, dovrebbero essere a carico del Governo Ottomano come per i prigionieri di guerra (210).

h) Per i morti nei massacri degli armeni, si dovrebbe anche aver alcun riguardo, come lo si fa per i pochi caduti alleati in guerra sul territorio Turco (art. 218-225).

i) Le sanzioni contemplate negli articoli 226-230 dovrebbero estendersi anche contro gli autori dei massacri; gli irrisorii processi simulati dal Governo Ottomano dopo l'armistizio non devono per niente giustificare quei misfatti;

j) I provvedimenti presi o contemplati sotto il titolo di Protezione delle Minoranze, dovrebbero essere più radicali e meglio garantiti per l'esecuzione

(149-151), né il Consiglio delle Nazioni, se non è assistito da forza, potrà garantirne l'esecuzione. Il fatto di nuovi massacri in zone occupate da alleati, spiega meglio l'inefficacia di queste disposizioni.

II. Indennità per i danni e restituzione di beni dovuta dalla Turchia

17 - Si sa che il Governo Ottomano dopo la deportazione e massacri degli armeni

a) confiscò tutti gli immobili con gli attrezzi, utensili e mobiglia;

b) tutti i depositi di somme e di oggetti preziosi nelle Banche;

c) spogliò le Chiese, Presbiterii, Episcopii, Scuole, Istituti;

d) fece spogliare i deportati stessi di tutto quello che avevano potuto prendersi seco, credendo ingenuamente di trasferirsi da un paese all'altro.

e) distrusse Chiese, Episcopi, Scuole, Edificii pubblici e privati, officine etc.

Dopo ciò promulgò la legge accennata nel Trattato (art. 144) *Sulle proprietà abbandonate.* Ora non basta annullare una tale legge, bisognerà imporre adeguata restituzione dei beni confiscati, ed indennità per i distrutti; la costituzione delle Commissioni senza assistenza di forze militari estere e di un Tribunale Superiore *ad hoc* e sul posto, non si otterrà nulla.

18 - Le difficoltà di recupero sono:

a) perdita di documenti e di titoli di proprietà;

b) scomparsa di eredi che possano reclamare, scomparsa di documenti di identità per eredi che si presentassero;

c) l'esistenza di beni su nomi di terzi;

d) perdita di atti privati, con cui gran numero di beni anche ecclesiastici erano a nome di privati per le difficoltà note in Turchia per tali proprietà. Le formalità prettamente legali non arriveranno far giustizia.

19 - Dispone il Trattato all'art. 288 che i beni, diritti ed interessi di antichi sudditi ottomani devono essere restituiti loro nello stato in cui si trovano; Ma se sono distrutti e la loro distruzione è negata dai Turchi e non si potrà ristabilire la natura della costruzione dello stabile per mancanza di testimonii uccisi e per scomparsa di documenti, come si dovrà farsi risarcire dei danni? così è di moltissimi beni ecclesiastici: Chiese, presbiterii, episcopi, oggi rasi al suolo. Perchè non mettere questa restituzione agli antichi sudditi ottomani sotto le medesime condizioni almeno del precedente articolo (287)?

20 - I beni che appartenevano a membri di una communità, morti o scomparsi dopo il 1º Agosto del 1914 senza lasciar eredi, potranno, dice l'art. 144 comma 3º essere attribuiti alla communità, invece che allo Stato. Osservo:

a) la Delegazione armena voleva che tali beni appartenenti a communità armene fossero attribuiti allo Stato Armeno: lo scrivente presentò una Nota reclamando che dovessero quei beni essere attribuiti ai rispettivi Dicasteri religiosi, cioè Patriarcati. Si dovrà insistere in questo senso per i beni di communità religiose. Quel *"Possono"* deve cambiarsi in *"devono"* nell'art. citato.

b) Tra i membri superstiti di queste communità da noi cattolici vi possono essere non-armeni, come p.e. in quella delle Suore di Trebizonda ve n'è una francese, la quale pur non volendo riprendere l'abito, vuol impossessarsi dei beni inscritti nei registri del catasto turco a nome dell'Istituto delle Suore Armene dell'Assunta; a questo scopo ha perfino ricorso al suo governo, e qualche impiegato francese la spingerebbe a ciò.

21 - Queste medesime difficoltà ed osservazioni valgono per gli oggetti, valori, archivi etc. Perduti o dispersi.

III. Interessi Religiosi.

22 - Per i Cattolici bisogna che la S. Sede trovi modi di assistenza nel ricupero dei Beni Ecclestici, onde non vengano negati ed appropriati dai Turchi, o usurpati dai non-cattolici, più forti sempre in tali contingenze, o dai Laici sotto nome di Beni Nazionali. Così all'art. 148 comma 2º non s'intende chi debbano essere i rappresentanti delle Communità, di cui si tratta, ed a cui devono essere versati i fondi - i Capi Religiosi? - Quelli muniti soltanto di Berat Ottomano ? - i Consigli Laici? - Chi devesi intendere per rappresentanti accreditati?

23 - Per gli interessi poi cattolici in genere nelle comunità di sudditi ottomani non basteranno

a) né la <u>libertà</u> di culto, di fede, religione o confessione proclamata nel Trattato (art. 141 comma 2º), né l'<u>eguaglianza</u> di sudditi (art. 145), poiché queste in massima ci erano anche prima ed i principii cattolici non si potevano far prevalere; né l'<u>autonomia</u> <u>ecclesiastica</u> inculcata nell'art. 149. Poiché

b) il Governo ottomano ha voluto sempre regolare le queszioni [*sic*] cattoliche con i criterii delle Chiese scismatiche, e l'eguaglianza in questo caso e sotto tale aspetto sarebbe disastrosa per i cattolici come è stata per lo passato;

c) la <u>libertà</u> poi è stata convertita in un abuso nelle queszioni [*sic*] di matrimonii misti, nelle queszioni [*sic*] di amministrazione ecclesiastica etc.

d) l'<u>autonomia</u> poi intesa nel senso scismatico ha creato nel seno della communità armeno-cattolica l'interminabile serie di queszioni [*sic*] tra laicato e Gerarchia , sotto pretesto di privilegii e diritti nazionali nelle Chiese Orientali autonome.

25 - All'art. 149 poi

a) bisognerebbe specificare la natura di detta <u>autonomia</u> nel senso d'indipendenza dall'<u>ingerenza</u> <u>governativa</u> per togliere così il pericolo dell'equivoco sopra accennato.

b) bisognerebbe specificare le prerogative ed indennità di carattere religioso che si vogliono mantenere, onde i cattolici non abbiano a presumere che quei privilegi siano nazionali o civili perchè emanati dal Governo. Sopra tali equivoci si basa l'incessante queszione [*sic*] nel seno della Communità armeno-cattolica, per cui immunità ecclesiastiche per la semplice ragione di essere state dal Governo riconosciute con atti ufficiali, sono riguardate spesso attribuzioni civili o nazionali ed i Vescovi e Patriarchi, aventi Berat o Firman sono stati presi per Capi Civili, emancipandoli così di fatto dalla S. Sede, ecco il senso a cui potrebbe essere convertita l'<u>Autonomia Ecclesiastica</u> del Trattato.

c) Se vi fossero privilegii civili accordati alle Communità, bisognerebbe separarli da quelli Religiosi ed affidarli magari a laici.

d) Quest'unico articolo per tutte le Confessioni e Chiese in Oriente, porta seco pregiudizievoli confusioni; il Patriarca Scismatico Armeno voleva p.e. estendere per tutta la Nazione lo Statuto della Chiesa sua, ho protestato objettando la diversità essenziale di amministrazione ecclesiastica della Chiesa Cattolica e di quella anche Protestante. La Delegazione mi diede ragione, ma io non potei esigere un articolo speciale per i Cattolici; la S.Sede lo potrà fare per cattolici d'Oriente in genere.

e) Inoltre è da notare che per gli armeni cattolici si hanno avuti diversi Berat Patriarcali in diverse date, più o meno differenti e perciò più o meno anche favorevoli; bisognerebbe quindi specificare quel Berat che garantirebbe meglio gli interessi cattolici, i privilegii e le immunità ecclesiastici di fronte ai scismatici carezzati dai Laici anche cattolici. - Tre sono stati i principali BERAT: 1) quello dell'anno 1830 concesso al Sacerdote Giacomo Valle, quando riconosciuta l'emancipazione della communità armeno-cattolica dal Patriarcato Gregoriano fu dovuto far riconoscere al Governo un Capo Religioso, che per intrighi dei Scismatici non fu il Primate nominato dalla S.Sede Mons. Antonio Nurigian.

2) quello del 1857 concesso al Primate Hassun, quale CAPO LEGITTIMO SPIRITUALE DEGLI ARMENI CATTOLICI NELLA SUA QUALITA DI ARCIVESCOVO PRIMATE DI COSTANTINOPOLI, come dice in precisi termini quel Berat, che si era potuto ottenere, all'infuori del Berat per il Patrik, in virtù dell'hatti-humayun menzionato nell'art. IX del Trattato di Parigi del 1856. Questo Berat è più importante del primo poiché era stato dato ad Hassun, quale Capo legittimo spirituale e quindi non era che un riconoscimento della giurisdizione ecclesiastica del Primate.

3) quello dell'anno 1867 conferito al medesimo Mons. Hassun il quale, eletto Patriarca anche di Cilicia, riuniva nella sua persona le due Sedi; ed è, credo, quest'ultimo che era passato nel corpo di Legge DESTUR, e sul suo modello si rilasciavano i Berat ai successivi Patriarchi, se non che il Governo dei Giovani Turchi dopo la Costituzione modificò quel Berat diminuendo di molto le attribuzioni patriarcali. Quale forma di riconoscimento di Capo Spirituale è certo migliore quella del secondo Berat, ma quale più completo è quello passato nel Destur, corpo di legge. Si sa poi la tendenza dei Giovani turchi, manifestata con atti più radicali durante la guerra, di voler togliere ogni aspetto nazionale-civile ai Patriarcati ed alle communità senza però esentarle

dal controllo governativo, ma sottoponendovi anche di più con sistema laicizzante di governo ed amministrazione delle Chiese cristiane.

26 - Avendo sott'occhio tutte le precedenti osservazioni si dovrebbe ottenere una modificazione dell'art. 149, come ebbi ad esporre anche alla S. Congregazione Pro Ecc. Orient., del seguente tenore:

"Il Governo ottomano s'impegna a riconoscere e a rispettare l'autonomia ecclesiastica, scolastica, AMMINISTRATIVA e GIUDIZIARIA di OGNI CHIESA E CONFESSIONE di minoranze etniche in Turchia, IN BASE DEI PRINCIPI RELIGIOSI E GERARCHICI DI QUELLE CHIESE E CONFESSSIONI. A questo fine e salvo disposizioni del presente Trattato, il Governo Ottomano conferma e manterrà integralmente per l'avvenire le prerogative, ATTRIBUZIONI e immunità di carattere religioso, AMMINISTRATIVO E GIUDIZIARIO riconosciute o concesse dai Sultani ai Capi Religiosi delle razze non musulmane IN CONFORMITA AI PRINCIPI GERARCHICI E RELIGIOSI DELLE RISPETTIVE CREDENZE, mercè speciali ordinanze o decreti imperiali (Firman, Hatti, Berat etc) disposizioni ministeriali o ordini del Gran Vizir etc.

27 - Al comma 2º poi avendo in vista la grave legge sul matrimonio emanata durante la guerra, direi: "Qualsiasi legge, regolamento, decreto o circolare del Governo Ottomano che importi abrogazione restrizione o modificazione delle dette prerogative e immunità, IN OPPOSIZIONE ANCHE AI PRINCIPII COSTITUTIVI, GERARCHICI E CONFESSIONALI DI OGNI CREDENZA NON MUSULMANA, sarà considerata a questo riguardo come nullo e senza effetto."

Queste sono le poche osservazioni che faccio in fretta pregando di farvi l'attenzione che merita l'oggetto grave del Trattato che forse sarà riveduto a Parigi.

[Translation]

One would have liked to work up an exposition of observations on the entire context of the Treaty of Sèvres but, given the precipitation of unexpected complications, that do not allow the situation of Armenia and the attitude of the Governments toward her as well as towards Turkey itself to be seen clearly, I will limit myself to three points only which, together with national interests, also entail religious ones, and I would especially like to involve in them the Secretariat of State, already so stressed with demands for this same cause.

These points can be reduced to three:

1 Situation of Armenia and of the Armenians in general;

2 Indemnity for the damages and restitution of assets owed by Turkey;

3 Religio-political interests;

I Situation of Armenia and of the Armenians in general

1 Armenia finds herself today in a state of invasion, and suffers the sad and disastrous consequences of it, analogous to those of the time of war; the

populations taken refuge there, that together with those of the country made up a very considerable number of Armenians, are once again on the way to being exterminated; the youth in particular is implacably condemned to death by the Turkish invaders with the same artifices of the past massacres: some run through with a sword directly, others put out of their homes naked and without shelter, freezing alive in the bad weather with an intense cold of 24 degrees below 0°; it is easy to imagine how others, relegated to the Turkish centers of Anatolia, may be treated. The little news that has arrived confirms this.

2 - The Bolsheviks, masters of the country, are not remedying the situation; Russian in spirit, Jewish in their recent intentions, they easily tolerate the extermination of this too-visible population.

3 - One should not attribute to the Armenians the responsibilities of Sovietism, then, imposed on the Armenian Government, that are prejudicial to the rights of Armenia recognized up until now.

4 - Armenia has suffered this invasion because of her tenacious fidelity to the Entente powers, by whom, in the Treaty of Sèvres, she is considered as one of the contracting Allies.

5 - Therefore, in any potential revision of the Treaty, the conditions for Armenia must be improved and not worsened, and at least the provisions made in art. 88-93 must be held firm.

6 - The formula adopted today in some political environments, to settle things based on reality, is unjust in the case of the act carried out by force on the weak; that reality should be the justice owed to the oppressed;

7 - Therefore, to Armenia must be recognized:

1) the right of existence, to be guaranteed against the unjust determination of her inhuman enemies to annihilate her;

2) the right to independence as a free state;

3) her territory in the Caucasus and in the Provinces of Asia Minor with access to the sea (88–93)

8 - Kurdistan, which historically has not existed, should not be constituted to the detriment of Armenia and of her territorial rights, rendering them more exposed on that side as well, to a circle of another race bloodthirsty and inimical out of hatred, including anti-Christian hatred.

9 - In Cilicia, unjustly granted to Turkey, conditions of secure domicile must be created for all the Christians, with a privileged position for the Armenians, who have title to imprescriptible rights there.

10 - The clever division of the Ottoman Government into two Governments, into that of rebel Kemalists and that of the impotent Sultan, neither one accountable for mutual acts, has made it clear that the Turk will never submit to any of the conditions of the Treaty, just as they did not abide by any of the clauses of the armistice, with impunity.

11 - The sole sanction provided by art. 36 regarding the occupation of Constantinople cannot suffice; to the Turks, the extermination of the Armenians is more important than the loss of Constantinople, fearing more an enemy at their backs, strengthened by the concentration caused by the restriction of territory, than the jealousy of Governments, a situation which is always retrievable.

12 - The restitution of territories occupied to Turkey's disadvantage: in the case of eventual restitution, they should be returned only after and against the fulfillment of her part of all the clauses of the obligations imposed on her regarding Armenia and the Armenians in general.

13 - Also the military arrangements made in the Treaty will be insufficient to guarantee the tranquility in Turkey and peace with surrounding countries:

a) How will they be able to demobilize the Turks when they shall be left to themselves, seeing as they were not able to do so when they were beaten? (153)

b) The Kemalists gave away the secret of an apparent demobilization, discharging the solders equipped with all their arms and ammunition, declaring all the Turks capable of bearing arms soldiers, thus the proscription (art. 164) will be ineffective.

c) This danger is even greater with the enrollment of volunteers, referenced in art. 165.

d) The Christians, who would not seem to be excluded from belonging to the army (*idem*), will find themselves effectively excluded, not having career officers as required by art. 167.

e) The Turks who were prisoners of war returned before the ratification of the Treaty were enrolled with the Kemalist troops; so to what end are articles 208-209?

f) The Kemalists today have also recruited the surviving Armenians re-entering their country and send them to die with impunity; who will give this a compassionate thought, at least?

14 – It will not be the academic declamations of the League of Nations that redress the deplorable evil; the true seed of the evil, inoculated in the Treaty itself, is found in the opportunistic and utilitarian arrangements of the Governments and in mutual jealousy.

15 - Arrangements for reforming the judiciary system in Turkey and rendering it more tolerant are nil, therefore it is necessary to at least contemplate this in the judicial reform which seeks to create a system in place of the capitulatory system; being Christian is a prejudicial factor against the Christians (136)

16 - Concerning the Armenians in general

a) They should not be treated as Ottoman subjects in all those articles in which those subjects are regarded as enemies, for example art. 239, 283, 284, 289, 291, etc

b) on the contrary, they must be recognized in all as subjects of allied power, in the sense of art. 290, 293 para. 2/308 etc, even though, at the time of the Treaty's ratification, the option had not been available.

c) The conditions of option of nationality must be more clear and generous:

• there will be a majority of Armenians, who will not be of the, or in the, territories separated, or to separate, from Turkey, therefore the provision of art. 123, 125 is not as it should be.

• having to relocate to the state of option within twelve months (art. 126) would be for the Armenians a new kind of deportation, if they were not conceded time and opportunity to secure their interests.

d) For the Armenians who will have to remain Ottoman subjects, the judiciary system in Turkey must be rendered more bearable (v. observ. n° 15), as the military service (v. observ. n° 13), as, indeed, all of civil life.

e) The Kemalists in the last invasion have been undoubtedly killing Armenian prisoners of war who were Ottoman subjects; they could also do this in Cilicia and elsewhere, if effective measures are not taken in the Treaty;

f) There are hundreds of thousands of Armenian orphans and women who still remain in the hands of the Turks; the allies chose not to continue the assistance begun on the Armenian research commissions; therefore, why not formulate at least art. 147 with more effective sanctions as in art. 215 at least.

g) The repatriation expenses of the detained Armenians who were turned out of their towns and their homes should be charged to the Ottoman Government as are those for the prisoners of war (210).

h) For those who have died in the massacres of the Armenians, there must also be some regard, as there is for the few allied soldiers fallen in war on Turkish soil (art. 218-225).

i) The sanctions contemplated in articles 226-230 should be extended also against the authors of the massacres; the derisory trials simulated by the Ottoman Government after the armistice must in no way stand in justice of those misdeeds;

j) The provisions made or contemplated under the heading of Protection of Minorities, should be more radical and better guaranteed as to their execution (149-151), nor can the Council of Nations, if it is not backed up by force, guarantee their execution. The fact of new massacres in areas occupied by allies better explains the inefficacy of these measures.

II. Indemnity for the damages and restitution of assets owed by Turkey

17 - It is known that the Ottoman Government after the deportation and massacres of the Armenians

a) confiscated all the real estate along with tools, utensils and furnishings;

b) all the deposits of cash and of valuables in the Banks;

c) despoiled the Churches, Presbyteries, Bishops' residences, Schools, Institutes;

d) had the deported themselves stripped of all that which they had been able to take with them, believing ingenuously to be relocating from one town to another.

e) destroyed Churches, Bishops' residences, Schools, public and private Buildings and workshops etc.

After which, it promulgated the law mentioned in the Treaty (art. 144), *On abandoned property*. Now, it is not enough to annul such a law; it is necessary to impose adequate restitution of the confiscated assets, and indemnity for those destroyed; the setting-up of Commissions will obtain nothing, without assistance from foreign military forces and from a Superior Court *ad hoc* and on site.

18 - The difficulties in recuperation are:

a) loss of documents and property titles;

b) disappearance of heirs who might make claim, disappearance of identifying documents for heirs who would present themselves;

c) assets being in the name of third parties;

d) loss of private deeds, with which a great number of assets, including ecclesiastical assets, were held in private name due to the known difficulties in Turkey with such properties. Purely legal formalities will not arrive at doing justice.

19 - The Treaty in art. 288 provides that the assets, rights and interests of former Ottoman subjects must be restituted to them in the state in which they were found; But if they are destroyed and their destruction is denied by the Turks and it is not possible to re-establish the nature of the construction of the building because witnesses have been killed and documentation has disappeared, how shall one obtain compensation for the damages? this is the case of many ecclesiastical assets: Churches, presbyteries, bishops' residences, today razed to the ground. Why not put this restitution to former Ottoman subjects under the same conditions, at least, of the preceding article (287)?

20 - The assets that belonged to members of a [religious] community, deceased or disappeared after August 1st, 1914, without leaving heirs, may, says art. 144, para. 3 be attributed to the community, rather than to the State. I observe:

a) the Armenian Delegation wanted that such assets belonging to Armenian communities be attributed to the Armenian State: this writer presented a Note protesting that those assets should be attributed to their respective religious Offices, that is, Patriarchates. It must be insisted in this sense for the assets of religious communities. That "*May*" should be changed into "*must*" in the art. cited.

b) Among the surviving members of these communities of us Catholics there may be non-Armenians, e.g., in that of the Sisters of Trabizon there is a Frenchwoman, who, though choosing not to retake the veil, wanted to take possession herself of the assets inscribed in the Turkish land registers in the name of the Institute of the Armenian Sisters of the Assumption; to this end she even made an appeal to her government; no doubt some French clerk put her up to it.

21 - These same difficulties and observations hold for objects, stock and bond certificates, archives etc. Lost or dispersed.

III. Religious Interests.

22 - For the Catholics, the Holy See must find means of assistance in the recuperation of Church Assets, such that they not be denied and appropriated by the Turks, or usurped by non-Catholics, always stronger in such contingencies, or by the Secular under the name of National Assets. Thus in art. 148 para. 2 it is not understood who the representatives of the Communities should be, that it is talking about, and to whom should be disbursed the funds - the Religious Leaders? - Those equipped only with an Ottoman *Berat*? - the Secular Councils? - Who should be intended by accredited representatives?

23 - For Catholic interests, then, in general in the communities of Ottoman subjects, it shall not suffice

a) neither the <u>freedom</u> of worship, of faith, religion or proclaimed confession in the Treaty (art. 141 para. 2), nor the <u>equality</u> of subjects (art. 145), since these for the most part already existed beforehand and Catholic principles could not be made to prevail; nor the <u>ecclesiastical autonomy</u> inculcated in art. 149. Since

b) the Ottoman Government has always wanted to rule on Catholic questions with the criteria of the schismatic Churches, and the equality in this case and under this aspect would be disastrous for the Catholics as it has been in the past;

c) the <u>freedom,</u> then, was converted into an abuse in the questions of mixed marriages, in the questions of ecclesiastical administration, etc.

d) the <u>autonomy,</u> then, intended in the schismatic sense, created within the Armenian-Catholic community the interminable series of questions between laity and Hierarchy, under the pretext of privileges and national rights in the autonomous Oriental Churches.

25 - In art. 149, then

a) the nature of said <u>autonomy</u> in the sense of independence from <u>governmental interference</u> must be specified, in this way removing the danger of misunderstanding mentioned above.

b) it is necessary to specify the prerogatives and indemnities of religious character that would be maintained, so that there is no chance of the Catholics' presuming that those privileges are national or civil just because they emanate from the Government. Upon such misunderstandings is based the incessant question within the Armenian-Catholic Community, by whom ecclesiastical immunities, for the simple reason of having been recognized by the Government with official acts, are often regarded as civil or national attributions, and the Bishops and Patriarchs, having *Berat* or *Firman*,[272] were taken for Civil Leaders,

---

[272] Translator's Note: *Berat* and *Firman* are types of Ottoman court rulings: the first, an investiture; the second, an imperial decree.

emancipating them thus in fact from the Holy See; that's the sense to which the Ecclesiastical Autonomy of the Treaty could be converted.

c) If there were civil privileges accorded to the Communities, they should be separated from Religious ones, and maybe entrusted to the laity.

d) This single article for all the Confessions and Churches in the Orient, brings with it prejudicial confusions; the Armenian Schismatic Patriarch wanted, for example, to extend the Statute of his Church over the whole Nation; I protested, presenting the objection of the essential diversity of ecclesiastical administration of the Catholic Church and even that of the Protestants. The Delegation agreed with me, but I was not able to obtain a special article for the Catholics; the Holy See will be able to for Catholics of the Orient in general.

e) Moreover, it should be noted that the Catholic Armenians have had different Patriarchal *Berat* on different dates, more or less different and with that also more or less favorable; it is necessary, therefore, to specify that *Berat* which would better guarantee Catholic interests, the ecclesiastical privileges and immunities in the face of the schismatics who are the pets of the Laity, Catholics among them. - The principal *BERAT* have been three: 1) that of 1830 conceded to the Priest Giacomo Valle, [since] when the emancipation of the Armenian-Catholic community from the Gregorian Patriarchate was recognized, it was necessary to identify to the Government a Religious Leader, who, due to the intrigues of the Schismatics, was not the Primate nominated by the Holy See, Mons. Antonio Nurigian.

2) that of 1857 conceded to the Primate Hassun, as LEGITIMATE SPIRITUAL HEAD OF THE ARMENIAN CATHOLICS IN HIS QUALITY OF ARCHBISHOP PRIMATE OF CONSTANTINOPLE, as that *Berat* says in precise terms, that was obtained, excluding the *Berat* for the *Patrik*,[273] under the *Hatti-humayun*[274] mentioned in art. IX of the Treaty of Paris of 1856. This *Berat* is more important than the first, since it was given to Hassun as legitimate spiritual Head, and was therefore a recognition of the ecclesiastical jurisdiction of the Primate.

3) that of 1867 conferred to the same Mons. Hassun who, elected Patriarch also of Cilicia, joined together in his person the two Sees; and it is, I believe, this last that had passed into the body of Law *DESTUR*, and on its model *Berat* were issued to successive Patriarchs, but the Government of the Young Turks after the Constitution modified that *Berat*, greatly diminishing the patriarchal attributions. As a form of recognition of a Spiritual Leader the second *Berat* is certainly better, but the more complete one is that which passed into the *Destur*,

---

273 Translator's Note: *Patrik*. Turkish name for the Eastern Orthodox patriarch.
274 Translator's Note: *Hatti-humayun*. The name of a particular Ottoman reform edict dealing with religious freedoms and organization within the empire.

body of law. One knows, anyway, of the tendency of the Young Turks, manifested by the most radical acts during the war, to want to take away every national-civil aspect from the Patriarchates and from the communities, without, however, exempting them from government control, but subjecting them to it even more with the laicizing system of government and administration of the Christian Churches.

26 - Keeping all the preceding observations in mind one should obtain a modification of art. 149, as I set forward also to the S. C. for the Oriental Church, in the following vein:

"The Ottoman Government commits to recognizing and to respecting the ecclesiastical, scholastic, ADMINISTRATIVE and JUDICIAL autonomy of EVERY CHURCH AND CONFESSION of ethnic minorities in Turkey, ON THE BASIS OF THE RELIGIOUS PRINCIPLES AND HIERARCHIES OF THOSE CHURCHES AND CONFESSIONS. To this end, and excepting provisions of the present Treaty, the Ottoman Government confirms and will fully maintain for the future the prerogatives, ATTRIBUTIONS and immunities of religious, ADMINISTRATIVE AND JUDICIAL character recognized or conceded by the Sultans to the Religious Leaders of the non-Muslim races IN CONFORMITY WITH THE HIERARCHICAL AND RELIGIOUS PRINCIPLES OF THE RESPECTIVE BELIEFS, by way of special ordinances or imperial decrees (*Firman, Hatti, Berat,* etc.) ministerial regulations or orders of the Grand Vizier, etc.

27 - At the 2° paragraph, then, having in sight the grave law on marriage issued during the war, I would say: "Whatever law, regulation, decree or circular of the Ottoman Government that imports abrogation, restriction or modification of said prerogatives and immunities, IN OPPOSITION ALSO TO THE CONSTITUTIONAL, HIERARCHICAL AND CONFESSIONAL PRINCIPLES OF EACH NON-MUSLIM BELIEF, will be considered in this regard as null and without effect."

These are the few observations I make in haste, asking that it be given the attention meriting the serious object of the Treaty that perhaps will be revised in Paris.

85

18 February 1921, Rome – draft of Gasparri's response to Naslian – AAEESS, *Asia* 57, 1, n° 16169

Insieme alla lettera della S.V. Ill. e Rma ho ricevuto gli annessi documenti, contenenti alcune sue opportunissime osservazioni sul trattato di Sèvres, per quanto si riferisce agli interessi della Chiesa Cattolica in Armenia od in quelle altre regioni di Oriente che si verranno a trovare definitivamente sotto il dominio o l'influenza dei Turchi.

La S.Sede, che ha mostrato sempre un interessamento speciale per la nobilissima nazione Armena, non mancherà certo di fare tutto il possibile, anche in questa circostanza, perché possano essere introdotte nel trattato di Sèvres alcune modificazioni in favore delle comunità cattoliche di Oriente; attese per altro le difficoltà del momento, mi sento in dovere di aggiungerLe che non sembra si possano nutrire soverchie illusioni che le dimande della Santa Sede saranno senz'altro soddisfatte da parte dei vari Governi interessati.

Intanto La ringrazio di quanto ha voluto comunicarmi e profitto ecc

[Translation]
Together with the letter from Y.M. Illus. and Rev. I received the accompanying documents, containing some of your very opportune observations on the treaty of Sèvres, as far as it refers to the interests of the Catholic Church in Armenia or in those other regions of the Orient that will come to find themselves definitively under the dominion or the influence of the Turks.

The Holy See, which has always shown a special interest for the most noble Armenian nation, shall certainly not fail to do everything possible, also in this circumstance, so that several modifications in favor of the Catholic communities of the Orient may be introduced into the treaty of Sèvres; foreseeing, however, the difficulties of the moment, I feel it my duty to add that it does not seem possible to harbor abundant illusions that the requests of the Holy See will be absolutely satisfied on the part of the various Governments involved.

Meanwhile I thank you for all that you have been pleased to communicate to me and I profit etc

86

3 February 1921, Geneva – Morsier to Gasparri – AAEESS, *Asia* 57, 1, n° 16180

Eminence,

La ligue internationale philarménienne prend la liberté de vous adresser l'appel inclus, que nous envoyons également indistinctement à toutes les Eglises chrétiennes et en particulier à Leurs Grandeurs les Evêques Suisses et nous vous serions reconnaissants de le recommander à la haute et bienveillante attention de Sa Sainteté le Pape Benoît XV.

En vous remerciant de l'accueil que vous voudrez bien faire à cet envoi, nous vous présentons, Eminence, l'expression de notre plus haute considération.

[signed]
Le sec.g.al A.de Morsier

Allegato al doc. n° 86, p. 327
[*Attachment* to doc. n° 86, p. 327]

APPEL AUX EGLISES!

L'Arménie, oppressée et persécutée depuis des siècles par les Turcs, n'est pas seulement la victime de la volonté de son dominateur, mais elle semble le jouet de la politique de l'Europe ainsi que de celle du Proche Orient. Il est évident que, si un terme n'est pas mis immédiatement aux injustices commises à l'égard de l'Arménie, cette nation n'existera plus, car elle risque d'être anéantie sous peu, par la convoitise de ses ennemis.

Les amis des Arméniens du monde entier, ne pouvant assister plus longtemps, sans protester, à ces abominations, se sont décidés d'unir leurs efforts en faveur de ce malheureux pays, espérant ainsi pouvoir lui porter un secours plus efficace, quelle que soit du reste sa destinée politique.

Dans ce but, les représentants des groupements philarméniens du monde entier se sont réunis à Paris en Juillet dernier et ils y ont décidé la fondation d'une Ligue internationale philarménienne. Cette Ligue a été constituée définitivement par un congrès philarménien international à Genève au mois de septembre 1920.

Le but de cette Ligue est d'avoir constamment l'oeil ouvert sur les événements d'Arménie et de sauvegarder ainsi, au mieux du possible, les intérêts de ce pays, de les défendre auprès de tous ceux qui pourraient les compromettre, enfin de renseigner le public sur la situation des Arméniens et de l'Arménie.

Au mois de novembre dernier le Comité Exécutif de cette Ligue a tenu, pendant plusieurs jours, ses premières séances à Genève. Il a adressé un appel aux Puissances Alliées en les suppliant de faire leur possible pour intervenir en faveur de l'Armenie dont la situation s'aggrave de jour en jour.

Ce même Comité s'est adressé également à la Société des Nations, dont les séances se tenaient à Genève à cette même époque, en lui exposant la situation de l'Arménie et en la priant d'user de toute son autorité pourqu'un terme soit mis au crime international, commis à l'égard de ce pays.

Dès lors le Comité n'a cessé de suivre de près les événements d'Arménie, de renseigner le public à cet égard et il ne se lasse pas d'attirer l'attention des gouvernements alliés et autres sur la gravité de la situation dans laquelle se trouve le peuple martyre

Ainsi la Ligue internationale philarménienne veille et veillera à l'avenir aux intérêts généraux qui concernent le peuple arménie en dehors de toute politique de parti ou de nation, et quelle que soit la solution de la question, elle prêtera à l'Arménie son concours pour assurer à ce jeune Etat tous les droits qui lui reviennent pour l'aider à se reconstituer.

Ce sera, nous l'espérons du moins, le travail de demain. Aujourd'hui, helas! nous épuisons tous nos moyens d'action pour tâcher d'obtenir qu'on arrête l'extermination des derniers restes de ce vaillant peuple.

Des appels au secours nous arrivent sans cesse de là-bas par lettres et par télégrammes.

C'est notre devoir de réveiller les consciences dans le monde entier, de renseigner le public sur les affaires arméniennes pourqu'il proteste énergiquement dans tous les milieux.

Nous nous adressons à vous et nous implorons votre appui.

Nous vous demandons instamment d'user de toute votre influence auprès de vos amis et des membres de vos Associations et Eglises pour les éclairer sur la situation des Arméniens et leur faire comprendre la responsabilité qui incombe à toute conscience humaine et chrétienne.

Nous vous adressons les Statuts de la Ligue en vous priant de faire connaître la présente lettre dans vos Conseils et Assemblées, leur demandant de donner leur adhésion morale et effective à la Ligue internationale philarménienne.

Tous dons et cotisations volontaires individuelles ou collectives, seront reçus avec reconnaissance.

87

10 February 1921, Tiflis – Moriondo to the pope – CO, 106, 3, 5, 2, n° 5313

Beatissimo Padre,

Dopo cinque mesi che sono a Tiflis, ricevetti finalmente, il 4 c.te, le prime lettere della S. Congregazione, nelle quali mi si dice fra l'altro che "la Santità Vostra, non ostante le criticissime circostanze, ha espresso parere che, per diverse considerazioni, io debba rimanere qui".

Dopo ciò è superfluo assicurare la S. Vostra che ubbidirò, come è mio sacro dovere.

Solo per obbedienza rinunciai con grave sacrificio alla Diocesi di Cuneo e venni qui, sebbene prevedessi le difficoltà che mi aspettavano e non condividessi per nulla l'ottimismo che traspariva dalle relazioni del precedente Visitatore né le rosee speranze concepite, in base a quelle, dalla S. Congregazione: cose tutte che esposi, prima di partire, a chi di ragione.

E solo per obbedienza ci rimarrò, finché piaccia alla Santità Vostra trasferirmi altrove, e le forze me lo consentiranno: benché ogni giorno più mi debba persuadere che troppo bene fondati erano i miei timori e che la mia permanenza e quel poco che posso svolgere della povera opera mia poco o nulla gioverà alla realizzazione delle sopradette speranze, fino a che dureranno le presenti condizioni.

Con me resterà il mio ottimo Segretario il P. Pietro Gagnor O.P. che benedico Iddio d'aver condotto meco e che mi è di grande aiuto.

Vivamente ringrazio la S.tà V. delle LL 20 mila inviatemi. La vita è qui carissima e le 1000 L mensili assegnatemi della S. Congregazione appena bastano per una settimana. Parimenti ringraziano la S.V. per mezzo mio i disgraziati Armeni del Caucaso delle Ltq 1000 trasmessemi dal Delegato Ap. di Costantinopoli, che sto loro distribuendo, meglio che si possa.

Dopo la Visita Pastorale della Diocesi di Cuneo, avevo proposto alla Concistoriale come capace e degno di esser Vescovo in qualche piccola Diocesi il Teol. D. Michele Viotti. Sapendo ora che è vacante la Diocesi di Susa oso far presente alla S.tà V. il suo nome, sicuro che farebbe bene in quella piccola Diocesi Piemontese più che altrove, mentre il Clero di Cuneo sarebbe lieto e certamente grato alla S.tà Vostra di veder uscir finalmente un Vescovo anche dalle sue file.

Nel bisogno che sento vivissimo di uno speciale aiuto di Dio, mi prostro ai piedi della S. Vostra implorandone la benedizione.

Della S. Vostra obbedientissimo Figlio = fr. N. Gabriele O.P. Vescovo

[Translation]

Most Blessed Father,

After five months in Tiflis, I received finally, on the 4th of this month, the first letters of the S. Congregation, in which I am told, among other things, that "Your Holiness, notwithstanding the most critical of circumstances, expressed the opinion that, for divers considerations, I must remain here".

After that, it is superfluous to assure Y. Holiness that I will obey, as is my sacred duty.

Only out of obedience did I renounce with grave sacrifice the Diocese of Cuneo and come here, even though I foresaw the difficulties that were waiting for me and I did not share in the least the optimism shown in the reports of the preceding Visitor nor the rosy hopes conceived, on their basis, by the S. Congregation: all things that I stated, before leaving, to those concerned.

And only out of obedience will I remain, until it should please Your Holiness to transfer me elsewhere, and my strength allows: even though every day more I am persuaded that my fears were too well-founded, and that my remaining here and what little I can carry out of my meager work will be of little or no use to the realization of the abovementioned hopes, as long as the present conditions persist.

With me will remain my excellent Secretary, F. Pietro Gagnor O.P., who I thank God to have brought with me and who is of great help to me.

I sincerely thank Y. Holiness for the 20 thousand L. sent me. Life is quite expensive and the 1000 L. monthly assigned me by the S. Congregation barely last a week. Equally, through me, the unfortunate Armenians of the Caucasus, thank Y.H. for the 1000 Turkish L. conveyed to me by the Ap. Delegate of Constantinople, that I am distributing as well as possible.

After the Pastoral Visit to the Diocese of Cuneo, I had proposed to the Consistory as capable and worthy of being Bishop in some small Diocese the Th.D. Michele Viotti. Knowing now that the Diocese of Susa is vacant, I venture to indicate his name to Y. Holiness, sure that he would do well in that small Piedmontese Diocese, better than anywhere else, while the Clergy of Cuneo would be happy and certainly grateful to Y. Holiness to finally see a Bishop come from their ranks as well.

In the need that I profoundly feel of a special help from God, I prostrate myself at the feet of Y. Holiness begging of you benediction.

Of Y. Holiness, most obedient Son = Fr. N. Gabriele O.P. Bishop

88

12 February 1921, Tiflis – Moriondo to Marini – CO, 106, 3, 2, n° 5293

Vicariato Apostolico del Caucaso

Eminenza,

Il giorno 4 Febbraio ricevetti finalmente quanto Ella e la S. Congregazione m'inviarono, in data 17 Dicembre cioè: lettere, Lr. 20000 dono del S. Padre, Lr. 25000 per Messe, Calendarii, più la Sua pregiatissima del 11 Novembre.

Di tutto ringrazio l'Eminenza Vostra e specialmente delle consolanti parole che mi scrive.

Quì [sic] la situazione è sempre press'a poco la medesima. Tuttavia, in considerazione di ciò che Ella mi scrive e in modo particolare per soddisfare il desiderio del S. Padre, continuerò a fare il sacrificio di rimanere al mio posto, adoprandomi del mio meglio per compiere quanto è possibile della missione affidatami. Voglio sperare che Dio gradirà il mio sacrificio e mentre mi darà le forze necessarie, vorrà benedire l'opera mia e far sì che presto le critiche condizioni presenti si mutino in meglio.

Non credo che l'Eminenza V. abbia giudicato le mie relazioni una semplice espressione d'impressioni mie soggettive, effetto di sconforto dell'animo; poiché quanto scrissi è purtroppo la realtà, provata da fatti quotidiani e condivisa da tutte le personalità politiche e diplomatiche europee che quì si trovano, e di cui sono prova le stesse notizie che la stampa europea dà di queste regioni.

In questi giorni vi è un po' più di tranquillità, in quanto che nei circoli politici si crede diminuito il pericolo d'un'invasione bolscevica, che un mese fa si temeva come imminente. Conferisce pure a questo miglioramento di situazione l'aver le potenze dell'Intesa riconosciuto l'autonomia della Georgia.

Il Governo però nulla promette di bene verso la religione, prima ancora d'aver votato la legge di separazione già la mette in pratica, impossessandosi dei beni religiosi. A nulla valgono le proteste e le minaccie, poiché ad ogni costo si vuol attuare il programma comunista e antireligioso del governo. Né vi è a sperare che simile governo cada, avendo in suo favore quasi tutto il popolo, compenetrato fino al midollo dei principii del socialismo.

La situazione economica è sempre gravissima, né si troverà facilmente una via di uscita, se le potenze europee non daranno alla Nazione aiuti finanziarii.

2. INVIO DI MISSIONARII. Poiché la S. Congregazione è di parere che, nonostante la esposta situazione, si continui nell'impresa, io penso che si potrebbe pure inviare i tre Missionarii Gesuiti, che già erano designati. Essi potranno essermi di qualche aiuto.

Il Revmo D. Antonoff, già Vicario Gener. è gravemente infermo, senz'alcuna speranza di guarigione. Non so ove trovare uno che gli succeda nell'ufficio di Parroco della chiesa polacca. Il Missionario di nazionalità polacca potrebbe sostituirlo e anche gli altri due, in mancanza di altro alloggio, potrebbero provvisoriamente abitare nella piccola casa parrocchiale, pur essendo a disposizione mia per i servizi cui potrei destinarli.

Se ciò crede opportuno la S. Congregazione dia loro gli ordini necessarii per la partenza.

L'invio di altri Missionarii, come già dissi, non credo che sia per ora conveniente.

I Polacchi residenti a Tiflis sono in gran parte partiti per la loro patria. Non ne resta che 2500 circa, i quali pure pensano di partire nella prossima primavera. Ve ne ha ancora un certo numero a Baku, forzati a rimanervi, perché le autorità bolsceviche non permettono loro di partire.

3. ACQUISTO D'UNA RESIDENZA. Riguardo all'acquisto d'una residenza propria è cosa difficile anche per me di dare un parere. Certo sarebbe buona cosa l'averla, perché si eviterebbero le tante noie e incomodi, che si hanno abitando in un alloggio privato, tanto più nelle circostanze in cui io mi trovo, e, mentre sarebbe meno costoso, sarebbe altresì più decoroso pel rappresentante della S. Sede. Ma tutto è così incerto e rischioso che non ardisco di pronunziarmi definitivamente. Tuttavia se la S. Congregazione stimasse che ciò sia conveniente, mi dia ordini in proposito.

È difficile l'inviare a Roma un progetto di compra e attenderne la decisione, poiché le migliori occasioni che si presentano sono sempre occasioni del momento, che non lasciano lungo tempo per decidere.

Non posso poi dire se la Società Americana, di cui mi si parla, possa o no possedere in Georgia, non sapendo io quale sia questa società. Credo però che tutte le società legalmente riconosciute abbiano questo diritto.

4. I CATTOLICI DI AKALKALAKI. Non ho stimato fin ora prudente decidere il passaggio dei cattolici della provincia di Akalkalaki dell'Amministrazione Eccl. Armena a quella Giorgiana, perché: 1 nel referendum che a tal fine promossi fra la popolazione vi furono, da parte degli Armeni e specialmente dei Giorgiani, delle mene e intrighi, che turbarono la necessaria libertà dei pareri. 2 Il governo bolscevico dell'Armenia aspira alla conquista di quella regione, e non è improbabile che vi riesca. Nel qual caso quelle popolazioni si troverebbero a mal partito e sarebbero probabilmente oggetto di vendette, se avessero rinnegato l'Armenia per la Georgia. Quindi a tempo più propizio, quando si potrà di persona visitare le popolazioni e rassicurarsi del lor libero volere, si potrà meglio risolvere la questione, che per ora stimo bene lasciar allo stato quo.

5. RITO. Quanto al rito: nelle città è sempre forte la corrente, che vuole il rito latino e osteggia il rito giorgiano. Solo nei villaggi si potrà, per ora, far qualche cosa per introdurre il rito giorgiano. Con prudenza quindi e quando qualche Sacerdote sarà in grado di celebrare con decoro, farà il primo tentativo in Akaldzike, dove son sicuro riuscirà bene.

Intanto la S. Congregazione mandi pure i parati di cui dispone.

Libri liturgici non si hanno che quelli della Chiesa Scismatica. Il Segretario del Revmo p. Delpuch e il P. Vardizé ne avevano esaminato una buona parte, che trovarono del tutto ortodossa. La S. Congregazione deve avere già questi libri, che erano stati inviati, per esame, anni fa dai P.P.Giorgiani di Cospoli. Se più non si ritrovassero ne manderò copia.

Nella Lettera Pastorale per la S. Quaresima ho creduto conveniente trattare l'argomento dell'Unità della Chiesa, e ho impartito ordini affinché nelle chiese di rito latino si osservi questo rito nella sua interità e si eliminino tutte quelle mescolanze di giorgiano che vi si erano introdotte. A semplice titolo di curiosità ne invio una copia.

6. SUORE GIORGIANE. Le Suore giorgiane di Cospoli mi han fatto formale dimanda di aprire una scuola elementare in Tiflis e un orfanotrofio in Akaldzike. Giudicando che esse potranno ben corrispondere allo scopo ho accordato loro la richiesta facoltà, che però tarderà ancor qualche tempo a mettersi in esecuzione. Prego intanto la S. Congregazione a darmi pure il suo parere in riguardo.

7. DISTRIBUZIONE DI DENARO PER BENEFICENZA. Ho ricevuto da Mons. Dolci, Deleg. Apost. di Cospoli la somma di Lire Turche 1000; parte del denaro inviato dal S.Padre per soccorrere gli Armeni. In una visita che feci alla Società Armena di Beneficenza diedi, a nome del S.Padre, una parte di essa, facendo distribuire l'altra parte nei paesi armeni devastati dalla guerra.

Ho pure visitato l'orfanotrofio della Croce rossa Giorgiana, cui lasciai pure una somma del danaro che m'era stato consegnato dalla S. Sede per beneficio degli orfani.

I giornali della città parlarono con encomio dell'una e dell'altra visita.

8. MEZZO DI CORRISPONDENZA. Il mezzo più sicuro per la corrispondenza è il Ministero; poiché la posta fa un servizio pessimo e molta corrispondenza va smarrita. Anche per l'invio del danaro il modo migliore e più vantaggioso si è di mandare valori in carta per mezzo del Ministero, come si è fatto ora. L'invio per mezzo della Banca causa sempre molta perdita.

Nella speranza di sovente ricevere lettere dell'Eminenza Vostra, mi raccomando alle sue preghiere ecc

[Translation]

Apostolic Vicariate of the Caucasus

Eminence,

On February 4th I finally received that which you and the S. Congregation sent me, dated December 17th, that is: letters, 20,000 L. gift of the Holy Father, 25,000 L. for Masses, Calendars, plus your most valuable [letter] of November 11th.

I thank Your Eminence for everything and especially for the consoling words that you write.

Here the situation is still more or less the same. Anyway, in consideration of that which you write me and particularly to satisfy the Holy Father's wish, I will continue to make the sacrifice of staying at my post, exerting myself as best I can to fulfill as much as possible of the mission entrusted to me. I would like to hope that God will appreciate my sacrifice and, while he gives me the necessary strength, will see fit to bless my work and let the current critical conditions soon change for the better.

I don't believe that Y. Eminence judged my reports a simple expression of my subjective impressions, a result of emotional discomfort, since what I wrote is unfortunately the reality, proven by day-to-day facts and shared by all the European political and diplomatic figures here, and to which the very same news that the European press gives about these regions attests.

These days there is a little bit more calm since in political circles the danger of a Bolshevik invasion, that a month ago was feared imminent, is believed to be diminished. The Entente powers' having recognized Georgia's autonomy also adds to this improvement of the situation.

The Government, however, promises nothing good for religion; even before having voted on the law of separation it is already putting it into practice, taking possession of religious assets. Protests and threats are worthless, since the government's communist and anti-religious program is to be implemented at all costs. Nor is there hope that such a government should fall, having in its favor almost all the people, pervaded to the core with principles of socialism.

The economic situation is still quite serious; a way out will not be easily found if the European powers do not give financial aid to the Nation.

2. SENDING OF MISSIONARIES. Since the S. Congregation is of the opinion that, notwithstanding the situation set forth, the undertaking is to be continued, I think that the three Jesuit Missionaries who have already been designated might also be sent. They will be of some help to me.

The Most Rev. D. Antonoff, formerly Vicar Gener., is seriously infirm, without any hope of recovery. I don't know where to find one to succeed him in the office of parish priest of the Polish church. The Missionary of Polish nationality could replace him and the other two, in the absence of other lodging, could also provisionally live in the small parish house, while being at my disposition for services to which I might assign them.

If they believe it opportune, let the S. Congregation give them the necessary orders for departure.

The sending of other Missionaries, as I already said, I don't believe to be convenient for now.

The Poles living in Tiflis have, in large part, left for their country. There remain only about 2500, who are themselves thinking of leaving next spring. There are still a certain number in Baku, forced to remain there because the Bolshevik authorities do not permit them to leave.

3. PURCHASE OF A RESIDENCE. Regarding the purchase of a residence, it is a difficult thing for me to even give an opinion on. Certainly it would be a good thing to have, because the many annoyances and inconveniences that one has living in a private lodging, even more so in the circumstances in which I find myself, would be avoided and, while it would be less costly, it would also be more decorous for the representative of the Holy See. But everything is so uncertain and risky that I do not dare to pronounce myself definitively. At any rate, if the S. Congregation should deem it convenient, do give me instructions in that regard.

It is difficult to send a purchase plan to Rome and await the decision thereof, since the best opportunities that present themselves are always opportunities of the moment, which do not allow a long time for deciding.

I cannot, then, say whether the American Company, of which I have heard spoken, may or may not own [property] in Georgia, not knowing myself what kind of company it is. I believe, however, that all legally recognized companies have this right.

4. THE CATHOLICS OF AKHALKALAKI. So far I have not considered it prudent to decide the passage of the Catholics of the province of Akhalkalaki from the Armenian Eccl. Administration to the Georgian, because: 1 in the referendum that I promoted to that end among the population there were, on

the part of the Armenians and especially of the Georgians, plots and intrigues that disturbed the necessary freedom of opinion. 2 The Bolshevik government of Armenia aspires to the conquest of that region, and it is not improbable that it should succeed. In that case, those populations would find themselves badly off, and they would probably be the object of vendettas if they had repudiated Armenia for Georgia. Therefore, in a more propitious moment, when it is possible to personally visit the populations and be assured of their free will, it will be possible to better resolve the question, which for now I consider best left in the *status quo*.

5. RITE. As to rite: in the cities, the trend that wants the Latin rite, and is hostile to the Georgian rite, is still strong. Only in the villages is it possible, for now, to do something to introduce the Georgian rite. With prudence therefore, and when some Priest is able to celebrate with decorum, he will make the first attempt in Akhaltsikhe where I am sure it will turn out well.

Meanwhile the S. Congregation should feel free to send the vestments that are available.

Liturgical books are not to be had other than those of the Schismatic Church. The Secretary of the Most Rev. F. Delpuch and F. Vardizé have examined a good part of them, which they found to be completely orthodox. The S. Congregation should still have these books, which had been sent for examination years ago by the Georgian Fathers of Constantinople. If they should not be found, I will send copies of them.

In the Pastoral Letter for Holy Lent I believed it convenient to address the subject of the Unity of the Church, and I imparted orders such that in the Latin rite churches this rite be observed in its entirety and that all those mixtures of Georgian that had been introduced be eliminated. Just for curiosity's sake I am sending a copy of it.

6. GEORGIAN SISTERS. The Georgian Sisters of Constantinople made a formal request to me to open an elementary school in Tiflis and an orphanage in Akhaltsikhe. Judging that they should correspond well to the purpose, I accorded them the requested faculty which, however, will still be somewhat delayed in being put into the works. I meanwhile ask the S. Congregation to also give me its opinion in regard.

7. DISTRIBUTION OF MONEY FOR CHARITY. I received from Mons. Dolci, Apost. Deleg. of Constantinople, the sum of 1000 Turkish Lire, part of the money sent by the Holy Father to assist the Armenians. In a visit that I made to the Armenian Beneficent Society I gave, in name of the Holy Father, a part of this, and I had the remainder distributed in the Armenian towns devastated by the war.

I also visited the Georgian Red Cross orphanage, where I also left a sum out of the money that had been consigned to me by the Holy See on behalf of the orphans.

The newspapers of the city spoke with praise both of one visit and of the other.

8. MEANS OF CORRESPONDENCE. The most secure means for correspondence is the Ministry; since the mails have awful service and a lot of correspondence goes missing. Also for the sending of money, the best and most advantageous way is to send paper instruments by way of the Ministry, as was just done. Sending by way of the Bank is always very expensive.

In the hope of often receiving letters from Your Eminence, I entrust myself to your prayers, etc.

89

13 February 1921, Tiflis – Moriondo to Marini – CO, 106, 3, 2, n° 5293

Eminenza,

Nel rapporto, unito alla presente, parlai delle Suore Giorgiane di Cospoli, che mi fecer dimanda di venir in Georgia a fondar una scuola e un orfanotrofio.

Ora, terminato appena il rapporto, vengo a sapere, per mezzo di lettere delle dette Suore, indirizzate a persone del Clero di quì, che il Revmo P. Delpuch, durante il suo soggiorno a Cospoli, avrebbe loro dichiarato che esse non saranno autorizzate a venir in Georgia, dove saranno invece inviate Suore francesi.

Non so quanto vi sia in ciò di vero ed io non vi presto troppa fede: Poiché non credo che il P. Delpuch abbia ancora ad intromettersi negli affari che riguardano le regioni soggette alla mia giurisdizione.

Ad ogni modo, credo bene far noto all'Eminenza V. che è mia convinzione, basata anche su quanto Ella stessa scrive; esser dette Suore di buon spirito, che le Suore Giorgiane siano le più adatte per incominciare l'opera di apostolato in Georgia, e quelle che potranno subito lavorare con frutto , colle opere che progettano di fondare. Conosco le Suore francesi per esperienza e dico sinceramente che poco mi piace il lor esagerato patriottismo, per cui sono prima missionarie della Francia e poi della Chiesa Cattolica.

Da informazioni molto attendibili seppi pure che il Revmo P. Delpuch aveva già gettati quì i germi del gallicismo, e fra altro aveva fatto serie promesse di aprir quanto prima una cappella ufficiale francese: e parecchie persone già mi dimandarono quando si aprirà questa cappella

Questo credo utile scriverle per renderla informata di tutto ed affinché l'Eminenza Vostra possa disporre ogni cosa per il meglio di questa Missione.

Le rinnovo i sensi della mia stima e devozione ecc.

[Translation]

Apostolic Vicariate of the Caucasus

Eminence,

In the report attached to the present I spoke of the Georgian Sisters of Constantinople, who made a request to me to come to Georgia to found a school and an orphanage.

Now, the report just finished, I come to find out, by way of letters from said Sisters addressed to members of the Clergy here, that the Most Rev. F. Delpuch, during his stay in Constantinople, had declared to them that they will not be authorized to come to Georgia, where instead French Sisters will be sent.

I do not know how much truth there is in this, and I do not give it too much credence, since I don't think that F. Delpuch would again interfere in affairs that regard the regions subject to my jurisdiction.

At any rate, I believe it best to make known to Y. Eminence that it is my conviction, based also on what you yourself write, said Sisters being of good spirit, that the Georgian Sisters are the most well-suited to beginning the mission work in Georgia, and those who will be able to quickly work fruitfully, with the institutions that they are planning to found. I know the French Sisters from experience and I say sincerely that I like very little their exaggerated patriotism, according to which they are first missionaries of France and then of the Catholic Church.

From very attendible reports I also found out that the Most Rev. F. Delpuch has already sown the seeds of gallicism here, and among other things had made a series of promises to open an official French chapel as soon as possible; many people have already asked me when this chapel will open.

This I believe useful to write to you so as to keep you informed of everything and so that Your Eminence may manage everything for the best of this Mission.

I renew to you my feelings of esteem and devotion, etc.

90

28 February 1921, Rome – Terzian to Cerretti[275]– AAEESS, *Asia* 57, 1, n° 17537

Eccellenza,

La Lega delle Nazioni nell'ultima sua generale riunione aveva invitato ad intervenire a favore dell'Armenia i Governi della Spagna e delle Repubbliche del Brasile e degli Stati Uniti. Questi Governi avevano prontamente aderito a quell'invito, perciò lo scrivente ha creduto opportuno interessare i sullodati Governi con un nuovo appello da parte sua in questi giorni della Conferenza di Londra, ove potranno essere prese definitive decisioni anche per l'Armenia. Gli Ambasciatori della Spagna e del Brasile accolsero molto benevolmente il mio ricorso, mi fecero però intendere che anche una parola del S. Padre ai loro rispettivi Governi sarebbe efficace allo scopo.

Quindi mi sono permesso ieri sera nell'udienza onorata da Sua Eminenza il Cardinale Segretario di Stato di pregarlo di voler interessare il Santo Padre in oggetto di un tale intervento. Sua Eminenza promise che oggi stesso

---

275 The original of this document was found in AAEESS, *Asia* 57 by Riccardi, *op. cit.*, note 140, p. 128.

inviterebbe da se gli Ambasciatori di Spagna e di Brasile per intendersi sul passo da fare in proposito.

Prego ora Vostra Eccellenza di voler ancora ricordare a Sua Eminenza l'affare, raccomandandolo anche per parte sua, urgendo realmente la necessità di un tale efficace appello del S. Padre ai tre Governi impegnati presso la Società delle Nazioni. Tale atto del Santo Padre, mentre confermerebbe sempre meglio l'alto suo interessamento per la disgraziata Armenia, darebbe anche a noi la soddisfazione di aver tentato tutti i mezzi per concorrere alla salvezza del nostro popolo.

I tre Governi intervenendo durante la Conferenza influirebbero molto sulle deliberazioni da prendere e potrebbero giovare assai alla causa nostra.

Voglia, Eccellenza, scusarmi l'insistenza, che del resto mi è imposta dall'imperiosità delle circostanze, mentre colgo l'occasione per rassegnarmi, con rinnovati sensi della più alta stima, di Vostra Eccellenza, ecc

[Translation]
Excellency,

The League of Nations in its most recent general meeting had invited the Governments of Spain and of the Republics of Brazil and of the United States to intervene in favor of Armenia. These Governments readily accepted that invitation, hence this writer believed it opportune to involve the above-named Governments in a new appeal on her behalf, in these days of the Conference of London, where definitive decisions could be taken regarding Armenia as well. The Ambassadors of Spain and of Brazil received my appeal very favorably; however, they led me to understand that just a word from the Holy Father to their respective Governments would be effective to this end.

Therefore I permitted myself yesterday evening in the audience honored by His Eminence the Cardinal Secretary of State to ask him to please interest the Holy Father in the object of such an intervention. His Eminence promised that this very day he would invite the Ambassadors of Spain and of Brazil to see him in order to establish an understanding about the steps to take in this regard.

I pray now that Your Excellency may be pleased to remind His Eminence again of the affair, entrusting it to him also on your behalf, really urging the necessity of such a powerful appeal of the Holy Father to the three Governments working with the League of Nations. Such an act of the Holy Father, while it would even better confirm his keen concern for the unfortunate Armenia, would give also to us the satisfaction of having attempted all means of contributing to the rescue of our people.

The three Governments intervening during the Conference would have a great influence on the deliberations to be made and could be extremely useful to our cause.

May it please you, Excellency, to excuse my insistence which, after all, is imposed upon me by the pressing nature of the circumstances, while I take the occasion to present myself, with renewed feelings of the most highest esteem, of Your Excellency, etc.

91

1 March 1921, Rome – Gasparri's handwritten draft to the Marquis of Villasireda[?], amb. of Spain to the Holy See [276]– AAEESS, *Asia* 57, 1, n° 17537

È stato riferito alla S. Sede che la Lega delle Nazioni, nell'ultima sua riunione generale aveva invitato la Spagna ad intervenire per la soluzione della questione Armena e che il Governo aveva aderito a tale invito.

Il S. Padre è del tutto certo che il Governo Spagnuolo, ispirandosi a quella larghezza e nobiltà di vedute che lo distingue, vorrà esaminare la questione anzidetta con quella equanimità, quella simpatia e quella benevolenza di cui è degno un popolo che ha tanto sofferto.

Ciononostante la Stessa Santità Sua mi ha dato il venerato incarico di raccomandare vivamente a Vostra Eccellenza la causa di quel misero popolo, in favore del quale Essa è intervenuta tante volte, e specialmente durante la guerra.

Profitto ben volentieri dell'incontro ecc.

[Translation]

It was referred to the Holy See that the League of Nations, in its most recent general meeting, had invited Spain to intervene regarding the solution to the Armenian question and that the Government had accepted that invitation.

The Holy Father is quite certain that the Spanish Government, prompted by that openness and nobility of views that distinguishes it, will want to examine the aforesaid question with that equanimity, that sympathy and that benevolence of which a people who have suffered so much is worthy.

Nevertheless, His Holiness himself gave me the venerated charge of energetically advocating to Your Excellency the cause of that poor people, in favor of which you have intervened so many times, especially during the war.

With great pleasure I profit from the encounter, etc.

92

1 March 1921, Rome – handwritten draft from Gasparri to Magalhas de Azevedo amb. of Brazil to the Holy See – *Ibid.*, n° 17537[277]

È stato riferito alla Santa Sede che la Lega delle Nazioni, nell'ultima sua riunione generale aveva invitato la Repubblica del Brasile ad intervenire per la

---

276 Copies of doc. nn° 91 and 92 were found in AAEESS, *Asia* 57 by Riccardi, *op. cit.*, note 140, p. 128.
277 V. note 276.

soluzione della questione armena e che il governo della Repubblica aveva aderito a tale invito.

Il Santo Padre è del tutto certo che il Governo brasiliano, ispirandosi a quella larghezza e nobiltà di vedute che lo distingue, vorrà esaminare la questione anzidetta con quella equanimità , quella simpatia e quella benevolenza di cui è degno un popolo che ha tanto sofferto.

Cionondimeno la stessa Santità Sua mi ha dato il venerato incarico di raccomandare vivamente a Vostra Eccellenza la causa di quel misero popolo, in favore del quale Essa è intervenuta tante volte, e specialmente durante la guerra.

Profitto ben volentieri dell'incontro ecc.

[Translation]

It was referred to the Holy See that the League of Nations, in its most recent general meeting, had invited the Republic of Brazil to intervene regarding the solution to the Armenian question and that the Government of the Republic had accepted that invitation.

The Holy Father is quite certain that the Brazilian Government, prompted by that openness and nobility of views that distinguishes it, will want to examine the aforesaid question with that equanimity, that sympathy and that benevolence of which a people who have suffered so much is worthy.

Nevertheless, His Same Holiness gave me the venerated charge of energetically advocating to Your Excellency the cause of that poor people, in favor of which you have intervened so many times, especially during the war.

With great pleasure I profit from the encounter etc.

93

3 March 1921, Rome – the Brazilian ambassador to Gasparri[278]— *Ibid.*, n° 17537

Eminentissime Seigneur,

J'ai eu l'honneur de recevoir la Note n° B-17537 du 1ᵉʳ mars courant.

Votre Eminence Révérendissime y porte à ma connaissance que le Souverain Pontife, informé de l'invitation, faite au Brésil par la Société des Nations, et acceptée par lui, de contribuer à la solution de la question arménienne, a voulu de Son côté adresser un pressant appel au Président de la République pour la cause de ce noble peuple chrétien, qui a déjà tant souffert,

---

278 A copy of this document was found in AAEESS, *Asia* 57 by Riccardi, *op.cit.*, note 140, p. 128.

et en faveur duquel Sa Sainteté Elle-même est intervenue à plusieurs reprises, spécialement pendant la guerre récente.

Je me suis empressé de transmettre par télégramme le contenu de cette Note à mon Gouvernement, qui sans aucun doute conformera sa conduite encore une fois à ses sentiments bien connus de déférence et de vénération envers la haute autorité morale du Saint Siège, ainsi qu'au culte de la veritable liberté et du droit, dont la Nation brésilienne a donné toujours et partout l'exemple.

Je me ferai un devoir de transmettre à Votre Eminence Révérendissime la réponse de mon Gouvernement, aussitôt qu'elle me sera parvenue.

Je saisis ecc

94

2 March 1921, Constantinople – telegr. from Moriondo to Marini – CO, 106, 5, 3, 2, n° 5287

Causa avvenimenti costretto partire Tiflis con legazioni straniere trovomi Cospoli aspettando ordini : Moriondo

[Translation]
Cause events constrained to leave Tiflis with foreign legations am in Constple awaiting orders : Moriondo

95

3 March 1921, Constantinople – Moriondo to Marini – CO, 106, 3, 5, 2, n° 5347

VICARIATO APOSTOLICO
DEL CAUCASO

Eminenza,

In data 12 Febbraio spedivo lettera, in cui accusavo ricevuta della risposta e del danaro dall'Eminenza Vostra inviatimi.

Dicevo in essa che la situazione della Georgia pareva alquanto migliorata e conforme al desiderio del S. Padre io sarei rimasto al mio posto, - che del resto mai avevo pensato abbandonare, senza ordine espresso della S. Congregazione - per compiere quanto le circostanze avrebbero permesso della mia missione.

Pochi giorni eran trascorsi, quando improvvisamente i Bolscevichi attaccarono la frontiera giorgiana e in breve tempo giunsero a pochi kilometri dalla capitale. Nell'imminenza del pericolo il governo esortò i rappresentanti delle Nazioni a lasciare la città e rifugiarsi in luogo sicuro.

Perciò con treno speciale, assieme al corpo diplomatico, partii la sera del 17 Febbraio, al momento in cui il nemico si trovava alle porte della città. Dopo tre giorni di pessimo viaggio arrivammo a Batum, ove contavo rimanere in attesa dello svolgersi degli avvenimenti. Ma colà non fu possibile di trovare alloggio, tanto la città era invasa da fuggiaschi. I Rappresentanti delle Nazioni si recarono a bordo delle navi da guerra già giunte in porto ed io trovai ospitalità a bordo del piroscafo Costantinopoli. Intanto le notizie che giungevano erano sempre peggiori, e siccome era omai perduta ogni speranza di arrestare le orde bolsceviche e d'altra parte i Kiemalisti occupavano le provincie giorgiane di Artakan e Artvin, sulle mosse di scendere verso Batum, credetti bene recarmi a Costantinopoli in attesa dell'esito finale degli avvenimenti.

Quivi giunto telegrafai subito all'Eminenza Vostra, chiedendo istruzioni sul da fare.

È cosa difficile prevedere quale sarà il risultato finale di quanto ora avviene. È però assai probabile che il Caucaso sia per lungo tempo ancora il campo di guerre e di lotte, che impediranno lo svolgimento dell'opera progettata dalla S. Congregazione. Ora che i Bolscevichi sono i padroni di quelle regioni, sarà ardua impresa allontanarneli o tentare un'opera di evangelizzazione cattolica nei loro dominii.

Non è improbabile che Bolscevichi e Kiemalisti, ora che si trovano a contatto immediato e si contendono più di una regione, abbiano a farsi guerra vicendevole.

Io credetti opportuno ritirarmi da Tiflis, secondo il consiglio del governo e di altri rappresentanti stranieri, perché se poco potevo fare nelle condizioni in cui mi trovavo, a nulla certo avrebbe più valso l'opera mia sotto la schiavitù e tirannia bolscevica; mentre per altro sarei rimasto, Dio sa fino a quando, isolato da tutti ed esposto ad ogni possibile evento.

Ho lasciato quale Vicario dei Cattolici giorgiani, caldei ecc. il Rev. P. Emmanuele Vardizé, bravo Sacerdote, zelante e abile negli affari, che mi fu di grande aiuto durante la mia permanenza in Georgia.

Causa gli avvenimenti non ricevetti più, dopo il 4 Febbraio, il corriere postale; per modo che la sola corrispondenza speditami in data 17 Dicembre mi pervenne. Se mai l'Eminenza Vostra avesse in seguito inviato istruzioni e ordini, che fosse per me necessario avere nelle attuali circostanze, La prego di volermi notificare d'urgenza dette istruzioni.

Spero che l'Eminenza vorrà quanto prima favorirmi d'una risposta e significarmi il da fare. Se l'Eminenza Vostra crede opportuno potrei venire a Roma per meglio riferire sulla verità delle cose.

Mentre le bacio ecc

[Translation]

APOSTOLIC VICARIATE
OF THE CAUCASUS

Eminence,

On February 12th I sent a letter, in which I acknowledged the receipt of the response and the money sent to me by Your Eminence.

I said, in this, that the situation of Georgia seemed somewhat improved and, complying with the Holy Father's wish, I would remain at my post—which, anyway, I would never have thought to abandon without express order of the S. Congregation—to carry out as much of my mission as the circumstances would have permitted.

Few days had gone by, when suddenly the Bolsheviks attacked the Georgian border and within a short time arrived a few kilometers from the capital. Given the imminence of the danger the government exhorted the representatives of the Nations to leave the city and take refuge in a safe place.

Whereupon, on a special train together with the diplomatic corps, I left the evening of February 17th, at the moment in which the enemy found themselves at the gates of the city. After three days of awful travel we arrived in Batum, where I had counted upon remaining, waiting for events to play themselves out. But there it was impossible to find lodging, for how overrun the city was with refugees. The Representatives of the Nations boarded some warships already come into port and I found hospitality on board the battleship Constantinople. Meanwhile, the incoming news was ever worse, and since by now all hope had been lost of stopping the Bolshevik hordes and at the same time the Kemalists occupied the Georgian provinces of Ardahan and Artvin, ready to descend towards Batum, I believed it best to go to Constantinople to wait for the final outcome of events.

Here arrived, I promptly telegraphed Your Eminence, asking instructions on what is to be done.

It is difficult to foresee what the final result will be of what is now happening. It is, however, quite probable that the Caucasus shall be, for a long while still, the arena of wars and of struggles that will impede the carrying out of the work projected by the S. Congregation. Now that the Bolsheviks are the masters of those regions, it will be an arduous task to drive them out or to attempt a mission of Catholic evangelization in their dominions.

It is not improbable that Bolsheviks and Kemalists, now that they find themselves in immediate contact and contend more than one region, might make war against one another.

I believed it opportune to retreat from Tiflis following the advice of the government and of other foreign representatives because, if I could do little in the conditions in which I was, certainly my work would be worth nothing under Bolshevik slavery and tyranny; while I would have remained, God knows how long, isolated from everyone and exposed to every possible event, besides.

I left as Vicar of the Georgian Catholics, Chaldeans etc. the Rev. F. Emmanuele Vardizé, a good Priest, zealous and able in business, who was of great help to me during my stay in Georgia.

Due to events, I have not received the postal courier since the 4th of February; so that only the correspondence sent to me on December 17th has arrived. If Your Eminence had perhaps sent further instructions and orders that would be necessary for me to have under the current circumstances, I pray it should please you to notify me urgently of said instructions.

I hope that Y. Eminence shall be pleased to soon favor me with a reply and indicate to me what is to be done. Should Your Eminence believe it opportune, I could come to Rome in order to better report on the truth of things.

While I kiss, etc.

96

4 March 1921, Rome – Mons. Assessor to Tedeschini – CO, 106, 3, 5, 2, n° 5287

Illmo e Revmo Mons. Federico Tedeschini
Sostituto della Segreteria di Stato di S.S.

Il sottoscritto Assessore della S.C. per la Chiesa Orientale, avendo appreso telegraficamente che Mons. Moriondo, Visitatore Apostolico del Caucaso, in vista dell'avanzata bolscevica nella Georgia si è trasferito a Costantinopoli, prega la S.V. Illma e Revma a nome dell'Emo Signor Card. Segretario di voler far telegrafare a Mons. Dolci invitandolo ad "avvertire Mons. Moriondo di aspettare lettere della S. Congregazione".

Chiedendo scusa del disturbo ecc.
firmato : Mons. Assessore

[Translation]
Most Illus. and Most Rev. Mons. Federico Tedeschini
Substitute of the Secretariat of State of the Holy See

The undersigned Assessor of the S.C. for the Oriental Church, having learnt telegraphically that Mons. Moriondo, Visitor Apostolic to the Caucasus, has moved to Constantinople in view of the Bolshevik advance into Georgia, asks Y. Most Illus. and Most Rev., in the name of the Most Emin. Card. Secretary, to be so pleased as to have telegraphed to Mons. Dolci an invitation for him to "advise Mons. Moriondo to wait for letters from the S. Congregation".

Asking forgiveness for the disturbance etc.
signed : Mons. Assessor

97

5 March 1921, Rome – Mons. Assessor to Moriondo – CO, 106, 3, 5, 2, n° 5287

Illmo e Revmo Mons. Natale Gabriele Moriondo
Visitatore Apostolico del Caucaso,

Mi è pervenuto il telegramma con il quale la S.V. mi ha annunziato il suo arrivo costì e in attesa di avere dalla S.V. un rapporto circa gli ultimi avvenimenti che hanno determinato la Sua forzata partenza dal Caucaso ho fatto telegrafare dalla Segreteria di Stato a Monsignor Dolci per notificarLe di attendere le varie lettere di questa S.C. che il P. Dionisio Kalatozoff, partito ieri sera, dovrà consegnare a V.S. e a Mons. Dolci.

In esse, infatti, già in previsione di quanto è avvenuto, si faceva conoscere alla S.V. come la S.C. avrebbe sommamente desiderato di saperLa rimasta nel Caucaso magari nel dominio dei kemalisti, sia per poter difendere a nome del S.Padre le persone e i beni dei cristiani, sia per evitare l'impressione spiacevole che potrebbe aversi dai cristiani del Caucaso nel ritenersi abbandonati dal loro autorevole Pastore.

Ma poiché ormai le circostanze Le hanno consigliato di recarsi a Costantinopoli, la S.C. non può che raccomandare alla S.V. di procurare con tutti i mezzi ordinari e straordinari che Le sarà possibile di mantenersi a contatto con il clero e con il popolo del Caucaso di qualunque rito e giurisdizione, confortandoli con i Suoi scritti e con i soccorsi che questa S.C. recentemente Le ha inviati e interessandosi attivamente di tutti gli abitanti di quella regione senza distinzione di religione e di nazionalità.

Qualora poi le circostanze migliorassero in qualche modo e rendessero possibile a V.S. di ritornare almeno a Batum, senza attendere al ritorno dalle autorità diplomatiche o consolari, ma senza esporsi certamente a temerarie avventure, procuri di tornare quanto prima vicino al Suo Gregge, pur confidando nell'assistenza e protezione divina del Supremo Pastore.

Approssimandosi frattanto la Pasqua la S.V. abbia presente di procurare i sacri olii in modo che a suo tempo possano esserne provveduti, non solo i Suoi sudditi, ma anche le Chiese dipendenti dall'Amministratore Apostolico armeno.

Riservandomi poi di darle particolari istruzioni in riguardo ai Religiosi e alle Religiose georgiane costì residenti, dopo che il P. Delpuch mi avrà inviato l'atteso suo Rapporto, penso che la S.V., anche a nome della S.Sede, farà cosa opportuna se, profittando del Suo soggiorno costì, vorrà interessarsi della loro situazione presente e della loro sistemazione futura e riferirmi il Suo illuminato parere su quanto sarebbe opportuno e possibile fare per assicurare ai due Istituti una vita regolare ed efficace per il bene dei cattolici georgiani.

Intanto augurandoLe di tutto cuore da Dio assistenza e conforto etc.

[Translation]

Most Illus. and Most Rev. Mons. Natale Gabriele Moriondo
Visitor Apostolic of the Caucasus,

I received the telegram with which you announced to me your arrival there and, in anticipation of having a report from you about the recent events that determined your forced departure from the Caucasus, I had the Secretariat of State telegraph Monsignor Dolci to notify you to wait for the various letters of this S.C. that F. Dionisio Kalatozoff, departed yesterday evening, is to consign to yourself and to Mons. Dolci.

In these, in fact, already foreseeing the course of events, it was made known to you how the S.C. would have desired exceedingly to know that you remained in the Caucasus, perhaps in the dominion of the Kemalists, both in order to be able to defend in the name of the Holy Father the persons and the assets of the Christians, and to avoid the unpleasant impression that the Christians of the Caucasus might have in considering themselves abandoned by their influential Pastor.

But since now the circumstances suggested that you go to Constantinople, the S.C. can do nothing but urge you to try, with all the means, ordinary and extraordinary, that shall be possible for you, to keep in contact with the clergy and with the people of the Caucasus of whatever rite and jurisdiction, comforting them with your writings and with the aid that this S.C. recently sent you, and actively concerning yourself with all the inhabitants of that region without distinction for religion or for nationality.

At such time, then, as circumstances improve in some way and render possible your return at least to Batum, without waiting for the return of the diplomatic or consular authorities, but without exposing yourself, certainly, to foolhardy risks, try to return as soon as possible close to your Flock, while trusting in the assistance and divine protection of the Supreme Shepherd.

In the meantime, as Easter is drawing near, remember to obtain the holy oils so that in due course not only your own subjects, but also the Churches dependent on the Armenian Apostolic Administrator, may be provided with them.

Reserving myself, then, to giving you particular instructions in regard to the Georgian Religious residing there after F. Delpuch has sent me his awaited Report, I think that you, also in the name of the Holy See, would do an opportune thing if, profiting from your sojourn there, you would be pleased to concern yourself with their current situation and with their future arrangements and to relate to me your enlightened opinion on how much would be necessary and possible to do to in order to assure the two Institutes of a steady and effective life for the good of Georgian Catholics.

Meanwhile wishing you whole-heartedly assistance and comfort from God etc.

98

9 March 1921, Roma – handwritten draft of the telegram from Gasparri to Kemal[279]– AAEESS, *Asia* 117, n° 17569

Kemal Mustafà Pascià
Angora
Au nom du Souverain Pontife j'ai l'honneur de faire appel à vos nobles sentiments d'humanité, en Vous conjurant de vouloir bien donner, aussitôt

---

[279] A copy of this document was found in AAEESS, *Asia* 117 by Riccardi, *op. cit.*, note 131, pp. 127–128.

que possible des ordres opportuns pour assurer le respect de la vie et des biens des Chrétiens du Caucase, de l'Asia Mineure et de l'Anatolie.Après tant de souffrance que l'humanité a endurée il est à souhaiter que la voix de la clémence et de la pitié s'impose partout.

99

12 March 1921, Angora – reply telegram from Kemal to the pope[280]– AAEESS, *Asia* 117, n° 17569 (In Turkish with) translation in French:

Sainte Papa Benoit Quinze
Rome
Au Nome de votre sainteté son Eminence le Cardinal Gasparini [*sic*] Il-à-transmis par dépêche votre appel en faveur des Chrétiens de l'Anatolie du Caucase et de l'Asie Mineure Stop L'obligation d'assurer la sécurité et le bonheur de tous le habitants de notre pays sans distinction de religion est pour nous un dévoir imperiux commandé par nos sentiments humanitaires ainsi que par la réligion musulmane Stop Par consequent les Chretiens de toutes les regions ou s'étendent l'autorité et l'influence du Gouvernement de la Grande Assemblée National de Turquie jouissent de la tranquilité la plus complete Stop La paix et la sécurité qui a l'interieur de nos Frontières régnent partout où une armée étrangere ne vient pas porter la dévastation et la mort constituent la preuve irrefutable de mes affirmations stopD'autre part pour mieux montrer l'invariabilité de notre politique sur cette question je prends la libérte de transmettre ci-dessous a votre Sainteté les declarations que j'ai faites à ce sujet dans le discours d'inauguration que j'ai prononcé le 24 avril 1920 a l'occasion de l'ouverture de la grande Assemblée Nationale de Turquie ainsique dans mon discours du premiér mars dernier au début de la seconde année de notre legislature

Moustafa Kémal
Président de la grande Assemblée Nationale deTurquie

Fragment de mon discours du 24 Avril 1920: C'est un principe fondamentail admis de touts temps chez nous de proteger les grecs et les arméniens de l'Anatolie et de leur assurer paix et bonheur tant qui ils s'absolument [*sic*] de faire opposition a la volonté Nationale et aux ordres du gouvernement stop même en fable [*sic*] des criminelles agressions commisses contre nos frères de race et de réligion par des forces Arméniennes tant régulier qu'irréguliers en Cilicie ainsi qu'en déhors de nos frontières orientales nous avont considére comme un dévoir primordial d'humanité d'assurer la sécurité la plus complete aux chrétiens qui vivent tranquillement a l'interieurs de notre pays stop Dans ces jours ou l'Anatolie Cernée est privée de tout moyen de

---

280 A copy of this document was found in AAEESS, *Asia* 117 by Riccardi, *op. cit.*, note 131, pp. 127–128.

communiques avec le monde exterieur nous avons considére que parmi les mesures enentiereles [*sic*] destinés a sauvegarder les interête superieurs de la patrie la protection de la population chretienne venait en première ligne et avons donné des instructions en ce sens a toutes les autorités competentes stop Fragment de mon discours du prémier mars 1921 messieurs les puissances de l'entente nous considerent comme un peuple inaple [*sic*] a former un état independant et prenant pretexte de cette fausse supposition ils tachent de demembrer notre pays et d'asservir notre nation stop ce qui les induit ainsi en erreur c'est la croyance qui ils ont de notre incapacite de nous gouverner nous mêmes stop or notre peuple privé depuis une année de tout appui et de toute aide ainsi que des formes administratives aux quelles il était habite dépuis des siècles à été éxpose à la plus grande de toute les calamites qu'un peuple peut subir stop malgré cela il s'administre actuellement de la façon la plus humaine la plus civilisée et la plus rispectueuse des droits et des libértés de chacun stop dans les parties envahies de notre pays nos ennémis se livrent sans arrêt a toutes sortes d'atrocités telles qu'assassinats deportations pillages et dévastations contre nos paisible compatriotes privés de tout moyen de defense tandis que par contre dans les parties du pays ou s'etende l'autorité du gouvernement de la grande assemblée nationale de Turquie tous les elements nous [*sic*] musulmans joissent de la paix et de la sécurite à l'abri de nos armes er de nos lois.

100

31 March 1921, Rome – the Brazilian ambassador to Gasparri – AAEESS, *Asia* 57, 1, n° 17537

Eminentissime Seigneur,

Faisant suite à ma note du 3 courant, j'ai l'honneur de porter à la connaissance de Votre Eminence Révérendissime que Son Excellence le Président de la République a pris le plus grand intérêt à l'appel que le Saint Père lui a adresseé en faveur de l'Arménie et que des instructions ont été données à l'Ambassadeur du Brésil à Paris, Président du Conseil Exécutif de la Société des Nations, de soutenir chaleureusement devant celle-ci la cause de l'infortuné peuple arménien.

Je saisis ecc

101

8 April 1921 – Memorandum of "The Armenia America Society" to the American Government – AAEESS, *Asia* 57, 1, n° 23279

L'Autonomie pour les Arméniens

1° - <u>L'appel à l'Amérique</u>:

Le Président de "The Armenia America Society" se trouvait à Genève pendant la récente session de l'Assemblée de la Société des Nations et le Directeur de la Société était à Londres pendant la récente Conférence des

Premiers Ministres, qui discutaient la révision du Traité de Sèvres. De toutes les discussions il devint évident que la question des dépenses mettait obstacle à l'organisation de l'administration et de la police de sûreté dans le Foyer arménien délimité par le Président Wilson. Nous sommes sûrs et certains que si le Gouvernement des Etats-Unis déclarait nettement qu'il participerait à un emprunt, dont le montant ne serait dépensé que sous la surveillance d'une Commission américaine, cette déclaration permettrait de mettre rapidement à l'exécution les clauses du Traité de Sèvres concernant la constitution d'une Arménie autonome en Turquie.

2º - <u>Le but à poursuivre pour l'Arménie.</u>

Conformément au Traité de Sèvres, une region des quatre Vilayets du Nord Ouest de la Turquie, devait être délimitée par le Président Wilson et jointe à la République Arménienne dont la capitale était Erivan en Transcaucasie. Les circonstances ont changé depuis la signature du Traité de Sèvres. On commence à voir que la sécurité des Arméniens de Turquie sera mieux assurés en les traitant séparément et en dehors de la situation de l'Arménie Russe.

Il ressort qu'il y a grande nécessité de travailler en vue de créer une Arménie autonome, ayant son centre à Erzeroum, indépendamment de l'attitude de la Russie. En outre la question de la Cilicie, dont la population est maintenant en grande partie arménienne, exige d'être envisagée tout à fait à part.

3º - <u>Argument de justice.</u>-

On commence à comprendre de tous les Alliés de la guerre dernière, les Arméniens ont souffert proportionnellement le plus, et qu'ils sont au premier rang pour la bravoure et leur dévouement à la cause des Alliés. Bien que ce ne soit pas de leur faute, les événements ont pris une tournure telle qu'ils sont menacés de se trouver dans une situation pire qu'avant la guerre, malgré qu'ils aient été du côté des vainqueurs. Il est vrai que les Etats-Unis n'étaient pas en guerre avec la Turquie, mais les Arméniens ont combattu et les Allemands et les Autrichiens et il y a un grand nombre de témoignages que leur campagne au Caucase et en Palestine ont efficacement contribué aux succès des Alliés en Turquie et par conséquent à la victoire en Europe Occidentale. Nous espérons que le peuple américain soutiendra le gouvernement dans cet effort de faire rendre justice à l'un des Alliés de la dernière guerre.

4º - <u>Argument de la Paix.</u>-

La création d'une Arménie autonome en Turquie est une condition essentielle pour le rétablissement de la Paix dans le Proche Orient. Ne pas leur rendre justice serait créer des motifs de trouble et d'insécurité. Les Etats-Unis sont intéressés au rétablissement de la paix, au point de vue de leur commerce, si même il n'y avait pas d'autres raisons, et c'est pourquoi nous pensons que le peuple des Etats-Unis voudra soutenir le Gouvernement dans le juste effort d'aider au rétablissement de la Paix. Ceci sera vrai surtout, si l'on arrive à établir qu'une assistance de cette nature n'entrainerait pas les Etats-Unis dans des embarras extérieurs.

5º - <u>Argument de l'intérêt du peuple Américain.</u>

Les Américains par les dons qu'ils ont faits par l'entremise du Near East Relief, ont en outre manifesté d'une manière admirable leur intérêt pour la race arménienne Nous croyons que le peuple des Etats-Unis voudra pour des motifs humanitaires soutenir le Gouvernement dans son juste effort pour accorder l'autonomie aux Arméniens.

6º - Le Programme (plate-forme) des Républicains.

En ce qui concerne les Arméniens la plate-forme des Républicains a déclaré ce qui suit: "Nous avons des sympathies profondes pour le peuple de l'Arménie et nous sommes prêts à leur venir en aide par tous les moyens convenables, mais le Parti Républicain s'opposera dans le présent et dans l'avenir à l'acceptation d'un mandat sur n'importe quel pays en Europe ou en Asie".

En essayant d'interpréter cette résolution, il nous semble qu'un emprunt, qui aura comme but l'organisation de l'administration dans le Foyer Arménien serait entièrement d'accord avec le vrai sens de ladite résolution et sans doute il s'en suivra tout naturellement un essai de faire réaliser la résolution de la plate-forme. Nous sommes convainçus que le peuple des Etats-Unis attend du Gouvernement une coopération avec les autres Puissances, en vue de faire rendre justice au peuple Arménien.

102

8 April 1921 – Policy proposed to the United States on behalf of the Armenians [anonymous] – AAEESS, *Asia* 57, 1, nº 23279

1º - Le Gouvernement des Etats-Unis accorderait à l'Arménie, comprenant la partie du territoire Ottoman désigné pour les Arméniens, un emprunt à être dépensé sous le contrôle d'une Commission Américaine, ou bien il participe à un emprunt, dans le but d'organiser l'administration et la force de police d'un Etat Arménien Indépendant.

2º - Les Etats-Unis discuteraient avec les Alliés des mesures par lesquelles on peut établir une paix durable en Asie Mineure et rendre justice aux Arméniens, qui étaient des Alliés dans la guerre dernière.

3º - Les Etats-Unis useraient de leurs bons offices auprès des Alliés afin d'obtenir la sécurité des Arméniens qui furent encouragés après l'armistice à s'établir en Cilicie, ou ils forment maintenant le trois quart de la population.

Discussion

Il y a au moins trois raisons, pour que les Etats-Unis adoptent une politique de reconstruction à l'égard du peuple arménien. La première est le fait que les Arméniens étaient des Alliés dans la dernière guerre et ont été reconnus comme tels dans le Traité de Sèvres. La seconde est l'importance qu'il y a pour la paix di monde à ce qu'une juste solution soit donnée aux questions du Proche Orient. La troisième est l'intérêt que ce peuple des Etats-Unis prend à la cause arménienne.

Une telle politique de reconstruction doit avoir comme but d'assurer aux Arméniens une zone géographique où ils puissent vivre en sécurité et travailler pour leur propre salut. Les régions qu'on envisage pour un telle zone géographique sont au nombre de trois, à savoir, l'Arménie de Russie, les Provinces arméniennes dans le Nord-Est de la Turquie et la Cilicie

1º - <u>Arménie Russe de Transcaucasie.</u> - L'Arménie Russe est actuellement sous la domination de Moscou, - ou est exposée à l'être à tout moment. Cette Arménie Russe dont le centre est sa capitale d'Erivan, pourrait être un point de départ excellent pour réaliser la constitution d'un Etat Arménien, à supposer cependant qu'il y ait une assurance du coté de la Russie qu'elle consentira à cette indépendance. Pour le moment on n'a pas une telle assurance et jusqu'à ce que la situation des Soviets s'éclaircisse, il semble que le sort des Arménien de Turquie, dont un grand nombre errent et se sont réfugiés un peu partout, doit être considéré séparément de la situation de l'Arménie de Caucase. Les Etats-Unis peuvent insister sur l'indépendance de l'Arménie du Caucase comme condition préalable de toute négociation avec le Gouvernement de Moscou. Les Etats-Unis ont reconnu la République Arménienne le 10 Août 1920 et le Sécretaire d'Etat, Mr. Colby a défini le point de vue américain en disant "que les frontières de la Russie devaient être respectées en y comprenant tout l'ancien Empire Russe à l'exception de …… et de tels autres territoires qui pourraient par un accord faire partie de l'Etat Arménien". Cette déclaration semble indiquer que l'indépendance de l'Arménie Russe fait partie de la politique des Etats-Unis.

2º - <u>Les Provinces arméniennes dans le Nord-Est de la Turquie</u>. - Ces provinces ou Vilayets étaient à l'origine au nombre de six. Les Arméniens ont été chassés de ces provinces et à tel point que, au moment ou le Traité de Sèvres fut signé, en août dernière, le Président Wilson fut autorisé à ne prendre en consideration que quatre vilayets dans les limites desquels il avait à déterminer les frontères de l'Arménie de Turquie. C'étaient les vilayets de Trebizonde, Erzeroum, Van, et Bitlis.

Conformément au Traité de Sèvres , l'Etat délimité ainsi par le Président Wilson devait être joint à la République Arménienne de Transcaucase. Le fait que cette République est devenue soviétique, même contre la volonté du peuple, a déterminé les Chefs de Gouvernement dans leur dernière Conférence à régler le sort de ces quatre vilayets, indépendamment de la situation en Transcaucasie. Les Premiers Ministres ont été d'avis que les frontières tracées par le Président Wilson contenaient plus de territoires qu'il n'était opportun pour un Etat Arménien et ils ont remis la tâche de fixer les frontières des dits quatre Vilayets au Conseil de la Société des Nations. Cette action rejette ce que le Président Wilson avait accordé et viole le Traité de Sèvres, puisque conformément à ce Traité l'arrêt du Président Wilson devait être définitif. Si les frontières sont révisées on devrait donner des compensations du coté du Vilayet de Kharpout et des routes nécessaires pour le commerce afin que l'Etat Arménien ait son existence économique assurée.

Les dépenses pour l'organisation de l'administration et de la gendarmerie dans cette région est une question qui soulève des difficultés pour la réalisation d'une autonomie arménienne et les Etats-Unis ne feraient qu'agir conformément aux promesses faites par les Républicains et les Démocrates dans leurs programmes (plates-formes) en émettant un emprunt pour le rapatriement des réfugiés, pour la constitution du gouvernement et pour le travail de reconstruction préliminaire. Le Gouvernement des Etats-Unis ne ferait que tenir les promesses faites par les deux programmes (plates-formes) des Républicains et des Démocrates, en entrant en pourparlers avec les Puissances Alliés pour mettre fin au scandale arménien.

3º - La Cilicie. - Ce pays a appartenu aux Arméniens, ayant formé le Royaume de l'Arménie mineure. Après l'armistice, les deux Gouvernements de la Grand-Bretagne et la France se sont joints pour encourager les réfugiés arméniens à s'établir en Cilicie, en leur montrant qu'elle deviendrait leur foyer. Actuellement les trois quart de la population y est arménienne. Même en 1912, d'après les statistiques des Turcs eux-mêmes, la population musulmane de la province d'Adana était de 185,000 contre une population chrétienne de 215,000. Aujourd'hui les troupes françaises occupent la Cilicie, mais ces troupes seront retirées et le pays sera abandonné aux Turcs. La raison donné pour ce retrait est la dépense que l'occupation entraîne, bien qu'il soit connu que la Cilicie est un pays extrêmement riche et que le Colonel Brémond, qui en a été dernièrement le Gouverneur militaire, rapporte que les revenus annuels normaux sont de 100,000,000 de Francs et que les dépenses normales d'administration ne sont que 30,000,000.

Si la France pouvait être assurée d'avoir les fonds nécessaires pour commencer à assumer le mandat de la Cilicie, il y aurait quelques raisons de croire qu'elle pourrait accepter sur la Cilicie un mandat distinct de celui de la Syrie. Le mandat de la Cilicie serait beaucoup plus rémunérateur que celui de la Syrie; il serait moins dificile à exercer et viendrait en aide à la France pour sa position en Syrie.

Le Gouvernement des Etats-Unis ne ferait que remplir les promesses faites dans les deux programmes (plates-formes) des Républicains et des Démocrates, en entreprenant avec la France l'émission d'un emprunt, agé sur les revenus de la Cilicie. S'il est impossible de trouver une Puissance mandataire, les Etats-Unis ne feraient que tenir les promesses faites dans les progammes (plates-formes) des deux partis, en usant de leurs bons offices à faire nommer un Gouverneur Chrétien en Cilicie, afin que les vies et les biens des Arméniens soient sauvegardés. Une pareille institution d'un gouverneur chrétien pour le Liban a donné sous le régime turc d'excellents résultats.

Le programme (plate-forme) des Républicains en ce qui concerne l'Arménie contenait la déclaration suivante:

"Nous avons des sympathies profondes pour le peuple arménien et nous sommes prêts à leur venir en aide par tous les moyens convenables, mais le Parti Républicain s'opposera dans le présent et l'avenir à l'acceptation d'un mandat quelconque sur un pays d'Europe ou d'Asie."

Le programme (plate-forme) des Démocrates en ce qui concerne l'Arménie dit:

"Nous exprimos notre profonde et sincère sympathie pour le malheureux peuple d'Arménie et nous espérons que notre Gouvernement se conformant à sa constitution et à ses principes, fera tout son possible et le necessaire pour leur venir en aide dans leurs efforts pour établir et maintenir un gouvernement qui leur soit propre"

103

8 April 1921 – Resolution proposed to the U. S. Congress [anonymous] – AAEESS, *Asia* 57, 1, n° 23279

RESOLUTION

Attendu que les Arméniens ont été officiellement reconnu dans le Traité de Sèvres comme Alliés dans la dernière guerre, et

Attendu que le traitement inhumain subi par les Arméniens pendant la guerre est dû au fait qu'ils ont épousé la cause des Alliés, et

Attendu que il importe au commerce et aux transactions des Etats-Unis qu'une paix durable soit établie en Asie Mineur , et

Attendu que la libération des Arméniens a été considérée comme un des buts de la guerre et que par le Traité de Sèvres un Etat indépendant arménien a été créé, et que les frontières de l'Etat Arménien prévu par les clauses de ce Traité ont été déjà délimitées par le Président des Etats Unis et

Attendu que le peuple des Etats-Unis a manifesté d'une manière non équivoque son intérêt au sort de l'Arménie chrétienne, par ses généreuses contributions aux secours qui leur ont été accordés et par la voie des programmes (plates-formes) de ses deux grands partis politiques, il a proclamé sa sympathie profonde pour le peuple d'Arménie et son désir de leur venir en aide par tous les moyens convenables, - il demande que le Congrès soit prié d'autoriser un emprunt fait par les Etats-Unis, cet emprunt ne dépassant pas 25 millions de dollars et étant destiné à la constitution d'un Etat Arménien autonome, créé dans l'Arménie de Turquie, sans attendre la solution de l'Arménie de Russie.

Il est décidé en outre que le Congrès sera prié d'autoriser le Président de conférer avec les Puissances Alliées et avec les représentants du peuple arménien en vue des démarches à faire pour constituer une Arménie autonome et pour décider la forme de l'administration et le système financier, afin de donner satisfactions aux justes réclamations des Arméniens.

Il est décidé en outre que le Président sera prié d'user de ses bons offices pour obtenir la sécurité des Arméniens réfugiés qui, depuis l'armistice, ont été rétablis en Cilicie.

104

16 April 1921, Rome – the Spanish ambassador to Gasparri – AAEESS, *Asia* 57, 1, n° 17537

Eminentisimo y Reverendisimo Senor,

Con referencia a la Nota de 1° de Marzo ùltimo sobre la cuestion armenia tengo la honra de poner en conocimiento de Vuestra Eminencia Reverendisima, que el Gobierno de S.M. siente la mas viva simpatìa hacia la Nacion Armenia, como lo ha demostrado acudiendo desde el primer momento al llamamiento del Consejo de la Sociedad de las Naciones, declarando que contribuirà gustoso a toda accion de orden moral y diplomatico encaminada al fin pacìfico perseguido con tanto celo por dicha Soceidad y que su interés hacia aquel pais ha sido vivamente estimulado por los sentimientos que ha tenido a bien expresar Su Santidad.

Aprovecho esta oportunidad para reitera a Vuestra Eminencia Reverendisima las seguridades de mi mas alta y respetuosa consideracion

105

3 May 1921, Rome – Kalatosoff to Marini – CO, 106, 3, 5, 2, n° 5638

Dato l'occasione di accompagnare ragazzi orfani, destinati pel Pont. Collegio Leonino armeno, per ordine espresso di Sua Eccza Monsignore Delegato Apostolico Angelo Dolci, eccomi, l'umilissimo servo di Vostra Eminenza di nuovo a Roma dalla mattina del giorno 25 aprile.

Le spese del mio viaggio *per la venuta* sono fatte dalla somma disposta a questo scopo da Mgr. Patriarca Paolo Terzian. Quanto al *mio ritorno*, mi disse Mgr. Delegato Dolci, che mi mando coi ragazzi, di rivolgermi alla Congregazione Orientale. Mi sono sempre pronto per ripartire al comando della Vostra Eminenza Reverendissima.

Quanto alla mia partenza pel Tiflis, luogo del mio servizio, ora sotto occupazione communista (bolscievika) stimo non superfluo di far qui la seguente relazione in proposito.

1. Come già avevo riferito da Costantinopoli, arrivato io colà ai 10 di marzo non potei proseguire per Batum, perché causa l'occupazione della Georgia e la guerra tra bolscieviki e kemalisti che si era scoppiata a Batum, il vapore doveva andare soltanto fino a Trebizonda. Si era saputo inoltre che già un vapore italiano era catturato dai bolscieviki nel porto di Batum. Così

pell'ordine del Delegato Apostolico Mgr Dolci e il consenso del Visit.Apost. nostro Mgr. Moriondo mi sono fermato a Costantinopoli aspettando fin alla prima possibilità di partenza.

2. Ai 13 aprile, dietro un invito officiale dei bolscieviki occupanti la Georgia col Batum, sono partiti al porto di Batum gli agenti delle società di navigazione italiane, per riaprire loro agenzie e riccominciare la circolazione regolare della navi-passagieri e merci.

Mi sono affrettato dal Sigr. Marco Ballovich gentillissimo agente del Lloyd-Triestino e dell'Adria a Batum, e consegnai ad esso 12500 lire italiane, che volle inviare a Tiflis Mgr. Moriondo: 6000 al D. Emm. Vardize suo vicario all'ordinariato georgiano cattolico, e 6500 a Don Antonio Kapoyan all'amministrazione armeno-cattolica. Inoltre gli *Oli Santi* pel tutto Caucaso, e la corrispondenza officiale e privata diretta a Batum e a Tiflis. La ricevuta data dal Sigr. M. Ballovich, ho rimesso a Sua Eccza Mgr. Moriondo, che mandò anche due lettere 1) a P. Emm. Vardize e 2) a Don Antonio Kapoyan, cogli necessarj istruzioni. Ne mandai anch'io communicando tutto necessario.

Il gentilissimo Sigr. M. Ballovich, mi ha promesso di scrivere una dettagliata relazione sulla situazione creata in Georgia in seguito all'occupazione bolscievica, e se si potrà e quando partire per Batum. Lui la lettera scriverà a Mgr. Moriondo, e ci manderà tutte le corrispondenze che lui riceverà indirizzate Batum e Tiflis. Per questa via anche la Sacra Congregazione potrà in avvenire farci arrivare i suoi desideratissimi ordini e disposizioni.

La lettera del Sigr. Ballovich si aspetta a Costantinopoli verso il quindici Maggio corrente, forse anche prima; ma le risposte da Tiflis, che saranno più interessante arriveranno a Costantinopoli verso il fine di questo mese, forse un po' prima.

Intanto, essendo tutto il necessario già spedito a Batum e a Tiflis, col permesso di Vostra Eminenza Reverendissima io potrei, sul mio viaggio di ritorno, soffermarmi 2-3 settimane nel nostro convento di San Lazzaro, per fare delle ricerche necessarie pel mio studio nella biblioteca dei manoscritti.

Al primo avviso di Mgr. Moriondo, partirò immediatamente per Costantinopoli, Batum e Tiflis.

3. Per quanto ho potuto consultare personaggi provenienti da Tiflis, Batum, Bakù, Odessa, Sebastopoli, Ekaterinodar e Novorossisk, anche parecchi bolscieviki giorgiani trovantisi a Costantinopoli, per poter facilmente e con sicurezza viaggiare sotto bolscievichi, anzi per essere garantito contro loro visite notturne e difficoltà di viaggio e comunicazione, sarebbe indispensabile esser munito d'una carta officiale della Segreteria di Stato di Sua Santità, essendo un prete cattolico, nella quale carta deve essere chiaramente indicata la funzione che vi vado esercitare per commissione [*sic*] di Sua Santità. Mi spiego: [...indecifrabile], che abracia [*sic*] tutti cattolici armeni nei confini della Russia del 1914; che Sua Santità mi comanda di visitare le istituzioni

cattoliche della Crimea, della Georgia e dell'Armenia, e del Caucaso di Nord, nei quali luoghi principalmente si trovano maggiormente gli armeni cattolici.

Con tale espressione di volontà di Sua Santità, ch'è ben rispettata anche presso i bolscieviki, avrò, naturalmente non senza rischio, la possibilità di vedere in che stato si trovano i cattolici, il clero e le chiese nostre nei luoghi sopraindicate. E questa visita, dopo tanta devastazione è addirittura indispensabile, perche temo che altrimenti i nostri cattolici subiranno molto danno religioso spirituale, e la visita gli reccherà grande consolazione e rilievo. Ed al tempo stesso avrò la facilità fare un rapporto minuzioso sullo stato attuale delle cose riguardanti il popolo, il clero e le chiese nostre, che regolarmente farò arrivare alla Sacra Congregazione.

Io sono spontaneamente disposto ad andar all'incontro ai pericoli di vita pel bene degli interessi della Santa Chiesa, ma prego umilmente di benevolere di munirmi delle carte e dei mezzi necessarie a quest'uopo per poter viaggiare, consolare, soccorrere. La Sacra Congregazione può fidare nel Suo umillissimo servo, che tutto sarà applicato in prò degli indigenti e niente pel proprio guadagno ed interesse privato.

4. Preghierei istantemente di elargire 2-5 mila lire ancora pel soccorso degli cattolici armeni di Crimea e Caucaso che sono rifugiati a Costantinopoli, ricci [sic] d'ieri oggi sprovvisti di tutto.

Bacio ecc

[Translation]

Given the occasion of accompanying orphan children, destined for the Armenian Leonine Pont. College by express order of His Exc. Monsignor Angelo Dolci, Apostolic Delegate, here I am, the most humble servant of Your Eminence, in Rome once again, since the morning of April 25th.

The expenses of my trip *coming* were taken from the sum destined for this purpose by Mgr. Patriarch Paul Terzian. As for my *return*, I was told by Mgr. Delegate Dolci, who sent me with the children, to address myself to the Oriental Congregation. I am always ready to leave again at the command of Your Most Reverend Eminence.

As far as my departure for Tiflis, my place of service, now under communist (Bolshevik) occupation, I do not deem it superfluous to make here the following report in that regard.

1. As I have already reported from Constantinople, having arrived there myself on the 10th of March, I could not proceed to Batum because, due to the occupation of Georgia and the war between Bolsheviks and Kemalists that had broken out in Batum, the steamship was to go only as far as Trabizon. It was known, moreover, that an Italian steamship had already been captured by the Bolsheviks in the port of Batum. Thus, by the order of the Apostolic Delegate Mgr. Dolci and the consensus of the Visit. Apost. our Mgr. Moriondo, I stopped in Constantinople, waiting for the first possibility of departure.

2. On April 13th, after an official invitation from the Bolsheviks occupying Georgia in Batum, the agents of the Italian navigation companies left for the port of Batum to reopen their agencies and recommence the regular circulation of ships—both passenger and merchant.

I hastened to Mr. Marco Ballovich, most kind agent of Lloyd-Triestino and of Adria at Batum, and consigned to him 12,500 Italian lire that Mgr. Moriondo wished sent to Tiflis: 6,000 to D. Emm. Vardizé his vicar at the Georgian Catholic bishopric, and 6,500 to Don Antonio Kapojan at the Armenian-Catholic administration. Also, the *Holy Oils* for the entire Caucasus, and the official and private correspondence directed to Batum and to Tiflis. The receipt, given by Mr. M. Ballovich, I remitted to His Exc. Mgr. Moriondo, who sent also two letters 1) to F. Emm. Vardizé and 2) to Don Antonio Kapojan, with the necessary instructions. I sent one also, communicating everything necessary.

The very kind Mr. M. Ballovich promised me to write a detailed report on the situation created in Georgia following the Bolshevik occupation, and whether and when it will be possible to leave for Batum. He will write the letter to Mgr. Moriondo, and will send us all the correspondence that he receives addressed to Batum and Tiflis. This way, even the Sacred Congregation will in the future have their most welcome orders and dispositions delivered to us.

The letter from Mr. Ballovich is expected in Constantinople around the fifteenth of this May, maybe even earlier; but the replies from Tiflis, which will be more interesting, will arrive in Constantinople towards the end of this month, perhaps a little sooner.

Meanwhile, all the necessary items having already been sent to Batum and to Tiflis, with the permission of Your Most Reverend Eminence I could, on my return voyage, stay for 2–3 weeks in our convent of St. Lazarus, to do some research in the manuscript library necessary to my study.

At the first notice of Mgr. Moriondo, I will leave immediately for Constantinople, Batum and Tiflis.

3. As far as I was able to consult personages coming from Tiflis, Batum, Bakù, Odessa, Sebastopol, Yekaterinodar and Novorossiysk, even a good number of Georgian Bolsheviks found in Constantinople, in order to be able to travel easily and with security under the Bolsheviks, or rather, to be insured against their nocturnal visits and travel and communication difficulties, it would be indispensable to be equipped with an official document from the Secretariat of State of His Holiness, being a Catholic priest, in which document should be clearly indicated the function that I am going there to perform on commission from His Holiness. I will explain: [...indecipherable], that embraces all the Armenian Catholics within the confines of 1914 Russia; that His Holiness commands me to visit the Catholic institutions of the Crimea, of

Georgia and of Armenia, and of the Northern Caucasus, in which places, principally, are found the greatest number of Catholic Armenians.

With such an expression of the will of His Holiness, who is well-respected even among the Bolsheviks, I will have, naturally not without risk, the possibility of seeing in what state Catholics, the clergy and our churches in the abovementioned places find themselves. And this visit, after so much devastation, is absolutely indispensable, because I fear that otherwise our Catholics will suffer much religious and spiritual damage, and the visit will bring them great consolation and relief. And at the time same I will have the opportunity to make a detailed report on the current state of things, regarding the people, the clergy and our churches, that I will duly have sent to the Sacred Congregation.

I am of my own accord disposed to risk my life for the good of the interests of the Holy Church, but I humbly ask that you should be so kind as to equip me with the documents and the means necessary to this purpose, to be able to travel, console, aid. The Sacred Congregation can trust in its most humble servant, that everything will be applied in favor of the indigent and nothing for personal gain and private interests.

4. I would pray you to bestow another 2–5 thousand lire immediately for aid to the Catholic Armenians of Crimea and the Caucasus who have taken refuge in Constantinople, rich yesterday, today lacking everything.

I kiss etc.

106

7 May 1921, Beirut – Giannini to Gasparri – AAEESS, *Asia* 57, 1, n° 21439

Eminentissimo Principe,

Accludo qui una delle solite corrispondenze che solevo inviare al Rmo Mons. Tedeschini, affinché sia pubblicata, se lo si crede espediente, nel l'"Osservatore Romano".

La corrispondenza è datata da Adana e riguarda la situazione della Cilicia, ove giorni fa mi recai non solo per amministrare la Cresima nelle nostre parrocchie di rito latino ma anche per rendermi conto della situazione divenuta addirittura angosciosa pei cristiani, dopo che nella Conferenza del Marzo a Londra la Francia s'impegnò a ritirar le sue truppe.

La corrispondenza mirerebbe ad eliminare questa eventualità, che io sinceramente e per buone ragioni giudico dannosa alla Francia non meno che alla popolazione cristiana del territorio che si vorrebbe abbandonare.

Fui scongiurato da innumerevoli persone di ogni classe e di ogni culto, con le lacrime agli occhi, di lavorare per questo scopo; e ne fui scongiurato specialmente nella mia qualità di rappresentante della Santa Sede, essendo ben note le paterne sollecitudini dell'Augusto Pontefice per tutti i cristiani, e singolarmente pei cristiani di queste regioni orientali.

Anche ultimamente fece ottima impressione la notizia dei passi fatti presso il capo dei sedicenti nazionalisti turchi di Angora, Kemal Pacha, a tutela dei cristiani. Si è sicuri che il suo rappresentante Bekir Sami Bey, recandosi in Vaticano, non avrà mancato di fare in proposito le più belle promesse, e di dare le più esplicite assicurazioni.

Ma alla dolce e riconoscente commozione che tutti provano nel vedere anche una volta il Padre universale della Cristianità interessarsi alle sorti dei figli suoi, non corrisponde la fiducia nel risultato delle paterne premure, posto che questo debba dipendere unicamente dal buon volere dei governanti turchi.

Né io posso dar torto a quei poveri cristiani, purtroppo ammaestrati da lunga dolorosissima esperienza. Conosco assai bene e da vicino il sunnominato Bekir Sami Bey, governatore a Beirut il primo anno della guerra. Non è un malvagio deliberatamente sanguinario come il suo immediato successore a Beirut. Anzi so che a qualcuno fece del bene, e riconosco che finché rimase qui non si avverarono certi orrori venuti dopo. Ma è anche lui un fanatico del turchismo panislamico, sebbene circasso di razza; né sarà mai capace di opporsi efficacemente a misure, qualunque esse siano, che il suo Governo reputi utili ai suoi scopi. Per le nostre Missioni fu inesorabile, come lo è anche adesso il Governo di Angora nel suo territorio.

Appunto il fatto che Bekir Sami Bey è circasso di razza è una delle prove che il sedicente nazionalismo di Angora, dinanzi al quale più o meno sinceramente s'inchinano i nostri politici europei, non è che una etichetta abilmente inventata pel bisogno della causa. Il concetto europeo della nazionalità è sin qui inpervio alle menti orientali. L'islamismo turchesco contro il cristianesimo: ecco la vera divisa del Governo di Angora. E l'Europa avrà ben a pentirsi di avergli ceduto la Cilicia, la quale tra le altre cose non è turca se non per una ben piccola parte della sua popolazione.

Checchessia di ciò, e benché io mi spieghi assai facilmente l'attuale politica della Francia e dell'Italia verso i Turchi, fatta nascere dagli altrui troppo ingordi appetiti e dall'odierna avversione delle due nazioni ad imprese guerresche, credo però che si possa ancora sperare; e questa speranza m'incoraggia ad implorare anche una volta l'aiuto della Santa Sede a pro' di quelle povere desolate popolazioni.

La Santa Sede sa molto meglio di me che cosa possa farsi di buono in proposito, e noi saremo sempre riconoscenti di tutto ciò che farà. Dal canto mio credo sarebbe utile far intendere a chi di dovere che insieme con l'onore anche il ben inteso interesse della Francia richiedono che non ritiri le sue truppe dalla Cilicia se non a patto di essere ragionevolmente sicura che la tranquillità per tutti sia veramente garantita. Se questo principio è seriamente accettato, le truppe francesi rimarranno ancora per lungo tempo in Cilicia.

L'Onore della Francia è impegnato, perché tutta la popolazione cristiana e parte anche della musulmana si è troppo compromessa con atti e parole nel tempo dell'occupazione francese; e dovrebbe pagarla ben cara, se fosse senz'altro abbandonata in mano dei Turchi, senza quelle solide garanzie che questi non possono dare.

V'è anche impegnato l'interesse della Francia, che non potrebbe aver mai la pace neppure in Siria, se la contigua Cilicia, specialmente coi limiti tracciati a Londra, fosse senz'altro consegnata al Governo turco essenziamente ispirato ai principi del panislamismo. Senza contare che solo la pingue Cilicia, bene amministrata, potrebbe compensare i sacrifici pecuniari della spedizione militare del Levante.

Né si creda che occorrano enormi sforzi per pacificare definitivamente questo paese: basterà qualche atto di ben decisa energia, mancato fin a qui, che provi ai Turchi la volontà ferma della Francia di farsi rispettare così in Cilicia come altrove.

L'Emza V. Rma certamente vede la somma importanza della cosa non solo al punto di vista cristiano e cattolico, ma anche umano e civile. Perciò senz'altro La prego di farne parola all'Augusto Pontefice, alla paterna bontà del Quale quelle povere popolazioni per mezzo mio supplichevolmente si raccomandano

E chinato al bacio ecc

[Translation]
Most Eminent Prince,

I enclose here one of the usual correspondences[281] that I have been in the habit of sending to the Most Rev. Mons. Tedeschini,[282] so that it might be published, if he believes it expedient, in "L'Osservatore Romano" ["The Roman Observer"].[283]

The correspondence is datelined Adana and regards the situation of Cilicia, where I went days ago not only to administer the Baptism in our Latin rite parishes, but also to get a sense of the situation which has become really distressing for the Christians after, in the Conference of March in London, France committed to pulling out her troops.

The correspondence would aim to eliminate this eventuality, that I sincerely and for good reasons judge damaging to France no less than to the Christian population of the territory that would be abandoned.

---

281 Not found.
282 Substitute of the Secretariat of State
283 Translator's Note: *L'Osservatore Romano*. Vatican-owned newspaper, reporting semi-officially on the activities of the Holy See.

I was implored by innumerable persons of every class and of every creed, with tears in their eyes, to work toward this end; and I was so beseeched especially in my quality as representative of the Holy See, the paternal concerns of the August Pontiff for all Christians, and particularly for the Christians of these eastern regions, being well-known.

Also recently, the news of the steps taken with the head of the self-styled Turkish nationalists of Angora, Kemal Pasha, in safeguard of the Christians, made an excellent impression. You may be sure that his representative Bekir Sami Bey, going to the Vatican, will not have failed to make the most beautiful promises in that regard, and to give the most explicit assurances.

But the sweet and grateful emotion that everyone feels in seeing once again the universal Father of Christianity involve himself with the fate of his children, does not correspond to faith in the outcome of the paternal considerations, given that this must depend solely on the good will of the governing Turks.

Nor can I possibly blame those poor Christians, unfortunately taught by long and very painful experience. I know closely and well enough the abovenamed Bekir Sami Bey, governor of Beirut the first year of the war. He is not deliberately bloodthirsty and wicked like his immediate successor in Beirut. In fact, I know that he did good for some and I recognize that, while he remained here, certain horrors that came afterwards were not realized. But he, too, is a fanatic of pan-Islamic Turkism, though Circassian of race; he will never be capable of effectively opposing measures, whatever they might be, that his Government considers necessary to its ends. Towards our Missions he was unforgiving, as is now too the Government of Angora in his territory.

Indeed, the fact that Bekir Sami Bey is of the Circassian race is one of the proofs that the self-styled nationalism of Angora, before which our European politicians more or less sincerely bow down, is nothing more than a label cleverly invented to serve the cause. The European concept of nationality is, up to now, impervious to oriental minds. Turkish Islam against Christianity: here is the real motto of the Government of Angora. And Europe will have great regrets in having ceded them Cilicia, which, among other things, is not Turkish if not for a rather small part of its population.

Whatever comes of this, and although I quite easily understand the current policy of France and of Italy towards the Turks, born of the too-voracious appetites of others and from the current aversion of the two nations toward warlike enterprises, I believe, however, that one might still hope; and this hope encourages me to beg once again for the help of the Holy See in favor of those poor desolate populations.

The Holy See knows much better than I what good can be done about it, and we will be ever grateful for all that it will do. For my part I believe it would be useful to make those concerned understand that along with her honor also the obvious interest of France demands that she not withdraw her troops from

Cilicia, if not on condition of being reasonably sure that peace for all is truly guaranteed. If this principle is accepted seriously, French troops will remain in Cilicia for a long time to come.

The Honor of France is at stake, because all the Christian population and even part of the Muslim one was too compromised with acts and words during the period of the French occupation; and should pay very dearly, if they were willingly abandoned to the hands of the Turks, without those solid guarantees that the latter cannot give.

There is also at stake the interest of France, that could never have peace, not even in Syria, if the contiguous Cilicia, especially with boundaries set down in London, were freely consigned to the Turkish Government fundamentally inspired by the principles of pan-Islamism. Without counting that the fat Cilicia alone, well-administered, could compensate for the pecuniary sacrifices of the military expedition to the Levant.

Nor is it believed that enormous efforts would be required to definitively pacify this country: it will suffice some act of clearly decisive energy, lacking up until now, that would prove to the Turks France's firm will to make themselves respected in Cilicia as elsewhere.

Y. Most Rev. Emin. certainly sees the utmost importance of the matter not only from the Christian and Catholic point of view, but also the human and civil. Therefore I ask that you speak about it as soon as possible to the August Pontiff, to the paternal goodness of whom those poor populations beseechingly entrust themselves by way of me

And bowed to the kiss etc.

107

14 May 1921, Beirut – Giannini to Gasparri – AAEESS, *Asia* 57, 1, n° 21439

Eminentissimo Principe,

Oggi stesso fu da me un ben noto personaggio armeno, il Sig. Archag Tchobanian, letterato di vaglia, poeta e conferenziere applaudito anche in francese, faciente parte della missione presieduta da Nubar Pascià, che in Europa sta difendendo la nobile e pietosa causa della tartassata agonizzante nazione armena. Egli sta facendo un giro d'ispezione in queste regioni, per tornarsene presto, via Costantinopoli, presso Nubar Pascià a Londra o a Parigi; e di passaggio per Beirut ha voluto vedere il Delegato Apostolico reduce dal recente viaggio in Cilicia di cui è parola nei precedenti fogli n. 15 e 16, per parlare con lui della causa che tanto gli sta a cuore, e per pregarlo d'insistere affinché la Santa Sede continui ad interessarsi con la sua antica benevolenza delle sorti della nazione armena.

Poiché nella mattinata il Sig. Tchobanian era stato telegraficamente informato che la popolazione di Zeitun, ben nota località dei dintorni di Marasc, trovavasi assediata dai nazionalisti turchi e in pericolo prossimo di soccombere e di essere quindi affatto sterminata; con angosciosa insistenza pregò il Delegato Apostolico di voler far subito tutto il suo possibile per evitare questo nuovo disastro.

Lì per lì, non sapendo che altro fare, io mi sono affrettato ad informar per iscritto l'Alto Commissario della Repubblica francese, invocando il sollecito benevolo intervento del suo Governo presso il Governo di Angora. Lo stesso passo ho fatto subito anche presso il Console generale d'Italia, che stasera stessa, basandosi sulla mia preghiera verbale, ha telegrafato nell'accennato senso al Ministero degli Esteri. E subito ne scrivo all'Emza V. Rma, sperando che la Santa Sede vorrà interessarsi della cosa, e pregando Dio che si faccia in tempo a salvare quella povera popolazione cristiana, reliquia scarsissima dei numerosi abitanti cristiani di quel distretto fatti nella maggior parte miseramente perire durante la guerra mondiale.

Seguitando poi il discorso sulle cose di Cilicia ed in genere sulla critica situazione della nazione armena, io, nel promettere al Sig. Tchobanian d'implorare la continuazione del benevolo appoggio della Santa Sede, gli accennai di sfuggita l'idea di passare per Roma nel ritornare in Europa, esibendomi, quando la proposta gli andasse, di dargli un biglietto di raccomandazione per ottenere una benevola udienza dall'Emza V. Rma. Egli accettò subito e con molta premura la mia proposta. Perciò, salvo casi imprevisti, egli passerà per Roma, e chiederà di essere ricevuto dall'Emza V. Rma, presentando il biglietto che gli ho promesso e che gli farò avere. L'Emza V. Rma vedrà poi se convenga procurargli anche una udienza presso Sua Santità.

Il Sig. Tchobanian non è cattolico, ma da uomo di non ordinario ingegno sa apprezzare il Cattolicismo.

Questa martirizzata nazione armena, che ebbe tante e così magnifiche promesse dagli Alleati dell'Intesa durante la guerra, adesso trovasi più o meno abbandonata da tutti. Sarà onore eterno della Santa Sede l'aver seguitato ad interessarsene attivamente, quando i potenti della terra stavano per abbandonarla affatto. E chi sa che ciò non possa anche essere avviamento ad un ritorno di questi figli separati nel seno della Madre comune? In ogni caso non sarà mai né superfluo né perduto tutto ciò che si potrà fare per impedirne il temuto esterminio.

Stamattina ho avuto una lunga conversazione con l'Ammiraglio de Bon, comandante in capo della flotta del Mediterraneo orientale, che da qualche giorno staziona nella rada di Beirut. Gli ho parlato molto della Cilicia, della quale egli s'interessa grandemente. Mi ha chiesto che gli precisassi per iscritto alcune cose dettegli a voce. Ed io gli ho mandato in proposito una Nota, di cui accludo qui copia a titolo d'informazione. Penso che l'egregio Ammiraglio, buon cattolico praticante, intenda mettere al corrente il suo governo.

Intanto l'evacuazione delle truppe francesi è pel momento ritardata. Ed io spero più che mai nell'aiuto di Dio e nell'efficacia della materne premure della Santa Sede.

Chinato al bacio ecc

Allegato al doc. n° 107, p. 367:

[Translation]

Most Eminent Prince,

Just today I was visited by a well-known Armenian personage, Mr. Archag Tchobanian, scholar of merit, poet and acclaimed lecturer also in French, member of the mission presided over by Nubar Pasha, who in Europe is defending the noble and piteous cause of the tormented and dying Armenian nation. He is making an inspection tour of these regions, to return soon, via Constantinople, to Nubar Pasha in London or in Paris, and, traveling through Beirut, wanted to see the Apostolic Delegate just back from the recent trip to Cilicia described in the preceding pages n. 15 and 16,[284] to speak with him about the cause that he takes so much to heart, and to pray that he insist such that the Holy See should continue, with its age-old benevolence, to concern itself with the fate of the Armenian nation.

Because in the morning Mr. Tchobanian had been telegraphically informed that the population of Zeytun, well-known locality in the vicinity of Marash, found themselves under siege by the Turkish nationalists and in imminent danger of succumbing and of being then entirely exterminated; with anguished insistence he begged the Apostolic Delegate to please do his utmost right away to avoid this new disaster.

Then and there, not knowing what else to do, I hurried to inform the High Commissioner of the French Republic in writing, invoking the prompt benevolent intervention of his Government with the Government of Angora. I immediately took the same step also with the Consul General of Italy who, this very afternoon, following my verbal request, telegraphed in the sense indicated to the Foreign Minister. And I write of it at once to Y. Most Rev. Emin., hoping that it should please the Holy See to concern itself with the matter, and praying to God that it should be in time to save that poor Christian population, scant relic of the numerous Christian inhabitants of that district, for the most part caused to perish miserably during the world war.

Continuing, then, the discussion about things in Cilicia and in general about the critical situation of the Armenian nation, I, in promising to Mr. Tchobanian to plead for the continuation of the Holy See's benevolent support, casually mentioned to him the idea of passing through Rome in returning to Europe, offering, when the suggestion appealed to him, to give

---

284 V. doc. n° 106, cit.

him a note of recommendation to obtain a benevolent audience with Y. Most Rev. Emin. He quickly and eagerly accepted my proposal. Therefore, barring unforeseen circumstances, he will come through Rome, and will ask to be received by Y. Most Rev. Emin., presenting the note that I promised him and that I will let him have. Y. Most Rev. Emin. will see, then, whether it is convenient to procure him an audience with His Holiness as well.

Mr. Tchobanian is not Catholic, but as a man of uncommon intelligence he is able to appreciate Catholicism.

This martyred Armenian nation, that had so many and such magnificent promises from the Allies of the Entente during the war, now finds herself more or less abandoned by all. It will be the eternal honor of the Holy See to have maintained an active interest, when the powerful of the earth were about to abandon her completely. And who knows that this might not also initiate a return of these separated children to the bosom of their common Mother? In any case, it shall never be either superfluous or wasted all that which might be done to impede their feared extermination.

This morning I had a long conversation with Admiral de Bon, commander in charge of the eastern Mediterranean fleet, which has been stationed in Beirut harbor for several days now. I talked to him quite a bit about Cilicia, in which he is greatly interested. He asked me that I precise for him in writing some of the things voiced to him. And I sent him a Note in that regard, of which I here enclose a copy for your information. I think that the distinguished Admiral, good praticing Catholic, intends to update his government.

Meanwhile the evacuation of the French troops is postponed for the moment. And I hope more than ever in the help of God and in the efficacy of the maternal care of the Holy See.

Bowed to the kiss etc

Attached to doc. n° 107, p. 367:

Le Délégué Apostolique de Syrie à Son Excel. l'Amiral de Bon

Le soussigné, faisant suite à l'entretien de ce matin, et pour répondre au désir de Monsieur l'Amiral, a l'honneur de lui exposer ce qui suit:

Le manque de statistiques régulières ne permet pas de donner des chiffres exacts sur la population de la Cilicie et sur ses fractions variées.

Toutefois, après des recherches consciencieuses, le soussigné croit pouvoir accepter les chiffres approximatifs suivants:

La population totale de la Cilicie atteint environ le chiffre de 550,000 habitants, dont 300,000 non chrétiens et 250,000 chrétiens.

Les non chrétiens sont loin d'être tous turcs: le plus grand nombre parmi eux - plus de cent mille- sont des Nosairis ou Alaouites. Cent mille, tout au plus, sont des turcs proprement dits. Le reste de la population non chrétienne se compose de kurdes, de cirkassiens, turkmanns, etc.Pour ce qui concerne les chrétiens, la très grande majorité est arménienne, tandis que les chrétiens d'autres races n'arrivent pas à cinquante mille. C'est pourquoi, le groupe national le plus nombreux et le plus compact qui soit en Cilicie est, sans contredit, celui des arméniens qui sont par ailleurs les plus anciens habitants de cette région.

On ne peut nier que les arméniens, comme du reste la presque totalité des habitants de cette vaste province, parlent communément le turc, sans négliger pour cela leur langue maternelle dont ils se servent constamment entre eux. Mais le fait qu'une langue est plus communément parlée ne peut, semble-t-il, octroyer des droits spéciaux à la partie de la population dont la dite langue est langue nationale.

Cela étant, on ne voit pas pourquoi le nationalisme turc serait en droit de réclamer pour soi l'hégémonie politique sur la Cilicie, vu que les turcs ne forment même pas le cinquième de la population cilicienne. Si l'hégémonie politique devait être reconnue, en Cilicie, pour des considérations de nationalité, à l'une des fractions ethniques de ce pays, celle-ci ne devrait être autre, semble-t-il, que la nation arménienne qui est la plus nombreuse, la plus compacte et la plus ancienne, comme il a été dit plus haut.

Mais si cela ne peut être, il serait au moins tout naturel que la Cilicie ne soit pas livrée comme una proie au nationalisme turc qui menace d'extermination les autres races, spécialement les arméniens. On pourrait, tout au plus, admettre, si l'on ne peut faire autrement, la <u>suveraineté</u> du Sultan sur la Cilicie qu'on érigerait en province autonome,avec un régime spécial, garanti par la France non seulement diplomatiquement mais encore par la présence permanente d'une garnison militaire, avec défense, à la Sublime Porte, d'y entretenir des milices.

La nécessité de cette solution de la question de Cilicie semble s'imposer, non seulement pour le bien du pays mais aussi pour le prestige et l'intérêt de la France.

108

18 June 1921, Beirut – Giannini to Gasparri – AAEESS, *Asia* 57, 1, n° 22655

Eminentissimo Principe,

Reduce dal viaggio all'interno da me accennato, alla vigilia della partenza, nel foglio del 19 maggio scorso, N. 18 e di cui quanto prima darò discarico, debbo subito ritornare sulla questione dei cristiani che tuttora gemono sotto il giogo turco o sono minacciati di dover tornare a subirlo, specialmente nella Cilicia.

Ne ho motivo pressante, se altro non vi fosse, in una lettera che trovo qui al mio ritorno; con la quale questo Alto Commissario della Rep. Franc., rispondendo, in data 24 Maggio, alla mia dimanda d'intervento a pro degli armeni di Zeitun di cui è parola nel mio foglio del 14 del detto mese N. 17, dopo aver notato che "une démarche isolée de la Rep. Fr. auprès du gouvernement d'Angora ne produirait aucun résultat heureux", conclude: "Votre Grandeur estimera peut-être avec moi que seule une démarche collective des Puissances pourrait faire impression et obtenir des garanties sérieuses pour l'ensemble des populations chrétiennes d'Anatolie et de Cilicie. L'initiative première des pourparlers serait, tout naturellement, dans les attributions du Saint Siège et Votre Grandeur est toute désignée pour mettre le Saint-Siège au fait de la question".

L'Emza V. Rma sa che io non ho aspettato il suggerimento di questo Alto Commissariato per compiere questo mio dovere, avendo ricevuto, come spero, i miei fogli del 7, 9, 14 e 19 Maggio scorso, coi relativi allegati. Ciò non ostante, volentieri profitto dell'occasione per ritornare sul doloroso argomento, anche perché parmi che si debba ad ogni costo evitare il pericolo di essere tacciati di non aver fatto tutto quello che potevamo per la salvezza di tanti miseri cristiani imploranti il soccorso della Santa Sede.

Se non che, nello stato presente delle cose, io sono più che mai convinto che un intervento amichevole, anche collettivo, delle Potenze, non porterebbe a gran che. Anzi riuscirebbe, forse, perfino dannoso a quei poveri cristiani, ai quali s'imputerebbe la imperdonabile colpa di averlo provocato. Il vedersi trattato come Potenza regolarmente riconosciuta, confermò il Governo di Angora nella persuasione che le Potenze europee, ormai esauste dai lunghi anni della guerra mondiale, non siano più al caso d'imporgli la loro volontà con la forza; e che perciò la condiscendenza usatagli non sia che pura debolezza. Ora il Turco che dinanzi alla forza prevalente s'inchina sino a terra, dinanzi alla debolezza, invece, sia reale sia apparente, diviene sconfinatamente arrogante. Già lo mostrò l'Assemblea di Angora con la risposta agli accordi, secondo noi deplorevoli, conclusi dai suoi mandatari nel Marzo scorso a Londra: appena un Napoleone I, dopo le sue più strepitose vittorie, avrebbe potuto parlare con tanta svergognata arroganza. E sempre peggio parleranno e agiranno, finché si pretenderà di guadagnarli con le buone maniere. E i poveri cristiani gementi sotto il loro giogo saranno sempre più maltrattati, malgrado tutte le più belle promesse, finché non si arrivi al loro totale sterminio.

Ormai non c'è via di mezzo, secondo il mio povero parere: o schiacciare con la forza l'idra panislamica e bolscevizzante di Angora, o rinunziare alla salvezza dei miseri resti della popolazione cristiana nei luoghi da essa infestati. E in questo caso l'idra velenosa aumenterà sempre più le sue dimensioni, sino ad invadere tutto l'Oriente, per poi precipitarsi sull'Occidente. Una vera catastrofe per la civiltà europea, se le Potenze europee non si affrettano a scongiurarla.

Per ciò che riguarda in particolare la Francia, se essa persisterà nella sua politica remissiva verso il Governo di Angora, non potrà neppure sperare di aver mai la pace in Siria. Le bande che sino a adesso infestano vasti territori nelle regioni di Hama e di Aleppo, sono intimamente legate con quel governo e da esso sussidiate con tutti i mezzi. Si volle essere condiscendenti, per risparmiare sangue e denaro, e ogni giorno le spese aumentano, e con esse, purtroppo, le vittime. E seguiterà sempre così, finché la Francia non si decida o a schiacciare il capo all'idra velenosa, o ad abbandonare affatto anche questo poco di Siria che le rimane, rosicchiata al nord dai turchi e al sud dagli inglesi.

Agitato dal pensiero di questo stato deplorevole di cose, prima di partire per Aleppo mi decisi a scrivere una lettera in proposito all'Emo Card. Dubois, di cui adesso accludo qui copia a titolo d'informazione, non avendo potuto farlo allora per la ristrettezza del tempo. A scriver questa lettera m'indusse, tra le altre cose, l'aver inteso che anche presso questo Alto Commissariato della Repubblica si deplorava la deficienza di un'azione illuminatrice nel mondo politico di Parigi, ove il Governo che sa, prigioniero dell'opinione pubblica contraria ad energiche imprese in questo Oriente, non osa far atti di energia, e tira innanzi con piccoli mezzi alla meglio, cioè alla peggio, nascondendo per quanto può le quotidiane dolorose vicende dell'Armata del Levante, senza decidersi né ad aumentarne le forze, in modo da renderla atta a menare un colpo decisivo, né a richiamarla in patria. Bisognerebbe dunque agire a Parigi sull'opinione pubblica, dicendo talquale la verità, affinché, visto che nessun serio uomo politico potrà assumersi la responsabilità di un ritiro delle truppe dalla Siria, un vero suicidio per la Francia, la stampa e i parlamentari finiscano con incoraggiare il Governo ad un supremo sforzo invece di seguitare a costringerlo ad un contegno indeciso che già arrecò tanti danni e più ne arrecherà in seguito, se dovesse durare. Per questo scopo scrissi la mia lettera all'Emo Card. Dubois.

Naturalmente ciò a cui io miro ha poco che fare con la usuale umana politica, che per sé stessa ben poco m'interesserebbe. Il mio scopo è salvare possibilmente tanti miseri cristiani, e in modo speciale i nostri nuclei di cattolici sparsi qua e là, e le nostre Missioni. Per dirne una, so che i Gesuiti di Adana hanno dal loro Superiore l'ordine di far partire le Suore e partire essi stessi, nel caso che le truppe francesi lascino la Cilicia e non si offrano solide garanzie per la loro sicurezza. E non posso far a meno di trovar ragionevole l'ordine.

L'armeno Sig. Tchobanian, di cui è parola nel mio foglio del 14 Maggio N. 17, lasciò Beirut prima del mio ritorno, per recarsi a Gerusalemme e quindi a Costantinopoli e a Parigi, passando possibilmente per Roma. Non so per altro quando possa arrivare costà. Ma rinnovo, in ogni caso, la raccomandazione a suo riguardo

E chinato al bacio ecc

[Translation]

Most Eminent Prince,

Back from the trip to the interior I had mentioned, on the eve of departure, in the letter of last May 19th, N. 18, and of which I will discharge myself as soon as possible, I must at once return to the question of the Christians who are still now groaning under the Turkish yoke or are threatened with having to go back to suffering it, especially in Cilicia.

For this I have a pressing motive, if there should be no other, in a letter that I find here upon my return; with which the High Commissioner of the French Rep., responding, dated May 24th, to my request for intervention on behalf of the Armenians of Zeytun of whom I give word in my letter of the 14th of said month, N. 17, after having noted that "*une démarche isolée de la Rep. Fr. auprès du gouvernement d'Angora ne produirait aucun résultat heureux*", concludes: "*Votre Grandeur estimera peut-être avec moi que seule une démarche collective des Puissances pourrait faire impression et obtenir des garanties sérieuses pour l'ensemble des populations chrétiennes d'Anatolie et de Cilicie. L'initiative première des pourparlers serait, tout naturellement, dans les attributions du Saint Siège et Votre Grandeur est toute désignée pour mettre le Saint-Siège au fait de la question*".

Y. Most Rev. Emin. knows that I did not wait for the suggestion of the High Commission to carry out this duty of mine, having received, as I hope, my letters of the 7th, 9th, 14th and 19th of last May, with their relative attachments. That notwithstanding, I profit willingly from the occasion to return to the painful subject, also because it seems to me that the danger of being accused of not having done all that we could for the safety of so many wretched Christians begging the assistance of the Holy See must be avoided at all costs.

If it were not that, in the present state of things, I am more than ever convinced that a friendly intervention, even collective, of the Powers, would not lead to much. In fact, it might even turn out to be, perhaps, damaging to those poor Christians, to whom would be imputed the unpardonable guilt of having provoked it. Seeing itself treated as a duly-recognized Power bore out the Government of Angora in its conviction that the European Powers, by now exhausted by the long years of the world war, are no longer in the condition to impose their will on it by force; and that therefore the indulgence shown them is nothing but pure weakness. Now the Turk, who in front of predominant force bows down all the way to the ground, in front of weakness instead, whether real or apparent, becomes boundlessly arrogant. Already the Assembly of Angora showed this with the reply to the accords, in our opinion deplorable, concluded by its agents last March in London: only a Napoleon I, after his most resounding victories, could have spoken with such shameless arrogance. And they will speak and act ever worse, as long as one expects to win them over with good manners. And the poor Christians groaning under their yoke will be ever more mistreated, despite all the most beautiful promises, until their total extermination is arrived at.

By now there is no middle way, in my humble opinion: either crush the pan-Islamic and Bolshevizing hydra of Angora by force, or renounce the safety of the poor remains of the Christian population in the places overrun by it. And in this case the poisonous hydra will grow ever larger in dimension, to the point of invading all the Orient, to then fall upon the Occident. A true catastrophe for European civilization, if the European Powers do not hasten to prevent it.

For that which regards France in particular, if she persists in her remissive policy towards the Government of Angora, she will not be able to even hope of ever having peace in Syria. The bands that have up until now infested vast territories in the regions of Hama and of Aleppo, are intimately tied to that government and completely subsidized by it. One wanted to be indulgent, to save on blood and money, and every day the expenses grow, and with them, unfortunately, the victims. And it will continue on like this, until France decides either to crush the head of the poisonous hydra, or to completely abandon even this small part of Syria that she has left, gnawed away at from the north by the Turks and from the south by the English.

Agitated by the thought of this deplorable state of things, before leaving for Aleppo I decided to write a letter on the matter to the Most Emin. Card. Dubois, of which I now enclose here a copy for your information, not having been able to do it earlier due to time constraints. I was induced to write this letter by, among other things, having understood that even at High Commission of the Republic here they deplored the lack of an illuminating action in the political universe of Paris, where the Government that knows, prisoner of a public opinion contrary to energetic enterprises here in the Orient, does not dare act with energy, and with small measures gets by for the best, that is, for the worst, hiding the painful daily vicissitudes of the Army of the Levant as much as it can, without deciding either to increase its forces, in such as way as to enable it to strike a decisive blow, or to call it back home. It would be necessary, therefore, to act on public opinion in Paris, telling exactly the truth just as it is, in order that—seeing as no serious politician will be able to assume the responsibility for a withdrawal of troops from Syria, a real suicide for France—the press and the parliamentarians end up encouraging the Government to a supreme effort instead of continuing to constrain it to the indecisive behavior that has already brought so much damage and will bring more to follow, should it last. For this reason I wrote my letter to the Most Emin. Card. Dubois.

Naturally that for which I aim has little to do with the usual human politics; that interests me very little for its own sake. My intent is to possibly save so many poor Christians, especially our centers of Catholics scattered here and there, and our Missions. To tell you of one, I know that the Jesuits of Adana have orders from their Superior to see that the Sisters leave, and to leave themselves, in the case that the French troops leave Cilicia and solid guarantees are not offered for their safety. And I cannot help but find the order reasonable.

The Armenian Mr. Tchobanian, who was mentioned in my letter of May 14th N. 17, left Beirut before my return, to reach Jerusalem and then

Constantinople and Paris, possibly passing through Rome. I don't know, by the way, when he might arrive there. But I renew, in any case, the recommendation in his regard

And bowed to the kiss, etc.

Allegato al doc. n° 108, p. 372:
[*Attached* to doc. n° 108, p. 372:]

A Son Eminence le Card. Dubois Archev. de Paris
Beyrouth, le 19 Mai 1921
Eminentissime Seigneur,

De retour d'un récent voyage en Cilicie, où deux cent cinquante mille chrétiens environ vivent dans l'angoisse, trop fondée malheureusement, d'une extermination totale, si ce pays devait être réellement évacué par les troupes françaises et remis entre les mains des turcs, conformément à la Conférence de Londres; je fais appel à votre coeur de chrétien, de Prélat et de français, implorant votre bienveillante intervention, pour empêcher l'exécution d'une décision non moins nuisible à cette pauvre population qu'aux intérêts de la France.

Je me rends parfaitement compte des raisons qui ont porté le Gouvernement Français à se montrer si condescendant envers les turcs dans la Conférence du mois de Mars dernier; et quand même je ne comprendrais pas ces raisons, je me garderais bien cependant de critiquer le Gouvernnement d'un pays qui a déjà fait tant de sacrifice pour le bien de ces régions d'Orient et auquel est dûe toute notre reconnaissance.

Toutefois, je crois qu'il y aurait de sérieuses considérations à faire avant que d'évacuer la Cilicie. Cette évacuation, si jamais elle devait avoir lieu, ne devrait se faire que si le territoire peut être remis à un Gouvernement responsable, sincèrement désireux de la tranquillité et efficacement capable d'y maintenir l'ordre et d'y assurer la sécurité de la nombreuse population chrétienne. Or, tel ne peut être, pour le moment du moins, un Gouvernement turc, et bien moins encore le Gouvernement d'Angora, lequel passe en Europe pour un Gouvernement nationaliste, mais n'est en réalité qu'un Gouvernement à base panislamique. Ce Gouvernement peut être très liberal en promesses, mais ses promesses resteront lettre morte, si une force étrangère ne l'oblige à les maintenir, en refrénant les extrémistes qui sont les maîtres à l'Assemblée d'Angora. C'est pour cela que même une partie considérable de la population musulmane de la Cilicie, amie sincère de la paix et ennemie des massacres, ne désire point le retour du régime turc.

D'autre part, bien que je ne sois ni homme politique, ni stratège militaire, je connais suffisamment ces pays et la mentalité des turcs d'Anatolie et des musulmans de Syrie, pour pouvoir dire, avec certitude, qu'en cédant à la

Turquie la Cilicie jusqu'à Killis, c'est-à-dire jusqu'aux portes d'Alep, la France ne sera jamais tranquille en Syrie. Les bandes qui donnent actuellement tant de travail aux troupes françaises dans les environs de Hama, ainsi que sur le territoire des Alaouites, sont pleinement d'accord avec les prétendus nationalistes d'Angora et, partant, avec le Gouvernement de Constantinople. Il n'y a pas à en douter. Et cet accord restera toujours en pleine vigeur, en dépit de tous les Traités internationaux, au grand préjudice de la Syrie et de la France, tant que cette dernière, au lieu de montrer de l'énergie, suivra une politique de condescendance envers les musulmans, ses ennemis irréductibles en Syrie et en Anatolie. Une condescendance qui passe pour de la faiblesse ne fera qu'accroître toujours plus l'audace et l'effronterie de ces ennemis irréconciliables de la France et de la civilisation européenne. Il en fut de même avec l'Emir Faiçal, aussi longtemps qu'on espérait le gagner par les bonnes manières.

Enfin, par la cession de la riche Cilicie, la France se prive d'un territoire qui peut seul compenser, en partie, les grands sacrifices en argent qu'elle est en train de faire pour l'Armée du Levant.

En résumé, des raisons d'humanité et d'intérêt bien compris demandent que la France ne quitte pas la Cilicie, au moins pour l'instant.

Les raisons de nationalité elles-mêmes ne sont point en faveur de l'élément turc. Les vrais turcs en Cilicie forment tout au plus le cinquième de la population totale. Ils sont à peine cent mille; tandis que les chrétiens, dont la très grande majorité est arménienne, en forment peu moins de la moitié: ils sont au nombre de deux cent cinquante mille environ. Ajoutons que les arméniens sont les plus anciens habitants de cette région. Donc, au point de vue national, la Cilicie est un territoire plus arméniens que turc.

Dans le cas donc où l'on ne pourrait faire mieux, je pense qu'il conviendrait d'ériger la Cilicie en province autonome sous l'égide de la France, laquelle devrait y maintenir une garnison. Le territoire pourrait resté sous la <u>suzeraineté</u> du Sultan, si l'on ne peut faire autrement, mais avec défense à la Sublime Porte d'y avoir des troupes propres, ainsi que cela se passait pour le Liban, sous l'ancien régime.

Pour obtenir ce resultat, il faudra quelques efforts, mais plus d'ordre morale que phisique. Il suffirà que la France montre une volonté énergique, ce qu'elle n'a pas fait jusqu'à présent. Du reste, les efforts qu'il faudra dépenser seront largement compensés par les résultats qu'on obtiendra. Et les ossements des soldats français qui sont mort jusqu'ici en Cilice, tressailliront dans leurs tombes, en voyant que leur sang n'a pas été versé en vain.

Je supplie Votre Eminence de vouloir bien user de toute son influence pour attirer l'attention des hommes politiques français sur cette grave question à laquelle de très hauts intérêts sont rattachée, qui touchent non seulement la France, mais aussi l'humanité.

Veuillez agréer, Eminentissime Seigneur, avec mes remerciements anticipés pour ce que vous voudrez bien faire pour cette juste cause, l'hommage etc.

109

5 July 1921, Rome – Gasparri to Giannini – AAEESS, *Asia* 57, 1, n° 22655

Ho ricevuto il Rapporto della Signoria Vostra Illma, N. 19, in data del 18 giugno, col relativo inserto, riguardante le condizioni presenti della Cilicia.

Nel significare alla S.V. che non ho mancato di prendere conoscenza delle notizie contenute in tale Rapporto, profitto ecc

[Translation]

I received the Report of Y. Most Illus., N. 19, dated June 18th, with relative enclosure, regarding the present conditions of Cilicia.

In conveying to you that I did not fail to take cognizance of the news contained in said Report, I profit, etc.

110

17 July 1921, Beirut – Giannini to Gasparri – AAEESS, *Asia* 57, 1, n° 24161

Eminentissimo Principe,

Fu qui giorni fa di passaggio, trattenendovisi per circa due settimane, un uomo politico francese assai noto, il Sig. Franklin-Bouillon, già Deputato alla camera e Presidente della commisssione per gli affari esteri e Ministro.

Adesso non è più nulla, ufficialmente. Ma, checchessia delle sue idee e della sua iscrizione nel partito radico-socialista, egli è e rimane uomo molto intelligente e tuttora assai in vista tra gli uomini politici del suo paese. Per quello poi che riguarda la Turchia, egli gode della riputazione di una competenza speciale, fondata sulle sue cognizioni concrete di uomini e di cose dell'impero ottomano, ove soggiornò lungamente e contrasse rapporti amichevoli con personaggi che anche oggi vanno per la maggiore. Perciò un due mesi fa si recò ad Angora, per riprender contatto con le antiche conoscenze e per esaminare sul posto lo stato delle cose sotto ogni rispetto. Non si trattava d'una missione ufficiale, ma il suo Governo non v'era estraneo.

Dopo essere rimasto nell'Anatolia circa un mese e mezzo, riprese la via del ritorno, traversando rapidamente la Cilicia e soffermandosi alquanto in Siria.

Appena arrivato a Beirut assistette alla ceremonia di ringraziamento del 3 corrente di cui è cenno nel mio rapporto del 7, N. 24. Dopo la ceremonia il Generale Gouraud volle presentarmelo, ed egli mi si mostrò molto grato delle poche parole che avevo detto in chiesa prima d'intonare il Te Deum.

Il 14 Luglio poi, in occasione del solito ricevimento solennissimo, il Generale volle di nuovo presentarmi a lui, e lo fece cercare apposta nella folla, dicendogli che io avevo da parlargli sulle cose di Siria e di Cilicia. Poiché l'ottimo Generale sa molto bene come io la penso, credette buono che dicessi i miei pensieri anche a questo inviato ufficioso del suo Governo. Anzi dopo qualche momento che la nostra conversazione era cominciata lo stesso generale volle prendervi parte, venendo a sedersi presso di noi nell'angolo di una delle sale della sua residenza di Beirut. Ma né il luogo né il tempo erano propizi per lunghi discorsi. Ad ogni momento v'erano distrazioni. La più grossa fu quella dell'arrivo del Patriarca foziano con numeroso seguito. E allora si decise, non essendovi più modo di riprendere né subito né in seguito la conversazione, che io avrei esposto per iscritto le mie idee. Ciò che feci, appena tornato a casa, con un piccolo promemoria che inviai il giorno dopo al Sign. Franklin-Bouillon per mezzo del Generale. I due già si trovavano nella villeggiatura di Aley sul Libano, ed io il giorno stesso, cioè il 15, partivo per questa mia residenza estiva, di dove mi sarebbe stato difficile inviare lo scritto. Dovetti dunque scrivere con molta fretta, per inviare il mio Promemoria da Beirut la mattina del 15.

Cercai d'intonare lo scritto alle esigenze particolari della mentalità del destinatario, di cui mi ero reso conto nel breve colloquio. Egli tornava dall'Anatolia tutto pieno e impressionatissimo dei miracoli di organizzazione civile e militare campiuti, secondo lui, dai nazionalisti turchi. Perciò, visto che i greci non contano e che né la Francia né le altre grandi Potenze sono disposte a combatterli armata mano: cosa, del resto molto ardua, sempre secondo lui; non v'è altra politica da seguire che quella di un'amichevole intesa, inviando ad Angora dei sagaci rappresentanti che tentino di arginare il fiume che non si può far ritornare indietro.

Per conto mio in primo luogo ho motivo di non credere troppo ai pretesi miracoli dei nazionalisti turchi, abilissimi mistificatori che certamente non mancarono di darla a bere, come suol dirsi, all'inviato francese quanto potevano: tanto più che pei suoi precedenti lo conoscevano ben disposto ad abbondare nel loro senso. Ma anche ammessi, in tutto o in parte, quei miracoli, si potrà tutt'al più convenire che oggi non sia più facile come due anni fa imporre con la forza la propria volontà ai nazionalisti turchi, e che quindi la miglior cosa sarebbe concludere con essi un'amichevole intesa. A patto però che si tratti d'un'intesa leale e durevole, che salvi gl'interessi essenziali della Francia, sì materiali che morali; compresa, tra questi ultimi, la doverosa tutela dei cristiani indigeni, e specialmente dei cattolici, il cui abbandono, dopo averli terribilmente compromessi, significherebbe la sparizione definitiva d'ogni prestigio francese nel Levante, a profitto di rivali che da tempo lo insidiano. Se la Francia non è disposta, ed io non credo che possa esserlo, a perder tutto, non solo in Cilicia ma anche in Siria, bisognerà che, più presto o più tardi, si decida ad imporre la sua volontà ai nazionalisti turchi con la forza. Cosa non del tutto agevole oggi, ne convengo, ma non certo superiore ai suoi mezzi, malgrado tutto. Del resto molto meno difficile oggi che dimani: senza contare che un buon colpo menato a tempo taglierebbe corto alla politica delle mezze misure praticata sin qui e che minaccia di perpetuarsi con successivo non mai interrotto dispendio di denaro e di sangue, molto maggiore di quello che si richiederebbe per dare il colpo di grazia, e di più nocevole oltre ogni dire al prestigio della Francia sì in faccia agli amici che ai nemici.

Queste le direttive a cui m'ispirai nello stendere in fretta il piccolo Promemoria di cui accludo copia non solo a titolo d'informazione ma anche perché spero che l'Emza V. Rma non mancherà, all'occasione, di continuare il Suo benevolo interessamento per le cose nostre di qua, tanto importanti al punto di vista religioso e sociale. Da uomini come il Sign. Franklin-Bouillon non c'è molto da sperare. Ma si può almeno tentare di indurli a riflettere un po' meglio sul multiforme problema. E se non con loro, forse con altri si potrà anche arrivare a qualcosa di meglio, con l'aiuto di Dio. Nel quale aiuto io seguito a sperar molto, malgrado tutto.

Chinato al bacio ecc

[Translation]
Most Eminent Prince,

Some days ago, passing through, remaining for about two weeks, a very well-known French politician was here, Mr. Franklin-Bouillon, formerly Representative to the house and President of the commission on Foreign Affairs and Minister.

Now he is nothing anymore, officially. But, whatever his ideas and [whatever you make of] his membership in the radical-socialist party, he is and remains a very intelligent man and still now is quite visible among the politicians of his country. For that which regards Turkey he enjoys the reputation of a special expertise, founded on his concrete knowledge of men and of matters of the Ottoman Empire, where he has spent a great deal of time and established friendly relationships with personages who even today are among the more important in the country. So, about two months ago he went to Angora, to make contact again with his old acquaintances and to examine on location the state of things in every respect. It did not have to do with an official mission, but his Government was not extraneous to it.

After having stayed in Anatolia about a month and a half, he undertook his return, quickly crossing Cilicia and stopping a while in Syria.

Just arrived in Beirut, he attended the thanksgiving ceremony of the 3rd of this month which is mentioned in my report of the 7th, N. 24. After the ceremony General Gouraud was pleased to introduce me to him, and he showed himself to be very grateful of the few words that I had said in church before singing the *Te Deum*.

On July 14th, then, in occasion of the usual formal reception, the General would again present me to him, and had him purposely sought out from amongst the crowd, telling him that I needed to speak with him about matters of Syria and of Cilicia. Since the good General knows very well my opinion, he thought it appropriate that I tell my thoughts to this unofficial envoy of his Government as well. In fact, a few moments into our conversation the general himself wanted to take part in it, coming to sit near us in the corner of one of the rooms of his residence in Beirut. But neither the place nor the time were propitious for long discussions. At every moment there were distractions. The biggest was that of the arrival of the Photian Patriarch with a numerous following. And then it was decided, there not being another chance to take up the conversation again, neither right away nor later on, that I would set out my ideas in writing. Which I did, as soon as I returned home, with a short memo that I sent the following day to Mr. Franklin-Bouillon by way of the General. The two were already at the vacation house in Aley and I was leaving the same day, that is, the 15th, for my summer residence here, from which it would have been difficult to send the letter. Thus I had to write with great haste, to send my Memorandum from Beirut the morning of the 15th.

I tried to match the letter to the particular demands of the recipient's mentality, of which I got a sense during our brief conversation. He returned from Anatolia all full of and very impressed with the miracles of civil and military organization accomplished, according to him, by the Turkish nationalists. Therefore, seeing as the Greeks don't count and since neither the French nor the other great Powers are disposed to fight them militarily: quite a difficult thing besides, again according to him; there is no other policy to follow than that of a friendly understanding, sending some sagacious representatives to Angora to try to contain the river that cannot be turned backwards.

In my opinion, in the first place, I have reason not to believe too much in the claimed miracles of the Turkish nationalists, skillful tricksters who certainly did not fail to reel in, as they say, the French envoy when they could: all the more so, in that from past example they knew him to be well-disposed to exaggeration on their behalf. But even admitting those miracles, in whole or in part, one may at the most agree that today it will not be as easy as it was two years ago to impose one's will upon the Turkish nationalists by force, and that therefore the best thing would be to come to a friendly agreement with them. On the condition, however, that it is a loyal and lasting agreement, that protects the essential interests of France, both material and moral; including, among the latter, the dutiful tutelage of the indigenous Christians, and especially of the Catholics, whose abandonment, after having terribly compromised them, would signify the definitive disappearance of all French prestige in the Levant, to the profit of rivals who have long been laying a trap for her. If France is not disposed, and I do not believe that she can be, to lose everything, not only in Cilicia but also in Syria, it will be necessary that, sooner or later, she decide to impose her will on the Turkish nationalists by force. Not a completely easy thing today, I agree, but not, certainly, beyond her means, despite everything. After all, much less difficult today than tomorrow: without taking into account that the right blow struck at the right time would curtail the politics of half-measures practiced up till now and which threatens to perpetuate itself with successive, uninterrupted expenditures of money and of blood, much greater than that which it would take to give the coup de grâce and, what's more, harmful beyond words to France's reputation whether in the face of friends or of enemies.

These were the precepts I took inspiration from in hurriedly writing out the short Memorandum of which I enclose a copy not only for your information but also because I hope that Y. Most Rev. Emin. will not fail, given the occasion, to continue your benevolent concern for our affairs here, so important from a religious and social point of view. From men like Mr. Franklin-Bouillon there is not much to hope. But one can at least try to induce them to reflect a little more upon the multiform problem. And if not with them, perhaps with others one can even arrive at something better, with the help of God. In whose help I continue to trust very much, despite everything.

Bowed to the kiss etc

Allegato al doc. n° 110, p. 379:
[*Attached* to doc. n° 110, p. 379:]

Mémoire
adressé à Mr. Franklin-Bouillon par le Délégué Apostolique de Syrie

Le soussigné, de nationalité italienne, ne se reconnaît, comme tel, aucun droit, et n'a, d'ailleurs, aucune velléité de s'occuper du côté purement politique de l'action française dans le Levant.

Mais, comme représentant du Saint Siège et comme chef religieux pour les latins du pays, il ne peut point se désintéresser du sort qu'on prépare aux chrétiens, specialement aux catholiques, en Sirie et en Cilicie. C'est pourquoi, lorsque la Commission wilsonienne d'enquête vint ici en 1919, il se permit de donner, de vive voix et par écrit, son avis en faveur de l'installation de la France en ce pays, en se basant sur les intérêts que la France y avait et qui concordaient parfaitement avec ceux du Saint Siège et des catholiques, dont il a la garde. Pour ce même motif, il se croit en devoir d'exprimer aujourd'hui son opinin fondée sur des bases solides, touchant la meilleure façon de protéger, en ces pays, les intérêts du Christianisme, et plus particulièrement du Catholicisme, qui concordent parfaitement, selon lui, avec ceux de la France.

Ayant assisté aux tristes événements qui se déroulèrent pendant la guerre, alors que de centaines de mille de chrétiens, en Syrie et en Cilicie, périrent par le glaive et la faim, sans autre crime de leur part que leur reconnaissant souvenir des bienfaits de la France; le soussigné ne peut qu'appréhender, avec horreur la possibilité de voir ces territoires retourner sous le régime turc, lequel se croira plus que jamais autorisé à sévir contre les chrétiens et spécialement contre les catholiques, ouvertement reconnus aujourd'hui comme partisans de l'oeuvre de civilisation entreprise dans ces contrées par le Gouvernement Français.

C'est pourquoi, il est profondement convaincu que dans les décision définitives qu'on va prendre concernant la politique à suivre en Syrie et en Cilicie, des questions de haute humanité se trouvent engagées qu'il importe de prendre en sérieuse consideration.

D'autre part, se rendant parfaitement compte des raisons graves qui justifient la répugnance actuelle de l'opinion publique en France de s'imposer de nouveaux sacrifices d'argent et de personnes pour ces pays, il trouve raisonnable qu'on veuille en finir avec une politique qui a déjà coûté beaucoup d'argent et de sang et qui menace d'en domander encore, Dieu sait pour combien de temps.

Cela étant donné, le soussigné ne voit plus que deux politiques à adopter: ou celle d'accord amical avec les turcs, obtenu a force de concessions plus ou moins pénibles de la part de la France; ou celle d'un dernier effort énergique qui dispense la France de faire dépendre du bon vouloir des turcs la sauvegarde de ses intérêts essentiels dans le Levant.

La première politique, préconisée par l'opinion publique en France, peut paraître de prime abord la plus rationnelle. Le soussigné reconnaît très volontiers qu'elle serait de beaucoup préférable à la seconde, si l'on pouvait réellement arriver à conclure avec les turcs un accord loyal et durable, sur la base d'une efficace sauvegarde de tous les intérêts matériels et moraux, les plus essentiels, de la France, qui sont les mêmes que ceux des chrétiens de Syrie et de Cilicie.

Mais il ne croit pas à la possibilité de cet accord loyal et durable, quoi qu'en disent les dirigeants actuels de la polique turque, qui se voient forcés, pour le moment, de se montrer conciliants, en quelque sorte, pour ne pas avoir la France contre eux, alors qu'ils ont assez d'ennuis ailleurs. Le soi-disant nationalisme turc, représenté actuellement par l'Assemblée d'Angora, ne se résignera jamais sincèrement, s'il ne veut pas se suicider, à considérer comme définitive la perte des territoires qui lui furent arrachés par la victoire des Alliés dans la dernière guerre. Il cherche maintenant à jeter de la poudre aux yeux avec le nouveau clichet du pantouranisme, inventé pour le besoin de la cause; tandis qu'en réalité le microbe qui l'excite est le traditionnel panislamisme, lequel aspire avant tout à restaurer l'empire turc tel qu'il était avant la dernière guerre, et puis à en étendre les limites même au delà des anciennes frontières, et à l'infini. C'est pourquoi, un accord qui serait conclu maintenant avec eux à force de concessions de la part de la France, ne serait tout au plus qu'une trêve, car il fortifierait matériellement et moralement le gouvernement d'Angora et donnerait à ses partisans la convinction que la France est faible et que la force se trouve de leur côté. Aussitôt qu'il n'aura plus les embarras avec lesquels il se trouve présentement aux prises, ce gouvernement, qu'il soit entre les mains de ses chefs actuels, ou qu'il tombe dans le pouvoir d'autres plus audacieux, reprendra par tout les moyens sa politique panislamique.

Nous avons éprouvé déjà les effects de cette politique, et les vaillantes troupes qui se battent depuis longtemps contre de soi-disants rebelles, au nord de la Syrie et en Cilicie, les sentiront toujours davantage. La Cilicie retrocédée et les frontières du nouvel empire turc étendues jusqu'aux portes d'Alep, il sera encore plus aisé au panislamisme triomphant de fomenter la révolte en Syrie où ses partisans sont déjà nombreux et le seront davantage dans la suite. On verra alors ce que vaudra l'accord avec le gouvernement d'Angora, tant pour les garanties qu'on lui imposera en Cilicie que pour ce qui regarde ses aspirations à la reconquête de la Syrie.

La reconquête de la Syrie spécialement est, pour le panislamisme turc, une question de vie ou de mort. Il serait absurde d'en douter. La Syrie est pour les turcs la seule voie qui conduit aux lieux saints de l'Islam, sans lesquels leur Kalifat est menacé de voir le terrain lui échapper sous les pieds.

En conséquence, l'accord amical conclu à force de concessions de la part de la France, portera infailliblement non seulement au sacrifice des intérêts matériels et moraux de la France en Cilicie, mais il conduira aussi à la perte de la Syrie.

Si la France peut se résigner à tout cela, il n'y a plus rien à dire. Mais, étant donné que le soussigné ne pense pas qu'il puisse se trouver jamais un homme d'Etat en France, qui considère d'un oeil tranquille la possibilité d'un tel désastre qui éteindrait pour toujours le prestige de son pays dans tout le Levant; il croit que pour conserver la Syrie, vu le peu de consistance des accords amicaux avec le gouvernement d'Angora, on devra suivre pour longtemps la politique des demi-mesures qui a déjà coûté tant d'argent et de sang sans jamais nous donner la paix; et l'on sera enfin obligé de recourir à cet effort énergique qu'on aura voulu éviter et qui coûtera beaucoup plus d'argent et de sang qu'aujourd'hui.

Le soussigné est convaincu qu'actuellement l'effort de la France pour imposer sa volonté aux turcs, au lieu de subir la leur, est plus d'ordre moral che matériel. Tant que les turcs voient que la France est encline aux accords malgré tout, ils enflent la voix et se montrent très exigeants, persuadés que cela servira avantageusement leurs visées tant vis-à-vis de la France à laquelle ils cherchent à arracher le plus de concessions possibles, qu'aux yeux de leurs partisans de Cilicie et de Syrie lesquels se sentent toujours plus soutenus dans leur révolte contre la France et réconfortés dans leur espoir de retourner sous un régime qui peut seul leur assurer l'ancienne suprématie oppressive sur les chrétiens du pays. Tandis que si la France montre, par la parole et par les faits, qu'elle entend imposer sa volonté parfaitement conforme aux droit imprescriptibles de l'humanité et de la civilisation, les turcs baisseront la voix et réfléchiront bien avant de s'engager dans un lutte inégale. Qu'on donne à l'héroique

Général Gouraud les moyens nécessaires et l'ordre de dégainer son épée, au besoin, et l'on verra qu'en peu de temps, et sans trop de sacrifices, l'ordre sera rétabli et consolidé en Syrie et en Cilicie; et alors on aura avec les turcs l'accord désiré, non tel qu'on voudrait le faire maintenant, mais vraiment solide et tel que le réclament les intérêts matériels et moraux de la France en ces pays.

D'ailleurs, un accord conclu dans ces conditions n'empêchera pas la France de se montrer généreuse envers la Turquie et de rétablir avec l'empire turc l'amitié traditionnelle qui fut si riche en bons fruits. Etant en état d'imposer sa volonté, la France pourra consentir, par exemple, à ce que la Cilicie retourne sous la suzeraineté du Sultan, en faisant de cette riche contrée une province autonome de l'empire, avec un régime à peu près similaire à celui de l'ancien Liban, garanti par une garnison française permanente. Cette mesure serait en somme justifiée, après tout, par le fait que les turcs, en Cilicie, sont une minorité, un cinquième de la population totale, partant moins nombreux que les chrétiens indigènes, malgré les massacres.

En rognant ainsi les ailes au panislamisme, on aura la paix non seulement en Cilicie mais en Syrie aussi. Et de la sorte la France aura rempli, en ces pays, la mission éminemment civilisatrice que lui assignent et ses traditions et les sacrifices de tant de ses fils qui ont travaillé pendant des siècles à répandre son influence. Et le monde lui sera reconnaissant d'avoir assuré dans ces pays et ailleurs le triomphe de la civilisation sur la barbarie.

Beyrouth, le 15 Juillet 1921
(Signé) f. F. Giannini

111

30 July 1921, Constantinople – Moriondo to Marini – CO, 106, 3, 5, 2, n° 6331

Eminenza,

Sono cinque mesi che mi trovo a Cospoli, in attesa di ordini, e la mia situazione diviene ogni dì più ambigua e per me grave, sì moralmente che economicamente, avendo tutt'ora con me il Segretario e il Domestico, che non licenziai, nella speranza di avere da un momento all'altro una destinazione.

Sarei perciò molto riconoscente all'Eminenza V. se si degnasse scrivermi una parola in proposito, che mi togliesse dall'incertezza in cui mi trovo e mi significasse il da fare.

La Georgia e il Caucaso, secondo le poche e schematiche notizie, che ricevetti dai Sacerdoti del luogo, versano in condizioni ognor più tristi. Il Bolscevismo vi regna tiranno: la miseria, la fame ed il colera decimano la popolazione, ormai impotente a reagire contro di chi la opprime.

Ho potuto inviare intenzioni di Messe, che ridussi da 5 a 10 Lr. ciascuna. Inviai pure una parte del danaro che ancora mi rimaneva della somma datami dalla S. Congregazione per il Clero e Fedeli. Ora per mezzo del P. Kalatosoff, che spero potrà giungere fino a Tiflis, invio altre Messe e l'ultimo residuo della detta somma.

Nell'attesa d'una sua cortese risposta, Le bacio ecc

[Translation]
Eminence,
I have been in Constantinople for five months awaiting orders, and my situation becomes ever more ambiguous and, for me, serious, both morally and economically, still having with me now the Secretary and the Domestic, whom I did not fire, in the hopes of having a destination from one minute to the next.

I would, therefore, be very grateful to Y. Eminence if he were to deign to write me a few words on the subject, that might remove me from the uncertainty in which I find myself and indicate to me what must be done.

Georgia and the Caucasus, according to the few and schematic pieces of news that I received from the Priests of the area, are in ever more sad conditions. Bolshevism reigns tyrannical there: poverty, hunger and cholera decimate the population, by now powerless to react against their oppressors.

I was able to send intentions of Masses, that I reduced from 5 to 10 Lr. each. I also sent a part of the money that still remained to me from the sum given me by the S. Congregation for the Clergy and Faithful. Now, by way of F. Kalatosoff, who I hope will be able to reach Tiflis, I send other Masses and the last remainder of said sum.

Awaiting your courteous reply, I kiss etc.

112

11 August 1921, Rome – handwritten draft of the encrypted telegr. from Gasparri to Dolci – AAEESS, *Asia* 117, n° 23784

Urge provvedere sicurezza cattolici Villaggio Artvin presso Batum. Sacerdote Giuseppo Vartanian già trucidato con ottanta cristiani passaggio fiume Ciorokh. Faccia passi opportuni presso governo Kemalista. Card. Gasparri

[Translation]
Urge provide safety Catholics Village Artvin near Batum. Priest Giuseppo Vartanian already slain with eighty Christians crossing river Chorokh. Take necessary steps with Kemalist government. Card. Gasparri

113

30 August 1921, Constantinople (Pera) – Naslian to Gasparri – AAEESS, *Asia* 117, n° 25108

Eminenza Reverendissima,
Dopo l'irreparabile disastro nazionale, che non accenna ancora trovar termine, i profughi Armeni superstiti, per assicurarsi la vita di fronte

all'incertezza dell'avvenire, sono in cerca di paesi ove possano essere ospitati allo scopo di trovar modo e mezzi di conservazione, di sviluppo fino a che le condizioni dell'Armenia possano consentirvi il loro ritorno.

Il Governo Brasiliano sembrerebbe favorevole ad accordare facilitazioni di viaggio e di prima istallazione a colonie armene che vi volessero accorrere. Il Rappresentante della repubblica Armena per l'America del Sud scrivendo in proposito da Rio-de-Janeiro al Patriarca Armeno Gregoriano, spera di riuscire nelle sue trattative su quest'oggetto con i Governi del Brasile, Chili ed Argentina e fa invito agli Armeni ad accedervi.

Un Comitato privato Armeno si è formato per aderire a quell'invito incoraggiato specialmente da competenti in materia e tra gli altri da qualche ex-delegato Agronomo del Governo Ottomano al Brasile, il quale ha dato ampie informazioni sulla vita agricola, industriale e commerciale di quel paese, per cui gli Armeni data la loro attitudine speciale per quella vita, sarebbero anche più decisi a rispondere all'invito.

Ma più che a trattative di un rappresentante loro, gli Armeni si affiderebbero a qualche più alta assicurazione in oggetto.

I Capi del Comitato sumenzionato conoscendo l'alta influenza che la Santa Sede può avere in quel Governo Cattolico, si sono indirizzati al nostro Patriarcato per pregarlo ad interessare cotesta Segreteria di Stato a favore di questo progetto sottomettendo alla benevola attenzione di Vostra Eminenza le varie condizioni le quali converrebbero agli emigranti: e cioè:

1) Che a questi si concedano dal Governo Brasiliano facilitazioni di viaggio.

2) Che si concedano gratuitamente dal Governo Brasiliano quanto occorre alla prima istallazione ed arezzi [sic] necessarii.

3) Non si sottomettano alle condizioni del regime detto la "Fagenda" [sic], con dispersione dei gruppi da emigrare.

4) Ma bensi si accordi a loro territorii in ragione di clima temperato e vicini alle reti ferroviarie, ove possano raggrupparsi da forma e villaggi o città armeni.

5) Si conceda a loro chiesa e scuola per conservarsi nel loro rito e nella lingua nazionale; non fanno difficoltà che il sacerdote sia cattolico e quindi siano assistiti da esso cattolicamente purche [sic] sia armeno.

6) Consenta il Governo brasiliano che essi possano permanere sudditi del Governo Armeno.

7) Finalmente sembrerebbe convenir meglio agli Armeni istallarsi a SAO PAOLO, a PARANA SANTA CATERINA, vicini agli elementi Portughesi.

Qualora Vostra Eminenza credesse dar seguito alla presente richiesta per mezzo del Nunzio Apostolico e dell'Ambasciatore del Brasile presso la S. Sede, pregherebbero i Capi del Comitato in oggetto di presentare gli Armeni quali superstiti di un popoli cristiano perseguitato, i quali vorrebbero ricostituirsi dall'inumane disastro d'esterminio a cui andarono vittime nel loro paese.

Confidando nella provvida benevolenza della S. Sede che abbraccia tutti i popoli, mentre domando mille scuse per la libertà presa del presente ricorso, ho l'alto onore di poter rinnovare ecc.

[Translation]
Most Reverend Eminence,

After the irreparable national disaster, that still does not look as if it will find an end, the surviving Armenian refugees, to secure their lives in front of the uncertainty of the future, are in search of countries where they can be hosted, with the goal of finding ways and means of maintaining themselves, of development until the conditions in Armenia might allow their return there.

The Brazilian Government would seem favorable to granting travel and settlement assistance to Armenian communities who would arrive there. The Representative of the Armenian Republic to South America, writing about it from Rio de Janeiro to the Armenian Gregorian Patriarch, hopes to succeed in his negotiations on this subject with the Governments of Brazil, Chile and Argentina and to invite the Armenians to come there.

A private Armenian Committee has formed to accept that invitation, encouraged especially by experts, among others by an ex-representative Agronomist of the Ottoman Government to Brazil, who gave ample information about the agricultural, industrial and commercial life of that country, whereby the Armenians, given their special aptitude for that life, would be even more decisive in responding to the invitation.

But more than in the negotiations of one of their representatives, the Armenians would trust some higher assurance on the matter.

The Heads of the aforementioned Committee, knowing the high degree of influence that the Holy See can have with that Catholic Government, addressed themselves to our Patriarchate to ask him to interest the Secretariat of State in favor of this project, submitting to the benevolent attention of Your Eminence the various conditions that would suit the emigrants: such as:

1) That to them is conceded travel assistance by the Brazilian Government.

2) That are conceded by the Brazilian Government all that is needed for settlement and necessary tools free of charge.

3) They are not submitted to the conditions of the regime called the *Fazenda*,[285] with dispersion of the emigrating groups.

---

285 Translator's Note: *Fazenda*. System whereby Brazilian land-grant plantations were populated with indentured servants (and, earlier, slaves).

4) But rather they be accorded territories based on the temperate climate and vicinity to railway networks, where they may assemble to form Armenian villages or cities.

5) They are conceded churches and schools to conserve for themselves their rite and national language; they won't create any problems should the priest be Catholic and they be assisted by him then in Catholic fashion, as long as he is Armenian.

6) The Brazilian Government consents that they should remain subjects of the Armenian Government.

7) Finally, it would seem to be more convenient for the Armenians to settle in SAO PAOLO, in PARANA SANTA CATERINA, near the Portuguese elements.

Should Your Eminence see fit to respond to the present request by way of the Apostolic Nuncio and of the Ambassador of Brazil to the Holy See, the Heads of the Committee in question would pray that the Armenians be presented as survivors of a persecuted Christian people, who would like to recover from the inhuman disaster of extermination of which they were going to be victims in their country.

Confiding in the provident benevolence of the Holy See that embraces all the peoples, while I ask a thousand pardons for the liberty taken in the present appeal, I have the high honor of being able to renew etc.

114

1 September 1921, Constantinople (Pera) – Naslian to Gasparri – AAEESS, *Asia* 117, n° 25109

Eminentissimo Signor Principe,

Contrariamente alle assicurazioni iterate dei kemalisti date alla S. Sede di rispettare la vita ed i beni dei Cristiani, notizie tristi di eccidi incalzano, e noi ritorniamo all'epoca degli anni micidiali della guerra mondiale.

Nuove deportazioni di Cristiani in genere, di Armeni in specie, dei superstiti appena rientrati in patria, nuovi massacri sono riportati da testimoni oculari e da lettere di fiducia.

Per cui mi son permesso tra gli altri ricorrere anche all'Alto Commissario Italiano rimettendogli la nota, di cui accludo copia. Da essa vedrà che i Kemalisti, non mettono distinzione veruna tra cattolici e non cattolici e proseguono il loro piano d'esterminio.

É da deplorare che la mala fede turca e le fallaci promesse ed assicurazioni, abbiano ora potuto neutralizzare le Potenze dell'Intesa, come durante la guerra vi avevano riuscito con la Germania e l'Austria. Mentre denunzio tale inumana impassibilità dei governi, prego V.E. di voler adoperarsi come meglio è possibile alla Santa Sede, per far prevalere la voce di giustizia , di pace e di pietà, presso chi di dovere.

Nell'angoscia e vivo dolore dei gravi casi deplorati ed in apprensione di più gravi minaccie, mentre imploro il pegno d'ogni consolazione la benedizione Apostolica dell'Augusto Padre della Cristianità intera, ho l'onore ecc

Allegata al doc. n° 113, p.392:

NOTA
sulla situazione degli Armeni nelle provincie

Si accertano le tristi notizie della ripresa dei massacri sistematici dei superstiti Armeni nelle provincie del dominio kemalistico.

A Artvin, nel Caucaso, che da quattro mesi in quà si trova nella zona d'invasione kemalistica, il Commando Turco nella prima metà di luglio ha intimato agli Armeni, per la maggior parte cattolici, di trasferirsi a Batum prendendo seco gli occorrenti beni mobili, senza poter alienare gli immobili, che dovrebbero restare al governo.

Su tale intimazione gli Artviniotti emigrano esposti a mille maltrattamenti e saccheggio durante il tragitto. In un primo convoglio composto di 100-120 persone, oltre la spogliazione di queste, viene con scelta premeditata separato ed ucciso il sacerdote novello Don Giuseppe Vartanian, protetto italiano, il quale dopo il corso degli studii superiori a Roma, ove aveva insegnato con lode in varii Istituti italiani, era destinato dai superiori maggiori a quella Missione di Artvin, ove si era recato un anno fa.

Dopo i fatti di Artvin, che interessavano in particolar modo questo patriarcato Armeno Cattolico, sopravvengono quelli di Merzifun, anche più gravi. dal 24 al 25 Giugno una banda turca scortate da Topal Osman di Ghirassonda, con lista in mano insegue gli Armeni; prima appicca fuoco al quartiere cristiano per obbligare a sortire dai loro domicilii gli abitanti e tutti quelli che furono fuori di casa vennero all'istante fucilati; dopo si passò a perquisire una ad una tutte le case e in tutti i loro nascondigli e quelli che furono ritrovati vennero strangolati. Sono da inorridire i particolari delle ignominie commesse contro le ragazze e donne giovani, le quali dopo essere sottomesse al disonore, sono state rinchiuse in massa in case e vi son state bruciate vive. Analoghi sono i fatti riportati per Havza ed i numerosi villaggi d'intorno, per Kavak e per Ciakalli sino a Samsun.

Topal Osman ha tentato per prima dar principio ai suoi misfatti da quest'ultima città, ma sembra per la prossimità a Costantinopoli e quindi per la facilità della divulgazione dei fatti, ha creduto più opportuno dar sfogo nell'interno del paese. Si dice pure che i maomettati di Samsun si siano opposti a quel ignobile carnefice, ma che tale opposizione sia stata una manovra per eludere i giudizi dell'opinione europea. Il fatto è che anche a Samsun tutti i cristiani individualmente sono registrati e numerati dalla gendarmeria turca e si stà in apprensione di una prossima deportazione e conseguente strage.

L'esterminio degli Armeni progettato dal Comitato giovane turco durante la guerra, eseguito sopra vasta scala da Talaat, Enver e compari, è ripreso oggi da

Kemal sui nostri superstiti innocui appena rientrati dal fatale esiglio. E se inallora il governo turco poté neutralizzare la Germania e l'Austria, incriminate per ciò quali complici dell'inumano progetto, dovremmo forse riguardare le Potenze, che combatterono per la liberazione dei piccoli popoli, impotenti oggi ad arrestare la prosecuzione del medesimo attentato di lesa umanità?

Pur riconoscendo la complicata situazione, il patriarcato Armeno Cattolico denunzia i fatti, previene di quanto minaccia ed implora efficace intervento ed interessamento di questo Alto Commissariato per salvare quanti ci restano. - Si raccomandano in particolar modo i Cattolici Armeni di Samsun, i quali con a capo il giovine Curato Don Gamsaragan e le due Religiose con le loro poche orfane, sono minacciati di morte insieme agli altri cristiani e si trovano già nell'elenco preparato dal governo kemalistico.

Quel sacerdote D. Giov. Gamsaragan, alunno anche esso della nostra Scuola Superiore Armena di Roma, tante volte beneficata dal Regio Governo Italiano, a cui rende servizii da non disprezzarsi nella propaganda della lingua, è anche esso novello che si è destinato a quella Missione circa da due anni in quà e posso assicurare che non è mai compromesso né implicato in affari e questioni politici, dedito soltanto al suo ministero. _ Le due Religiose, Suora Marta e Suora Eugenia sono rientrate anche esse due anni fa dai luoghi di esiglio, ove erano relegate nella deportazione del 1915 e sopravvivono alle 34 compagne esigliate insieme e massacrate dopo torture. Quindi una seconda deportazione di giovani suore, che già ne hanno traversato tutti gli orrori, equivarrebbe per esse la morte. L'Istituto così spento di quelle Suore è stato solo a sostenere l'insegnamento della lingua Italiana nelle sue scuole a Trebizonda.

Perciò si prega con istanza l'Alto Commissariato Italiano di voler adoperarsi come meglio può per salvare la vita ai cristiani in genere, ai cattolici in specie e più particolarmente al sullodato sacerdote e alle Religiose, insieme alle quattro o sei orfane da loro protette. Il Patriarcato Armeno Cattolico Sarebbe riconoscentissimo se si potesse farli venire quà.

Pera li 31 agosto 1921

[Translation]

Most Eminent Prince,

Contrary to the Kemalists' repeated assurances, given to the Holy See, of respecting the lives and assets of the Christians, sad news of pogroms come one after the other, and we return to the era of those deadly years of the world war.

New deportations of Christians in general, of Armenians in particular, of the survivors just re-entered into the country, new massacres are reported by eyewitnesses and by trustworthy letters.

Therefore, I permitted myself to, among other things, appeal to the Italian High Commissioner, entrusting to him the note of which I enclose a copy.

From it, you will see that the Kemalists do not draw any distinction between Catholics and non-Catholics and they persist in their plan of extermination.

It is deplorable that Turkish bad faith and their false promises and assurances have now been able to neutralize the Entente Powers, just as they had succeeded with Germany and Austria during the war. As I denounce such inhuman impassivity of the Governments, I pray that it please Y.E. to try as best as possible with the Holy See to see that the voice of justice, of peace and of mercy prevails with those concerned.

In anguish and keen distress for the serious, deplorable, events, and in apprehension of graver threats, while I beg the token of every consolation, the Apostolic blessing of the August Father of all Christianity, I have the honor etc

Attached to doc. n° 113, p. 392:

NOTE
on the situation of the Armenians in the provinces

The sad news is verified, of the resumption of systematic massacres of surviving Armenians in the provinces under Kemalist dominion.

In Artvin, in the Caucasus, which has been in the area of Kemalist invasion for the last four months, the Turkish Command in the first half of July ordered the Armenians, for the most part Catholics, to relocate to Batum taking with them the necessary personal property, without being able to transfer or convey their real estate, which would pass to the government.

Under such order, the Artvin residents emigrated, exposed to a thousand mistreatments and depredations during the journey. In an initial convoy composed of 100-120 persons, besides the dispossession of these, with premeditated choice came to be separated out and killed the new priest Don Giuseppe Vartanian, protected Italian, who, after attending secondary school in Rome, where he had then taught with honors in various Italian Institutes, was destined by the major superiors to that Mission in Artvin, where he had gone a year ago.

After events in Artvin, which particularly interested this Armenian Catholic patriarchate, those of Merzifon arose, even more serious. From the 24th to the 25th of June, a Turkish band escorted by Topal Osman of Giresun, with list in hand, pursued the Armenians; first they set fire to the Christian quarter to force the inhabitants to leave their homes, and all those that were outside were instantly shot; afterwards they went on to search all the houses and in all their hiding places one by one, and those who were found were strangled. The particulars are horrifying, of the ignominies committed against the girls and young women who, after being submitted to the dishonor, were shut up *en masse* into houses and were burned alive therein. Analogous are the facts reported for Havza and the numerous villages around it, for Kavak and for Sakalli all the way to Samsun.

Topal Osman tried first to initiate his misdeeds in this latter city, but it seems that, due to its proximity to Constantinople and therefore due to the ease with which news of the facts would spread, he believed it more opportune to unleash himself in the interior of the country. It is also said that the Mohammedans of Samsun opposed that ignoble executioner, but that such opposition had been a maneuver to elude the judgments of European opinion. The fact is that even in Samsun all the Christians are individually registered and numbered by the Turkish gendarmerie and there is apprehension of an upcoming deportation and consequent massacre.

The extermination of the Armenians planned by the Young Turk Committee during the war, executed on a vast scale by Talaat, Enver and companions, is taken up again today by Kemal upon our innocuous survivors just returned from fated exile. And if previously the Turkish government was able to neutralize Germany and Austria, incriminated insofar as complicit in the inhuman project, should we perhaps regard the Powers, that fought for the liberation of minority peoples, today impotent to arrest the continuation of the same crimes against humanity?

Though recognizing the complicated situation, the Armenian Catholic patriarchate denounces the facts, anticipates the degree of threat, and begs the effective intervention and involvement of this High Commission to save those remaining to us. We particularly recommend to you the Armenian Catholics of Samsun, who are headed up by the young Curate Don Gamsaragan and the two Nuns with their few orphans; they are threatened with death along with the other Christians and already find themselves on the list prepared by the Kemalist government.

That priest, D. Giov. Gamsaragan, also an alumnus of our Armenian High School in Rome, assisted so many times by the Royal Italian Government, to which it rendered valuable services in the propagation of the language, is also new; he was sent to that Mission about two years ago, and I can assure you that he was never compromised nor implicated in political affairs and questions, [but] devoted solely to his ministry. The two Nuns, Sister Marta and Sister Eugenia, also returned two years ago from places of exile where they were relegated in the deportation of 1915, and survived their 34 companions exiled together and massacred after torture. Therefore a second deportation of young sisters, who have already been through every horror, would be equivalent to death for them. The Institute of those Sisters, thus extinguished, was alone in sustaining the teaching of the Italian language in its schools in Trabizon.

Therefore the Italian High Commission is petitioned to try its utmost to save the lives of the Christians in general, of the Catholics in particular and most particularly of above-named priest and of the Nuns, together with the four or six orphans under their protection. The Armenian Catholic Patriarchate would be very grateful if it were possible to have them come here.

Pera, August 31st, 1921

115

27 [October 1921?] Constantinople – art. from the Armenian newspaper *Joghovurti Tsain* – AAEESS, *Asia* 117

Angora, 27 Gelaleddin Arif bey, deputato di Erzerum, nella seduta di ieri del grande Assemblea Nazionale, ha presentato il seguente disegno di legge col quale si vuol annullare i diritti ed i privilegi delle minoranze, che per la sua importanza e passata all'ordine del giorno.

A - I privilegi ed i diritti delle minoranze, acquisiti da parte delle minoranze in epoche diverse per Ordini (Firman) dei Sultani, sono annullate.

B - Le minoranze della Turchia, non potranno aver nessun diritto e privilegio, salvo quelli riconosciuti dal patto nazionale e quelli riconosciuti da trattati fra le potenze dell'Intesa e quelle Alleate.

C - L'esecuzione della legge presente si affida alla Grande Assemblea Nazionale.

[Translation]

Angora, 27th Gelaleddin Arif Bey, representative of Erzerum, in yesterday's session of the Grand National Assembly presented the following legislation which would annul the rights and the privileges of the minorities; due to its importance it became the order of the day.

A - The privileges and the rights of the minorities, acquired on the part of the minorities in different periods by Orders (*Firman*) of the Sultans, are annulled.

B - The minorities of Turkey shall not have any right or privilege, save those recognized by the national pact and those recognized by treaties between the powers of the Entente and those of the Allies.

C - The execution of the current law is entrusted to the Grand National Assembly.

Un des membres de l'Assemblée Nationaliste turque d'Angora vient de présenter un projet de loi portant abolition de tous les Firmans octroyés, pendant plus de cinq siècles, aux patriarches (Chefs religieux) des diverses Communautés Chrétiennes de l'Empire Ottoman.

Or ces Firmans confèrent aux patriarches un droit de juridiction pour le réglement de toutes les affaires concernant le statut personnel de leurs ouailles.

Et il ne s'agit pas là d'un privilège, comme le prétendent à tort les jeunes turcs.

En matière de statut personnel, les principes et les règles du droit musulman sont en contradiction absolue avec les principes et les règles des peuples chrétiens. C'est en raison de cette incompatibilité de lois et de moers que les Sultan avaient reconnu la nécessité d'une juridiction spéciale aux chrétiens. Et c'est la même raison qui oblige le gouvernement Français à accorder un droit de juridiction analogue aux chefs religieux des musulmans d'Algerie. Le Chéri (droit coranique) admet la bigamie, la répudiation; il reconnaît comme légitimes les enfants nés d'une concubine etc...Les juges musulmans ne connaissent pas et ne peuvent pas appliquer d'autres lois. A moins de vouloir saper e détruire les bases de la famille chrétienne il serait impossible de laisser à ces juges le pouvoir de régler les questions de validité de mariage, de filiation, de séparation, de divorce.

C'est ce que les jeunes turcs ont essayé de faire pendant la guerre. C'est dans le même esprit et afin de provoquer la dissolution de la famille et mettre le désordre dans la société chrétienne que le projet de loi en question vient d'être déposer sur le bureau de l'Assemblée d'Angora.

Et veut-on savoir à quelle occasion cette proposition de loi a été faite?

Ce fut au moment de la discussion par l'Assemblée d'Angora de l'accord signé le 20 0ctobre 1921 par M. Franklin-Bouillon au nom de la France - "Puisque l'Art. 6 de l'accord Franco-Turc suffira désormais à assurer les droits des minorités, disait l'auteur du projet, les Firmans n'ont plus raison d'être!"

D'après l'Art. 6 de l'accord les chrétiens ne jouiront en Cilicie que des droits reconnus, par traité, aux minorités de certains pays, comme la Pologne, la Roumanie..., c'est-à-dire égalité de droits civils et politiques, liberté de culte, usage de la langue nationale, entretien d'écoles. Mais la Pologne et la Roumanie sont des Etats Européens dans lesquelles les minorités étnhiques ont les mêmes moers et coutumes sociales que la race dominante. Les dispositions internationales qui les concernent n'ont pas prévu la nécessité (qui s'impose en pays musulman) d'un statut personnel spécial et d'une juridiction particulière aux chrétiens.

Vouloir remplacer les anciens Firmans par des garanties aussi incomplètes (garanties qui sont d'ailleurs inscrites dans les lois fondamentales de la Turquie) ce n'est rien moins qu'une supercherie, comme tant d'autres dont les jeunes turcs sont coutumiers).

En ces matières le Traité de Sèvres doit être entièrement maintenu se l'on veut que les sociétés chrétiennes puissent exister en Turquie.

Une autre condition sine qua non del la vie et de la sécurité de ces communautés ainsi que du maintien de la paix en orient, c'est la constitution d'une gendarmerie mixte telle que le prévoit le dit Traité de Sèvres. Après les massacres affreux perpétrés pendant la grande guerre, après le conflit gréco-tuic et aussi après les encouragements donnés aux chrétiens depuis l'armistice, les haines, l'exaspération, l'esprit de révolte et le sentiment de peur sont devenus trop violents de part et d'autre. Une cohabitation n'est plus possible entre musulmans et chrétiens sans une intervention organisée, permanente et effective de la part des Alliés.

Il y va non seulement de l'exsistance des chrétiens obligés de vivre en Turquie mais de l'intérêt bien entendu des turcs eux-mêmes, de la stabilité de leur Gouvernement et, par conséquent - on ne saurait trop le répéter - du repos et de la paix en Europe.

116

10 November 1921 – Memorandum for Mons. Pizzardo (Substitute Sec. of State) – CO, 106, 3, 5, 2, n° 5278

Mons. N. Gabriele Moriondo, attualmente Visitatore Apostolico del Caucaso dall'aprile u.s. ha lasciato Tiflis in occasione dell'occupazione bolscevica della Georgia e si è recato a Costantinopoli in attesa di disposizioni da parte della S. Sede.

Egli, sia a voce per mezzo del suo segretario venuto in Roma, sia con lettera privata ha fatto sapere alla S.C. per la Chiesa Orientale che non intende di ritornare nel Caucaso e attende invece un'altra destinazione dalla S. Sede.

Attesa tale disposizione di animo di Mons. Moriondo, Mons. Papadopulos crederebbe opportuno appagare la lunga attesa di quel Prelato, ordinando che la S.C. per la Chiesa Orientale annunzi alla S.C. Concistoriale che potrà disporre di Mons. Moriondo per una Diocesi d'Italia a lui conveniente.

Tale decisione sembrerebbe poi urgente

1° perché la S.C. per la Chiesa Orientale non può lasciare a lungo oltre 50000 cattolici di diverso rito senza un capo che abbia cura del clero e del popolo che invoca assistenza dalla S. Sede trovandosi esposto a dure prove.

2° perché essendosi sparsa la voce che Mons. Moriondo è rimasto a Costantinopoli per succedere a Mons. Dolci parrebbe opportuno procedere al trasferimento di Mons. Moriondo prima che abbia luogo la nomina di un nuovo Delegato

[Translation]

Mons. N. Gabriele Moriondo, currently Visitor Apostolic to the Caucasus since this past April, has left Tiflis in occasion of the Bolshevik occupation of Georgia and has gone to Constantinople awaiting orders on the part of the Holy See.

He, both verbally by way of his secretary come to Rome and by private letter, has made known to the S.C. for the Oriental Church that he does not intend to return to the Caucasus and instead attends another destination from the Holy See.

Expecting such a state of mind from Mons. Moriondo, Mons. Papadopulos would believe it opportune to satisfy the long expectation of that Prelate, ordering that the S.C. for the Oriental Church announce to the S.C.

Consistorial that it may make available to Mons. Moriondo an Italian Diocese convenient to him.

Such a decision would thus seem urgent

1º because the S.C. for the Oriental Church cannot leave more than 50,000 Catholics of different rites for long without a leader to take care of the clergy and of the people who beg assistance from the Holy See, finding themselves exposed to difficult trials.

2º because, the rumor having been spread that Mons. Moriondo has remained in Constantinople to succeed Mons. Dolci, it would appear opportune to proceed to Mons. Moriondo's transfer before the nomination of a new Delegate takes place

117

27 November 1921, Rome – handwritten letter from Tchobanian to Gasparri
– AAEESS, *Asia* 117, nº [?]

Eminence,

Monseigneur Giannini, que j'ai eu l'honneur de connaître à Beyrouth, vous avait annoncé mon passage à Rome lors de mon retour à Paris et la démarche que je devais faire auprès de votre Eminence au sujet des chrétiens de Cilicie. A mon grand degret, je n'ai pu réaliser ce projet, que j'avais pourtant à coeur; les circostances m'ont obligé de rentrer directement à Paris, au lieu de passer par Constantinople a Rome. Je prie Votre Eminence de vouloir bien m'en excuser.

Je sais, du reste, que Mgr. Giannini, qui défend avec toute la noblesse de son grand coeur et toute la vigueur de son esprit élevé la cause douloureuse et sacré des chrétiens d'orient, et qui m'a accordé un si généreux et cordial appui dans ma mission à Beyrouth, a exposé mieux que je ne saurais le faire, dans ses rapports adressés au Saint-Siêge, la situation précaire des chrétiens de Cilicie et les graves périls qui les menaceraient au cas où les troupes françaises évacueraient cette contrée. Je sais que S. S. le Souverain Pontife a fait tout ce qui était en son pouvoir pour conjurer ce désastre, pour faire ajourner l'évacuation; je connais la haute et magnanime sollicitude que Sa Sainteté a témoigné à l'Arménie et à sa cause nationale, pendant la guerre et depuis l'armistice; tous les arméniens de Cilicie, et du monde entier, le savent et lui en sont profondément reconnaissants, de même que nos compatriotes qui se trouvent sous le joug du gouvernement kemaliste, dans les provinces de Kharpout et de Sivas, ou à Marache et Ourfa, savent que si les malheureuses conditions d'esclaves auxquelles ils étaient exposés se sont à un moment donné un peu adoucis, ils le doivent avant tout à l'intervention du Sa Sainteté. Cette gratitude de mes compatriotes de Cilicie et de tout le Levant, je regrette de n'avoir pu venir l'exsprimer par votre entremise à Sa Sainteté. M. Diran Bey Noradounghian, conseiller de la Délégation Nationale Arménienne, fils du

Président de la Délégation, se rendra dans quelques jours à Rome pour remplir ce devoir au nom de la Délégation et au nom de toute notre nation.

Il vous exposera la terrible situation où se trouvent les christians de Cilicie depuis la conclusion de l'accord franco-kémaliste et adressera au Saint-Siège un appel suprême en faveur de ces malheureux.

Nous avons déjà eu l'honneur de faire connaître à Son Excellence Mgr. Cerretti les plus récents informations, si alarmantes, que nous avons reçues de là-bas, et nous l'avons prié de vouloir bien les transmettre au Saint-Siège, ainsi que la substance de la requête que la Délégation a adressée au gouvernement français à la suite de la conclusion de l'accord d'Angora. Mgr. Cerretti nous a dit que le Saint Père avait déjà fait le possible et qu'à présent, après la signature de l'accord il était difficile d'intervenir et d'obtenir une modification de ces arrangements. Nous reconnaissons la justesse et la délicatesse de cette remarque, que Mgr. Cerretti a faite du reste avec une évidente tristesse, mais nous pensons, ainsi que nous le lui avons dit, que les intérêts supérieurs et l'existence même de la chrétienté et de la civilisation étant menacés par l'état de choses que résultera da l'application rapide et littérale de l'accord, le Souverain Pontife pourrait, sans choquer aucune susceptibilité, élever sa voix paternelle pour montrer le péril et conseiller une généreuse prudence. Les populations chrétiennes, affolées, avant même qu'on ait commencé l'évacuation, demandent aux Puissances d'envoyer des transports pour leur donner la possibilité de quitter le pays; abandonnant leurs biens, leurs terres, leurs trésors, ces malheureux veulent se jeter n'importe où, pour être loin des bourreaux turcs dont le retour les épouvante, préférant la ruine, les privations, la mort par la misère et les épidémies aux massacres atroces et aux déportations qui sont inévitables.

D'ailleurs, même si la crainte des massacres n'était pas fondée, la pensée seule de retomber sous la domination de ceux qui ont fait périr avec des procédés d'une barbarie préhistorique un million de nos compatriotes, rend la vie impossible, après le retrait des troupes françaises, à ces infortunés débris des déportations, qui, ayant survécu par miracle, groupés en Cilicie par les soins même du gouvernement français, s'étaient cru définitivement libérés du cauchemar turc.

La France qui a assumé de si grands sacrifices, pendant la guerre, pour la cause de la liberté, a été amenée à cette douloureuse décision par suite, avant tout, de la crise financière dont elle souffre. Nous savons que la France - et nous bien en sommes reconnaissants - a subi depuis l'armistice d'importantes pertes en hommes et en argent pour protéger les chrétiens de Cilicie; elle déclare ne plus pouvoir supporter cette charge. Nous en sommes navrés, car la tutelle français sur la Cilicie était le voeu le plus cher des populations chrétiennes et même de tous les musulmans modérés. Ce qui redouble notre douleur, c'est que ce départ ait été décidé sans que des garanties réelles soient obtenues pour la sécurité des chrétiens. La promesse du gouvernement d'Angora de respecter les droits des minorités est la seule garantie qui figure dans l'accord, et cette garantie n'en est pas une.

Ce qui, en outre, nous rend profondement pénible cette évacuation de la Cilicie, c'est qu'elle a lieu avant la réalisation du Foyer national arménien, dont la constitution a été décidée en mars dernier par le Conseil suprême et dont l'Assemblée générale de la Société des Nations a consacré encore une fois le principe par une motion votée à l'unanimité. Si l'évacuation avait eu lieu après la fondation de ce Foyer, nous aurions pu transférer dans ce refuge national de notre race nos frères et soeurs de Cilicie. Ce désastre arrive à un moment où l'Arménie transcaucasienne se trouve sous le joug des bolchéviks, l'Arménie turque est aux mains des kémalistes, et pas un pouce de terre arménienne n'exsiste où notre race puisse trouver cette sécurité et cette liberté dont ses immenses sacrifices et sa vaillante conduite pendant la guerre l'ont rendue digne et que tous les gouvernements alliés lui ont solennellement promises.

Ce que nous sollicitons maintenant du gouvernement français, est une chose bien modeste, bien raisonnable et modérée, c'est de vouloir bien avoir la chevaleresque bonté d'ajourner l'évacuation au moins pour quelques mois (l'exode de cette masse de pauvres êtres en plein hiver serait si pénible). Les alliés vont bientôt se réunir leur Conseil suprême pour régler les problèmes d'orient dans leur ensemble; ils donneront aussi, nous en avons le ferme espoir, - car supposer le contraire serait déshonorer l'humanité, - un solution équitable au problème de la libération du peuple arménien. Nous supplions le gouvernement français d'assumer un dernier sacrifice, d'ajourner l'évacuation jusqu'au réglement total de la question d'orient.

Les démarches que nous avons faites auprès d'éminentes personnalités françaises ont été favourablement acouillies, et nous avons l'impression que cette cause n'est pas perdue, que le grand coeur du peuple français s'apercevant du péril qu'il ne voyait pas au premier moment, ne restera pas sourd à l'appel des chrétiens de Cilicie et voudra faire le noble geste que nous demandons, si une grande voix s'élève pour l'encourager dans cette voie et pour inviter les alliés à aider la France dans cette lourde tâche.

C'est bien le manque d'une concorde absolue, d'une entente étroite et d'une action commune des alliés à l'égard du problème turc, qui a créé cette douloureuse et dangereuse situation en Orient. Jamais la chrétienté n'avait été aussi profondément humiliée devant l'Islam coalisé et menaçant, que dans les conjonctures présentes. Et si les kémalistes, après un retrait prématuré des troupe françaises, rentrat en Cilicie en vaiqueurs et voient ceux qui hier, à l'heure de la victoire, declaraient que les peuples chrétiens ne seraient plus placés sous la domination turque, abandonner à leurs bourreaux les populations chrétiennes, leur arrogance, leur fanatisme, leur mégalomanie panislamique prendront de telles proportions, qu'il ne sera plus possible aux chrétiens d'Orient ou d'Occident, de vivre dans l'Empire Ottoman. Votre Eminence doit savoir que les Jésuites eux-mêmes sont décidés à transférer en Syrie leurs établissements de Cilicie, si les troupes françaises évacuerent ce pays.

L'union entre les trois grandes nation alliés qui sont à la tête de la chrétienté et de la civilisation avec l'aide amicale de l'Amérique, pourrait facilement mettre un frein à ce débordement de l'orgueil et de la fureur panislamiques et conjurer le péril qui menace l'existence de la chrétienté en orient et compromet son prestige dans le monde entier.

Qui peut, avec plus d'autorité et avec une plus sereine et majestueuse éloquence, adresser aux alliés cet appel à l'Union devant le danger qui les menace tous, sinon Celui qui est la plus grande voix de la chrétienté? Nous nous adressons à cette haute et noble puissance spirituelle, du fond de notre détresse, et nous l'adjurons d'exercer son action conciliatrice sur les alliés, afin que s'élevant au dessus des rivalités qu'engendrent des intérêts matériels secondaires, ils voient la communauté de leurs intérêts essentiels et de leurs devoirs sacrés, et que par une entente fraternelle ils sauvent l'honneur de la civilisation.

Si ces quelques lignes d'un modeste poète d'Arménie paraissent à votre Eminence dignes d'être présentées à Sa Sainteté, je vous serais reconnaissant d'attirer sur elles la haute attention du Saint Père.

Je me permets de vous envoyer, avec cette lettre, un exemplaire de mon ouvrage *La Roseraie d'Arménie* que je dédie à Sa Sainteté comme un humble hommage de gratitude et de respectueuse admiration, et je prends la liberté d'offrir à votre eminence quelques-uns de mes ouvrages en témoignage de reconnaissance, car je sais la part si importante que votre Eminence a cordialment prise à l'action du Saint-Siège, durant toute cette grande crise, en faveur du chrétiens d'Orient.

Veuilles agréer, ecc

118

28 November 1921, Paris – G. Noradounghian to Gasparri – AAEESS, *Asia* 117, n° 26036 A.E.

Eminence,

J'ai l'honneur de porte à votre haute connaissance que le Délégation Nationale Arménienne a chargé M. Diran Noradounghian, Conseiller de cette Délégation, ancien premier Secrétaire d'Ambassade, de se rendre à Rome déposer au pied du Trône Pontifical les hommages respectueux et l'expression émue des sentiments de reconnaissance de la Nation Arménienne pour toutes les bontés témoignées à son égard par Sa Sainteté et exposer la situation présente des chrétiens en Orient.

La Delegation Nationale Arménienne aime à penser qu'il plaira à Votre Eminence de réserver à son représentant un bienveillant accueil et qu'Elle daignera lui témoigner Sa haute confiance durant la mission dont il est chargé.

Je vous prie, Eminence, de vouloir bien agréer les assurances de ma plus haute et respectueuse considération et de mon profond dévouement.
[Signed] Le Président G. Noradounghian
Allegato al doc. n° 118
Proposta del Signor Noradounghian
da firmare dai deputati e senatori delle Potenze

[*Attachment* to doc. n° 118
Proposal of Mr. Noradounghian
to be signed by the representatives and senators of the Powers][286]

Nous soussignés, profitant de cette reunion du Conseil Suprême qui a pour but de restaurer la paix en Orient, venons d'un même coeur, unis devant cette sainte cause de la paix comme nos enfant l'ont été dans la mort, prier respectueusement le Conseil d'ecouter notre voix qui se permet de lancer cet appel afin que soit toujours plus reyonnante la splendeur du Droit et plus haute la dignité de la Justice.

C'est l'heure de prouver que les peuples libres savent faire régner le Droit! Comment répondrait-on de l'avenir si une réunion de représentants de nations victorieuses ne tenait pas les premesses solennelles faites par leurs Gouvernements et laissait commettre quelque chose d'injuste!

Il s'agit de l'exécution d'engagements formels qui à maintes reprises ont été faites par les Puissances, membres du Conseil Suprême, à leurs alliés, les Arméniens, fils de la doyenne des nations, de libérer leur patrie du joug turc, leur patrie qui fut l'avant garde de la civilisation, héritiére légitime de l'humanisme antique, et qui s'est montrée cette fois-ci encore fidèle à son passé.

L'Arménie a été la symbole et la synthèse de toutes les horreurs de la guerre.

En automne 1914, les turcs envoyèrent des émissaires au Congrès national des Arméniens siégeant à Erzeroum et lui firent la promesse d'accorder l'autonomie à l'Arménie, si les Arméniens s'engageaient à aider activement la Turquie durant la guerre. A cause du courageux refus des Arméniens ceux-ci ont été systématiquement massacrés en 1915 et 1916 par le Gouvernement jeune-turc. "Les deux tiers de la population 700.000 hommes, femmes, enfants ont été exterminés par les méthodes les plus infernales et avec sang

---

[286] Published, together with the names of the Italian senators who were signatories (Luzzatti, Boselli, Scialoja, Torigiani, Arsour, Aortis, Verraris, Wollemberg, Rava, Lorta, Tassoni) and of Orlando, by Naslian, *op. cit.*, vol. II, pp. 946-948.

froid", dit le 3 octobre 1918 dans sa lettre au Vicmte Bryce, le Secrétaire adjoint aux Affaires Etrangères Anglais.

De même les arméniens de Russie firent la sourde oreille aux tentatives des chefs tatars et autres de se joindre à eux dans une révolte contre la Russie au moment de la déclaration de guerre. Plus de 200.000 arméniens combattaient dans l'armée russe. Après l'écroulement de cette Armée (fin 1917) de nombreux volontaires arméniens se chargèrent de la défense du front du Caucase et retardèrent pendant de longs mois l'avance des Turcs rendant ainsi un signalé service à l'armée britannique de Mésopotamie.

Enfin, la France forma, d'accord avec la Délégation Nationale Arménienne de Paris une légion de volontaires arméniens appelée plus tard "Legion arménienne" qui sous les ordres des officiers français prit part à la campagne de Palestine et merita pour sa bravoure et sa résistance les hommages du Commandant français et du Maréchal Lord Allenby, le Commandant en Chef.

A l'armistice les autorités alliées transportèrent en Cilicie les réfugiés arméniens d'Egypte, de Palestine, ainsi qu'un grand nombre de déportés qui se trouvaient dans les déserts de Syrie. Près de 180.000 arméniens s'établirent ainsi en Cilicie et vécurent confiant sous la pretection française sur cette terre, dite petite Arménie, si longtemps captive dont les alliés venaient de briser les liens.

Le 10 Août 1920, l'Arménie était admise au traité de Sèvres comme signataire et l'art. 88 de ce traité déclarait "l'Arménie un Etat libre et indépendant" les frontières de cet état étant laissés à l'arbitrage du Président Wilson.

Depuis la signature du traité de Sèvres, la République Arménienne a été attaquée par les troupes kémaliste qui lui ont enlevé plusieurs territoires (Kars, etc.). D'autre part les Bolcheviks occupèrent le pays. Aucun territoire de l'Arménie turque ne put non plus être liberé.

La victoire finale de l'Entente n'a donc pas apporté aux arméniens la délivrance promise, et alliés fidèles, ceux-ci ne purent recueillir ce qui leur était dû!

Devant cet etat de choses, le Conseil Suprème réuni à Londre en mars 1921 décida la création en Arménie turque d'un foyer national arménien dont les frontières seraient délimitées par une Commission nommée par la Société des Nations, et en Septembre dernier l'Assemblée de la Société des Nations, par un vote unanime, opina également pour la création de ce "home" national arménien.

Un nouveau malheur attendait les Arméniens établis en Cilicie depuis trois ans. Par l'accord Franco-Kémaliste, la France évacuait cette province et remettait aux Kémalistes même la partie qui en vertu du traité de Sèvres devait rester sous mandant français.

On se représente l'angoisse terrible de ces malheureux chrétiens qui, au nombre de près de 250.000, ne pouvant se soumettre de nouveau à un joug qui a été si féroce et si barbare, fuient en masse, sans savoir même où pouvoir se rendre, devant l'imminence de la plus inquiétante des probabilités.

On se rend compte qu'il y a eu dans la tragedie arménienne des alternatives, des rémissions courtes et à peine sensibles, des recrudescences, les plus grande espoirs, suivis des plus lourdes déceptions! Et pourtant rien n'a pu ébranler ce peuple antique parce qu'il a toujours gardé cette force d'âme que Mirabeau appellait le "fanatisme de l'espérance" et qu'une foi invincible l'a soutenu, la foi dans sa destinée!

Certes si nous n'ignorons point que les nations vraiment dignes de s'appartenir arrivent à l'indépendance à travers le martyre nous savons aussi que la civilisation nous a enseigné le respect de la liberté individuelle, la fidélité à la parole donnée, la défense des opprimés, toutes sortes de disciplines morales d'où résulte l'éminente dignité du genre humain.

Aussi souhaitons nous, avec toute la ferveur de nos sentiments envers l'Arménie, qu'au milieu des redoutables inconnues actuelles il existe au moins une certitude: que le Conseil Suprème libère cette terre d'Orient dont le destin de ses habitants chrétiens a été une honte pour toute la Civilisation et que les larmes- et peut-être le sang- que versent encore en ce moment les Arméniens, coulent pour la dernière fois!

L'Humanité, la Justice, le Droit, interessés à cette sainte cause, attendent du Conseil Suprème l'inéluctable liberation de l'Arménie de Turquie.

119

3 March 1922, Rome – Agagianian to Papadopulos – CO, 106, 3, 5, 2, n° 7439

A Sua Eccellenza Illma Revma Mons. Isaia Papadopoulos,
Vescovo di Grazianopoli, Assessore della S. Congregazione
"Pro Ecclesia Orientali"
Eccellenza Reverendissima,

Spinto oltreché da un intimo affetto del cuore, dalle lettere anche continue ed insistenti dei nostri indimenticabili sacerdoti della Missione Armeno-cattolica del Caucaso, - i quali si lamentano dello stato quasi d'abbandono in cui sono lasciati essi e la Missione, mentre i protestanti coll'oro e col pane si impiantano su larga scala nelle città e villaggi aprendo oltre gli orfanotrofi etc, numerose *cappelle* e così si approfittano dello sfascelo della Chiesa scismatica per guadagnare nuovi proseliti - mi prendo la libertà di ripetere quanto scrissi a V. Eccellenza ultimamente, pregandoLa vivamente perché voglia benignamente prendere dei provvedimenti quanto prima, se non si vuol correre il pericolo di perdere quel poco che è rimasto ed il molto che si può fare.

1) È necessario, senza più oltre differire, dare un Capo responsabile a questa Missione.

2) Giacché c'è una grande mancanza di sacerdoti per la cura d'anime, conviene domandare alle nostre Congregazioni Religiose che destinino due o tre Missionari per colmare i vuoti colà prodotti.I Sacerdoti specialmente originari del Caucaso ci vanno con entusiasmo per salvare ed assistere i loro fratelli in mezzo a tante sofferenze.

3) La presenza di un Delegato Apostolico nel Caucaso, nelle condizioni presenti, è il più ed il meglio che si possa fare per l'incoraggiamento dei Cattolici d'ogni rito e per studio da vicino di opera di propaganda cattolica nel Caucaso e per esso nella Russia. Esso sarebbe rispettato anche dai Bolscevichi e da qualunque Governo, perché Rappresentante del Papa, di cui ormai è immensa la venerazione anche fra gli eterodossi, e perché sarà simbolo vivente della carità inesausta della S.Sede verso i derelitti ed orfani.

4) Il Signor Gregorio Evanguloff, Commissario per l'Istruzione del Governo di Erivan, in un incontro coi nostri Sacerdoti a Tiflis, ha detto "vengano pure loro, noi li aiuteremo in tutto quel che possiamo".

Mentre m'apresso al bacio del S. Anello, nutro ferma fiducia che V. Eccellenza non mancherà di prendere la più favorevole e sollecita cura del sovraesposto, e mi dichiaro ecc

firmato : Sac. Francesco L. Agagianian - V. Rettore del Collegio Armeno

[Translation]

To His Excellency Most Illus. Most Rev. Mons. Isaia Papadopoulos,
Bishop of Gratianopolis, Assessor of the S. Congregation
for the Oriental Church
Most Rev. Excellency,

Prompted as much by an intimate, heartfelt affection as by the continuous and insistent letters from our unforgettable priests of the Armenian-Catholic Mission of the Caucasus—who complain of the state of near-abandonment in which they and the Mission are left while the Protestants with gold and with bread are setting themselves up on a grand scale in the cities and villages, opening, beyond orphanages, etc., numerous *chapels* and so they profit from the ruin of the schismatic Church to win new proselytes—I take the liberty of repeating what I wrote to Y. Excellency recently, strongly requesting that measures would please be taken as soon as possible, if the risk is not to be run of losing the little that remains and the much that can be done.

1) It is necessary, without further delay, to give this Mission a responsible Leader.

2) Seeing as there is a great dearth of priests to tend to souls, it would be advisable to ask our Religious Congregations that they destine two or three Missionaries to fill in the voids produced there. The Priests, especially those originally from the Caucasus, go there with enthusiasm to save and assist their brothers in the midst of so much suffering.

3) The presence of an Apostolic Delegate in the Caucasus, under current conditions, is the most and the best that can be done in order to encourage Catholics of every rite, and to study close at hand the work of Catholic propaganda in the Caucasus and, through him, in Russia. He would be respected even by the Bolsheviks and by any Government whatsoever, being Representative of the Pope, of whom the veneration is immense even among the heterodox, and because he will be a living symbol of the inexhaustible charity of the Holy See towards orphans and the destitute.

4) Mister Gregorio Evangouloff, Education Commissioner of the Government of Erevan,[287] in a meeting with our Priests in Tiflis, said "send them along; we will help them in any way that we can."

As I approach to kiss the Holy Ring, I harbor the unswerving faith that Y. Excellency shall not fail to take the most favorable and solicitous care of the above, and I declare myself etc.

signed: F. Francesco L. Agagianian - Vice Rector of the Armenian College

120

13 May 1922, Smyrna – open letter from Krouzian to Pope Pius XI – AAEESS, *Asia* 117

Lettre ouverte éditée dans le journal arménien "Arevelian Mamoul" du 13 Mai 1922 N° 2854 e adressée:

A Sa Sainteté Pie XI.

Souverain Pontife de l'Eglise Catholique et Apostolique Romaine

Très Saint Père,

Le fait d'avoir pris, moi, un simple particulier, la liberté de me prosterner aux pieds de votre Sainteté, est le résultat de cette ferme conviction que les dignitaires suprême de Dieu, dépositaire des vertus divines du Maître, veulent bien condescendre à prêter leurs oreilles aux doléances et aux supplications des humbles et des malheureux. Et quoique je ne puisse pas prétendre à être reconnu pour le jeune Samuel, j'ose quand même porter un message de l'Eternel au Grand Prêtre Heli. I Samuel. III.

Je suis un arménien à qui fut imparti le rôle douleureux d'être le témoin oculaire et la victime des atrocités inouïes, que l'imagination turque a su inventer pour anéantir la chrétienté de l'Orient Moyen.

Je fus le scribe endolori des femmes et de jeunes filles bestialement outragées par les Turcs, et j'ai enrégistré le martyre des millions d'enfants innocents et de jeunes hommes.

Une force providentielle nous soutenait pourtant, nous, les survivants de ces hécatombes, dans toutes nos épreuves; car nous nous nourrissions de l'espoir de la victoire finale de la justice. Cette force provenait de notre

---

287 V. note 251.

espérance séculaire et de notre confiance en les Puissances, aux côtés des quelles nous nous étions rangés avec nos légion de braves. Et Arara uni à l'Ararat, sanctifiés par nos drapeaux teints de notre sang, saluèrent allégrement l'aube de la justice victorieuse.

La politique, pourtant, qui ne connait ni honneur et ni probité, qui ne sait respecter ni la parole donnée et ni la sainteté de l'engagement pris, a nié tout cela; elle a trahi et livré à l'ennemi irréconciliable de la chrétienté les anciens peuples martyrs de l'Orient.

La France a oublié, la première, les anciens et les nouveaux sacrifices des Arméniens et leurs dévouement sans borne. La France fut la Première à s'unir des liens d'amitié aux ennemis de Jésus-Christ, en transgressant les terribles commandements divins, répétes des centaines de fois dans les Ecritures Saintes. Deutéronome VII…

Nous avons porté nos plaintes devant le Trône de Seigneur contre ces iniquités des hommes d'Etat de la France, et nous ne doutons point du chatiment qui les attend. Nous ne voudrions pas, certes, le souhaiter; mais nous ne doutons non plus que les turcs "seront" pour eux "un aigillon dans leurs côtes et des épines dans leurs yeux". Josué XXIII, 13, jusqu'à ce qu'ils retournent à l'Eglise contre la quelle ils se sont révoltés, à l'hierarchie qu'ils ont méconnue et à la justice de la gloire de la quelle ils se sont dépouillés.

Il est bien regrettable et doublement désespérant pour nous de constater que l'Italie aussi ait mis son sceptre victorieux sous les pieds de l'Antichrist, qui a écrasé des millions des fils du Saiveur sous ses dents; elle s'humilie devant la Bête condamnée. Daniel VII.7. Elle pactise avec les infidels pour s'assurer des intérêts matériels à Van, à Bitlis et à Erzroum, qui sont les patrimoines des orphelins et des veuves. Ne ce sont pas les villes qui devraient revenir, conformément à la décision consacrée par l'assentiment même de l'Italie, aux Arméniens qui, tout en étant les propriétaires d'un lot plus grand encore, les ont achetés plusiers fois de leur sang?

Toutes les sources d'intérêts économiques sont-elles taries pour l'Italie pour qu'elle songe à convoiter l'Arménie et qu'elle la recoive de la main de l'usurpateur?

L'Italie, qui est un pays religieux à un si haut degré et un pays croyant par excellence, ne peut elle pas voir, même sous la clarté rayonnante du Vatican, le message de Dieu? "Malheur à ceux qui décrettent des décrets d'iniquités, et qui écrivent pour ordonner la violence; pour refuser justice aux pauvres, et pour ravir le froit aux malheureux de mon peuple; pour faire des veuves leurs butins, et pour piller les orphelins". Esaie X. 1_2." Ne parle point aux oreilles d'un insensé… ne déplace pas la borne ancienne, et n'entre point dans les champs des orphelins". Proverbes XXIII. 9-10. Combien de conseils et de principes dogmatiques des Saints Pères de l'Eglise et combien d'expériences de la vie quotidienne viennent confirmer ces lois inouables et éternelles!

Nous espérions, avec beaucoup de raison, que l'Italie, en notre qualité de frères déshérités, d'alliés et de compagnons d'armes, aurait pris la défense de notre sainte cause. Mais, helas! elle aussi a suivi le pas de sa soeur cadette dans le chemin de perdition et elle a suspendu sa couronne de laurier de la corne brisée du Vaincu, et elle exigent maintenant, toutes les deux, que les épaves des peuples chrétiens martyrisés soient livrées à leurs bourreaux, qui sont aussi infidéles à leur propre religion qu'ils sont ennemis de l'Evangile, et, par conséquent, féroces, sauvages et sanguinaires.

Nous n'attendons donc rien, très Saint Père, de leur politique dépourvue de sens moral et des spéculateurs matérialistes de nos malheur; ceux-ci sont ou des apostats avérés ou de ceux "qui dévorent les maisons des veuves, en affectant de faire de longues prières". Saint Luc XX. 47. Nous sommes les victimes de la chrétienté. Notre juge est Jesus-Christ Lui-même et notre protectrice Sa Sainte Eglise, et, pour cette raison, nous faisons appel, en la sainte personne de Son Souverain Pontife, à la conscience du monde entier chrétien.

Je ne suis qu'une pauvre épave sauvée du naufrage de l'Arménie et, le coeur navré, je m'adresse, en qualité du plus humble serviteur des serviteurs de Dieu, au monde chrétien, comme un vil métal qui fait réveiller les esprits alourdis par les préoccupations de la vie matérielle, comme une matière sans valeur quelconque qui fait retentir dans leurs coeurs la parole divine: "Faites droit et justice; délivrez l'oprimé de la main de l'opresseur". Jérémie XXII.8.

"Tes princes sont des rebelles et des compagnons de voleurs; tous ils aiment les présents et courent après les récompenses; ils ne font pas droit à l'orphelin, et la cause de la veuve ne vient pas jusqu'à eux"Esaie I.23...

"Ils sont engraissés...ils ne jugent pas la cause, la cause de l'orphelin..."Jérémie V. 28.

O Souverain Pontife! voila que nos ennemis farouches ont décidé d'anéantir complètement la chrétienté de l'Asie Mineure, conformément aux Psaumes 83.1-9. et d'en exterminer les survivants.

Les coupoles superbement élancées des basiliques de Saint Pierre et de Saint Paul sont elles écroulées comme les églises réduites en monceaux de ruines de l'Arménie, et l'amour chrétien, l'ascendant moral, la compassion et l'émulation sont ils devenues des cendres en même temps que nos gaies maisons patriarcales?

Nous connaissons tous, très Saint Père, vos pleurs et votre deuil tant sur nous: victimes sans soutiens, que sur les chevaliers sans coeurs. Mais vous avez plus que les pleurs. Vous avez vos conseils et remontrances pontificaux, vous avez vos ordonnances et commandements. E si ceux-ci restent impuissants à secouer le monde pour sauver le troupeau torturé et sanctifié, vous pourriez alors sortir à la porte du temple et crier: "Maudit celui qui déplace la borne de son prochain! Et tout le peuple répondra: Amen!" Deuteronome XXVII. 17.

Je baise respectueusement la plante de vos pieds.

[Signed] Kh. Krouzian

121

15 March 1922, Constantinople – telegram from Mons. Cesarano to the S. C. Oriental Church – CO, 106, 3, 5, 2, n° 7506/7439

Padre Dionissio Kalatozoff giunto Costantinople supplico istruzioni
[Father Dionissio Kalatozoff reached Constantinople begs instructions]

122

18 March 1922, Rome – Mons. Assessor [Papadopoulos] to Cesarano – CO, 106, 3, 5, 2, n° 7506/7439

Non appena giunto il telegramma con il quale V.S. si è compiaciuta annunziarmi l'arrivo del P. Dionisio Kalatozoff, ho pregato la Segreteria di Stato di risponderLe che questa S. Congregazione non ritiene necessario il proseguimento del viaggio del P. Kalatozoff sino a Roma, ma desidera che egli mandi sollecitamente le importanti notizie promesse a questa S.C. in un rapporto scritto e che ne attenda costì la risposta, se sarà necessario.

La S.V. potrà anche ascoltare quanto a voce il P. Kalatozoff Le potrà riferire sulle condizioni religiose e politiche del Caucaso e sui provvedimenti che si desiderano e avrà la bontà di interessarsi anche di quanto sarà in Suo potere e di riferire a questa S.C. quanto, a suo giudizio, crederà opportuno in proposito.

Sarebbe poi desiderio di questa S.C. che il sullodato Padre tornasse prima della settimana santa a Tiflis per non privare i fedeli armeni della sua assistenza nella ricorrenza della Pasqua. Si attenda perciò che egli invii quanto prima il rapporto, che, secondo lui, non poteva scrivere da Tiflis senza compromettersi. La S.C. potrà poi rispondere subito ai punti più urgenti del rapporto, rimettendo le altre questioni alla venuta del nuovo Visitatore e Amministratore Apostolico del Caucaso che si conta partirà da Roma nel giugno prossimo.

Intanto, ringraziandoLa del Suo interessamento in proposito etc.

[Translation]

As soon as the telegram arrived with which you were pleased to announce to me the arrival of F. Dionisio Kalatozoff, I asked the Secretariat of State to respond to you that this S. Congregation does not retain necessary the continuation of F. Kalatozoff's voyage as far as Rome, but desires that he promptly send the important news promised to this S.C. in a written report and that he await there the response, if necessary.

You might also listen to what F. Kalatozoff can recount to you in person about the religious and political conditions of the Caucasus and about the desired provisions, and have the goodness to concern yourself also, as much as is within your power, and to relate to this S.C. that which, in your judgment, you shall believe opportune in regard.

It would be, then, the wish of this S.C. that the above-named Father return to Tiflis before Holy Week, in order not to deprive the faithful Armenians of his assistance on the occasion of Easter. It is expected, therefore, that he send as soon as possible the report that, according to him, he could not write from Tiflis without compromising himself. The S.C. shall then respond quickly to the most urgent points in the report, putting off the other questions until the arrival of the new Visitor and Apostolic Administrator of the Caucasus, who should be leaving from Rome next June.

In the meantime, thanking you for your interest in the matter etc.

123

[n.d.] – Constantinople – secret handwritten report of F. Kalatosoff to the S. Congr. – CO, 106, 3, 5, 2, n° 7632, pp. 9–12 and 15–16

[...] [pp. 9–12]

3. Un'altra cosa segretissima ho saputo da un importante comunista ritornato da Moska (dopo la IX assemblea generale dei comunisti) in questo gennajo. Nelle sezioni : del culto e quella delle informazioni, si è costituito un agenstur speciale per penetrare nel Vaticano e nelle diverse alte instituzioni cattoliche di Roma, si è deliberato di vegliare sui mezzi e vie di communicazione e d'influenza di quegli istituti sul clero e popolo cattolico della Russia. Si sono accorti d'un inclinazione generale verso il cattolicismo, che intendono impedire, discreditando la buona fama del clero centrale, spiegando tutti i buoni atti con "gesuitismo" (furberia). Occorre essere attenti sui copisti, perché copie di varj atti importanti non vadano trasmessi (venduti) ai agenti informatori comunisti, che pagano caro, disponendo di somme in oro. Si parla (cosa incredibile) di parecchi ecclesiastici già entrati in relazione.Si comprano impiegati delle poste centrali, importanti, per controllare le corrispondenze tra persone importanti.. Al mio arrivo qui, le sezioni di controllo: inglese e francese, mi hanno pregato molto gentilmente di darle delle informazioni necessarie sulla situazione, ed a loro vice m'hanno prevenuto d'una buonissima organizzazione comunista esistente a Cospoli e dappertutto all'estero, perché io sia attento. Già insieme con me arrivò qui un comunista giorgiano, nominato ora in capo all'*istituto centrale del Commercio Riunito del Caucaso*, che fa quì i veci d'un ambasciatore bolscievico-comunista. Lui è Germano Mgalobliscivili, il compagno di studj del mio fratello (che sta ora a Nizza). Lui mi ha parlato di molte cose (inter nos) e mi ha fatto meraviglia del compromisso communista che si usa dappertutto. Tra altri, si vede che hanno portato dalla Russia nel Caucaso parecchi diecine di signorine belle ed istruite, che sono penetrate in tutte le classi dell'abitazione, ed alla

maniera d'un radio telegrafo, fanno sapere al centro militare di tutto che si pensa e si passa nel popolo, negli operai e nelle alte famiglie. Ogni movimento è controllato.

4. La nomina di un Visitatore Apostolico nuovo, è stato per noi una somma consolazione. Ma prego umillissimamente [sic], giacché non vengo a Roma, di voler bene prendere in considerazione, quanto segue. Era più facile per me di *dire*, ma sono costretto a *scriverle*.Imploro l'indulgenza della S. Congregazione per questa mia temerità, che mi permetto solo e solo pel bene della Santa Chiesa ed il bene del clero e della gregge cattolica:

Se già il nuovo Visitatore Apostolico non è stato nominato, sarebbe utile di far la scelta d'una persona che ci venga *di sua buona volontà*, che abbia *la pazienza di ascoltare quelli* che verranno a ricorrere al suo ajuto, *sia deciso di rimanervi almeno cinque anni*, che sappia *almeno un po' di russo, il francese poi senza dubbio*.

È più che indispensabile, che il segretario suo sia anche lui una persona di cuore e pensieri larghi, pazientosa, accessibile, sincero, buono. Non saprei dire il perché (siccome io ero assente dal Caucaso l'anno scorso) ma il Rev.mo Don Pietro segretario di Sua Ecc. Mgr. Moriondo, ha lasciato brutta memoria di se anche nella colonia italiana, che lo chiamano un impostore, persona maligna e priva di tatto. A lui si attribuisce la fuga di Sua Ecc.za.

Quanto alla partenza precipitosa di Sua Ecc.za si ridono i comunisti. Il secondo comissario di Aff. Esteri della Georgia, Toroscielidze m'ha detto:

"Ci ha sdegnato molto la fuga del Rappresentante del Papa di Roma. Lui essendo un capo cattolico, anche in caso di pericolo non doveva lasciare sua gregge, tanto più che era rappresentante di Papa, che fa tanto bene a tutti quanti del mondo. Noi non siamo selvaggi carnivori; sappiamo bene chi si dovrà esser fucilato, chi risparmiato, ossequiato. Ma lui ancora era un italiano, e noi siamo in tanta amicizia coi italiani!"

Essendo dato che il Visitatore Apostolico deve essere un europeo ed indi impossibile generalmente che sappia l'armeno ed il giorgiano.Occorre almeno che sapesse abbastanza il russo, o che volesse impararlo. Questa lingua fa veci del francese nel Caucaso.

Bisogna che il Visitatore Apostolico abbia il diritto di issare la *bandiera della S.Sede*. Abbia carte diplomatiche almeno per una semplice rappresentanza. Essere solo incaricato religioso non basta; non sarà ora rispettato. Bisogna che sia munito d'una certa somma

[…] [pp. 15–16]

5. Coll'arrivo del Visitatore Apostolico sta anessa [sic] la questione della sua dimora. In Tiflis non ci sono case libere, neanche camere libere; tutto è requisito, occupato. Questa è la questione più difficile ad essere risolta senza l'intervento del Regio Rappresentante d'Italia Cav. Franzani [o Franzoni?],(ch'è un allievo della Scuola Nazarena di Roma, un uomo buono,

ma apatico).Senza dubbio occorrerà ricorrere al suo intervento per via del Ministero degli Aff. Esteri. Dall'altra parte sarebbe bene di mandarmi una speciale carta officiale, incaricandomi di questo affare, per prossimo arrivo del Vis. Apost. Rappr. del Papa (non scrivendovi niente di altre cose). Con questa carta, insieme col cav. Franzani faremo il nostro possibile, perché fino a giugno la casa, ovvero 3-4 camere siano pronti in un luogo centrale, decente all'alto suo ufficio.

Ma ripeto deve essere un uomo affabile, sociabile, non asceta ritirato nella sua camera. In Tiflis non si desidera aver un frate esemplare, ma un uomo attivo (come Gesù) che "sa bere e mangiare", con tutta modestia, s'intende. È luogo a dire che il Rev.mo P. Delpuch, è stato un Visit. Apost. esemplare, che ha avuta una vastissima influenza, è rimasto indimenticabile da tutti quanti che lo hanno conosciuto. Che ha dato l'occasione ai giornali locali di lodar tanto il cattolicismo, e di constatare che tutte altre chiese avevano l'inevitabile obbligo di basarsi un giorno prima su quella chiesa granda [sic] di Roma per non rischiare il prossimo crollo completo. Suo zelo eclesiastico e l'atteggiamento affabile d'un discepolo di Cristo, ha lasciato profonda influenza anche sul cattolicossato della Georgia e anche quella d'Armenia. Non lo possono dimenticare, sebbene corto fosse stato il suo soggiorno in quegli paraggi.

Io domando di nuovo scuse perché mi sono permesso di estendermi lungamente sulla questione del Visitatore Apostolico. Ma mi duole molto che Sua Ecc.za Mgr. Moriondo nonostante suo spirito santo e zelato, ed esemplare religiosità, in seguito della sua vita ritirata, trista ed ascettica [sic] e la sua poca affabilità, ha lasciato di se [sic] una memoria meschina anche nei circoli europei. Per occupare un posto diplomatico centrale ci vuol tutt'altro; la santità dev'essere accompagnata con un po' di laicità modesta e vastezza delle idee che si vuole propagare, e addatarsi al milio [sic] dove si lavora.

[Translation]

[...] [pp. 9–12]

3. Another extremely confidential thing I heard from an important communist back from Moscow (after the ninth general assembly of the communists) this January. In the departments: of worship and that of information, a special agency has been formed to penetrate the Vatican and various high Catholic institutions in Rome; it was decided to keep a watch on those institutions' ways and means of communication and of influence on the clergy and Catholic people of Russia. They became aware of a general inclination towards Catholicism which they intend to impede, discrediting the good reputation of the central clergy, explaining away all their good deeds as "Jesuitism" (cunning). A sharp eye must be kept on the copyists, so that copies of various important documents may not be transmitted (sold) to communist

agent informers, who pay dearly, with sums of gold at their disposition. They say (an incredible thing) that they have already entered in contact with several ecclesiastics. They buy off workers in the central post offices, important, in order to monitor the correspondence between important people... Upon my arrival here, the control sections: English and French, asked me very kindly to give them some necessary information about the situation, and in turn they warned me about a very good communist organization existing in Constantinople and everywhere abroad, so that I might be careful. Already arrived here together with me is a Georgian communist—nominated now to be head of the *central institute of Reunited Commerce of the Caucasus*—who is taking on the function of a Bolshevik-communist ambassador here. He is Germano Mgaloblisсivili, a schoolmate of my brother (who nows lives in Nice). He spoke to me of many things (*inter nos*) and he astonished me with the communist compromise that is normal everywhere. Among other things, one sees that they have brought from Russia into the Caucasus several dozens of beautiful and educated misses, who have penetrated into every class of abode and, in the manner of a radio telegraph, have let the military headquarters know everything that is thought and that happens among the people, within groups of workers as well as in upper-class families. Every movement is monitored.

4. The nomination of a new Visitor Apostolic was a great consolation for us. But I most humbly pray, seeing as I am not coming to Rome, that you please take into consideration that which follows. It would be easier for me to *say*, but I am forced to *write it to you*. I beg the indulgence of the S. Congregation for my temerity here, that permits me exclusively for the good of the Holy Church and the good of the clergy and of the Catholic flock:

If the new Visitor Apostolic has not already been nominated, it would be useful to make the choice of a person who would come here *of their own good will*, having the *patience to listen to those* who will come in appeal of his aid, *be decided to remain here at least five years,* knowing *at least some Russian, then French, undoubtedly.*

It is more than indispensable that his secretary also be a person of generous heart and thoughts, patient, accessible, sincere, good. I couldn't say why (since I was absent from the Caucasus last year) but the Most Rev. don Pietro, secretary to His Exc. Mgr. Moriondo, left a bad impression of himself even among the Italian community, which called him an impostor, a malign person devoid of tact. His Exc.y's flight is attributed to him.

As far as the precipitous departure of His Exc., the communists are laughing over it. The deputy commissioner of Foreign Aff. of Georgia, Toroshelidze, said to me:

"The flight of the Representative of the Pope from Rome outraged us. He, being a Catholic leader, was not supposed to leave his flock even in the event of danger, more so in that he was the representative of the Pope, who does so much good for everyone in the world. We are not savage carnivores; we know very well who must be shot, who saved, who revered. But he was still an Italian, and we are on very friendly terms with the Italians!"

It being given that the Visitor Apostolic must be a European and therefore generally impossible that he would know Armenian and Georgian, it is necessary that at least he should know Russian well enough, or that he should want to learn it. This language stands in stead of French in the Caucasus.

It is necessary that the Visitor Apostolic have the right to raise the *flag of the Holy See*. Have diplomatic papers at least for a simple representation. Being only a religious envoy is not enough; he will not now be respected. It is necessary that he have a certain sum at his disposition

[...] [pp. 15–16]

5. With the arrival of the Visitor Apostolic is connected the question of his residence. In Tiflis there are no available houses, not even available rooms; everything is requisitioned, occupied. This is the most difficult question to be resolved without the intervention of the Royal Representative of Italy Cav.[288] Franzani [or Franzoni?], (who is an alumnus of the Nazarene School of Rome, a good man, but apathetic). Without a doubt it will be necessary to resort to his intervention by way of the Ministry of Foreign Aff. On the other hand, it would be good to send me a special official document, charging me with this matter, regarding the upcoming arrival of the Vis. Apost. Rep. of the Pope (not writing therein anything to do with other things). With this document, together with Cav. Franzani we will do our best such that by June a house, or rather 3–4 rooms, will be ready in a central location, conforming to his high office.

But I repeat, it must be an affable man, sociable, not an ascetic withdrawn to his room. In Tiflis it is not desirable to have an exemplary monk, but an active man (like Jesus) who "knows how to eat and drink", with all modesty it's understood. It must be said that the Most Rev. F. Delpuch, was an exemplary Visit. Apost., who had a vast influence; he has remained unforgettable by all those who met him. Who gave the opportunity to local newspapers to praise Catholicism so much, and to observe that all other churches had the inevitable obligation of entrusting themselves to the great church of Rome quickly, in order not to risk a forthcoming complete collapse. His ecclesiastical zeal, and the affable attitude of a disciple of Christ, made a profound influence also on the Catholicosate of Georgia and also that of Armenia. They will not forget him, however brief his stay in those parts was.

I ask again pardon because I have permitted myself to write at length on the question of the Visitor Apostolic. But it pains me very much that His Exc. Mgr. Moriondo, notwithstanding his holy and zealous spirit, and exemplary religiousness, left a poor memory of himself even in European circles, owing to

---

288 Translator's Note: *Cavaliere*. An Italian honorific title; a type of knighthood.

his withdrawn, sad and ascetic life and his scarce affability. In order to occupy a key diplomatic post the exact opposite is needed; sanctity must be accompanied by some modest secularism and sense of expansiveness of the ideas that one wants to propagate, and adapt itself to the milieu where one is working.

124

13 November 1922, Rome – The Director General of the *Fondo per il Culto*[289] [signature illegible] to Gasparri – AAEESS, *Asia* 117, n° 10228

Informazione

Il Ministro Kemalista a Roma Gelaleddin Arif ha riferito con compiacimento che il Santo Padre, ricevendo Miss Ellison, una scrittrice inglese convertita al Cattolicismo che si reca ad Angora, l'ha incaricata di portare a Mustafa Kemal la Sua benedizione speciale ed i ringraziamenti per il favore dimostrato durante i recenti avvenimenti al cattolicismo.

Avendo Miss Ellison ricordato un pensiero espresso da Benedetto XV all'indiano Mehemet Alì, che cioè il movimento islamico disegnatosi e sviluppatosi dopo la guerra non è forse un movimento fanatico di lotta religiosa, ma un riflesso di quell'ardente ritorno all'idealismo - per reazione contro il materialismo prebellico - che agita il mondo intero, Pio IX [sic!] ha caldamente approvato questo concetto.

Continuando la conversazione Gelaleddin Arif ha detto che il Governo nazionalista non tollererà più le mene del Patriarcato ecumenico e probabilmente non tollererà nemmeno la sua presenza in Costantinopoli. Trattamento analogo sarà usato verso il Patriarcato armeno. Perché i due Patriarcati hanno svolto un'azione che li rende incompatibili con la ricostituzione dello Stato ottomano. Non ha esitato ad aggiungere che se si potrà mettere la mano su Melezio subirà la stessa sorte del metropolita di Smirne, che è stato giustiziato.

Anche verso la chiesa ortodossa autocefala turca, ha detto Gelaleddin, il Governo nazionalista conserva qualche diffidenza; perché sa che le chiese

---

289 Translator's Note: *Fondo per il Culto* (Worship Foundation/Fund). A state entity formed in 1866 under the Italian Ministry of Justice, charged with managing expropriated church assets of the Papal States, mingled with public aid, to make up a government-overseen endowment. According to the Vatican's web site, its director in 1922 would have been Baron Carlo Monti, an old school friend of Benedict XV, and his confidential go-between in relations with the Italian government.

ortodosse in generale si sono sempre ispirate a propositi prima ancora politici che religiosi.

Le stesse prevenzioni non esistono per i cattolici anche perché, a differenza degli ortodossi che fanno capo a podestà civili (Grecia, Russia) essi riconoscono per loro un'autorità puramente spirituale. Se scomparirà, egli ha detto, anche quella larvata protezione che la Francia pretende sui cattolici, le simpatie turche per questi ultimi sarebbero anche maggiori.

Ha concluso augurandosi che, dopo la pace, la Santa Sede intensifichi la propaganda volta a romanizzare gli ortodossi di Turchia e specialmente quelli che non parlano il greco e sono indubbiamente dei veri Turchi.

[Translation]
Bulletin

The Kemalist Minister in Rome, Gelaleddin Arif, reported with some satisfaction that the Holy Father, receiving Miss Ellison, an English writer converted to Catholicism who traveled to Angora, charged her with bringing Mustafa Kemal his special blessing and thanks for the favors demonstrated to Catholicism during the recent events.

Miss Ellison recalled a thought expressed by Benedict XV to the Indian Mehemet Alì, that the Islamic movement that designed and developed itself after the war is not, perhaps, a fanatical movement of religious struggle, but a reflection of that ardent return to idealism—as a reaction against pre-war materialism—that is convulsing the whole world; Pius IX [sic!][290] has heartily approved of this concept.

Continuing the conversation, Gelaleddin Arif said that the nationalist Government will no longer tolerate the intrigues of the Ecumenical Patriarchate and probably will not even tolerate its presence in Constantinople. Analogous treatment will be given to the Armenian Patriarchate. Because the two Patriarchates have carried out activities that render them incompatible with the reconstitution of the Ottoman State. He did not hesitate to add that if he were able to get his hands on Melezio,[291] he would suffer the same fate as the metropolitan bishop of Smyrna, who was put to death.

The nationalist Government also, said Gelaleddin, reserves some distrust towards the Autocephalous Turkish Orthodox Church, because it knows that the orthodox churches in general have always been based more on political intentions than religious ones.

The same preconceptions do not exist for the Catholics, not least because, unlike the orthodox who head up civil administrations (Greece, Russia), they

---

290 Translator's Note: "[sic!]" found in the original.
291 Translator's Note: Meletius IV, Ecumenical Patriarch of Constantinople from 1921 to 1923.

recognize themselves as having a purely spiritual authority. If even that vague protection that France claims to offer the Catholics were to disappear, he said, Turkish sympathies for these latter would be even greater.

He concluded in hoping that, after the peace, the Holy See intensifies propaganda aimed at Romanizing the orthodox of Turkey, especially those who do not speak Greek and are undoubtedly real Turks.

125

14 November 1922, Rome – draft of Gasparri's reply – AAEESS, *Asia* 117, n° 10228

In ordine all'informazione dell'Ecc.mo Sig. Direttore del Fondo per il Culto, in data 14 corrente, si fa presente che il colloquio, come è stato riferito dal Signor Gelaleddin Arif, non corrisponde, sia nella sostanza sia nei termini, a quel che realmente nella conversazione fu detto.

Il Santo Padre si è infatti limitato a ripetere le sue raccomandazioni a Kemal Pascià, già note al pubblico, cioè: 1° che egli si studiasse, per quanto è da lui, di evitare nuovi spargimenti di sangue; 2° che desse ordine affinché nei suoi territorii fossero rispettate le persone e le istituzioni cristiane, specialmente cattoliche.

[Translation]

With regard to the bulletin of the Most Exc. Director of the *Fondo per il Culto*, dated the 14th of this month, note that the conversation as reported by Mr. Gelaleddin Arif does not correspond, either in its substance or in its terms, to that which was actually said in the conversation.

The Holy Father, in fact, limited himself to repeating his recommendations to Kemal Pasha already known to the public, that is: 1° that he study, as far as is possible, to avoid further bloodshed; 2° that he give orders such that Christian, and especially Catholic, persons and institutions be respected in his territories.

LIST OF DOCUMENTS FROM THE VATICAN ARCHIVES

ASV = Vatican Secret Archives (*Archivio Segreto Vaticano*)
AAEESS = Archives of the Sacred Congregation for Extraordinary Ecclesiastical Affairs (*Archivio della Sacra Congregazione per gli Affari Ecclesiastici Straordinari*)
CO = Archives of the Sacred Congregation for the Oriental Churches (*Archivio della Sacra Congregazione per le Chiese Orientali*)

1

5 March 1918, Rome – Der Abramian to the pope – AAEESS, *Asia* 57, 2, nº 59711

> Describes a massacre of Russian Armenians in Trabizon and asks the pope's intervention such that no others occur.

2

6 March 1918, Rome – Der Abramian and others to the pope – AAEESS, *Asia* 57, 2, nº 59712

> After the armistice between Russia and the Central Empires, new massacres are feared in the part of Armenia returning to Turkey. They ask for the pope's intervention.

3

8 March 1918, Paris – telegr. from Nubar to the Vatican – AAEESS, *Asia* 57, 2, nº 57889

> Asks for the intervention of the Holy See on behalf of the lives of the Armenians in the part of Armenia returning to Turkey.

4

9 March 1918, Rome – Gasparri's reply to Nubar – AAEESS, *Asia* 57, 2, nº 57889

> Assures that even prior to Nubar's telegram he had taken steps.

5

11 March 1918, Paris – Nubar to Gasparri – AAEESS, *Asia* 57, 2, nº 60608

> Confirms the news of the Turkish massacres.

6

13 March 1918, Paris – telegr. from Nubar to Gasparri – AAEESS, *Asia* 57, 2, n° 59729

> Thanks the cardinal and the pope for the interventions on Armenia's behalf.

7

19 March 1918, Constantinople (received 22 June 1918) – Dolci to Gasparri – ASV, *Guerra* [War] 1914–18, 244,112, n° 66827

> Describes the colloquium with the German ambassador Bernstorff and with the Turkish foreign minister to prevent Turkish reprisals in the territories reoccupied after the armistice; he also asked that the Turkish press not arouse anti-Armenian hatred (*v.* newspaper *Hilal* of 14 March 1918). It would appear that the Turkish government is disposed towards amnesty, but then the Armenian population, aside from some guerrilla fighters, has almost entirely fled to Russia.

8

24 June 1918, Rome – handwritten draft from Gasparri to Dolci – ASV, *Guerra* [War] 1914–18, 244, 112, n° 66827

> Thanks the Apostolic Delegate for the action taken and for the detailed report.

9

20 March 1918, Monaco – Schiappi to Gasparri – AAEESS, *Asia* 57, 2, n° 63502

> Refers the German chancellor's response to Pacelli regarding the Armenian Turks: the Turkish government has promised to treat the Armenians with clemency provided they submit; the Church should work in that direction.

10

29 March 1918, Constantinople – Dolci to Gasparri – AAEESS, *Asia* 57, 2, [n° ?]

> Relates having succeeded in preventing the deportation of the Armenians of Angora.

11

15 May 1918, Constantinople – The sultan to the pope – ASV, *Guerra* [War] 1914–18, 244, 112, n° 67801

> French translation of the sultan's letter. Responding to the pope's letter, he assures his goodwill toward peaceful Armenians.

12

14 June 1918, Constantinople – Dolci to Gasparri – *Ibid.*, n° 67801

Transmits the sultan's reply to the pope.

13

20 June 1918, Rome – handwritten draft from Gasparri to Dolci – *Ibid.*, n° 67801

The reply transmitted from the sultan to the pope.

14

21 June 1918, Tiflis (received in September) – Kalatosoff and Kapojan to Der Abramian – AAEESS, *Asia* 57, 2, n° 81691

On the conditions in Turkish Armenia during the passage from Russian occupation to Turkish reoccupation.

15

22 June 1918, Rome – Manna to Gasparri – ASV, *Guerra* [War] 1914–18, 244 K 12 c, 306, n° 66909

The Chaldean bishop asks whether it is possible send the aid offered by the Armenian community in England to Christians in the Caucasus and in Persia by an alternate route, rather than through Russia, because of the events in that country. In addition, it passes on the rumors of the Nestorian patriarch's killing.

16

25 June 1918, Rome – Gasparri to Manna – *Ibid.*, n° 66909

Replies that he will explore the possible alternate routes for sending aid from the English Armenians.

17

26 June 1918, Rome – Gasparri to Maglione – *Ibid.*, n° 66909

Conveys to Dolci an encoded telegram in which he asks confirmation of the rumors regarding the killing of Nestorian patriarch.

18

26 June 1918, Constantinople – Dolci to Gasparri – AAEESS, *Austria* 576, n° 69471

Reports an article from the Turkish newspaper *Hilal* about the Caucasian states, with an interview of the Azerbaijani delegate to the Constantinople conference, which mentions good relations among the new states and between Azeri and Turks. Mentions that Armenia does not yet have a government.

19

9 July 1918, Rome – telegram from Gasparri to Pacelli – ASV, *Guerra* [War] 1914–18, 244 K 12 c, 306, n° 68898

Enquires about the possibility of sending aid to Persia and to the Caucasus.

20

August 1918, Monaco – Pacelli to Gasparri – ASV, *Guerra* [War] 1914–18, 244 K 12 c, 306, n° 68898

Theoretical willingness of the Imperial Government to sending aid, but doubts feasibility especially regarding Persia.

21

18 July 1918, Constantinople – Dolci to Gasparri – AAEESS, *Asia* 57, 2, n° [...]61

Relates the visit he has had from the Armenian government delegation.

22

9 August 1918, Constantinople – Dolci to Gasparri – AAEESS, *Asia* 57, 2, n° 81286

Reports that he has returned the Armenian delegation's visit.

23

31 August 1918, Lugano – de Ritter to Gasparri – AAEESS, *Asia* 57, 2, n° 81693

Relays to Gasparri the response of von Dandl, the Bavarian prime minister.

24

29 August 1918, Monaco – von Dandl to Gasparri – AAEESS, *Asia* 57, 2, n° 81693

Relates the feelings of compassion for the suffering of the Eastern Christians that had motivated the Bavarian government to contact the Chancellor of the Empire in order to obtain an intervention in favor of the Armenians in particular. After the dispatch of Gasparri's promemoria such intervention was urgently requested once again, obtaining assurances of decisive action in that regard.

25

28 September 1918, Rome – Gasparri to de Ritter – n° 81693

Thanks for the letters transmitted.

26

28 September 1918, Rome – Gasparri to Dolci – AAEESS, *Russia* 505, n⁰ 81691

Cover letter accompanying the sum of 10,000 francs destined for poor Catholic Armenians, to be distributed by the two vicars in Tiflis: Dionigi Kalatosoff and Antonio Kapojan. Above all, instruction to Dolci to intervene with the government such that Turkish troops (and Turkish gangs) stop their persecutions of the Armenians.

27

24 October 1918, Constantinople – Dolci to Gasparri – AAEESS, *Russia* 540 bis, n° 85097

Informs of the visit made to him by two commissions (Armenian and Georgian) to ask for diplomatic recognition of the two republics on the part of the Holy See.

28

24 October 1918, Constantinople – Dolci to van Rossum – CO, 106, 4, 2, 3, n° 1191

Recounts to the prefect of *Propaganda Fide* the visit made to him by the two delegations, Armenian and Georgian, to whom he proposed the opportunity of embracing Catholicism remaining in their respective Eastern rites. Both delegations would like to establish relations with the Holy See in order to have its political support.

29

26 October 1918, Constantinople – Dolci to Gasparri – AAEESS, *Asia* 57, 2

D. has conveyed to the Armenian delegates the pope's express wish that the Armenian Catholic patriarch be present in Armenia personally or through a substitute. Enthusiasm on the part of the Armenian government and of the Catholic patriarch Terzian.

30

4 November 1918, Constantinople – Dolci to Gasparri – AAEESS, *Asia* 57, 2

Enthusiasm in the Armenian press for the pope's decision regarding the Catholic patriarch.

31

10 November 1918 – Memorandum for the American ambassador to Rome – AAEESS, *Asia* 57, 2, n° 84492

The right of Armenia to an independent rebirth and her usefulness to the allied cause and in particular to that of America.

32
25 October 1918, Constantinople – Dolci to Gasparri – AAEESS, *Asia* 57, 1, n° 85098

> Tells of massacres of Armenians in Baku and asks the pope's intervention.

33
27 November 1918, Rome – Gasparri to the Count de Salis – AAEESS, *Asia* 57, 2, n° 84211

> In the pope's name, asks that Great Britain send food to Armenia.

34
21 January 1919, Rome – de Salis to Gasparri – n° 84211

> Promises the shipment of humanitarian aid to the Armenians.

35
20 December 1918, Rome – Damadian to Gasparri – AAEESS, *Asia* 57, 2, n° [?]

> Thanks the Holy See for all it has done and asks for ongoing support as the Armenians continue to struggle for their freedom.

36
3 January 1919, Rome – Damadian to Gasparri – AAEESS, *Asia* 57, 2, n° [?]

> Asks the support of the Holy See for the reunification of *all* of Armenia, from the Caucasus to the Mediterranean.

37
28 January 1919, Constantinople – Dolci to Marini – CO, 105, 3, 5, n° 1525

> Secretly gained knowledge, and obtained a copy, of a letter from Terzian to Clémenceau, Wilson, Lloyd George and to the king of Belgium.

38
15 January 1919, Constantinople – copy of the letter from Terzian to Clémenceau, Wilson, Lloyd George and to the king of Belgium – *Ibid.*, n° 1525

> Pleads the case for Armenian independence, then indicates three conditions under which unity, order and development of the new state may be assured: freedom of conscience (that is, that no religion be recognized as the official state religion); freedom to re-organize the ecclesiastical provinces; and reparations for the immense damages, including material damage, suffered during the Turkish persecutions.

39
24 February 1919, Constantinople – Dolci to Marini – CO, 106,4,3 n° 1667

> Relays an article from the French newspaper *Renaissance*, which talks about a letter the pope had supposedly sent to Wilson asking for maximum support in the cause of Armenian independence.

40

[?] March 1919, Constantinople – Dolci to Gasparri – AAEESS, *Asia* 57, 1, n° [?]

Relates the visit that the *Locum-Tenens* of the Armenian Apostolic Patriarchate made to Dolci, in order to thank the Holy Father for his action on behalf of the Armenians.

41

6 March 1919, Constantinople – Dolci to Gasparri – AAEESS, *Asia* 57, 1, n° [?]

Communicates the visit made to him by the Armenian Apostolic Patriarch Zaven in thanksgiving for the pope's action on his behalf. Dolci relates having made him aware of the pontifical letter to the sultan.

42

18 March 1919, Constantinople – Dolci to Gasparri – ASV, *Guerra* [War] 1914–18, 244, 69, n° 90014

Conveys the translation of an article from the Armenian newspaper *Erivan* regarding the support of the Holy See for Armenian independence and the steps taken in that direction with the USA.

43

18 March 1919, Constantinople – Dolci to Gasparri – ASV, *Guerra* [War] 1914–18, 244, 69, n° 90034

Translation of an article from the Armenian newspaper *Vercin Lur* regarding Dolci's humanitarian intervention on behalf of sixty-one Armenians who had been condemned to death.

44

28 March 1919, Constantinople – Dolci to Gasparri – ASV, *Guerra* [War] 1914–18, 244, 69, n° 89948

Gives notice of an article from the Armenian newspaper *Nor Ghiank* which published the pope's address to the consistory of March 10 with the headline: "The Holy Pope's Speech for the East".

45

16 May 1919, Constantinople – Dolci to Gasparri – AAEESS, *Russia* 505, n° 1120

Passes on the transcription of F. Kalatosoff's letter of March 2 1919 from Tiflis, in which he acknowledges the receipt of a check sent by the pope and describes the miserable conditions of the population as well as of the Catholic clergy, along with the difficulties of the Apostolic Administrator in distributing aid in such a vast country without means of communication, neither the postal service nor the telegraph functioning; he bids Dolci to ask the Armenian and Georgian delegations in Constantinople for the restoration of government aid.

46

27 June 1919, Constantinople – Dolci to Card. Marini – CO, *Armeni e Caucaso* [Armenians and the Caucasus], 105, 3, 5, n° 2375

> Relates the protests in the Armenian and Greek press over the massacres of Armenians committed by Azeri in Karabakh (in Shushi, Aresh, etc.). The Armenian foreign minister has protested and put pressure on Gossy, English commander in the Caucasus, who, it appears, had the Azeri governor responsible for the massacres arrested.

47

30 June 1919, Rome – Marini to Gasparri – AAEESS, *Russia* 540 bis, n° 97077

> Requests for passports for F. Delpuch (of the White Fathers Missionaries of Africa), Visitor Apostolic to the Caucasus.

48

1 July 1919, Rome – Der Abramian to Gasparri – AAEESS, *Russia* 540 bis, n° 92975

> Sends a copy of the comments sent to the Congregation of the Eastern Church, dated 28 June 1919.

49

28 June 1919, Rome – Der Abramian to Assessor Mons. Papadopoulos – *Ibid.*, n° 92975

> Against the sending of a Visitor Apostolic to Armenia; better that he be sent to Georgia and that he discreetly look after Armenia, as well.

50

2 October 1919, Constantinople – Dolci to Gasparri – AAEESS, *Asia* 117, n° 10228

> Dolci unable to leave Constantinople for treatment, as he had wished, because of the alarm caused by Kemal in Anatolia with his military operations and interruptions of communications particularly between the Christians of Angora and their bishop Bahabian. Reports on the discussion with Admiral Robert, British High Commissioner, from which D. deduces: the imminent fall of Damad Ferid's cabinet, the western powers' forthcoming withdrawal from Turkey, the unlikelihood of immediate danger to Christians. Additionally, little sympathy for Georgian, Armenian and Ukrainian independence, for fear of German influence. D. affirms having energetically defended the independence of these small states, against the reconstitution of a Greater Russia which would be extremely dangerous for religious freedoms.

51

21 October 1919, Erevan – Delpuch to the Armenian foreign minister – AAEESS, *Asia* 126, n° 3643

> Says that the pope wishes for peace and freedom for the Armenians, and is ready to establish the best of relations with them. In exchange, precise guarantees for the Catholic Church in the country.

52

3 November 1919, Erevan – Alkhatissian and der Akopian to Delpuch – *Ibid.*, n° 3643

> In response to Delpuch's letter, thanks the pope and assures that the Catholic Church would have complete freedom. Asks in return that support for the Armenian cause be maintained.

53

21 November 1919, Tiflis – Delpuch to Papadopolus – *Ibid.*, n° 3643

> Report to the S. C. for the Oriental Church on his visit to the three Caucasian republics and on the cordial (almost triumphal) welcome received.

54

27 November 1919, Tiflis – Delpuch to Khatissian – CO, 106, 2, 3, n° 3228

> Thanks the Armenian president for the warm reception and assures that the pope will do everything possible to sustain the cause of the Armenian people, that for what they have gone through and how they have behaved they have every right to take their place among the free peoples.

55

[n.d., Perhaps January, 1920] – Relation of Delpuch to the S. C. for the Oriental Church – CO, 106, 2, 3, n° 3516

> Refers Khatissian's request for an official representative of the Holy See in the Transcaucasus. In consideration of the limited number of Latin-rite Catholics, he proposed a prelate with the title of Visitor Apostolic with a principal headquarters in Tiflis, and a secondary one in Erevan. Kh. accepted.
>
> D. adds that perhaps the title of Visitor Apostolic is a bit ambiguous; for the local population an Apostolic Delegate would be better. He then reports on the individual provinces and religious questions.

56

[n.d.] – Relation of Card. van Rossum on the Delpuch report – CO, 106, 2, 3, n° 3825

> He is in favor of sending an Visitor Ap. rather than an Ap. Delegate to the Caucasus, for a couple of reasons: *religiously speaking* a Visitor has more extraordinary powers (because everything needs to be reorganized); *politically speaking* a Delegate has jurisdiction over one or more states, but the Peace Conference has not yet established the boundaries of the three republics.

57

13 January 1920, Constantinople – Dolci to Marini – CO, 106, 2, 3, n° 3172

> Refers what Delpuch had told him about promises to the Church made by the former Russian undersecretary for the Caucasus and about the penetration of American Protestants.

58

15 January 1920, Rome – Gasparri to the Armenian prime minister and foreign minister – AAEESS, *Asia* 126, n° 3643

> Communicates the pope's contentment with Delpuch's reception and his prayers for Armenian independence; asks freedom for the Church.

59

20 January 1920, Constantinople – Cesarano to Gasparri – AAEESS, *Asia* 57, n° 1066

> The Monophysite patriarch tells of his trip to the Paris Peace Conference in support of the Armenian cause and asks that a representative of the Armenian Catholics also be sent.

60

28 January 1920, Rome – Gasparri to Cesarano – *Ibid.*, n° 1066

> Authorizes the dispatch of Naslian along with the Apostolics to the Peace Conference.

61

29 February 1920 – article in *La Croix* about Delpuch's trip – CO, 106, 2, 3, n° [?]

> Mentions the warm reception given to Delpuch.

62

6 March 1920, Rome – Papadopulos to Mons. B. Cerretti – AAEESS, *Asia* 126, n° 3643

> Proposes letters of congratulation from the Holy See to the three Transcaucasian republics upon their recognition, although not definitive, on the part of the Peace Conference.

63

12 March 1920, Paris – Naslian to French Catholic public opinion – AAEESS, *Asia* 57, 2, n° [?]

Letter to the bishops urging them to influence Catholic public opinion in their respective dioceses in favor of the Armenian cause.

64

13 March 1920, Paris – Naslian to the French foreign minister– AAEESS, *Asia* 57, 2, n° [?]

Asks protection for the rights of Armenian nationals and of Catholics.

65

3 April 1920, London – Aharonian to Gasparri – AAEESS, *Asia* 57, 2, n° 4764

Cover letter for the gift of two copies of an historical Armenian atlas.

66

[?] April 1920, Rome – Gasparri to Aharonian – *Ibid.*, n° 4764

Thanks for the historical atlases.

67

5 April 1920, Paris – Naslian to Gasparri – AAEESS, *Asia* 57, 2, n° 5288

Describes the work at the Peace Conference. Expresses substantial approval, with some reservations for that part of the treaty that regards Armenia's obligations.

Attached: – The Conference of London to the Armenian Delegation – *Ibid.*, p. 262–269

Document forwarded to the Armenian delegation, to have their observations regarding the Armenian government's obligations pertaining to religious or ethnic minorities, and to the economic and customs preferences to be accorded the member states of the League of Nations.

68

6 April 1920, Paris – Ahmed Riza to the pope – AAEESS, *Asia* 57, 1, n° [?]

Asks that the pope intercede on behalf of "unjustly accused" Turks.

69

13 April 1920, Rome – Tigran Nazarian to the pope – AAEESS, *Asia* 57, 1, n° 5293

The delegate of the Armenians of Karabakh and Zanguezur asks that the pope intervene at the Peace Conference of San Remo against the annexation of Karabakh to Azerbaijan.

70

27 May 1920, Paris – Naslian to Mons. [Papadopulos ?] – CO, 106, 2, 3, n° 4363

Speaks of religious and administrative questions, then of the Armenian situation: in the Caucasus there is the threat of definitive extermination, the Tartars are at one with the Turks. Captain Poidebard, a Jesuit on his way back from Erevan, told him that the final catastrophe is imminent, especially after the Bolshevik invasion, and he recommends intervention on the part of the Holy See. They are also very worried at Trabizon and Samsun. The Turks have been making threats against Naslian at Constantinople.

71

1 June 1920, Constantinople – Dolci to Gasparri – AAEESS, *Austria* 576, n° 7232

Accounting of the audience with the Grand Vizier Damad Ferid Pasha regarding the Peace Treaty imposed on Turkey. Dolci adds that the Grand Vizier is loathed by the Kemalists, who have become very strong.

72

18 June 1920, Rome – handwritten draft from Gasparri to Dolci – *Ibid.*, n° 7232

Approves of the discretion shown by D. in the audience with the Grand Vizier.

73

8 June 1920, Paris – Boghos Nubar to the pope – AAEESS, *Asia* 57, 1, n° 8131

Asks the pope's intervention against the danger of borders that would block Armenia in among traditionally enemy countries, cutting her off from all possibility of receiving aid and strangling her commercially and financially.

74

8 July 1920, Rome – handwritten draft from Gasparri to the Count de Salis – *Ibid.*, n° 8131

Following Nubar's appeal to the pope regarding Armenia's borders, asks the British plenipotentiary minister and extraordinary envoy to the Holy See to use his influence to prevent the strangulation of Armenia.

75

9 July 1920, Rome – handwritten draft from Gasparri to Nubar – AAEESS, *Asia* 57, 1, n° 8132

By order of the Holy Father, he did not fail to take the requested steps with the English minister on behalf of the Armenian people.

76

10 October 1920, Paris – Historical commentary by Nubar – AAEESS, *Asia* 57, 1, n° 13508

Despite the fact that the Armenians fought against the Turks alongside the Entente, it had decided, with the Treaty of Sèvres, to abandon the Armenians of Cilicia to the hands of the Turks. The National Armenian Delegation asks for at least administrative autonomy over the region, under the control and protection of France.

77

20 October 1920, Paris – Terzian to Gasparri – AAEESS, *Asia* 57, 1, n° 19169

Letter accompanying another [not found], from Nubar to the pope.

78

6 November 1920, Rome – handwritten draft of Gasparri to Nubar – AAEESS, *Asia* 57, 1, n° 13138

Says that the Holy Father has already taken steps to signal the new dangers threatening "their dear country".

79

21 November 1920, Rome – Naslian to Cerretti – AAEESS, *Asia* 57, 1, n° 13508

Due to the disastrous situation of which he brings news, he begs the Holy See's intervention in favor of Armenia.

Attached: Naslian's notes regarding the Holy See's intervention in favor of Armenia.

80

28 November 1920, Rome – Gasparri to Terzian – AAEESS, *Asia* 57, 1, n° 1316

Acknowledges receipt and assures that he has acted forcefully and repeatedly according the Armenians' wishes and that he will continue to do so.

81

18 December 1920, Tiflis – Mons. Moriondo to Card. [Marini?] – CO, 106, 2, 3, n° 4999

The undoing of Armenia is noted. The government will be Bolshevik, therefore certainly not favorable to the Church. Asks to be able to come away because he can do nothing now and less in the future. Informed of Kemalist violence against the Armenians, he protested to commanders, even in the pope's name. They made him promises, "let us hope they are not merely words"...

82

23 January 1921, Rome – Delpuch to Marini – CO, 106, 3, 5, 2, n° 5145

Cover letter for a conveyed communication from Evangouloff, former tzarist minister for the Caucasus, a non–Catholic Armenian, but with great sympathy for the Catholic Church.

83

23 October 1920, Tiflis – Evangouloff to Delpuch – *Ibid.*, n° 5145

On the eastern mentality regarding nationality and religious affiliation. Gives various suggestions, among which that of sending the Mekhitarist fathers from the see of Vienna as well as the sisters of the Immaculate Conception of Constantinople to Alexandroupolis, because of their knowledge of the language, etc.

84

25 January 1921, Rome – Naslian, notations on the Treaty of Sèvres – AAEESS, *Asia* 57, 1, n° 16169

Observations about 1.) the Armenian situation and the Armenians in general; 2.) indemnity for damages and the restitution of goods on the part of Turkey; 3.) religio-political interests.

85

18 February 1921, Rome – Gasparri to Naslian – *Ibid.*, n° 16169

In response to what N. has sent him regarding the Treaty of Sèvres, assures as to the Holy See's special pro-Armenian interest, but feels obliged to add that one shouldn't delude oneself that the requests of the Holy See will be satisfied.

86

3 February 1921, Geneva – Morsier to Gasparri – AAEESS, *Asia* 57, 1, n° 16180

Cover letter of the Appeal to the Churches on the part of the *Ligue International Philoarmenienne*.

Attached: Appeal to the Churches for humanitarian aid for Armenia

87

10 February 1921, Tiflis – Moriondo to the pope – CO, 106, 3, 5, 2, n° 5313

Declares that he will remain in the spirit of obedience, but with great sacrifice, as he deems it impossible to do anything given the current conditions. Issues thanks on behalf of the Armenians for various offerings from the pope.

88

12 February 1921, Tiflis – Moriondo to Marini – CO, 106, 3, 2, n° 5293/52

Says he will make the sacrifice of remaining because the pope has asked it of him. For the meantime, the eventuality of a Bolshevik invasion seems diminished, not least because the Entente Powers have recognized Georgia.

89

13 February 1921, Tiflis – Moriondo to Marini – CO, 106, 3, 2, n° 5293

Regarding the Georgian sisters (pro) and the French sisters (con).

90

28 February 1921, Rome – Terzian to Cerretti – AAEESS, *Asia* 57, 1, n° 17537

Advises the Secretary for Ecclesiastical Affairs of the Holy See that he has interested the governments of Spain, Brazil and the United States, on the occasion of the Conference of London. Asks that the Holy Father also speak to these governments and asks Cerretti to remind Gasparri to do so, as he has promised.

91

1 March 1921, Rome – Gasparri to the Marquis of Villasireda[?] Spanish ambassador to the Holy See – *Ibid.*, n° 17537

Transmits the pope's pressing appeal for Armenia to the Spanish government.

92

1 March 1921, Rome – Gasparri to M. de Azevedo, Brazilian ambassador to the Holy See – *Ibid.*, n° 17537

In the name of the pope, directs a pressing appeal for Brazil to support the Armenian cause.

93

3 March 1921, Rome – the Brazilian ambassador to Gasparri – *Ibid.*, n° 17537

Acknowledges receipt of the note of March 1st in which Gasparri informed him that the pope was addressing a strong appeal to the president of Brazil on behalf of Armenia. Assures to have sent it by telegram.

94

2 March 1921, Constantinople – telegram from Moriondo to Marini – CO, 106, 3, 5, 2, n° 5287

Cause events forced to leave Tiflis with foreign legation am in Constple awaiting orders.

95

3 March 1921, Constantinople – Moriondo a Marini – CO, 106, 3, 5, 2, n° 5347

Warns that due to the Bolshevik conquest of Georgia he has been constrained, along with other diplomats, to abandon the Caucasus. A fluid political situation, however, the Bolsheviks seem firmly installed. In any case his mission in the Caucasus, whether the fighting continues or whether the Bolsheviks win, cannot go forward. Not to be excluded that the Bolsheviks and Kemalists go to war, now that they are face to face.

96
4 March 1921, Rome – Mons. Assessor [Papadopulos] to Tedeschini – CO, 106, 3, 5, 2, n° 5287

> Asks that he telegraph Dolci to advise Moriondo to wait for orders from the Holy See before making other movements.

97
5 March 1921, Rome – Mons. Assessor to Moriondo – CO, 106, 3, 5, 2, n° 5287

> Declares that the Holy See would have preferred that he remain in Kemalist territory to help the Christians. At any rate, he is to maintain the closest possible contacts with his faithful, and be ready to return as soon as is feasible.

98
9 March 1921, Rome – handwritten draft of the telegram from Gasparri to Kemal – AAEESS, *Asia* 117, n° 17569

> Appeal in the pope's name on behalf of Christians in the Caucasus, Asia Minor and Anatolia.

99
12 March 1921, Angora – telegram from Kemal to the pope – *Ibid.*, n° 17569

> Restates promises of protection regarding the Greeks and Armenians.
>
> *Attached*: Excerpts from Kemal's speeches at the Turkish National Assembly regarding Greek and Armenian minorities.

100
31 March 1921, Rome – the Brazilian ambassador to Gasparri – AAEESS, *Asia* 57, 1, n° 17537

> The Brazilian president communicates that, following the pope's appeal, he has given instructions to the ambassador in Paris, President of the Executive Council of the League of Nations, to strongly uphold the Armenian cause.

101
8 April 1921 [n.p.] – Memorandum from the Armenia America Society to the American government – AAEESS, *Asia* 57,1, n° 23279

> Regarding the maintaining of some amount of autonomy in Turkish Armenia

102
8 April 1921 – Policy proposed to the United States on behalf of the Armenians [anonymous] – *Ibid.*, n° 23279

> Favoring the concession of a loan for the expenses necessary for the formation of a free, or at least autonomous, Armenia in Turkish territory.

103

8 April 1921 – Resolution proposed to the U. S. Congress [anonymous] – *Ibid.*, n° 23279

Policy proposal to the United States regarding the Armenians.

104

16 April 1921, Rome – the Spanish ambassador to Gasparri – AAEESS, *Asia* 57,1, n° 17537

Responds to Gasparri's note of March 1st about the Armenian question, assuring his government's unconditional support of the Armenian cause.

105

3 May 1921, Rome – Kalatosoff to Marini – CO, 106, 3, 5, 2, n° 5638

Describes the chaos into which the Caucasus has descended, in particular Georgia. To carry out his mission he needs an official document from the Secretary of State, since only the pope has authority, even with the Bolsheviks. Grave difficulties with transportation and connections.

106

7 May 1921, Beirut – Giannini to Gasparri – AAEESS, *Asia* 57, 1, n° 21439

Relates his convictions about the Kemalists and the serious danger for all Christians, and in particular for the Armenians, from the part of Kemalist pan-Islamism. Insists that the Holy See intervene with France so that they not abandon Cilicia.

107

14 May 1921, Beirut – Giannini to Gasparri – *Ibid.*, n° 21439

Reports on conversations held with the Armenian scholar Tchobanian and with Admiral de Bon, commander in charge of the eastern Mediterranean fleet, who asked him for a comment in the form of a memorandum regarding Cilicia.

Attached: memorandum for Admiral de Bon on France's interests in not abandoning Cilicia for political and strategic motives.

108

18 June 1921, Beirut – Giannini to Gasparri – AAEESS, *Asia* 57, 1, n° 22655

Observes that if France persists in its remissive policy towards the Angora government, she shall never be able to hope of peace in Syria. He wrote a letter, which he encloses, to the cardinal of Paris, Dubois, asking that he raise awareness among French politicians and public opinion about the cruel destiny that faces Cilicia.

Attached: Giannini's letter to the cardinal of Paris Dubois, on France's moral obligation not to abandon the Christians of Cilicia.

109

5 July 1921, Rome – Gasparri to Giannini – *Ibid.*, n° 22655

Acknowledges receipt of reports sent him regarding the situation in Cilicia.

110

17 July 1921, Beirut – Giannini to Gasparri – AAEESS, *Asia* 57, 1, n° 24161

Relates his meeting with Franklin Bouillon, during which he urged the (unofficial, but influential) French government envoy to Angora not to abandon Christians to Kemalist reprisals, if for no other reason than that it would severely compromise French prestige.

Attached: the memorandum given to Bouillon on the question of Cilicia

111

30 July 1921, Constantinople – Moriondo to Marini – CO, 106, 3, 5, 2, n° 6331

Reminds that he has been waiting for orders for five months. By now the Caucasus is in the hands of the Bolsheviks, the people are impoverished and in chaos. He has been able to send some aid, but asks for precise orders, making it understood that he wishes repatriation.

112

11 August 1921, Rome – handwritten draft of an encrypted telegram from Gasparri to Dolci – AAEESS, *Asia* 117, n° 23784

That Dolci should intervene with the Kemalist government over the massacres at Artvin and Batum.

113

30 August 1921, Constantinople – Naslian to Gasparri – AAEESS, *Asia* 117, n° 25108

The Brazilian government is disposed to accept Armenian refugees. Conditions asked by the Armenians are: travel facilitation, retention of Armenian citizenship, etc.

114

1 September 1921, Constantinople – Naslian to Gasparri – AAEESS, *Asia* 117, n° 25109

Notwithstanding all their promises, the Kemalists carry out massacres as their predecessors had done.

Attached: memorandum on the massacres of Armenians in Turkish Armenia at the hands of the Kemalists

115

27 [October 1921?] Constantinople –article from the Armenian newspaper *Joghovurti Tsain* – AAEESS, *Asia* 117

> Gelaleddim Arif Bey, deputy of Erzerum to the National Assembly, has presented legislation that would annul minorities' rights.
>
> *Attached*: comment in French [anonymous]

116

10 November 1921 – Pro-memoria for Mons. Pizzardo [Substitute Secretary of State] – CO, 106, 3, 5, 2, n° 5278

> Mons. Moriondo abandoned Georgia after the Bolshevik takeover, and does not want to return there; the Consistorial Congregation must be notified in order that they find him a diocese in Italy, and quickly, because: I) 50,000 Catholics cannot remain without a pastor; another must be sent; and II) rumors have spread that he will replace Dolci in Constantinople, which isn't true, thus he must leave.

117

27 November 1921, Paris – Tchobanian a Gasparri – AAEESS, *Asia* 117, n° [?]

> Regarding the Christians of Cilicia and the action of the Holy See in their favor, anticipating the dreaded withdrawal of French troops as per the Franco-Kemalist accord of Angora. The Kemalist government's promise to respect the rights of the deported is not attendible.

118

28 November 1921 – G. Noradunghian to Gasparri – AAEESS, *Asia* 117, n° 26036 A.E.

> Letter of introduction for his son, Diran, sent by the Armenian National Delegation to render homage to the pope and laying out the situation of the Eastern Christians.
>
> *Attached*: Proposal-appeal to the senators and representatives of the Entente Powers in occasion of the meeting of the Supreme Council for peace in the Orient. Describes Armenia's situation in contrast with the resolutions solemnly undertaken by the Powers.

119

3 March 1922, Rome – Agagianian to Papadopulos – CO, 106, 3, 5, 2, n° 7439

> [Agagianian, then deputy director of the Armenian College, future patriarch; Papadopulos, Assessor of the S. Congr. Oriental Church]
>
> After various considerations of a pastoral nature, restates the importance of an Apostolic Delegate to the Caucasus to encourage the Catholics and revive evangelization. Given the generosity and impartiality

demonstrated by the Holy See, he would be well accepted and respected even by the communists.

120

13 May 1922, Smyrna – open letter from Krouzian to Pope Pius XI – AAEESS, *Asia* 117, n° [?]

Published in the newspaper *Arevelian Mamoul*, asks for pressure on western countries, in particular Italy, on behalf of Armenia.

121

15 March 1922, Constantinople – telegram from Cesarano to the S. C. Oriental Church – CO, 106, 3, 5, 2, n° 7506/7439

Father Kalatosoff, having reached Constantinople, begs further instructions.

122

18 March 1922, Rome – Mons. Assessor [Papadopulos] to Cesarano – *Ibid.*, n° 7506/7439

Reply to Cesarano's telegram. The Secretariat of State bids him to notify F. Kalatosoff that it is not deemed necessary for him continue his voyage all the way to Rome, but that he should immediately send the important news promised and wait in Constantinople for a reply. [Cesarano should] obtain a report [from Kalatosoff], even verbal, on the religious and political conditions in the Caucasus and the desired provisions, and send a summary to the S. Congregation. It is then desired that F. Kalatosoff return to Tiflis before Holy Week in order not to deprive the faithful of his presence at Easter. Therefore, send the report at once; the S. Congr. will respond right away to the most urgent items, putting off the rest until the arrival of the new Visitor and Administrator for the Caucasus who should be leaving from Rome in June.

123

[n.d.] Constantinople – secret report of F. Kalatosoff to Marini – CO, 106, 3, 5, 2, n° 7632

Long report dealing mainly with religious questions and with the qualities that the new Ap. Visitor and his secretary should have. Warns that an Armenian communist has told him that the party has decided to infiltrate the religious orders and, above all, the Vatican itself.

124

13 November 1922, Rome – The Director General of the *Fondo per il Culto* [signature illegible] to Gasparri – AAEESS, *Asia* 117, n° 10228

> Informs that Gelaleddin Arif, Kemalist minister to Rome, had told him that Pope Pius XI, in an interview with an English writer who was going to Angora, had affirmed knowing of the Kemalists' sympathies for the Catholics.

125

14 November 1922, Rome – handwritten draft of Gasparri's response to the Director General of the *Fondo per il Culto* – n° 10228

> Disavowal of Arif's reporting regarding the pope's words, which were limited to repeating recommendations to Kemal to avoid further bloodbaths and to respect Christian persons and institutions.

BIOGRAPHICAL GLOSSARY*

AGAGIANIAN, FRANCESCO (Cardinal GREGORY PETER XV, Armenian Catholic Patriarch of Cilicia).

AHARONIAN, AVETIS (1866–1948). Dashnak exponent, first president of the Armenian Parliament, led the Delegation of the Republic at the peace conference with the Turks, in 1918. In 1919 he was permanent delegate to the Paris Peace Conference. In that capacity, he signed the Treaty of Sèvres for Armenia in 1920. In vain, he opposed the 1923 Treaty of Lausanne. He died in exile in Marseille.

DELLA CHIESA, GIACOMO (BENEDICT XV) (1854–1922). Elected pope on September 3, 1914. To defend the Armenians from Turkish persecutions he sent Sultan Mohammed V two letters, one in 1915 and another in 1918. August 1st, 1917, he sent a Note to the Belligerent Powers with concrete proposals for ending the war. The message, however, went unheeded. In the same year, he published the Code of Canon Law. In 1921 he re-established the diplomatic relations with France that had been interrupted at the beginning of the century.

DELPUCH, ANTONIO, a monk of the White Fathers Missionaries of Africa, Visitor Apostolic in the Caucasus at the end of 1919.

DOLCI, ANGELO MARIA, bishop of Gubbio and then of Amalfi, he was the first Apostolic Delegate of the Holy See in Constantinople (1914–22).

ENVER PASHA, (1881–1922). Exponent of the Young Turks. In 1914 he was Minister of War. After 1918 he led a revolt against the Soviets in Turkistan, in which he died.

GASPARRI, PIETRO (1852–1934). Cardinal and Secretary of State from 1914 to 1930. In 1929 he concluded the Concordat with the Italian state.

GIANNINI, F., Apostolic Delegate to Beirut

KEMAL, MUSTAFA (ATATURK) (1881–1938). Turkish general and politician. Between 1919 and 1922 he reconquered Greek-occupied Anatolia and Thrace for the Turks. In 1923 he founded the republic of which he was president, with dictatorial powers, until his death. He radically modernized Turkey.

KHATISSIAN, ALEXANDER (1876–1945). A Dashnak exponent, he was prime minister of the Armenian Republic from 1919 to 1920. He signed the Peace Treaty of Alexandroupolis with the Kemalists in 1920. After the rise of a communist regime in Armenia he moved to Paris.

---

* For certain individuals, it was only possible to ascertain their title held during the period of study.

KALATOSOFF, DIONIGI, Mekhitarist monk, Apostolic Vice-administrator of the Caucasus (1917–?)

MOHAMMED V (1844–1918). Sultan of Turkey from 1909, during the government of the Young Turks who deprived him of all power. Under his reign, the Italo-Turkish war (1911) and the Balkan wars (1912–13) took place, Turkey participated in the First World War, and the first massacres and deportations of Armenians occurred.

MORIONDO, NATALE GABRIELE. Dominican, Bishop of Cuneo, Visitor Apostolic to the Caucasus between 1920 and 1921.

NASLIAN, JEAN. Bishop of Trabizon, representative of the Armenian Catholics at the Conference of Paris, Visitor Apostolic in Turkey from April of 1921 until 1928, he organized the transfer of the Armenian Catholic patriarchy of Cilicia from Constantinople to Beirut.

NUBAR, BOGHOS (1851–1930). Son of a rich Armenian three times Prime Minister of Egypt, charged by the Catholicos with founding the Armenian National Delegation in Paris in 1912. This had the task of co-ordinating philo-Armenian activities and of sensitizing Europe to the Armenian problem. In 1916 he organized the Eastern (later Armenian) Legion, which fought alongside the Entente against the Turks. In 1919 he joined, with his National Delegation, the Delegation of the Armenian Republic at the Paris Peace Conference. In 1921 he retired to private life.

SHAHUMIAN, STEPAN (1878–1918). In 1902 founded the Union of Armenian Social Democrats. Elected to the Central Committee of the Bolshevik party in 1917, he was nominated Commissar for Caucasian Affairs by Lenin. Forced to take refuge in Baku, in 1918, he founded a Commune there, with the support of the Dashnak and the opposition of Azeri population, from April to July of 1918. The entry of the Turks into Baku forced him to escape by sea but, disembarked at Ashkhabad, he was executed by anti-Bolshevik troops.

SHANT, LEVON (1869–1951). Headed the Armenian Republic's delegation to Moscow in 1920, to negotiate an accord with Lenin's government. After the Sovietization of Armenia he went into exile in Beirut, where he died.

TERZIAN, PAUL PETER XIII. Armenian Catholic Patriarch of Cilicia.

WILSON, TH. WOODROW (1856–1924). U.S. president (1912–1920) belonging to the Democratic party. In 1917 he intervened in the First World War on the side of the Entente. Supported a peace founded on the principles of equality and of democracy (expressed in the "14 Points"). Also promoted the institution of the League of Nations.

BIBLIOGRAPHY

Vatican Archives Consulted:

Vatican Secret Archives (*Archivio Segreto Vaticano*), indicated by the letters ASV, War 1914–18 (*Guerra 1914–1918*), *rubrica* [heading] 244, folders 69 and 112; *rubrica* 244, K 12 c, folder 306

Archives of the Sacred Congregation for Extraordinary Ecclesiastical Affairs (*Archivio della Sacra Congregazione per gli Affari Ecclesiastici Straordinari*), otherwise known as the Vatican Secretariat of State, indicated by the letters AAEESS, position *Asia* 57, 1 and 2; *Asia* 117; *Asia* 126; *Austria* 576; *Russia* 505; *Russia* 540 bis

Archives of the Sacred Congregation for the Oriental Churches (*Archivio della Sacra Congregazione per le Chiese Orientali*), indicated by the letters CO, Armenians in general and the Caucasus (*Armeni in genere e Caucaso*), positions V and IV, *rubrica* 105, folder 3, 5; *rubrica* 106, folder 2, 3, folder 3, 2, folder 3, 5, folder 3, 5, 2

Published Works:

— — *Armin T. Wegner e gli Armeni in Anatolia, 1915. Immagini e testimonianze*, Milano 1996.

BASMADJIAN, K. J., *Histoire Moderne des Arméniens, depuis la chute du royame jusqu'au Traité de Sèvres (1375-1920)*, Paris 1922.

BASMADJIAN, V., *Les Arméniens: réveil ou fin?*, Paris 1979.

BRJUSOV, V., *Annali del popolo armeno* (trad., introd. e note di A. Ferrari), Milano 1993.

CARR, E. H., *La rivoluzione bolscevica 1917-1923*, Torino 1964.

CROCE, G. M., *I rappresentanti pontifici a Costantinopoli (1814-1922). Tra missione e diplomazia*, in Mutafian Cl. (a cura di), Roma-Armenia. Catalogo della Mostra Vaticana, Roma 1999.

DADRIAN, V., *Storia del genocidio armeno. Conflitti nazionali dai Balcani al Caucaso*, ed. it. a cura di A. ARSLAN e B. L. ZEKIYAN, Milano 2000.

DADRIAN, V. N., *Genocide as a Problem of National and International Law: The WWI Armenian Case and its Contemporary Legal Ramifications*, Yale, CT, 1989.

DEDEYAN G. (ed.), *Storia degli Armeni*, ed. it. a cura di B. L. ZEKIYAN e A. ARSLAN, Milano 2002.

Documenti Diplomatici Italiani, I-V, Firenze 1998-2005.

FERRARI, A., *Alla frontiera dell'impero. Gli armeni in Russia (1801-2005)*, Milano 2000.

FERRARI, A., *L'Ararat e la gru. Studi sulla storia e la cultura degli armeni*, Milano 2003.

HARTUNIAN, A. H., *Neither to Laugh Nor to Weep: A Memoir of the Armenian Genocide*, Cambridge, Mass., 1986.

HOVANNISIAN, R. G., *The Republic of Armenia*, t. 4, Berkeley, 1994.

IMPAGLIAZZO, M., *Una finestra sul massacro. Documenti inediti sulla strage degli armeni (1915-1916)*, Milano 2000.

LANG, D. M., *Armeni. Un popolo in esilio*, Bologna 1989.

LANG, D. M. and WALKER, CH. S., *The Minority Rights Group. Report n. 32: the Armenians*, London 1987.

MACLER, F., *Quatre conférences sur l'Arménie faites en Holland*, Paris 1932.

MANDELSTAM, A. N., *La Société des Nations et les Puissances devant le problème Arménien*, Paris 1926.

MECERIAN, J., *Le génocide du peuple arménien. Le sort de la population arménienne de l'Empire Ottoman. De la Constitution Ottoman au Traité de Lausanne 1908-1923*, Beyrouth 1965.

MORGENTHAU, H., *Ambassador Morgenthau's Story: The Documented Account of Armenian Genocide*, New York 1975.

MOROZZO DELLA ROCCA, R., *Le nazioni non muoiono. Russia rivoluzionaria, Polonia indipendente e Santa Sede*, Bologna 1992.

MOROZZO DELLA ROCCA, R., *Santa Sede e Russia rivoluzionaria*, in *Benedetto XV e la pace 1918*, a cura di RUMI, G., Brescia 1990.

MUTAFIAN, CL., *Metz Yeghern. Breve storia del genocidio degli armeni*, Milano 1995.

NASLIAN, J., *Les mémoires de Mgr. Jean Naslian sur les événements politico-religieux en Proche-Orient de 1914 à 1928*, , 2 tomi, Beyrouth 1951.

OHANIAN, P., *Turquia, Estado Genocida (1915-23). Documentos*. Tomo I, Buenos Aires 1986.

PASDERMADJIAN, H., *Histoire de l'Arménie; depuis les origines jusqu'au Traité de Lausanne*, III ed., Paris 1971.

PIPES, R., *The Formation of the Soviet Union: Communism and Nationalism 1917-1923*, Cambridge, Mass.,1964.

POIDEBARD, A., *Le Transcaucase et la République d'Arménie dans les Textes Diplomatiques du Traité de Brest-Litovsk au Traité de Kars*, Paris 1923, Appendices 1924.

POIDEBARD, A., *Rôle militaire des Arméniens sur le front du Caucase après la défection de l'armée russe (decembre 1917-novembre 1918)*, Paris 1920.

Pontificio Collegio Armeno, *Memorie 1883-1958*, Venezia 1958.

RICCARDI, A., *Benedetto XV e la crisi della convivenza multireligiosa nell'Impero Ottomano*, in *Benedetto XV e la pace 1918*, a cura di RUMI, G., Brescia 1990.

SIDARI, F., *La questione armena nella politica delle Grandi Potenze (dal Congresso di Berlino al Trattato di Losanna 1878-1923)*, Padova 1962.

SUNY, R. G., *Making Nations in Transcaucasia*, in fondazione Giangiacomo Feltrinelli, *Annali,* a. XXVIII (1992), Milano 1993.

SUNY, R. G., *Armenia in the Twentieth Century (Occasional Papers in Armenian Studies),* Chico, Calif., 1983.

TCHOLAKIAN, A., *Armenia: State, People, Life,* New York 1975.

TER MINASSIAN, A., *La République d'Arménie,* Bruxelles 1989.

TERNON, Y., *Gli Armeni 1915-1916: il genocidio dimenticato*, tr. it. Milano 2003.

WALKER, C. J., *Armenia: The Survival of a Nation,* New York 1983.

ZEKIYAN B. L., *Questione armena? Per puntualizzare la situazione attuale: schizzo di una sintesi storica*, in idem, *L'Armenia e gli armeni, Polis lacerata e patria spirituale: la sfida di una sopravvivenza*, Milano 2000.

ZEKIYAN, B. L., *Armenia. Incontro con il popolo dell'Ararat,* Venezia 1987.

www.ingramcontent.com/pod-product-compliance
Lightning Source LLC
Chambersburg PA
CBHW021134230426
43667CB00005B/108